The Princeton Review®

SAT Subject Test™
CHEMISTRY
PREP

17th Edition

The Staff of The Princeton Review

PrincetonReview.com

Penguin
Random
House

The Princeton Review
110 East 42nd St, 7th Floor
New York, NY 10017
E-mail: editorialsupport@review.com

Published in the United States by Penguin Random
House LLC, New York, and in Canada by Random
House of Canada, a division of Penguin Random
House Ltd., Toronto.

Terms of Service: The Princeton Review Online Companion Tools ("Student Tools") for retail books are available for only the two most recent editions of that book. Student Tools may be activated only once per eligible book purchased for a total of 24 months of access. Activation of Student Tools more than once per book is in direct violation of these Terms of Service and may result in discontinuation of access to Student Tools Services.

ISBN: 978-0-525-56895-7
ISSN: 2687-7600

SAT Subject Tests is a trademark owned by the
College Board, which is not affiliated with, and
does not endorse, this product.

The Princeton Review is not affiliated with Princeton
University.

Editor: Orion McBean
Production Editors: Jim Melloan and Sarah Litt
Production Artist: Bob McKeehen

Printed in the United States of America.

10 9 8 7 6 5 4 3 2 1

17th Edition

Editorial

Rob Franek, Editor-in-Chief
David Soto, Director of Content Development
Stephen Koch, Survey Manager
Deborah Weber, Director of Production
Gabriel Berlin, Production Design Manager
Selena Coppock, Managing Editor
Aaron Riccio, Senior Editor
Meave Shelton, Senior Editor
Chris Chimera, Editor
Eleanor Green, Editor
Orion McBean, Editor
Brian Saladino, Editor
Patricia Murphy, Editorial Assistant

Penguin Random House Publishing Team

Tom Russell, VP, Publisher
Rebecca Holland, Publishing Director
Amanda Yee, Associate Managing Editor
Ellen Reed, Production Manager
Suzanne Lee, Designer

Acknowledgments

The Princeton Review would like to give a sincere thanks to Stacey Cowap for her awesome edits to this edition.

Special thanks to Adam Robinson, who conceived of and perfected the Joe Bloggs approach to standardized tests and many of the other successful techniques used by The Princeton Review.

Contents

Get More (**Free**) Content
at **PrincetonReview.com/prep**

As easy as **1·2·3**

1 Go to PrincetonReview.com/prep and enter the following ISBN for your book:

9780525568957

2 Answer a few simple questions to set up an exclusive Princeton Review account. *(If you already have one, you can just log in.)*

3 Enjoy access to your **FREE** content!

Once you've registered, you can...

- Take a full-length practice PSAT, SAT, and ACT

- Get valuable advice about the college application process, including tips for writing a great essay and where to apply for financial aid

- If you're still choosing between colleges, use our searchable rankings of *The Best 385 Colleges* to find out more information about your dream school.

- Download the comprehensive study guides and a variety of printable resources, including: additional bubble sheets and the formulas reference guide

- Check to see if there have been any corrections or updates to this edition

Need to report a potential **content** issue?

Contact **EditorialSupport@review.com** and include:

- full title of the book
- ISBN
- page number

Need to report a **technical** issue?

Contact **TPRStudentTech@review.com** and provide:

- your full name
- email address used to register the book
- full book title and ISBN
- Operating system (Mac/PC) and browser (Firefox, Safari, etc.)

Look For These Icons Throughout The Book

 ONLINE ARTICLES

 PROVEN TECHNIQUES

 APPLIED STRATEGIES

Part I
Orientation

Chapter 1
Introduction

The SAT Subject Tests are one-hour exams that assess a student's knowledge of a particular academic subject. Not all colleges require the subject tests, and some subject tests are more appropriate for certain students than for others. The format and content of a given test falls within certain guidelines, and you should prepare accordingly. In this chapter, we will answer some basic questions about the SAT Subject Test in Chemistry and how you should prepare for it.

WHAT ARE THE SAT SUBJECT TESTS?

The SAT Subject Tests are a series of tests administered by the College Board. Unlike the regular SAT, the SAT Subject Tests are designed to measure knowledge in very specific areas. Many colleges require that you take one or more of these tests in order to qualify for admission; but even at colleges that do not require that you take them, administrators view student performances on the tests as an important factor that contributes to the decision to grant or withhold admission. Additionally, at some schools, a high score on one or more of the tests might enable you to "place out" of certain required college courses. For example, if you do well on the SAT Subject Test in Chemistry, you might be exempt from fulfilling the science requirement at one or more of the schools to which you're applying!

Which SAT Subject Tests Should I Take?

The colleges that do require you to take the SAT Subject Tests will expect you to take two or three of them. In order to find out which tests are required by the colleges or specific programs at colleges to which you're applying, you can ask your guidance counselor, call the admissions office of the colleges, or check in college guidebooks. Alternately, you can visit the College Board website at **sat.collegeboard.org** and use their college search engine to look up the colleges you're interested in; each school on this search engine has a profile in which this information is provided.

Once you find out which, if any, tests are required, part of your decision making is done. The next step is to find out which of the tests will show your particular strengths. After all, the SAT Subject Tests are given in a variety of subjects: Literature, U.S. History, World History, Biology, Chemistry, Physics, French, German, Spanish, Modern Hebrew, Italian, Latin, Japanese, Korean, Chinese, and English Language Proficiency. You should take the tests on which you think you'd score the highest. If you're fluent in Chinese, take the SAT Subject Test in Chinese. If, however, you're most comfortable in the world of moles, atoms, and titrations, take the SAT Subject Test in Chemistry.

When Are the Tests Offered, and How Do I Register for Them?

The SAT Subject Tests are usually administered in August, October, November, December, May, and June at test centers around the country. Since not all of the tests are offered at each administration, be sure to check the dates and details on the College Board website carefully. You'll want to take the test on a date that's as close as possible to the end of your coursework in the subject. For example, if your chemistry course ends in June, take the June test. If it ends in May, take the test in May or June—whichever date falls the soonest after your course has ended.

You can register for these tests either through the College Board website or through regular mail. To register by mail, ask your guidance counselor for the appropriate forms, which you'll need to mail in by the date listed on the College Board website—generally about five weeks before the test. You can register late, but late registration ends about four weeks prior to the test week and will cost you an additional fee. The costs of registering for an individual SAT Subject Test are $26 for the first test and $22 for any additional test.

You'll need to arrive at the test center pretty early—by 7:45 A.M., unless your admission ticket says otherwise. Your first test will begin between 8:30 and 9:00 A.M., and since each test is an hour long, if you take the maximum of the three tests that you're allowed to take at each sitting, you'll be done by 12:30 P.M. If you're taking just one or two tests, you can leave as soon as you've finished.

One final, but important, note—College Board allows you to change your mind about what test you'd like to take *on* the test day (except for the language test with listening). This means that if you aren't sure which test you'll feel more confident taking, you can study up until test day and then make your decision at the last moment.

How Is the Test Scored, and What Does the Score Mean?

As with the regular SAT, the SAT Subject Tests are scored on a scale from 200 to 800, where 200 is the lowest and 800 is the highest; the exception to this rule is the English Language Proficiency Test, which is scored on a scale from 901 to 999.

Subject tests that do not involve written responses (such as the SAT Subject Test in Chemistry) are graded by a computer. The computer simply adds up the number of questions you answered correctly and subtracts from this number one-quarter of the number of questions you answered incorrectly. (It doesn't count questions that you skipped either way.) This determines your raw test score. The raw score is then converted to a scaled score.

So, what's a good score on the SAT Subject Test in Chemistry? Well, a good score is one that falls in or above the range that the colleges you are interested in state as desirable. On the scale from 200 to 800, 500 is considered the average score of all test takers. If you score higher than this, your performance on the test is above average—if you score lower, then your performance is below average. Along with your regular score, you'll receive a percentile rank; this is another indication of how you fared in relation to all of the other test takers. If you receive a percentile ranking of 60 percent, that means that you scored higher than 60 percent of test takers and lower than 40 percent of test takers. But keep in mind that even if your score is below average or below the range that the schools of your choice list as being desirable for entrance, this doesn't necessarily mean that you won't get into these schools. Your scores on the SAT Subject Tests are not the only factor that goes into the admissions decision.

A Couple of Words About Score Choice™

You can choose which SAT Subject Test (and regular SAT) scores you want colleges to see by using Score Choice™. This is great news! So if, for example, you take the French test followed by the Chemistry test, but don't think the Chemistry test went very well, you can simply opt to have that Chemistry score withheld from the schools to which you are applying.

Score Choice is optional for students—this means that you have to opt in and actively choose which specific tests you want to send to colleges. If you choose not to use Score Choice, then all of the scores on file for you will automatically be sent when you request that score reports be sent to the colleges you're applying to.

Students should still feel comfortable sending all scores, since most colleges consider a student's best score.

A searchable list of colleges and their requested SAT score submission requirements, as well as more information on Score Choice, can be found at the College Board website at **www.collegeboard.com**.

When Can I See My Test Results?

A set period of time after you take the test, your score will be released online. To find out when your score will be made available, please visit **sat.collegeboard.org**. A hard copy of your score report is also sent to you, as well as to your high school, through regular mail approximately three to five weeks after the test date. How will colleges get your test results? Well, when you first register for the SAT Subject Tests, you're allowed to give the names of four schools to which you'd like your scores sent. If you want additional schools to receive your scores, you can request this through the College Board website, which will cost you an additional fee per each request. You can also phone in a request, but this costs more.

WHAT IS THE PRINCETON REVIEW?

The Princeton Review is a test-preparation company founded in New York City, but we have offices across the country and abroad. We've developed the techniques you'll find in our books, courses, and online resources by analyzing actual tests and testing their effectiveness with our students. What makes our techniques unique is that they're based on the same techniques that the test writers use when they write the tests. We don't want you to waste your time with superfluous content; we'll give you only the information you need to get a great score. You'll also learn to avoid common test traps, think like the test writers, find answers to questions you're unsure of, and budget your time effectively. You need to do only two things: (1) learn chemistry the way the subject test tests it, and (2) approach the test strategically.

POINT 1: LEARN CHEMISTRY THE WAY THE SUBJECT TEST TESTS IT

The SAT Subject Test in Chemistry, among many other subjects, tests the concept of Gibbs free energy.

If you sat and read your chemistry textbook to prepare for this test, you'd read a whole lot of material relating to Gibbs free energy that definitely will *not* be tested. You'd see diagrams such as this.

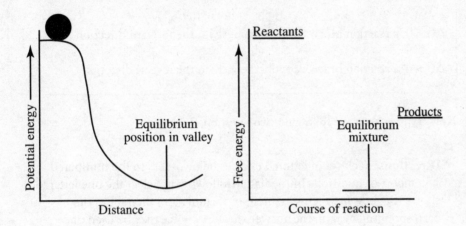

And you'd read text such as this.

We may consider free-energy change in a spontaneous reaction much as we consider the potential energy change that accompanies the rolling of an ordinary ball down a hill. The ball is driven down the hill by the potential energy within a gravitational field. By analogy, the free energy within a chemical system decreases continuously over time . . . blah, blah, blah . . . ultimately reaching a minimum. When potential energy is at a minimum, the reaction reaches its equilibrium.

We might best illustrate the concept by reference to the formation of ammonia from its elements hydrogen and . . . blah, blah, blah . . . . Imagine that a particular number of moles of nitrogen react with three times the number of hydrogen atoms. The formation of ammonia will not be complete because . . . blah, blah, blah . . . . An equilibrium will be attained by the system, and at equilibrium the reaction chamber will contain a mixture of . . . blah, blah, blah . . . . At that time there can be no additional spontaneous formation of ammonia because the system has reached a minimum state of free energy that . . . blah, blah, blah . . . . Free energy is a state function, and that is why . . . blah, blah, blah . . . .

The text would go on and on, intimidating and boring you, but offering nothing that raises your test score. You'd get so sick of it that you'd stop reading.

When we teach you about Gibbs free energy, we tell you exactly what you have to know to raise your test score. As we do that, we give you opportunities to practice on realistic chemistry problems, to make sure you're with us at every step. The most important thing for you to remember about Gibbs free energy is that it is symbolized as ΔG, and that if ΔG is negative, the reaction proceeds spontaneously in the forward direction, but if it's positive, the reaction proceeds spontaneously in the reverse direction.

Gibbs Free Energy

$\Delta G < 0$ a reaction proceeds spontaneously in the forward direction

$\Delta G > 0$ a reaction proceeds spontaneously in the reverse direction

---

Now try to answer the following two questions:

Directions: Each set of lettered choices below refers to the numbered statements or questions immediately following it. Select the one lettered choice that best fits each statement or formula and then fill in the corresponding oval on the answer sheet. A choice may be used once, more than once, or not at all in each set.

GFE- The available energy of a substance that can be used in a chemical transformation or reaction.

quizlet ↓

Questions 1-2 refer to the following.

(A) Heat of formation
(B) Work
(C) Entropy
(D) Gibbs free energy
(E) Enthalpy

enthalpy: the internal energy of the system + the product of pressure/volume

1. Must be negative if reaction proceeds spontaneously in forward direction

   ~~entha~~ GFE

2. Must be positive if reaction proceeds spontaneously in reverse direction

   GFE

Both answers are (D), and you know that simply by making the associations we talked about. The computer that grades your test doesn't care if you know why the answer is (D); it just wants to see the (D) oval filled in on your answer sheet.

POINT 2: APPROACH THE TEST STRATEGICALLY

It isn't enough to study chemistry the way the SAT Subject Test in Chemistry tests it; you must also study the questions themselves. You will need to understand the way they're designed and be familiar with certain techniques that systematically lead to correct answers.

When you sit down to take this test, you won't know the answers to all of the questions. But in Chapter 2 of this book, we'll show you ways to choose the correct answer even if you don't know it right away. We'll present eight strategies that will help you "outsmart" the test and its writers. Then, in Chapters 3 through 14, we'll show you over and over again how to use them.

Our strategies are powerful stuff. They teach you how to find the right answers logically and systematically—in much the same way that a detective solves a crime.

WHAT ABOUT PRACTICE AND PRACTICE TESTS?

This book is interactive. Over and over again you show us what you've learned. We check your progress page by page, paragraph by paragraph, and make sure you're with us every step of the way. If you're not, we help you figure out *why* you're not.

You might notice that our book cover is unlike most others. It doesn't promise you six, seven, or eight full-length practice tests. It would be easy for us to fill our pages with simulated test after simulated test, but testing yourself repeatedly with practice tests won't raise your score. You'll just prove that you can get the same score over and over again.

However, Parts II and V of this book are made up of three full-length tests, complete with explanations, that are just like the real SAT Subject Test in Chemistry. As you work your way through these tests, you'll become more comfortable with the test content and when you sit down to take the real test on test day, you'll be more than prepared.

SHOULD I BUY PRACTICE MATERIAL FROM THE COLLEGE BOARD?

Sure! If you want to take more than the three tests in this book, the College Board publishes a book called *The Official SAT Subject Test Study Guide in Chemistry*. Take the chemistry test that's in their book, and see how easy it is after you've worked through our book. It should be a piece of cake.

Head over to the College Board's website, **collegeboard.org**, for more information and practice questions.

Chapter 2
Test Strategies

The SAT Subject Test in Chemistry always examines the same areas of chemistry using three different question types. Your job is to know what to expect from the test, not only in terms of specific content, but also in terms of how the test is written and how you can use that information to your advantage. In this chapter, we will discuss the breakdown of the test and general strategies you can use.

CRACKING THE SAT SUBJECT TEST IN CHEMISTRY

The SAT Subject Test in Chemistry is made up of 85 multiple-choice questions, and you have one hour to answer them. You're not allowed to use a calculator on this test, but you won't need one. The test is divided into three sections: Parts A, B, and C, and each section is made up of a different type of question. Let's take a closer look at these parts.

Part A: Classification Questions

The first 20 to 25 questions you'll see on the exam fall under the category of what the College Board calls classification questions. In this type of question, you'll see a list of five words or phrases lettered A through E, followed by three to five questions. But sometimes the questions aren't really questions; they're phrases. Your job is to match the phrase in the "question" with a word or phrase that appears in the list A through E. Forget about chemistry for a minute, and see how it works.

Directions: Each set of lettered choices below refers to the numbered statements or questions immediately following it. Select the one lettered choice that best fits each statement or answers each question and then fill in the corresponding oval on the answer sheet. A choice may be used once, more than once, or not at all in each set.

Questions 1–4 refer to the following.
(A) Red light
(B) Swimming pool
(C) Piano
(D) Fire engine
(E) Ocean liner

1. Musical instrument that involves keyboard outside and strings inside

2. Motor vehicle designed to assist in effort to extinguish flames

3. Sea vessel that carries passengers across large bodies of water

4. Water-filled pit designed for recreational or athletic activities

The answers, of course, are (C), (D), (E), and (B). Now let's move on to see what the questions in Part B look like.

Part B: Relationship Analysis Questions ✗ *Part B of test*

The questions that make up Part B of the exam won't ask you to decide among (A), (B), (C), (D), or (E). Relationship analysis questions consist of two statements with the word BECAUSE in between them. You're supposed to figure out if the statements are true or false. If both are true, you're also expected to figure out whether the word BECAUSE belongs there. Once again, forget about chemistry for a second so we can show you how the questions work. The questions in Part B of the exam are numbered in a peculiar manner. This section begins with the number 101, though there are only 85 questions in the whole test!

Directions: Each question below consists of two statements, I in the left-hand column and II in the right-hand column. For each question, determine whether statement I is true or false <u>and</u> whether statement II is true or false and fill in the corresponding T or F ovals on your answer sheet. <u>Fill in oval CE only if statement II is a correct explanation of statement I.</u>

CE?
On your answer sheet for Part B, you'll see ovals marked T and F for true and false, but the "because" circle is marked CE, which stands for **Cause/Effect**. You're looking to see if I and II have a cause-and-effect relationship.

	I		II
101.	If one takes a shower, one gets wet	BECAUSE	the shower head releases water that falls on the individual taking the shower.
102.	If one walks rapidly, one will be in motion	BECAUSE	automobiles burn gasoline.
103.	A boat will sink if it fills with water	BECAUSE	it is impossible for a boat to develop a leak.
104.	President Lincoln died of natural causes	BECAUSE	Lincoln was president during the Civil War.
105.	Omaha, Nebraska, is the capital of the United States	BECAUSE	Omaha is the largest city in the entire world.

Question 101 Both statements are true, and the "because" belongs there. You get wet in a shower *because* the shower pours water on you.

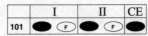

Question 102 Both statements are true. If you walk, you move, and automobiles do burn gasoline. But the "because" doesn't belong there. A walker doesn't move *because* automobiles burn gasoline. The statements have nothing to do with one another.

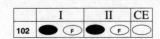

Question 103 A boat will sink if it fills with water. That's true. But the second statement is false. Boats *can* develop leaks.

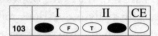

Question 104 The first statement is false. Lincoln was murdered. The second statement is true. He was president during the Civil War.

Question 105 Both statements are false. Omaha is not the capital of the United States, and it isn't the largest city in the world.

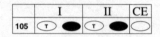

Now let's talk about the third and final section of the exam, Part C.

Part C: Five-Choice Completion Questions

The remaining 40–50 questions (a majority of the test) are ordinary looking multiple-choice questions such as the one below.

28. Which is the formula of a compound?

   (A) HCl
   (B) He
   (C) Cu
   (D) O_2
   (E) Br_2

Here, the answer is (A). A **compound** is a chemical combination of two or more elements. (We'll talk more about that later.) This type of question is straight-forward: you read the question and choose the answer choice that best answers the question.

Now that you know what kinds of questions you'll see on the SAT Subject Test in Chemistry, let's talk about the strategies you can use to tackle these questions.

STRATEGY #1: STUDY THE RIGHT STUFF IN THE RIGHT WAY

One important strategy for preparing to take this exam is to study only the concepts that will be tested. In Chapters 3 through 14, we will take a look at all the subjects that are certain to appear on the test and explain them in a way that's specifically designed to help you answer the test questions.

What topics do we cover? Well, the same topics that the College Board lists on their website as being covered.

I. Structure of Matter (25% of the questions will be on this topic): atomic theory and structure; periodic relationships; chemical bonding and molecular structure; nuclear reactions

II. States of Matter (16%): kinetic molecular theory of gases; gas laws; liquids, solids, and phase changes; intermolecular forces; solutions, concentration units, solubility, and colligative properties

III. Reaction Types (14%): acids and bases; oxidation-reduction; precipitation

IV. Stoichiometry (14%): mole concept and Avogadro's number; empirical and molecular formulas; percent composition, stoichiometric formulas; limiting reagents

V. Equilibrium and Reaction Rates (5%): gas equilibria and ionic equilibria; Le Châtelier's principle; equilibrium expressions; rate of reactions

VI. Thermochemistry (6%): energy changes in chemical reactions and physical properties; Hess's Law; entropy

VII. Descriptive Chemistry (12%): physical and chemical properties of elements and their familiar compounds; chemical nomenclature; chemical reactivity and products of chemical reactions; simple examples from organic chemistry and environmental chemistry

VIII. Laboratory (8%): equipment; measurements; procedures; observations; safety; calculations; interpretations of results

As you can see, we do not include everything there is to know about chemistry. We are here to strengthen and refresh your knowledge in the specific areas that will be important on the test.

STRATEGY #2: DO THE EASY ONES FIRST

In each of the three sections of the SAT Subject Test in Chemistry, the easier questions tend to come first and the harder ones come later. When you begin each section, answer as many of the "easy" questions as you can, but when they start to become more difficult, go on to the next section and do the same. Once you've answered all of the relatively easy questions in all the sections, go back to each section and start answering the more difficult ones.

This strategy makes sense because all questions are worth the same amount; answering a hard question correctly won't get you more points than answering an easy one correctly. If there's a chance that you might not be able to get to every question on the exam in the 60 minutes you're given, make sure you at least answer the ones you're sure to get right, first!

You don't need to answer every question to get a good score on the SAT Subject Test in Chemistry. It's possible to leave 30 questions blank and still score near 600 if you do well on the questions you *do* answer.

STRATEGY #3: TAKE A GUESS!

As we told you in the last chapter, in calculating your "raw score" (from which it then calculates your scaled score), the test does the following:

1. Gives you one point for each question you answer correctly

2. Deducts $\frac{1}{4}$ of a point for each question you answer incorrectly

3. Doesn't count questions you didn't answer

Because one-quarter of a point is deducted for any question you answer incorrectly, you should definitely guess the answer to any question for which you can eliminate at least one of the five answer choices. If you can eliminate one answer choice and then take a guess, then you will have a one-in-four chance of choosing the correct answer. If you can eliminate two answer choices, your odds of choosing correctly go to one-in-three.

As you read Chapters 3 through 14, you'll see that all of our techniques and strategies teach you to eliminate wrong choices. After you've done that, use guessing to your advantage.

STRATEGY #4: MAKING ASSOCIATIONS
(TYPE A, B, AND C QUESTIONS)

One helpful strategy for learning the key chemistry concepts that will show up on the test is to make associations between terms and concepts. What are we talking about? Well, let's forget chemistry, just to make the point. You may have learned in school that Teddy Roosevelt was a "trustbuster." You might not know what trusts are, how he busted them, why he wanted to bust them, or why anyone cares if trusts get busted. But if you learned to associate the name Teddy Roosevelt with the phrase "trustbuster," you would be able to answer a test question that looks like this.

3. Theodore Roosevelt believed in

(A) creating trusts
(B) destroying trusts
(C) making trusts larger
(D) communism
(E) socialistic economics

The association you learned to make—"Teddy Roosevelt" with "trustbuster"—allowed you to choose the correct answer: (B).

This strategy will also be useful on the SAT Subject Test in Chemistry; many questions will test your ability to associate one word or phrase with another. For example, suppose you had no idea what was meant by "pH," "acid," or "base," and you had just learned to associate

> **pH less than 7 with:** acid
>
> **pH greater than 7 with:** base

You'd be able to answer a test question that looked like this:

28. Which of the following solutions is most acidic?

(A) A solution of phosphoric acid at pH 4
(B) A solution of sodium hydroxide at pH 11
(C) A solution of hydrochloric acid at pH 5
(D) A solution of acetic acid at pH 6
(E) A solution of aqueous ammonia at pH 9

Whatever else you know about acids and bases, you know that (A) is right because, among the listed solutions, it has the lowest pH.

Throughout our teaching of SAT Chemistry, we will show you what associations to make, how to make them, and how they will point you to the right answers on test day.

STRATEGY #5: REPHRASE THE QUESTION (TYPE A AND C QUESTIONS)

In the questions seen in Parts A and C on the exam, the test writers will obscure the information in the question to make it harder to read. They are trying to mess you up! Don't fall for it.

To understand this type of trap, read the two sentences below.

1. In any dynamic chemical equilibrium, the removal of product will drive the equilibrium to the right and thus increase the concentration of product, while the concentration of reactants will decrease.

2. If a dynamic chemical equilibrium is subjected to withdrawal of product, the concentration of reactants will diminish, and the concentration of product will become greater.

These two statements mean exactly the same thing, but their wording is very different. Many of the words and phrases in statement 2 have the same meaning as those in statement 1, but they're disguised—they're camouflaged.

subjected to withdrawal of product	*means*	the removal of product
concentration of product will become greater	*means*	increase the concentration of product
concentration of reactants will diminish	*means*	the concentration of reactants will decrease

So, What About It?

When you learn something, whether it's chemistry or anything else, you tend to learn it in certain particular phrases. For instance, maybe you think of an element as "a substance that cannot be broken into any simpler substance." Fine. But if you're too attached to that particular way of stating it, look what happens when you try to answer the following question.

25. Which of the following best describes the characteristics of an element?

(A) It is capable of existing in relatively simple molecular forms.

(B) It exists only in molar quantities.

(C) It will always react with any other element.

(D) It is a fundamental form of matter.

(E) It is more reactive if the surrounding entropy is high.

If you're too attached to the way that you usually describe elements, you might not see the right answer although (a) you do know it, and (b) it's staring you in the face. The right answer to this question is (D). To say that an element is a fundamental form of matter is, more or less, to say it can't be broken down into simpler substances. The words aren't the same, but the meaning is.

Basically bullshit

Many students who know what an element is might still not answer this question correctly. This is because they'll look quickly through the choices and not see anything they recognize—this throws them into "answer-choice panic," and they'll pick something that "sounds right"—something that has the word "simple" in it, such as (A).

That's too bad. Students who do know the content sometimes choose the wrong answer simply because they fall for the camouflage trap.

Here's another example from a type C question. Suppose you know that if you add heat to a sample of gas molecules, each molecule, on average, starts bouncing around faster than it did before. But you're accustomed to stating it this way:

> *The average kinetic energy of gas molecules is directly proportional to the absolute temperature of the gas.*

If you're married to that statement, what's going to happen when you see the question below?

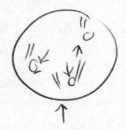

Heat

molecule

Bouncing around.

26. Which of the following is *always* increased by the addition of thermal energy to a sample of gas in a closed container?

    (A) Ideal gas constant
    (B) Average speed of gas molecules
    (C) Molecular weight of gas molecules
    (D) Volume of gas sample
    (E) Volatility

You know that increased heat increases average kinetic energy, but the answer has been camouflaged.

average speed of gas	*means*	average kinetic energy of molecules
addition of thermal energy	*means*	increasing the temperature

Maybe you're not used to thinking of the "addition of thermal energy" resulting in an increase in temperature. When it comes to gases, you're also not accustomed to thinking of "average speed of gas molecules" as reflecting the average kinetic energy. Although you know your chemistry, you might not realize that the right answer to this question is (B). You might decide to pick some crazy answer such as (A) or (D). Why? Because you fell into the trap.

Here's the Good News: You Can Rephrase It Yourself

To avoid the trap, keep some simple rules in mind.

- Remember that there's usually more than one way to say something.
- When you see a question that asks about a topic you've studied, don't fall apart just because the answer doesn't leap out at you right away.
- Relax. Realize that the right answer is probably camouflaged by words that are different from the ones you have in mind. Calmly search for them, and chances are, they *will* leap out at you.

In other words, keep an open mind. Don't expect test makers to use your words. Remember that the same concept or idea can be expressed in many different ways. Keep the concepts you know in mind, and don't get too attached to the words you use to express them.

Another Way out of the Trap:
Translate and Work Backward

Suppose you *do* try to keep an open mind on a particular question, and it just doesn't seem to work; the right answer isn't coming to you, although you know your chemistry. For questions in Part A, here's what you can do: look through all of the answer choices, and restate them in your own words. Below, we've listed five possible answer choices you might see in Part A of the exam. Below each answer choice, we've included one way of restating the answer.

(A)   Ideal gas constant
It's the letter R in the equation PV = nRT. It equals about 0.082 $\frac{L \cdot atm}{mol \cdot K}$.

(B)   Average speed of gas molecules
It's the speed at which gas molecules are moving around in a tank or container—it has to do with how much energy they have. It goes up with higher temperature and down with lower temperature.

(C)   Molecular weight of gas molecules
It's the weight (expressed in amu) of a gas molecule.

(D)   Volume of gas sample
It's the space the gas sample takes up—equal to the size of the container.

(E)   Volatility
It has to do with how easily a liquid below its boiling point evaporates when it's sitting around.

Now look at each of the following questions:

Questions 1–4 refer to the following.

1. Is always increased by the addition of thermal energy to a sample of gas in a closed container

   Average speed of gas molecules

2. Can be related to the pressure of a gas sample by the ideal gas law

   Volume of gas sample

3. Property associated with vapor pressure

   Volatility

4. Depends on the formula of a gas but not its temperature

   Molecular weight of gas molecule

Read the questions carefully, one by one, and compare them with the answer choices that you've put into your own words.

1. Hopefully you realize that "thermal energy" means heat. Now, which of the answer choices (stated in your own words) has to do with a factor that's affected by the addition of heat? Choice (B) does—it says that the average speed of gas molecules increases as heat (thermal energy) is added to the system and decreases as heat is taken away from a system. The answer to question 1 is (B).

2. If you know the ideal gas law (covered in Chapter 8), you would simply look among the answer choices for one of the variables from the equation, $PV = nRT$. In this equation, P = pressure, V = volume, n = number of moles of gas, R = the ideal gas constant, and T = temperature. Volume is the variable listed among the answer choices, so the correct answer is (D).

3. You should associate vapor pressure with the degree to which a liquid will evaporate at a temperature that's below its normal boiling point—and lo and behold, this is similar to how you've paraphrased (E): volatility. The answer is (E).

4. Read the question, and then look at the answer choices. Which of the choices, when stated in your words, mentions a characteristic of a gas that depends on its formula but not its temperature? Well, (C) looks like the most likely—the weight of a gas molecule does depend on its identity (formula) but not on its temperature. None of the other answer choices make any sense, so choose (C).

STRATEGY #6: AVOIDING THE TEMPTATION TRAP

Suppose we gave this question to a seven-year-old:

27. Which of the following best expresses the effect of Gibbs free energy on the spontaneity of a chemical reaction?
    (A) When Gibbs free energy is negative, the reaction proceeds spontaneously in the forward direction.
    (B) When Gibbs free energy is negative, the reaction proceeds spontaneously in the reverse direction.
    (C) George Washington was the first president of the United States.
    (D) Gibbs free energy affects the spontaneity only of exothermic reactions.
    (E) Gibbs free energy affects the spontaneity only of endothermic reactions.

Truth Isn't Always Right
Although (C) is a true statement, it doesn't answer the question that's being asked. That's how the test traps you. Make sure you're *always* answering the question posed on the test.

The child won't know what any of this means, but she *will* probably know that George Washington was the first president. So she'll choose (C); it's something she knows. She fell into the "temptation trap." The test writer stuck something into the answer choices that was familiar to the student; it was so familiar that the student chose it although it has nothing to do with the question.

What's That Got to Do with Me and the SAT Subject Test in Chemistry?

A lot. The temptation trap usually rears its head on questions from Parts A and C of the exam. On the day you take the test, there will be many things you know and some that you don't know. When you meet up with a type C question that's stumping you, you might reach out and grab an answer choice that "sounds familiar" although it has nothing to do with the question.

Suppose you know that adding an acid to a base increases the hydrogen ion concentration of the solution. Now, look at this question.

26. Which of the following will definitely occur if a quantity of acetic acid is added to a solution of potassium hydroxide at pH 11?
    (A) The number of free protons per liter of solution will increase.
    (B) Titration will tend to neutralize the solution.
    (C) The acetic acid will act as a weak base.
    (D) Acetate ion will precipitate out of solution.
    (E) The pH will remain constant.

The correct answer is (A), but if the answer to this question doesn't leap right out at you, you might decide to make a dash for something you know. Choice (B), by itself, is a true statement with which you might be familiar; titration between an acid and a base does tend to neutralize a solution. You might say to yourself, quickly, quietly, and almost unconsciously: "I've heard that statement. It sounds right." But (B) is wrong because it doesn't answer the question.

You Can Avoid the Temptation Trap

When you find yourself ready to choose an answer because it sounds right, stop to look at the question again carefully. Then take another look at the answer choices to see if another one, although in camouflage, is really a better answer to the question.

Let's think about the question we just looked at. We're adding an acid to a base. We know that we'll be lowering the pH of the solution—increasing the hydrogen ion concentration. Choice (A) says exactly that—in camouflage. Instead of referring to hydrogen ions, it refers to free protons. Instead of referring directly to concentration, or pH, it talks about increasing the number of protons per liter of solution. The right answer is (A), and you knew it, but you might not have chosen it. Why? Because panic led you straight into the temptation trap. Don't let that happen!

How Would You Say It?
Put the answers in your own words to avoid the camouflage trap.

STRATEGY #7: DIVIDE AND CONQUER

Let's take another look at the instructions to Part B.

Directions: Each question below consists of two statements, I in the left-hand column and II in the right-hand column. For each question, determine whether statement I is true or false and whether statement II is true or false and fill in the corresponding T or F ovals on your answer sheet. Fill in oval CE only if statement II is a correct explanation of statement I.

Now let's look at a question that has nothing to do with chemistry, to show how the divide and conquer strategy works.

	I		II
101.	All persons must breathe	BECAUSE	oxygen is necessary to human survival.

Here's what to do.

Step 1: Look at the first statement by itself and decide whether it's true or false. It's true. That means we fill in the oval marked T.

Step 2: Look at the second statement by itself. Is it true or false? It's true. That means we fill in the second oval marked T.

Step 3: Put the statements together, join them with the "because," and then decide if the sentence makes sense. "All persons must breathe *because* oxygen is necessary to human survival."

Does it make sense? Yes. So you would fill in the oval marked CE.

Try this question.

	I		II
102.	It is unlawful to drive while drunk	BECAUSE	most automobiles in the United States are powered by internal combustion engines.

Step 1: Look at statement I by itself. Is it true or false? It's true. We fill in the first oval marked T.

Step 2: Look at statement II by itself. Is it true or false? It's true. We fill in the second oval marked T.

Step 3: Now put them together. "It is unlawful to drive while drunk *because* most automobiles in the United States are powered by internal combustion engines."

Does it make sense? No. So we do not fill in the oval marked CE.

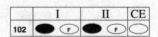

Let's do another one.

I		II

103. All Americans are   BECAUSE   no foreign country has ever
      exactly alike in their   made a valuable contribu-
      beliefs   tion to civilization.

Step 1: Look at statement I by itself. Is it true or false? It's false.
Step 2: Look at statement II by itself. Is it true or false? It's false.

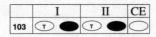

Notice that if either statement I or statement II is false, then there can be no cause-and-effect relationship, and you don't have to worry about filling in the CE oval.

When it comes to the divide and conquer strategy, use step 3 only if you determine that both statements are true.

STRATEGY #8: PROCESS OF ELIMINATION

We saved the best for last! Process of Elimination (or POE) is the most important strategy you have for the SAT Subject Test in Chemistry. It involves deciding what the bad answers are and crossing them off, instead of just looking for the right answer. Here's how it works.

Try the following question:

    1.   What is the French word for "eggplant"?

What? You don't know? Well then, you'd better guess at random. (By the way, there are no questions about vegetables, French or otherwise, on the SAT Subject Test in Chemistry. We're just using this question to make a point.)

If you really don't know the answer to a question, of course, you should always guess. But before you choose an answer at random, take a look at the problem the way you would see it on the test.

    1.   What is the French word for "eggplant?"
       (A) のみもの
       (B) すきやき
       (C) Aubergine
       (D) デザート
       (E) $&%()@@

Suddenly the question looks a lot easier, doesn't it? You may not have known the correct answer to this question, but you certainly knew four answers that were incorrect.

POE in Practice

Process of Elimination (POE for short) enables you to make your guesses really count. Incorrect answer choices are often easier to spot than correct ones. Sometimes they are logically absurd; sometimes they are the opposite of the correct answer. If you find a wrong answer, eliminate it. While you will rarely be able to eliminate all of the incorrect answer choices, it is often possible to eliminate one or two, and each time you can eliminate an answer choice, your odds of guessing correctly get better.

Try another question.

1. What is the capital of Malawi?
   (A) New York
   (B) Lilongwe
   (C) Paris
   (D) Kinshasa
   (E) Chicago

This time you could probably eliminate only three of the answer choices. However, this means that you are down to a fifty-fifty guess—much better than random guessing.

POE is a tremendously powerful tool. We refer to it in every single chapter of this book, and explain how to use it on a variety of specific question types.

Letter of the Day

Which makes more sense—guessing the same letter every time or switching around? If you think you're better off switching around, think again. As counterintuitive as it may seem, you will pick up more points consistently if you always guess the same letter. Sure, you won't get all of your random guesses correct, but you'll get some points. On the contrary, if you vary your guess answer, you might get some correct, but you might miss all of them just as easily.

It doesn't matter what letter you pick as your Letter of the Day. Contrary to popular opinion, you won't get more questions right if you guess (C) rather than any other choice. Go crazy, guess (A) or (E) on the next test you take. Just be consistent.

LET'S GET GOING

In Chapters 4 through 14, we'll teach you chemistry with our own special tailored-to-the-subject-test method. All along the way we'll ask you subject test–type questions. Then, in Part III, we'll explain the answers, showing you how to use knowledge and strategy to earn a high score.

Chapter 3
Some Basic Stuff

Some of the questions that appear early in each part of the SAT Subject Test in Chemistry will ask about the basic properties of matter and how they're measured. In this chapter, we'll review some basic terms: mass, volume, density, pressure, energy, temperature, and specific heat, and we'll show you how to approach the sometimes scary-looking questions that cover these topics on the exam.

MASS

Think about a sample of any type of matter, whether it's a hunk of solid, a glass of liquid, or a container of gas. The **mass** of any of these samples refers to the amount of matter in the sample, while **matter** simply refers to anything that occupies space and has mass.

> To convert grams to kilograms, just move the decimal point three places to the left. To convert kilograms to grams, move the decimal point 3 places to the right.
>
> 585 g = 0.585 kg
>
> To convert grams to milligrams or liters to milliliters, move the decimal three places to the right. To convert milligrams to grams or milliliters to liters, move the decimal point three places to the left.
>
> 1.524 g = 1,524 mg
> 2.4 L = 2,400 mL

Mass is measured in grams. One gram is nearly equal to the weight of a paper clip—for heavier samples it's often more convenient to use kilograms (1 kg = 1,000 grams), while for very small samples, it's convenient to use milligrams (1 mg = 1/1,000 gram). For any particular substance, a sample of greater mass means a sample with more atoms or molecules in it. (For now, think of atoms and molecules as tiny pieces of matter. We'll talk more about them later.) Two different samples of the same substance that have different masses must be made up of different numbers of atoms or molecules; for example, ten water molecules have greater mass than seven water molecules. Eight carbon dioxide molecules have greater mass than four carbon dioxide molecules.

For the SAT Subject Test in Chemistry, there's nothing more you need to know about mass itself. It represents the quantity of matter that makes up a sample. It's usually measured in grams, kilograms, or milligrams.

VOLUME

Again, suppose we're thinking about a sample of matter—solid, liquid, or gas. When we say volume, we're talking about how much room the sample takes up in space. The SAT Subject Test in Chemistry usually measures volume in liters (L) or milliliters (mL; 1 mL = 1/1,000 L—also keep in mind that 1 mL = 1 cm^3, or cubic centimeter).

How a sample is measured depends on what state it's in—whether it is a solid, liquid, or gas. When the sample is a liquid, we can determine its volume by pouring it into a graduated cylinder or any other measuring flask.

If the sample is a solid, we can immerse it in a liquid and see how much liquid it displaces. In other words, we can compare the original volume of the liquid and the volume of the solid/liquid combination, knowing that the difference will be equal to the volume of the solid.

For samples of gas, the volume of the gas is always equal to the volume of its container, since a gas always expands to fill its container. How do we learn the volume of the container? Well, if the volume isn't marked on the container, we can just treat the container as a solid object and find out its volume by immersing it in a liquid.

DENSITY

The property of density is intrinsic to a substance; substances such as water, lead, carbon dioxide, or ethyl alcohol, for example, all have different densities. **Density** is a measure of the ratio of an object's mass to its volume.

Generally, if we say "water is heavy," we mean that water has a high density relative to other substances. Ten kilograms of water occupy a relatively small volume—about 10 L. When we say "feathers are light," we mean that feathers have a low density relative to other substances. Ten kilograms of feathers occupy a relatively large volume.

How do we measure density? We measure it in units that reflect mass per volume. That means we might measure it in g/L, or mg/L, or kg/mL, or any other combination that represents mass per volume. We calculate density using the following formula:

$$\text{density} = \frac{\text{mass (kg)}}{\text{volume (m}^3)}$$

Consider a 2 mL sample of substance X and a 2 mL sample of substance Y. The sample of substance X weighs 8 grams, and the sample of substance Y weighs 6 grams. Therefore:

$$\text{Density X} = \frac{8 \text{ g}}{2 \text{ ml}} = 4 \text{ g/mL}$$

$$\text{Density Y} = \frac{6 \text{ g}}{2 \text{ ml}} = 3 \text{ g/mL}$$

All this means is that every 1 mL of substance X weighs 4 grams, and every 1 mL of substance Y weighs 3 grams. So, for this example, 5 mL of X weighs 20 grams, and 15 grams of Y occupies a volume of 5 mL.

At a given temperature, a certain mass of a substance that is a solid or a liquid has a fixed volume. This means that for liquids and solids at a given temperature, density does not vary. The same is not true of gases. A sample of any gas will expand to fill its container. We can double the volume of the container without changing the mass of the sample of the gas, and the density will decrease by a factor of two.

PRESSURE

When test writers say "pressure," they are usually talking about (1) the force that a sample of gas in a closed container exerts on the container walls, or (2) a solid or liquid standing in an environment and the force that a gas is exerting on the walls of the environment and everything in it—including the surface of the solid or liquid.

(1)   (2)

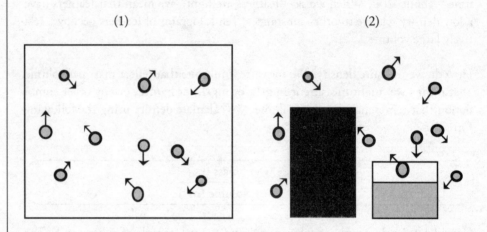

So, what units do we use to express pressure? A few. There are torr, millimeters of mercury (mmHg), and atmospheres (atm): 1 torr and 1 mmHg are equal, and 760 torr (or 760 mmHg) = 1 atm.

Pressure Basics
- Units of pressure: standard pressure = 760 torr = 760 mmHg = 1 atm
- Pressure is measured with a barometer or a manometer

Any question on the exam that contains any of the above terms will in some way be concerned with pressure. So when you see such a question, think pressure and you'll be on the right track.

What instruments are used to measure pressure? The barometer and the manometer. Both the barometer and manometer involve the use of the liquid metal mercury (Hg) to determine atmospheric pressure.

ENERGY

You will have to know a few things about energy for the SAT Subject Test in Chemistry. First, remember that energy exists in different forms, but it is always defined as the ability to do work or transfer heat. Energy can exist as heat, light, kinetic energy, or chemical bond energy. When we say kinetic energy, we're talking about the energy that an object possesses by virtue of the fact that it is moving. A moving bus, train, or car has kinetic energy. When we deal with chemistry, we're usually thinking about molecules that move; moving molecules have kinetic energy. The faster molecules move, the higher their kinetic energy.

What units are used to describe energy?

- calories (cal)
- joules (J) or kilojoules (1 kJ equals 1,000 J)

One calorie (1 cal) is equal to slightly more than 4 J (4.186 J to be specific).

What instrument is used to measure energy?

- a calorimeter

Keep the following things in mind when considering energy:

- Kinetic energy is the energy contained in the movement of molecules. The greater the kinetic energy, the faster the movement and the higher the temperature of the molecules.
- Chemical bonds contain energy. Breaking bonds requires energy; forming bonds releases energy.
- Heat is the transfer of kinetic energy from one thing to another.
- A calorimeter measures energy.

TEMPERATURE AND SPECIFIC HEAT

What exactly is heat? When you touch something warm, you feel heat, but what is that? Technically, **heat** is defined as the flow of energy from a body at a higher temperature to one at a lower temperature. If a particular sample of a substance experiences an increase in temperature, then you can say that particular sample has experienced an increase in heat content. So what exactly does temperature measure? Temperature measures the average kinetic energy of molecules in a sample; as the molecules in a sample move more quickly, the temperature of that sample increases.

For certain substances, the addition of a large amount of heat will have only a small effect on their temperature, while for other substances, the addition of a small amount of heat will have a dramatic effect on their temperature. The **heat capacity** of a substance refers to the amount of heat it must absorb for its temperature to be raised 1°C. Different substances have different heat capacities, and the heat capacity of a substance is described by its specific heat. The **specific heat** of a substance is the heat capacity of 1 gram of the substance.

Here's an equation that puts together all of the terms we just reviewed.

$$q = mc\Delta T$$

In this equation:

q = heat

m = mass

c = specific heat

ΔT = the difference between initial and final temperatures
(Δ means change or difference)

For example, it takes 1 calorie of heat to raise the temperature of 1 gram of water by 1°C. So we say that the specific heat of water is 1 cal/g • °C. The specific heat of carbon is 0.033 cal/g • °C, so it takes 0.033 calorie to raise the temperature of 1 gram of carbon by 1°C.

Now suppose you take 40 grams of water and 40 grams of carbon and add 200 calories of heat to each sample. Because water has a significantly higher specific heat than carbon, the input of the same amount of heat to both samples will result in a greater increase in temperature in the carbon sample than in the sample of water. See the calculations below.

$$\Delta T = \frac{q}{mc}$$

Same Equation, Different Form

Notice that this is the same equation we just gave you. We just shuffled things around a bit.

$$\Delta T_{carbon} = \frac{(200 \text{ cal})}{(40 \text{ g})\left(.033 \dfrac{\text{cal}}{\text{g} \cdot \text{°C}}\right)} = 151.5\text{°C}$$

$$\Delta T_{water} = \frac{(200 \text{ cal})}{(40 \text{ g})\left(1 \dfrac{\text{cal}}{\text{g} \cdot \text{°C}}\right)} = 5\text{°C}$$

Carbon increases in temperature by 151.5°C, but water increases in temperature by only 5°C. Why? Because the specific heat of water is roughly 30 times that of carbon.

Similarly, if we have equal masses of water and carbon and we want to raise the temperature of each sample by the same amount, we'll have to put about 30 times more heat into the water than we have to put into the carbon.

We've been talking about temperature in °C, and when we think of specific heat, that's the right unit of temperature to use. But, for this test, you also need to know about another temperature scale: degrees Kelvin (K). The Kelvin scale is also called the "absolute temperature" scale. How do you convert °C to K?

$$K = °C + 273$$
$$0 \ K = -273°C$$
$$0°C = 273 \ K$$

Temperature: average kinetic energy; °C and K
Specific heat: the amount of heat required to raise the temperature of 1 gram of a substance by 1°C; cal/g • °C

And remember, when it comes to heat content, temperature is a *reflection* of, but not a direct *measure* of, heat content. Heat content is not measured in °C. It's measured in calories, joules, or kilojoules.

HOW THE SAT SUBJECT TEST IN CHEMISTRY WILL TEST YOU ON ALL THIS

The SAT Subject Test in Chemistry writers sometimes make their questions look more difficult than they are by trying to catch you off guard and steer you off course. They might, for instance, use camouflage and temptation traps. Try the ten subject test–type questions that follow, keeping the techniques from Chapter 2 in mind. You can find the answers to the following questions in the beginning of Part IV.

DRILL 1

Question Type A

Questions 1–4 refer to the following.

(A) Volume
(B) Temperature
(C) Density
(D) Pressure
(E) Mass

1. Is a quantity that allows one to calculate mass if density is known

2. Always varies with the number of molecules present in a sample of a particular substance

3. Can be expressed as kilograms per liter

4. Is a measure of the average kinetic energy of a substance's molecules

Question Type B

<table>
<thead>
<tr><th></th><th>I</th><th></th><th>II</th></tr>
</thead>
</table>

101.   If the density of a solid substance and its volume are both known, mass can be calculated   BECAUSE   for any substance, the relationship between mass and volume varies directly with sample size.

102.   For any substance, solid, liquid, or gas, mass increases as volume increases   BECAUSE   density represents mass per volume.

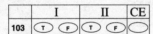

103.   If substances X and Y have specific heats of 0.2 cal/g · °C and 0.6 cal/g · °C, respectively, then 10 g of substance X has less heat content than 10 g of substance Y   BECAUSE   a substance with a relatively low specific heat will, when heated, experience less change in its temperature than a substance with a relatively high specific heat.

<table>
<thead>
<tr><th></th><th>I</th><th>II</th><th>CE</th></tr>
</thead>
<tbody>
<tr><td>103</td><td>T   F</td><td>T   F</td><td>◯</td></tr>
</tbody>
</table>

Question Type C

24. Two solid objects are of equal volume, but object A has density = X, and object B has density = (0.5)(X).

    Which of the following is true concerning objects A and B?

    (A) Objects A and B are of equal density.
    (B) Object B has twice the density of object A.
    (C) Objects A and B are of equal mass.
    (D) Object A has one half the mass of object B.
    (E) Object A has twice the mass of object B.

25. The specific heat of a substance is approximately 0.5 cal/g · °C. If 30 calories of heat are absorbed by 15 g of the substance at 30°C, its temperature will become

    (A) 19°C
    (B) 32°C
    (C) 34°C
    (D) 60°C
    (E) 90°C

26. Ten grams of oxygen gas are in a rigid 5 L vessel. If 2 g of oxygen gas are added to the vessel and temperature is kept constant, which of the following characteristics of the gas will increase?

    I.   Mass
    II. Density
    III. Pressure

    (A) I only
    (B) III only
    (C) I and II only
    (D) II and III only
    (E) I, II, and III

Summary

o   Mass is a measure of the amount of matter in a sample and is measured in grams or kilograms.

o   Volume is the amount of space something takes up and is measured in cubic centimeters, milliliters, or liters.

o   Density is a measure of the mass something has per unit volume, and is given by:

$$\text{density} = \frac{\text{mass (kg)}}{\text{volume (m}^3)}$$

o   Pressure is force per unit area and describes how much a sample of gas or liquid pushes on the surfaces the sample is in contact with.
   •   Standard pressure is 760 mmHg = 760 torr = 1 atm.
   •   Atmospheric pressure is measured with a barometer. Pressure in the laboratory is measured with a manometer.

o   Energy is measured in calories and joules, where 1 calorie = 4.186 joules.

o   Chemistry is concerned with two types of energy: kinetic energy is the energy of motion of molecules, and bond energy is the energy stored in a chemical bond.

o   Temperature is measured in degrees Celsius and Kelvin, where K = 273 + °C.

o   Specific heat is the amount of energy required to raise the temperature of 1 gram of substance 1 degree Celsius.

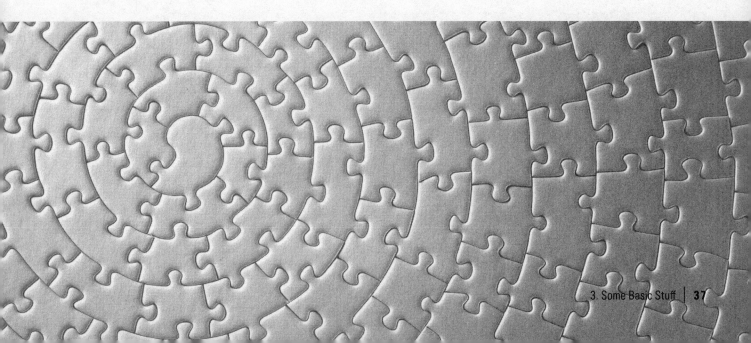

Part II
Practice Test 1

Practice Test 1

PRACTICE SAT SUBJECT TEST
IN CHEMISTRY–TEST 1

You are about to take the first of three practice SAT Subject Tests in Chemistry. The bubble sheet can be found near the back of the book; feel free to tear it out for use. (Just don't lose it!)

After answering questions 1–23, which constitute Part A, you'll be directed to answer questions 101–116, which constitute Part B. Then you will begin again at question 24. Questions 24–70 constitute Part C.

When you're ready to score yourself, refer to the answer key and scoring instructions on pages 60 and 74. Full explanations regarding the correct answers to all questions start on page 61.

SAT SUBJECT TEST IN CHEMISTRY

MATERIAL IN THE FOLLOWING TABLE MAY BE USEFUL IN ANSWERING THE QUESTIONS IN THIS EXAMINATION.

DO NOT DETACH FROM BOOK.

PERIODIC TABLE OF THE ELEMENTS

1 H 1.0079																	2 He 4.0026
3 Li 6.941	4 Be 9.012											5 B 10.811	6 C 12.011	7 N 14.007	8 O 16.00	9 F 19.00	10 Ne 20.179
11 Na 22.99	12 Mg 24.30											13 Al 26.98	14 Si 28.09	15 P 30.974	16 S 32.06	17 Cl 35.453	18 Ar 39.948
19 K 39.10	20 Ca 40.48	21 Sc 44.96	22 Ti 47.90	23 V 50.94	24 Cr 52.00	25 Mn 54.938	26 Fe 55.85	27 Co 58.93	28 Ni 58.69	29 Cu 63.55	30 Zn 65.39	31 Ga 69.72	32 Ge 72.59	33 As 74.92	34 Se 78.96	35 Br 79.90	36 Kr 83.80
37 Rb 85.47	38 Sr 87.62	39 Y 88.91	40 Zr 91.22	41 Nb 92.91	42 Mo 95.94	43 Tc (98)	44 Ru 101.1	45 Rh 102.91	46 Pd 106.42	47 Ag 107.87	48 Cd 112.41	49 In 114.82	50 Sn 118.71	51 Sb 121.75	52 Te 127.60	53 I 126.91	54 Xe 131.29
55 Cs 132.91	56 Ba 137.33	57 *La 138.91	72 Hf 178.49	73 Ta 180.95	74 W 183.85	75 Re 186.21	76 Os 190.2	77 Ir 192.2	78 Pt 195.08	79 Au 196.97	80 Hg 200.59	81 Tl 204.38	82 Pb 207.2	83 Bi 208.98	84 Po (209)	85 At (210)	86 Rn (222)
87 Fr (223)	88 Ra 226.02	89 †Ac 227.03	104 Rf (261)	105 Db (262)	106 Sg (266)	107 Bh (264)	108 Hs (277)	109 Mt (268)	110 Ds (271)	111 Rg (272)	112 § (277)						

§ Not yet named

*Lanthanide Series	58 Ce 140.12	59 Pr 140.91	60 Nd 144.24	61 Pm (145)	62 Sm 150.4	63 Eu 151.97	64 Gd 157.25	65 Tb 158.93	66 Dy 162.50	67 Ho 164.93	68 Er 167.26	69 Tm 168.93	70 Yb 173.04	71 Lu 174.97
†Actinide Series	90 Th 232.04	91 Pa 231.04	92 U 238.03	93 Np 237.05	94 Pu (244)	95 Am (243)	96 Cm (247)	97 Bk (247)	98 Cf (251)	99 Es (252)	100 Fm (257)	101 Md (258)	102 No (259)	103 Lr (262)

GO ON TO THE NEXT PAGE

<u>Note:</u> For all questions involving solutions and/or chemical equations, assume that the system is in pure water unless otherwise stated.

Part A

Directions: Each set of lettered choices below refers to the numbered statements or questions immediately following it. Select the one lettered choice that best fits each statement or answers each question, and then fill in the corresponding oval on the answer sheet. A choice may be used once, more than once, or not at all in each set.

Questions 1–4 refer to the following.

(A) Thermometer
(B) Conductivity tester
(C) Volumetric flask
(D) Buret
(E) Graduated cylinder

1. May be used in combination with a calorimeter to compare the specific heats of two substances

2. Is used to measure the volume of a solid by water displacement

3. Useful for adding small quantities of acid into a base

4. Is considered precise at a specific volume

Questions 5–9 refer to the following.

(A) Nucleic acids
(B) Proteins
(C) Carbohydrates
(D) Lipids
(E) Electrolytes

5. Always amphoteric in nature

6. Usually speed up the rate of a cellular reaction

7. Deoxyribose in DNA nucleotides belongs to this family of biologically important molecules

8. Always ionic in nature

9. Tend not to be water soluble, and aggregate into droplets or molecular bilayers

GO ON TO THE NEXT PAGE →

Questions 10–13 refer to the following.

(A) $Ag^+ + Br^- \rightarrow AgBr$

(B) $^{14}_{6}C \rightarrow {}^{14}_{7}N + {}^{0}_{-1}e$

(C) $^{234}_{92}U \rightarrow {}^{230}_{90}Th + {}^{4}_{2}He$

(D) $^{30}_{15}P \rightarrow {}^{30}_{14}Si + {}^{0}_{1}e$

(E) $2HgO \rightarrow 2Hg + O_2$

10. Represents the decomposition of a compound into its constituent elements

11. Represents alpha decay

12. Represents an oxidation-reduction reaction

13. Causes the neutron-to-proton ratio in a nucleus to be lowered

Questions 14–16 refer to the following.

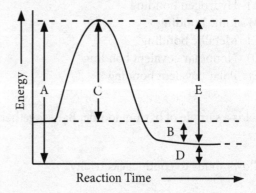

14. Is the activation energy of the reverse reaction

15. Is the enthalpy change of the forward reaction

16. Represents energy of the activated complex

GO ON TO THE NEXT PAGE

Questions 17–20 refer to the following.

    (A) Hydrogen bonding
    (B) Ionic bonding
    (C) Metallic bonding
    (D) Nonpolar covalent bonding
    (E) Polar covalent bonding

17. Holds a sample of barium iodide, BaI_2, together

18. Allows solids to conduct electricity

19. Attracts atoms of hydrogen to each other in an H_2 molecule

20. Responsible for relatively low vapor pressure of water

Questions 21–23 refer to the following.

    (A) Iron(III) chloride, $FeCl_3(s)$
    (B) Iodine, $I_2(s)$
    (C) Sodium hydroxide, $NaOH(s)$
    (D) Sucrose, $C_{12}H_{22}O_{11}(s)$
    (E) Graphite, $C(s)$

21. Gives off a purplish vapor as it sublimes

22. Can conduct electricity in the solid state

23. Its dissolution in water is highly exothermic

GO ON TO THE NEXT PAGE

PLEASE GO TO THE SPECIAL SECTION LABELED CHEMISTRY AT THE LOWER RIGHT-HAND CORNER OF THE ANSWER SHEET YOU ARE WORKING ON AND ANSWER QUESTIONS 101–116 ACCORDING TO THE FOLLOWING DIRECTIONS.

Part B

Directions: Each question below consists of two statements, I in the left-hand column and II in the right-hand column. For each question, determine whether statement I is true or false and whether statement II is true or false, and fill in the corresponding T or F ovals on your answer sheet. Fill in oval CE only if statement II is a correct explanation of statement I.

EXAMPLES:

	I		II
EX 1.	H_2SO_4 is a strong acid	BECAUSE	H_2SO_4 contains sulfur.
EX 2.	An atom of oxygen is electrically neutral	BECAUSE	an oxygen atom contains an equal number of protons and electrons.

SAMPLE ANSWERS

	I		II		CE
EX 1	●	F	●	F	○
EX 2	●	F	●	F	●

	I		II
101.	Carbon is a nonmetal	BECAUSE	carbon atoms can bond with each other.
102.	Two isotopes of the same element have the same mass number	BECAUSE	isotopes have the same number of protons.
103.	The density of a sample of water is doubled by doubling its mass	BECAUSE	compared to a gas, the molecules in a liquid are relatively far apart.
104.	Sodium and cesium exhibit similar chemical properties	BECAUSE	their atoms have the same number of valence electrons.
105.	An endothermic reaction can be spontaneous	BECAUSE	both enthalpy and entropy changes affect the value of a reaction's Gibbs free energy change.
106.	The $4s$ orbital fills before the $3d$ orbitals	BECAUSE	subshells fill in order from lower to higher energy.

GO ON TO THE NEXT PAGE ➡

I   II

107.	Calcium acts as a reducing agent when it reacts with bromine	BECAUSE	mass is conserved in a chemical reaction.
108.	If an acid is added to pure water, it increases the water's pH	BECAUSE	adding an acid to water raises the hydrogen ion concentration in the water.
109.	Covalent bonds must be broken for a liquid to boil	BECAUSE	heat must be released for a liquid to change into a gas.
110.	Alpha particles can be detected using a Geiger counter	BECAUSE	all radioactive elements are highly chemically reactive.
111.	As ice absorbs heat and begins to melt, its temperature remains constant	BECAUSE	the absorbed heat is consumed by the breaking of intermolecular interactions.
112.	When a solute is added to pure water, the vapor pressure of the water will decrease	BECAUSE	all solutes dissociate into positive and negative ions.
113.	The rate of a reaction is accelerated by increasing temperature	BECAUSE	a large equilibrium constant favors the formation of product.
114.	Hydrofluoric acid, HF(aq), is a weaker electrolyte than hydrochloric acid, HCl(aq),	BECAUSE	fluorine has a lower electronegativity than chlorine.
115.	A nonpolar molecule can have polar bonds	BECAUSE	polar bonds can be symmetrically arranged in a molecule so that there are no net poles.

GO ON TO THE NEXT PAGE

RETURN TO THE SECTION OF YOUR ANSWER SHEET YOU STARTED FOR **CHEMISTRY** AND ANSWER QUESTIONS 24–70.

Part C

Directions: Each of the questions or incomplete statements below is followed by five suggested answers or completions. Select the one that is best in each case and then fill in the corresponding oval on the answer sheet.

24. What is the number of protons and neutrons in an atom with mass number 89 and atomic number 39 ?

    (A) 50 protons and 50 neutrons
    (B) 50 protons and 39 neutrons
    (C) 39 protons and 89 neutrons
    (D) 39 protons and 50 neutrons
    (E) 39 protons and 39 neutrons

$$\ldots C_4H_{10}(g) + \ldots O_2(g) \rightarrow \ldots CO_2(g) + \ldots H_2O(l)$$

25. When the above equation is balanced using the lowest whole-number terms, the coefficient of CO_2 is

    (A) 2
    (B) 4
    (C) 8
    (D) 10
    (E) 13

26. Which of the following is closest in mass to a proton?

    (A) Alpha particle
    (B) Positron
    (C) Neutron
    (D) Electron
    (E) Hydrogen molecule

27. What is the approximate percentage composition by mass of the element oxygen in the compound $HClO_4$?

    (A) 16%
    (B) 32%
    (C) 50%
    (D) 64%
    (E) 75%

28. If two atoms that differ in electronegativity combine by chemical reaction and share electrons, the bond that joins them will be

    (A) metallic
    (B) ionic
    (C) a hydrogen bond
    (D) nonpolar covalent
    (E) polar covalent

29. When the temperature of a 20-gram sample of water is increased from 10°C to 30°C, the heat transferred to the water is

    (A) 600 calories
    (B) 400 calories
    (C) 200 calories
    (D) 30 calories
    (E) 20 calories

30. What is the oxidation state of chromium, Cr, in the compound potassium dichromate, $K_2Cr_2O_7$?

    (A) +1
    (B) +2
    (C) +3
    (D) +6
    (E) +12

31. An aqueous solution with pH 5 at 25°C has a hydroxide ion (OH^-) concentration of

    (A) 1×10^{-11} molar
    (B) 1×10^{-9} molar
    (C) 1×10^{-7} molar
    (D) 1×10^{-5} molar
    (E) 1×10^{-3} molar

GO ON TO THE NEXT PAGE

$$2H_2O(g) \rightarrow 2H_2(g) + O_2(g)$$

32. The volume of water vapor required to produce 44.8 liters of oxygen by the above reaction is

  (A) 11.2 liters
  (B) 22.4 liters
  (C) 44.8 liters
  (D) 89.6 liters
  (E) 100.0 liters

33. When 190 grams of $MgCl_2$ are dissolved in water and the resulting solution is 500 milliliters in volume, what is the molar concentration of $MgCl_2$ in the solution?

  (A) 2.0 *M*
  (B) 4.0 *M*
  (C) 8.0 *M*
  (D) 12.0 *M*
  (E) 16.0 *M*

34. When a fixed amount of gas has its Kelvin temperature doubled and its pressure doubled, the new volume of the gas is

  (A) four times greater than its original volume
  (B) twice its original volume
  (C) unchanged
  (D) one-half its original volume
  (E) one-fourth its original volume

35. In 12.4 hours, a 100 gram sample of an element decays so that its mass is 25 grams. What is the approximate half-life of this radioactive substance?

  (A) 1.6 hours
  (B) 3.1 hours
  (C) 6.2 hours
  (D) 24.8 hours
  (E) 49.6 hours

36. In the equation $Q \rightarrow {}^{4}_{2}He + {}^{216}_{85}At$, the species represented by Q is

  (A) ${}^{220}_{87}Fr$
  (B) ${}^{212}_{83}Bi$
  (C) ${}^{220}_{87}At$
  (D) ${}^{212}_{83}Fr$
  (E) ${}^{216}_{85}Bi$

37. A compound with a molecular weight of 56 amu has an empirical formula of CH_2. What is its molecular formula?

  (A) C_2H_2
  (B) C_2H_4
  (C) C_4H_8
  (D) C_4H_{10}
  (E) C_6H_{12}

38. The change in heat energy for a reaction is best expressed as a change in

  (A) enthalpy
  (B) absolute temperature
  (C) specific heat
  (D) entropy
  (E) kinetic energy

$$\dots NF_3(g) + \dots H_2O(g) \rightarrow \dots HF(g) + \dots NO(g) + \dots NO_2(g)$$

39. When the equation for the reaction above is balanced, how many moles of NF_3 would be required to react completely with 6 moles of H_2O ?

  (A) 0.5 mole
  (B) 1 mole
  (C) 2 moles
  (D) 3 moles
  (E) 4 moles

GO ON TO THE NEXT PAGE

40. Which characteristic is associated with bases?

    (A) React with metal to produce hydrogen gas
    (B) Donate an unshared electron pair
    (C) Always contain the hydroxide ion in their structure
    (D) Taste sour
    (E) Formed by the reaction of a nonmetal oxide and water

41. An element has the following properties: shiny, brittle, poor electrical conductivity, and high melting point. This element can be best classified as a(n)

    (A) alkali metal
    (B) halogen
    (C) metalloid
    (D) transition metal
    (E) noble gas

42. Which of the following forward processes produces a decrease in entropy?

    I. $H_2O(g) \rightarrow H_2O(l)$
    II. $Fe^{2+}(aq) + S^{2-}(aq) \rightarrow FeS(s)$
    III. $2SO_3(g) \rightleftharpoons 2SO_2(g) + O_2(g)$

    (A) I only
    (B) III only
    (C) I and II only
    (D) II and III only
    (E) I, II, and III

43. Which of the following will raise the boiling point of a sample of water?

    (A) Heat the water
    (B) Mix gasoline into the water
    (C) Bring the water sample to a higher altitude
    (D) Place the water sample on a magnetic stirrer
    (E) Dissolve table sugar into the water

44. Elements H and J lie in the same period. If the atoms of H are smaller than the atoms of J, then compared to atoms of J, atoms of H are most likely to

    (A) exist in a greater number of isotopes
    (B) exist in a lesser number of isotopes
    (C) exist in a greater number of oxidation states
    (D) have a greater positive charge in their nuclei
    (E) have a lesser positive charge in their nuclei

$$\ldots Al(s) + \ldots O_2(g) \rightarrow \ldots Al_2O_3(s)$$

45. When the equation representing the reaction shown above is completed and balanced and all coefficients are reduced to lowest whole-number terms, the coefficient of $O_2(g)$ is

    (A) 1
    (B) 2
    (C) 3
    (D) 4
    (E) 6

46. Which of the following solids has a brilliant blue color?

    (A) $Ca(OH)_2$
    (B) KCl
    (C) NaBr
    (D) Fe_2O_3
    (E) $CuSO_4$

47. Twenty-five percent of element X exists as ^{210}X and 75 percent of it exists as ^{214}X. What is the atomic weight of element X in amu?

    (A) 85
    (B) 211
    (C) 212
    (D) 213
    (E) 214

GO ON TO THE NEXT PAGE

48. A 600-milliliter container holds 2 moles of $O_2(g)$, 3 moles of $H_2(g)$, and 1 mole of He(g). Total pressure within the container is 760 torr. What is the partial pressure of O_2?

    (A) 127 torr
    (B) 253 torr
    (C) 380 torr
    (D) 507 torr
    (E) 760 torr

$$Fe(OH)_3(s) \leftrightarrows Fe^{3+}(aq) + 3OH^-(aq)$$

49. The ionic solid $Fe(OH)_3$ is added to water and dissociates into its component ions, as shown above. The solubility product expression for the saturated solution is

    (A) $K_{sp} = [Fe^{3+}][OH^-]$

    (B) $K_{sp} = [Fe^{3+}][3OH^-]$

    (C) $K_{sp} = [Fe^{3+}][3OH^-]^3$

    (D) $K_{sp} = [Fe^{3+}][OH^-]^3$

    (E) $K_{sp} = \dfrac{[Fe^{3+}][OH^-]^3}{[Fe(OH)_3]}$

50. Which of the following electron configurations represents an atom of magnesium in an excited state?

    (A) $1s^2 2s^2 2p^6$
    (B) $1s^2 2s^2 2p^6 3s^2$
    (C) $1s^2 2s^2 2p^5 3s^2 3p^2$
    (D) $1s^2 2s^2 2p^6 3s^1 3p^1$
    (E) $1s^2 2s^2 2p^6 3s^1 3p^2$

51. All of the following when added to water will produce an electrolytic solution EXCEPT

    (A) $N_2(g)$
    (B) $HCl(g)$
    (C) $KOH(s)$
    (D) $NaI(s)$
    (E) $CaCl_2(s)$

$$NH_3(aq) + H_2CO_3(aq) \leftrightarrows NH_4^+(aq) + HCO_3^-(aq)$$

52. In the reaction represented above, NH_4^+ acts as a(n)

    (A) indicator
    (B) hydrate
    (C) acid
    (D) base
    (E) salt

53. Which species has the ground state electron configuration $1s^2 2s^2 2p^6 3s^2 3p^6$?

    (A) Sulfide ion, S^{2-}
    (B) Bromide ion, Br^-
    (C) Neon atom, Ne
    (D) Chromium ion, Cr^{3+}
    (E) Potassium atom, K

54. Which of the following species is amphoteric?

    (A) Na_3PO_4
    (B) HCO_3^-
    (C) KOH
    (D) HNO_3
    (E) $C_2O_4^{2-}$

GO ON TO THE NEXT PAGE

55. An ideal gas has a volume of 10 liters at 20°C and a pressure of 750 mmHg. Which of the following expressions is needed to determine the volume of the same amount of gas at STP?

(A) $10 \times \dfrac{750}{760} \times \dfrac{0}{20}$ L

(B) $10 \times \dfrac{750}{760} \times \dfrac{293}{273}$ L

(C) $10 \times \dfrac{760}{750} \times \dfrac{0}{20}$ L

(D) $10 \times \dfrac{760}{750} \times \dfrac{273}{293}$ L

(E) $10 \times \dfrac{750}{760} \times \dfrac{273}{293}$ L

Questions 56 and 57 pertain to the phase diagram for substance Z below.

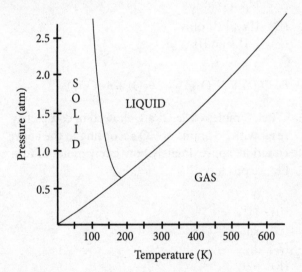

56. Substance Z is at 0.5 atm and 200 K. If the pressure on substance Z is steadily increased and its temperature is kept constant, what phase change will eventually occur?

(A) Condensation
(B) Freezing
(C) Melting
(D) Sublimation
(E) Vaporization

57. The normal boiling point of substance Z is closest to

(A) 100 K
(B) 200 K
(C) 300 K
(D) 400 K
(E) 500 K

58. The shape of a PCl_3 molecule is described as

(A) bent
(B) trigonal pyramidal
(C) linear
(D) trigonal planar
(E) tetrahedral

59. What volume of 0.4 M $Ba(OH)_2$ (aq) is needed to exactly neutralize 100 milliliters of 0.2 M HBr(aq)?

(A) 25 mL
(B) 50 mL
(C) 100 mL
(D) 200 mL
(E) 400 mL

60. Which of the following is true regarding the aqueous dissociation of HCN, $K_a = 4.9 \times 10^{-10}$ at 25°C?

   I.   At equilibrium, $[H^+] = [CN^-]$
  II. At equilibrium, $[H^+] > [HCN]$
 III. HCN(aq) is a strong acid.

(A) I only
(B) II only
(C) I and II only
(D) II and III only
(E) I, II, and III

GO ON TO THE NEXT PAGE

61. Which of the following atoms has the largest second ionization energy?

    (A) Silicon, Si
    (B) Calcium, Ca
    (C) Chlorine, Cl
    (D) Iron, Fe
    (E) Sodium, Na

Question 62 refers to the overall reaction and half-reactions with standard reduction potentials below.

$$2H_2O(l) \rightarrow 2H_2(g) + O_2(g)$$

$$\Delta H° = + 572 \text{ kJ/mol}$$

62. Given the enthalpy change for the above reaction, what would the enthalpy change for

    $$H_2(g) + \frac{1}{2}O_2(g) \rightarrow H_2O(l) ?$$

    (A) – 286 kJ/mol
    (B) + 286 kJ/mol
    (C) – 1044 kJ/mol
    (D) + 1044 kJ/mol
    (E) + 572 kJ/mol

63. The reaction of zinc metal, Zn, and hydrochloric acid, HCl, produces which of the following?

    I. $H_2(g)$
    II. $Cl_2(g)$
    III. $Zn^{2+}(aq)$

    (A) II only
    (B) III only
    (C) I and II only
    (D) I and III only
    (E) I, II, and III

Questions 64 and 65 refer to the following reaction.

$$2H_2S(g) + 3O_2(g) \rightleftharpoons 2SO_2(g) + 2H_2O(g) + \text{heat}$$

64. For the above reaction, the equilibrium concentration of $SO_2(g)$ can be increased by

    (A) adding neon gas
    (B) increasing the temperature
    (C) adding a catalyst
    (D) increasing the concentration of $H_2O(g)$
    (E) increasing the concentration of $O_2(g)$

65. Which of the following is increased by decreasing the volume of the reaction system?

    I. Rate of reaction
    II. Equilibrium concentration of reactants
    III. Value of K_{eq}

    (A) I only
    (B) III only
    (C) I and II only
    (D) II and III only
    (E) I, II, and III

$$Fe_2O_3(s) + 3CO(g) \rightarrow 2Fe(s) + 3CO_2(g)$$

66. When 3 moles of Fe_2O_3 are allowed to completely react with 56 grams of CO according to the above equation, approximately how many moles of iron, Fe, are produced?

    (A) 0.7
    (B) 1.3
    (C) 2.0
    (D) 2.7
    (E) 6.0

GO ON TO THE NEXT PAGE

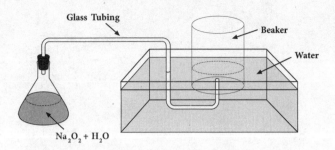

$$2Na_2O_2(s) + 2H_2O(l) \rightarrow 4NaOH(aq) + O_2(g)$$

67. Sodium peroxide, Na_2O_2, and water react in the flask at 25°C according to the equation and in the diagram above. If water levels are equal inside and outside the beaker, then the gas pressure inside the beaker is equal to the

(A) pressure of oxygen gas collected
(B) vapor pressure of water at 25°C
(C) sum of pressure of oxygen gas collected and atmospheric pressure
(D) sum of vapor pressure of water at 25°C and atmospheric pressure
(E) sum of pressure of oxygen gas collected and vapor pressure of water at 25°C

68. Which of the following molecules has the strongest carbon-to-carbon bond?

(A) C_2H_2
(B) C_2H_4
(C) C_2H_6
(D) C_3H_8
(E) C_4H_{10}

$$N_2O_4(g) \rightleftharpoons 2NO_2(g)$$

The following concentration data were gathered for the above reaction at 5 minute intervals from the start of an experiment:

Time After Start of Experiment	$[N_2O_4]$	$[NO_2]$
0 min (start)	0.00 M	0.50 M
5 min	0.10 M	0.33 M
10 min	0.20 M	0.20 M
15 min	0.25 M	0.15 M
20 min	0.28 M	0.13 M
25 min	0.28 M	0.13 M

69. If the experiment was carried out in a closed system at constant temperature, then during which time interval (from the start of the experiment) did the reaction most likely achieve equilibrium?

(A) 0 min (start) to 5 min
(B) 5 min to 10 min
(C) 10 min to 15 min
(D) 15 min to 20 min
(E) 20 min to 25 min

70. The emission spectrum of an element can be created when atoms of that element are

(A) reacted with a different atom to form a new molecule
(B) fired from a machine into a patch of metal foil
(C) change phase
(D) exposed to an outside energy source
(E) cooled to extremely low temperatures

STOP

If you finish before time is called, you may check your work on this section only.
Do not turn to any other section in the test.

Practice Test 1:
Answers and
Explanations

PRACTICE TEST 1 ANSWER KEY

Question Number	Correct Answer	Right	Wrong	Question Number	Correct Answer	Right	Wrong
Part A				*Part C*			
1.	A	_____	_____	24.	D	_____	_____
2.	E	_____	_____	25.	C	_____	_____
3.	D	_____	_____	26.	C	_____	_____
4.	C	_____	_____	27.	D	_____	_____
5.	B	_____	_____	28.	E	_____	_____
6.	B	_____	_____	29.	B	_____	_____
7.	C	_____	_____	30.	D	_____	_____
8.	E	_____	_____	31.	B	_____	_____
9.	D	_____	_____	32.	D	_____	_____
10.	E	_____	_____	33.	B	_____	_____
11.	C	_____	_____	34.	C	_____	_____
12.	E	_____	_____	35.	C	_____	_____
13.	B	_____	_____	36.	A	_____	_____
14.	E	_____	_____	37.	C	_____	_____
15.	B	_____	_____	38.	A	_____	_____
16.	A	_____	_____	39.	E	_____	_____
17.	B	_____	_____	40.	B	_____	_____
18.	C	_____	_____	41.	C	_____	_____
19.	D	_____	_____	42.	C	_____	_____
20.	A	_____	_____	43.	E	_____	_____
21.	B	_____	_____	44.	D	_____	_____
22.	E	_____	_____	45.	C	_____	_____
23.	C	_____	_____	46.	E	_____	_____
				47.	D	_____	_____
Part B				48.	B	_____	_____
101.	T, T			49.	D	_____	_____
102.	F, T			50.	D	_____	_____
103.	F, F			51.	A	_____	_____
104.	T, T, CE			52.	C	_____	_____
105.	T, T, CE			53.	A	_____	_____
106.	T, T, CE			54.	B	_____	_____
107.	T, T			55.	E	_____	_____
108.	F, T			56.	A	_____	_____
109.	F, F			57.	C	_____	_____
110.	T, F			58.	B	_____	_____
111.	T, T, CE			59.	A	_____	_____
112.	T, F			60.	A	_____	_____
113.	T, T			61.	E	_____	_____
114.	T, F			62.	A	_____	_____
115.	T, T, CE			63.	D	_____	_____
				64.	E	_____	_____
				65.	C	_____	_____
				66.	B	_____	_____
				67.	E	_____	_____
				68.	A	_____	_____
				69.	D	_____	_____
				70.	D	_____	_____

PRACTICE TEST 1 EXPLANATIONS

Part A

1. **A** When we talk about specific heat, we're talking about the amount of heat necessary to produce a change in temperature. The calorimeter can be used to measure heat input or output, and the thermometer, (A), would be used in combination with it to ascertain the associated change in temperature.

2. **E** A graduated cylinder can be used to help find the volume of an irregularly shaped solid. How? Fill the graduated cylinder with water and read the water's volume. Next, add the solid. The difference between the volume of both the water and solid and the volume of the water alone is the volume of the solid.

3. **D** When an acid and base are combined, think titration, and when you consider titration remember that a buret is typically used to deliver small amounts of acid into a base and vice versa.

4. **C** Volumetric flasks are used to measure an exact volume that matches the size of the flask.

5. **B** An amphoteric molecule can act either as an acid or a base. Proteins are polypeptides made from amino acids, and all amino acids have both an acid group (carboxylic acid group) and a base group (amino group). Therefore, proteins are always amphoteric.

6. **B** The speed of any chemical reaction can be increased by reducing the activation energy for that reaction. This is done through the addition of a catalyst. Enzymes are a type of biological catalyst, and all enzymes are also proteins.

7. **C** Deoxyribose is a ribose sugar molecule missing an oxygen atom. As with all molecules with the suffix *-ose,* ribose is a carbohydrate. In general, proteins tend to have the suffix *-in* (or *-ase* if they are an enzyme) and nucleic acids have the suffix *-ine* (except for uracil).

8. **E** Electrolytes are substances that increase the electrical conductivity of water by dissolving in solution to form ions. Therefore, all ionic compounds, or salts, are electrolytes.

9. **D** Most lipids are insoluble in water. For example, fat-based oils (such as corn oil), a subfamily of lipids, form droplets in water. Several other fat derivatives form double-layered sheets in water; this type of lipids serves as the principle structural element in cell membranes.

10. **E** Don't let phrases such as "constituent elements" throw you off course. The question asks you to identify a situation in which a compound is broken down into its elements. Mercury(II) oxide, HgO, is decomposed into the elements mercury, Hg, and oxygen, O_2, in (E).

11. **C** When a radioactive atom undergoes alpha decay, it loses 2 protons and 2 neutrons. That means that its atomic number decreases by 2, and its mass number decreases by 4. That's exactly what has happened here. Uranium (atomic number = 92, mass number = 234) has been converted to thorium (atomic number = 90, mass number = 230).

12. **E** The phrase "oxidation-reduction reaction" describes a reaction in which one atom loses electron(s) to another. The atom that loses electrons is oxidized, and the one that gains electrons is reduced. In HgO, the oxidation state of Hg is +2 and that of oxygen is –2. HgO is decomposed into the free elements Hg and O_2, each of which has an oxidation state of 0. So the oxidation state of Hg goes from +2 to 0; it has been reduced. Oxygen has been oxidized; its oxidation state has changed from –2 to 0. This is clearly a redox reaction.

13. **B** Look at (B). In an atom of carbon-14 there are 8 neutrons and 6 protons, a ratio greater than 1. In nitrogen-14, the neutron-to-proton ratio is 7:7 or equivalent to 1. Choice (B) is an example of beta decay. As you can see, beta decay causes the neutron-to-proton ratio to decrease.

14. **E** The activation energy of forward and reverse reactions is always characterized by the "hump" that you see in pictures of this kind. It's the energy necessary to get the reaction going. The reactants of the reverse reaction have energy that is expressed by the flat portion of the curve to the right of the hump. For a reaction to occur, these reactants must gain an energy equal to that represented by the top of the hump. This energy that must be acquired is represented by (E). Remember that catalysts reduce activation energy and the rate of the reaction.

15. **B** The enthalpy change of a reaction is the amount of heat the reaction absorbs or gives off. In this case, the reactants begin at one energy level (represented by the flat portion of the curve to the left of the hump), and the products are associated with another (represented by the flat portion of the curve to the right of the hump). The difference represents the enthalpy change of the reaction (which, in this case, is negative—the reaction liberates heat; it's exothermic).

16. **A** Recall that the activated complex represents the highest energy state reactants achieve as they are transformed into new substances. So the energy of the activated complex is measured from the very bottom of the diagram to the top of the activation energy barrier. This distance is represented by (A).

17. **B** BaI_2 is composed of a metal (Ba) and nonmetal (I) bonded together. This is an ionic compound that held together by—surprise—ionic bonding.

18. **C** You may be tempted to go with "ionic bonding" here, but resist that impulse. The ions in an ionic solid are too restricted in their movement to conduct a charge, so (B) is incorrect. Now think: what solids conduct electricity? Metals, of course. And why can copper wire be used to conduct electricity? Because the metallic bonds that hold a sample of copper together do so through the motion of many free electrons, which can conduct electricity as they move.

19. **D** Don't be fooled by (A). Hydrogen bonds occur *between,* not *within* molecules. A hydrogen molecule consists of nonmetal hydrogen atoms in a bond. Nonmetals form covalent bonds, and identical nonmetal atoms form nonpolar covalent bonds.

20. **A** Water's vapor pressure (its tendency to evaporate) is low compared to other similarly sized molecules. What keeps molecules together in the liquid state? Intermolecular forces do, and the intermolecular force most prevalent in water is hydrogen bonding. Since hydrogen bonds are a relatively strong intermolecular force, water molecules are significantly attracted to each other, and water does not evaporate readily.

21. **B** You might be asking yourself: purplish vapor? How am I supposed to know that? Unfortunately there will be a few questions on the test that will test your familiarity with the properties of certain substances. We hope your experiences in chemistry lab will carry you through. If not, don't panic. You'll see only a few of these types of questions. Iodine is a grayish-purple solid that gives off a similarly colored vapor as it sublimes.

22. **E** If you don't know that graphite, a form of carbon, can conduct electricity, you can still get the answer by eliminating the other choices. Choices (A) and (C) are ionic solids—they can conduct electricity in solution or in the molten state, but not as solids. Choices (B) and (D) (table sugar) are molecular solids. You wouldn't expect molecular solids to be particularly conductive. That leaves graphite, which is a network solid.

23. **C** If you've dissolved sodium hydroxide pellets in a beaker of water and felt the side of the beaker, you know that the process gives off heat.

Part B

101. **T, T** Use the divide and conquer strategy. Carbon is a nonmetal, so statement I is true. Do carbon atoms bond with each other? They sure do. Otherwise we wouldn't have oils, waxes, fossil fuels, diamonds, and literally thousands of different substances. Now, does the sentence make sense? No. Metal atoms can also bond with each other, so this ability is not unique to nonmetals. Fill in both true ovals, but not the CE oval.

102. **F, T** Isotopes of the same element do not have the same mass number, but since they are the same element, their atomic numbers (the number of protons) are identical. The first statement is false and the second is true.

103. **F, F** Divide and conquer. At a given temperature, the density of water stays the same whether we have 10 grams or 20 grams, so statement I is false. Statement II is also false: molecules in the liquid (and solid) state are much closer than they are in the gaseous state.

104.   **T, T, CE**

Both sodium and cesium are in the alkali metal family. As such, they have similar chemical properties, so statement I is true. Statement II is also true: alkali metals such as sodium and cesium have 1 valence electron in their atoms. Do the two statements make sense when they are combined? Do sodium and cesium exhibit similar chemical properties because their atoms have the same number of valence electrons? Yes, so fill in oval CE.

105.   **T, T, CE**

Divide and conquer. Can an endothermic reaction be spontaneous? Have you ever seen an ice cube melt at room temperature? That's a spontaneous endothermic process, so the first statement is true. What about the second statement? Remember that the change in Gibbs free energy, ΔG, depends on enthalpy change, ΔH, and entropy change, ΔS: $\Delta G = \Delta H - T\Delta S$. Statement II is also true. Does the second statement explain the first? Yes, it does. That ice cube melts at room temperature because the increase in entropy for the process overcomes the change to a higher energy state. Fill in the CE oval.

106.   **T, T, CE**

The first statement is true. The $3d$ orbitals are of higher energy than the $4s$ orbital, so the $4s$ orbital fills first. Evaluate the second statement. It is true. Subshells do fill in order of lower to higher energy. Does the second statement explain the first? Yes, it does. The $4s$ orbital fills before the $3d$ orbitals because it is lower in energy. Fill in oval CE.

107. **T, T** Divide and conquer. Here's what happens when calcium and bromine react: $Ca + Br_2 \rightarrow CaBr_2$. Bromine's oxidation state decreases from 0 to –1; it is reduced. Calcium (which is oxidized) is responsible for reducing bromine. In other words, calcium acts as a reducing agent. Statement I is true. Look at statement II. Is mass conserved in a chemical reaction? Yes. If it weren't, there would be no need to balance equations. Both statements are true. Does statement II explain why statement I is true? No, it doesn't. Do not fill in oval CE.

108. **F, T** Adding an acid to water increases the hydrogen ion concentration in the water, which means that the water's pH is *reduced*. The first statement is false and the second is true.

109. **F, F** For a liquid to boil, the intermolecular forces in the liquid must be overcome, not the bonds within individual molecules. When water boils, its H_2O molecules are still intact. While we're considering boiling, take a look at statement II. You need to heat water to make it boil, so boiling absorbs, not releases, heat. Both statements are false.

110. **T, F** Divide and conquer. A Geiger counter is used to detect radioactive particles, so statement I is true. Be careful with statement II. Radioactive elements have atoms with unstable nuclei. However, that has nothing to do with an atom's valence electrons. Radon (Rn) is a perfect example. The nuclei of radon atoms emit alpha particles. However, radon is a noble gas. Radon atoms have filled valence shells and are therefore unreactive chemically. Statement II is false.

111.   **T, T, CE**

The first statement is true. If the temperature of a substance didn't remain constant during melting there would be no such thing as a melting point. Instead, at a given pressure, a substance would melt over a range of temperatures. Statement II is also true. The heat absorbed by the ice is being used to break intermolecular hydrogen bonds, so the temperature does not rise although heat is being added. Does the second statement explain the first? Yes, it does. Since the average kinetic energy of molecules stays constant during a phase change (such as melting), the temperature also remains constant. Fill in the CE oval.

112. **T, F** The first statement is true. Adding a solute to a solvent reduces its freezing point, raises its boiling point, and reduces its vapor pressure. The second statement is false. Some, but not all, solutes dissociate into positive and negative ions.

113. **T, T** Divide and conquer. Statement I is true. A reaction will proceed more quickly if its temperature is raised. Look at the second statement. A large K_{eq} absolutely means that a reaction favors the forward reaction or, in other words, favors product formation. Both statements are true. Put them together. Does the second explain the first? No, it doesn't. The first deals with reaction rates (kinetics) and the second with equilibrium. These are different areas of chemistry, so don't fill in CE.

114. **T, F** Hydrofluoric acid is not one of the six common strong acids; thus, it will partially ionize and is a weak electrolyte. Hydrochloric acid is a strong acid, and it ionizes completely. So HCl(*aq*) is a strong electrolyte. Statement I is true. The second statement is false. Remember that electronegativity values decrease down a given column. So from fluorine to chlorine, electronegativity decreases.

115.   **T, T, CE**

The first statement is true. An example of this is the carbon tetrachloride molecule, CCl_4. It consists of four polar bonds. However, the bonds are arranged such that the overall molecule is nonpolar. Therefore, the second statement is true. Since the second statement explains the first, fill in the CE oval.

Part C

24. **D** The atomic number is the number of protons in the nucleus, and the mass number is the sum: number of protons + number of neutrons. If the atomic number is 39 and the mass number is 89, then the number of neutrons in the nucleus must be (89) – (39) = 50.

25. **C** On this question, we use the "plug-in" balancing strategy (a strategy we'll explain in Chapter 5 but let's dive in here and we'll explain it thoroughly later in the book). Since there are at least 4 carbon atoms on the left, the coefficient of CO_2 cannot be 2, so eliminate (A). If the coefficient of carbon is 4, place a 1 in front of C_4H_{10} to keep carbons in balance. This will give 10 hydrogens on the left. If you put a 5 in front of H_2O on the right, you then have 13 oxygens on the right. The only way you can get 13 oxygens on the left is to place $\frac{13}{2}$ in front of O_2 on the left. This puts all the elements in balance, but violates the rule of using only whole numbers, so (B) is wrong. However, if you multiply the coefficients we just determined by 2, you will maintain balance and have all whole numbers. So the balanced equation becomes: $2C_4H_{10}(g) + 13O_2(g) \rightarrow 8CO_2(g) + 10H_2O(l)$.

26. **C** The mass of a proton is approximately 1 amu, and this is very nearly the mass of a neutron. Both a positron and an electron are much lighter than 1 amu. A hydrogen molecule weighs roughly twice as much as a proton, and an alpha particle weighs about four times as much.

27. **D** Add up the mass of 1 mole of this substance. From the periodic table, we know that

  • 1 mole of hydrogen atoms has a mass of about 1 g.

  • 1 mole of chlorine atoms has a mass of about 35 g.

  • 4 moles of oxygen atoms have a mass of about 64 g.

  The total gram-molecular weight of this substance, then, is 100 g. Oxygen's contribution is 64 g, which means the compound is 64 percent oxygen by mass.

28. **E** As soon as you hear the term *electron sharing*, you know you're dealing with a covalent bond, so eliminate (A), (B), and (C). The fact that the two atoms differ in electronegativity tells you that one has more attraction for the shared electrons than the other. The result? A polar covalent bond—the molecule has a negative and a positive pole.

29. **B** Use $q = mc\Delta T$ to compute the amount of heat transfer. For water, the specific heat, c, is about 1 calorie/g • °C, so a 20 g sample of water experiencing a 20°C increase in temperature has (20 g)(1 calorie/g • °C)(20° C), or 400 calories of heat, transferred to it.

30. **D** Remember the oxidation state rules. An oxygen atom usually has a –2 state. Potassium atoms are always given a +1 state. In $K_2Cr_2O_7$, there are 2 potassium atoms and 7 oxygen atoms. So potassium atoms contribute 2(+1), or a state of +2. Oxygen atoms contribute 2(–7), or –14. For $K_2Cr_2O_7$ to be neutral, each chromium atom must have a state of +6.

31. **B** If the pH is 5, then $[H^+]$ is 1×10^{-5} moles/L. Water's ion product is 1×10^{-14} at 25°C, meaning that the product $[H^+] \times [OH^-]$ is 1×10^{-14}. So $[OH^-] = (1 \times 10^{-14})/(1 \times 10^{-5}) = 1 \times 10^{-9}$ moles/L. Choice (B) is correct.

32. **D** Based on the balanced equation, the ratio of water vapor consumed to oxygen produced is 2 moles H_2O to 1 mole O_2. The volume of gas will also be in this 2:1 ratio. So 89.6 liters of $H_2O(g)$ are required to produce 44.8 liters of $O_2(g)$.

33. **B** Molarity refers to moles of solute per liter of solution. You have 500 milliliters of solution, but you don't know how many moles of solute you have. First figure out the mass of 1 mole of $MgCl_2$. Looking at the periodic table, you can see that 1 mole of Mg has a mass of 24.3 g. Two moles of Cl have a mass of about 71 g. One mole of $MgCl_2$, therefore, has a mass of 95.3 g.

    You can then determine the moles of $MgCl_2$ by dividing the mass of the sample by the molar mass of the compound: 190 g/95.3 g = 2.0 mol. Finally, divide the moles of the sample by the volume of the solution (in liters) to determine the concentration of the solution: 2.0 mol/0.500 L = 4.0 M. The correct answer is (B).

34. **C** Think of the ideal gas equation: $PV = nRT$. What does this equation tell you? It means that volume is directly related to Kelvin temperature and inversely related to pressure. Doubling a gas's Kelvin temperature will double its volume if other variables are held constant. Doubling a gas's pressure will halve its volume if other variables are held constant. So the effect on volume of doubling pressure cancels out the effect of doubling Kelvin temperature, and the net result is that the gas's volume will stay the same.

35. **C** After 1 half-life, a 100 g sample will have a mass of 50 g. After 2 half-lives, it will have a mass of 25 g, which is the expiration of 2 half-lives. If 2 half-lives = 12.4 hours, then 1 half-life = 6.2 hours.

36. **A** This is alpha decay, in which a radioactive atom loses 2 protons and 2 neutrons. The loss of 2 protons means the atomic number decreases by 2, which means it *was* 87 before it decayed. The element with an atomic number of 87 is Fr (francium). The loss of 2 neutrons together with the loss of 2 protons means that the mass number has decreased by (2) + (2) = 4. The mass number is now 216, which means that it *was* 220. Notice that (C) has the right numbers, but not the right element. Remember that the atomic number uniquely identifies an element, so an atomic number of 87 must be francium, no matter what the mass number is. This also means that an element can have several different mass numbers, collectively called isotopes.

37.   **C**   The empirical formula tells you that the ratio of carbon to hydrogen is 1:2, so look for an answer that reflects the same ratio. Only (B), (C), and (E) do that, so eliminate (A) and (D). Now, among (B), (C), and (E), look for the one whose molecular weight is 56 amu. Look at the periodic table. Every carbon atom has an atomic weight of 12 amu, and every hydrogen atom has an atomic weight of 1 amu. Rather than pursue algebra, just try the three choices.

38.   **A**   Don't fall into the temptation trap and pick (B). Temperature differences can indicate the direction of heat flow. However, temperature is not a direct measure of heat energy. Instead, associate heat energy with enthalpy.

39.   **E**   On this test, the easiest way to balance an equation is by plugging in the answers. The test writer tells you that the coefficient in front of H_2O is 6, so put that in there. Now, see which of the answer choices, if placed in front of NF_3, would result in a balanced equation. If, for instance, you try (B), you'd have 1 mole of N on the left, which would give 3 moles of F on the left. In order to have 3 moles of F on the right, you'd have to put a 3 in front of the HF on the right. That means you'd have 3 moles of H on the right and 12 moles of H on the left. This is way out of balance.

Suppose you try option (D) and put a 3 in front of the NF_3 on the left. That gives 9 moles of F on the left, which means you'd have to put a 9 in front of the HF on the right. That in turn would provide 9 moles of H on the right when you have 12 moles of H on the left. Once again, this is out of balance.

Now, try (E). Put a 4 in front of NF_3 on the left, which gives 12 F on the left and means that you must put a 12 in front of the HF on the right. That gives 12 H on the right, balanced by 12 H on the left. The coefficients for both NO and NO_2 would be 2, which would balance both the nitrogens (N) and the oxygens (O).

40.   **B**   Make sure you can distinguish between an acid and a base. A base can donate an unshared electron pair, according to the Lewis definition, so (B) is correct. Choices (A), (D), and (E) are characteristics of acids. And what about (C)? Not all bases contain the OH^- ion in their structure—NH_3 is an example.

41.   **C**   The substance described has some metallic characteristics (shiny and high melting point) and some nonmetallic ones (brittle and poor electrical conductivity). It sounds like something that's between a metal and a nonmetal such as a metalloid or semimetal. This is a general description of the metalloid silicon.

42.   **C**   The freer molecules are to move around, the greater the entropy of the state. Equation I goes from a gas (very high entropy) to a liquid (more ordered, less entropy). That's a decrease in entropy. Equation II also involves an entropy decrease. Here, ions go from being able to move throughout a solution to being restricted in the solid state. Equation III shows an entropy *increase* because it is increasing the moles of gas (2 on left and 3 on right). I and II illustrate an entropy decrease, and the correct answer is (C).

43. **E** Choices (A) and (D) will not change water's boiling point. Remember that when a solute is dissolved in solution, the solution's boiling point will be raised (and its freezing point lowered). Only (E) involves dissolving a solute into water. Sugar water boils at a higher temperature than pure water under identical conditions. Why doesn't the addition of gasoline into the water have the same effect? Gasoline molecules are nonpolar and will not dissolve in water. As for (C), increasing the altitude of the water will decrease its boiling point.

44. **D** The question concerns periodic table trends and, in particular, atomic radius. As you move from left to right across a period, atomic radius decreases. So, within a period, the higher the atomic number, the smaller the atomic radius.

    This question is a perfect example of the camouflage trap. You might be thinking higher atomic number, and the correct answer is phrased as "greater positive charge in its nucleus." But keep the blinders off your brain. You know the answer—just remember that there's more than one way of expressing it.

45. **C** Aluminum is a metal, and oxygen is a nonmetal. They react to form an ionic compound. Aluminum (in the 3A group) forms a +3 ion. Oxygen (in the 6A group) forms a −2 ion. They will produce aluminum oxide, Al_2O_3. When the equation is balanced, you'll get $4Al(s) + 3O_2(g) \rightarrow 2Al_2O_3(s)$.

46. **E** Many colored compounds contain a transition metal (an element from the d region of the periodic table). Choices (A), (B), and (C) are ionic solids that possess an active metal (an element from the s region). These compounds appear white (for instance, $NaCl$ or table salt). Choice (D) is rust, which is not blue. $CuSO_4$ contains the transition metal copper (Cu), and its crystals are bright blue.

47. **D** Remember that the atomic weight of an element is the weighted average of all the different isotopes an element exists in. If 50 percent of element X had a mass of 210 amu and 50 percent had a mass of 214 amu, the weighted average would be 212 amu. Notice that you are told element X exists as ^{214}X more than half of the time. So the answer must exceed 212. However, since element X also exists in an isotope with a mass less than 214, expect that its atomic weight is less than 214 amu. Only (D) has a mass greater than 212 amu and less than 214 amu.

48. **B** The container holds a total of 6 moles of gas. Oxygen (O_2) constitutes one-third of that content. If you know how to work partial pressure problems, you know that oxygen's contribution to the total 760 torr of pressure is one-third: 760 torr/3 = approximately 253 torr.

49. **D** Since you're considering the dissolution of an ionic solid into water, you need to consider the solubility product expression. The solubility product constant, K_{sp}, will equal the product of aqueous ion concentrations raised to their coefficients. (Remember that solids are not expressed.) This is the relationship expressed in (D).

50. **D** The normal electron configuration for magnesium would be $1s^2 2s^2 2p^6 3s^2$. Since the question is talking about an "excited" magnesium atom in which one electron has been pushed up into a higher energy state, look for a configuration that shows one electron in a higher state than it should be. The total number of electrons should still be equal to magnesium's atomic number, but the location of one electron should be "elevated."

Choice (D) is just what you're looking for. Total number of electrons? Twelve, just as it should be. But look at the last entry. Instead of $3s^2$, it has $3s^1 3p^1$. The last electron has been elevated to the $3p$ subshell.

51. **A** To form an electrolytic solution, the solute must dissociate into ions. Adding $HCl(g)$ to water will produce hydrochloric acid, which ionizes into H^+ and Cl^- ions. Choices (C), (D), and (E) are all ionic solids, which will break into mobile ions upon dissolution in water. When $N_2(g)$ is dissolved into water, no ions are produced, and the resultant solution is nonelectrolytic.

52. **C** The double arrow indicates that the reaction is reversible. NH_4^+ is a reactant of the reverse reaction; if NH_4^+ donates a proton to HCO_3^-, NH_3 and H_2CO_3 are formed. Since NH_4^+ donates an H^+ ion (or proton) to another substance, it acts as an acid according to the Brønsted-Lowry definition.

53. **A** Add the superscripts to get the total number of electrons in the species: $2 + 2 + 6 + 2 + 6 = 18$. Which of the choices also has 18 electrons? A quick check of the periodic table shows that a sulfur atom has 16 electrons. Adding two more electrons gives the S^{2-} ion a total of 18 electrons.

54. **B** For a substance to be amphoteric, it must be able to donate and receive an H^+ ion. Eliminate (A) and (E)—these species don't have an H^+ ion to donate. Choice (C), KOH, is a strong base. You wouldn't expect it to ever act as an acid. Likewise, HNO_3 (D) is a strong acid that you would not expect to behave as a base. That leaves HCO_3^-. Note that it can act as an acid and become the carbonate ion, CO_3^{2-}, or it can act as a base and become carbonic acid, H_2CO_3.

55. **E** The ideal gas equation is $PV = nRT$. When the amount of gas does not change, n becomes a constant, like R. A little algebra gives $\dfrac{PV}{T} = nR$. Since $\dfrac{PV}{T}$ is equal to a constant, it will not change with time.

Consider that you are dealing with two points in time. At first, the gas has a volume of 10 liters at 20°C or (293 K) and 750 mmHg. So here, $\dfrac{PV}{T} = \dfrac{(750)(10)}{(293)}$. Later, the gas is under STP conditions, so $T = 273$ K and $P = 760$ mmHg. Now, $\dfrac{PV}{T} = \dfrac{(760)(V)}{(273)}$. If you set initial $\dfrac{PV}{T} =$ final $\dfrac{PV}{T}$, you get $\dfrac{(750)(10)}{(293)} = \dfrac{(760)(V)}{(273)}$. Rearranging and applying some algebra gives $V = 10 \times \dfrac{750}{760} \times \dfrac{273}{293}$ L. This is (E).

56. **A** Use the phase diagram. At 0.5 atm and 200 K, substance Z is a gas. If you maintain this temperature and increase the pressure, you can draw a vertical line from the point (0.5 atm, 200 K). Eventually that vertical line will cross into the liquid region. This means that, under steadily increasing pressure, substance Z (starting at 0.5 atm and 200 K) will condense. Condensation is the phase change from gas to liquid.

57. **C** The normal boiling point is the temperature at which the phase change from liquid to gas occurs, at a pressure of 1 atm. If you extend a horizontal line from the 1.0 atm mark on the "pressure" axis and see where it intersects the liquid-gas boundary, you'll get the normal boiling point. Doing so on this phase diagram shows a normal boiling point of about 300 K.

58. **B** Phosphorus is the central atom in PCl_3. A phosphorus atom needs 3 electrons to complete its valence shell. It gets 3 electrons by forming covalent bonds with 3 chlorine atoms. The PCl_3 molecule has the following structure:

Of the four electron pair sites around phosphorus, one is a lone pair. This gives the PCl_3 molecule a trigonal pyramidal shape.

59. **A** First, consider the neutralization that occurs between HBr and $Ba(OH)_2$.

$$2HBr + Ba(OH)_2 \rightarrow BaBr_2 + 2H_2O$$

Notice that for every 2 moles of HBr, only 1 mole of $Ba(OH)_2$ is needed for neutralization. You have 0.1 liters (or 100 milliliters) of 0.2 M HBr. This means you have 0.1 liters × 0.2 mole/liter, or 0.02 mole of HBr. You need 0.01 mole of $Ba(OH)_2$ to neutralize 0.02 mole of HBr. Twenty-five milliliters of 0.4 M $Ba(OH)_2(aq)$ has 0.025 liters × 0.4 mole/liter, or 0.01 mole of $Ba(OH)_2$.

60. **A** K_a indicates a weak acid. That means statement III is false, and therefore you can eliminate (D) and (E). It also means that most HCN remains as intact molecules, as opposed to H^+ and CN^- ions, so statement II is false. POE tells you that statement I must be true. And it is: $HCN \rightleftharpoons H^+ + CN^-$. Notice that the molar ratio of H^+ to CN^- is 1:1.

61. **E** Ionization energies get very large once you try to remove core electrons, which are attracted more strongly to the nucleus than valence electrons. So an atom with a very high second ionization energy would be expected to have just 1 valence electron: the second electron to be removed from such an atom would have to be a core electron. Among the choices, only sodium atoms have a single valence electron.

62.   **A**   When the reaction is flipped, the sign flips and become negative. Also, if all of the coefficients on the substances in the reaction are divided by two, then so is the value.

63.   **D**   Remember that many metals react with acids to produce hydrogen gas. Your first step should be to write out the reaction. Here it is: $Zn(s) + 2HCl(aq) \rightarrow ZnCl_2(aq) + H_2(g)$. Notice that the products of this reaction are $Zn^{2+}(aq)$, $Cl^-(aq)$ (from $ZnCl_2$), and $H_2(g)$.

64.   **E**   This is a Le Châtelier's principle question. How can you produce crowding on the left side of the equation and drive equilibrium to the right (increasing the SO_2 concentration)? Don't be fooled by (C): catalysts *do not affect equilibrium,* but changing concentrations *does* influence equilibrium. Increasing the concentration of O_2 will produce crowding on the left side and lead to an increase in the concentration of SO_2.

65.   **C**   The decrease in volume will increase the pressure in the reaction chamber, causing a shift to the right. This temporarily decreases the concentration of the reactants, however, once equilibrium is established the ratio of the products to the reactants will be the same as it was prior to the volume change. As the volume of the chamber is smaller, that means the concentration of the reactants and products will increase. The rate of reaction will also increase, because the molecules will collide more often in a smaller chamber.

66.   **B**   When quantities are given for more than one reactant, you must see which is limiting. Fifty-six grams of CO (molecular weight = 28 amu) are 2 moles of CO. Since the stoichiometric ratio of Fe_2O_3 to CO is 1:3 (based on coefficients from the balanced equation), CO is limiting. (You would need more than 9 moles of CO based on the 1:3 ratio for Fe_2O_3 to be limiting in this case.) The ratio of CO to Fe is 3:2. So 2 moles of CO will produce about 1.3 moles of Fe. You could quickly estimate this as between 1 and 2 to save time and still get the answer.

67.   **E**   Consider what gases are being collected in the beaker. Oxygen gas is flowing in from the reaction. Water vapor, $H_2O(g)$, is also entering the beaker from the evaporation of water. The pressure exerted by $H_2O(g)$ is equal to the vapor pressure of water. The total gas pressure in the beaker is, therefore, the sum of the pressure of oxygen gas collected and vapor pressure of water (at 25°C in this particular problem).

68.   **A**   If you draw the structure of acetylene, C_2H_2, you'll see that the carbon atoms must share three pairs of electrons to achieve stable octets.

$$H - C \equiv C - H$$

So C_2H_2 has a triple bond. None of the other molecules contains a triple bond. Since this is the strongest type of carbon-to-carbon bond, (A) is correct.

69. **D** Equilibrium is attained when the concentrations of all species become constant. The concentrations of N_2O_4 and NO_2 stay the same from the 20-minute mark to the 25-minute mark. This means equilibrium was achieved before the 20-minute mark. Since the concentrations of N_2O_4 and NO_2 are different from the 15-minute mark to the 20-minute mark, equilibrium was not achieved at exactly 15 minutes from the start of the reaction; equilibrium was attained between 15 and 20 minutes after the start of the reaction.

70. **D** An emission spectrum is created when electrons in an excited state fall back to their ground state. For the electrons to become excited, an outside energy source is required to overcome their attraction to the nucleus.

HOW TO SCORE PRACTICE TEST 1

When you take the real exam, the proctors will collect your test booklet and bubble sheet and send your answer sheet to a processing center, where a computer looks at the pattern of filled-in ovals on your answer sheet and gives you a score. We couldn't include even a small computer with this book, so we are providing this more primitive way of scoring your exam.

Determining Your Score

STEP 1   Using the answer key, determine how many questions you got right and how many you got wrong on the test. Remember: questions that you do not answer don't count as either right or wrong answers.

STEP 2   List the number of right answers here.

(A) _____

STEP 3   List the number of wrong answers here. Now divide that number by 4. (Use a calculator if you're feeling particularly lazy.)

(B) _____ ÷ 4 = (C) _____

STEP 4   Subtract the number of wrong answers divided by 4 from the number of correct answers. Round this score to the nearest whole number. This is your raw score.

(A) _____ – (C) _____ = _____

STEP 5   To determine your real score, take the number from Step 4 above, and look it up in the left column of the Score Conversion Table on the next page; the corresponding score on the right is your score on the exam.

PRACTICE TEST 1
SCORE CONVERSION TABLE

Raw Score	Scaled Score	Raw Score	Scaled Score	Raw Score	Scaled Score
85	800	45	620	5	390
84	800	44	620	4	390
83	800	43	610	3	380
82	800	42	610	2	380
81	800	41	600	1	370
80	800	40	590	0	370
79	800	39	590	−1	370
78	790	38	580	−2	360
77	780	37	580	−3	360
76	780	36	570	−4	350
75	780	35	560	−5	340
74	780	34	560	−6	340
73	780	33	550	−7	330
72	770	32	550	−8	330
71	770	31	540	−9	320
70	750	30	530	−10	310
69	750	29	530	−11	310
68	740	28	520	−12	300
67	740	27	520	−13	300
66	740	26	520	−14	290
65	730	25	510	−15	280
64	730	24	510	−16	280
63	710	23	500	−17	270
62	710	22	500	−18	270
61	710	21	490	−19	260
60	700	20	480	−20	250
59	700	19	480	−21	250
58	690	18	470		
57	690	17	470		
56	680	16	460		
55	680	15	450		
54	680	14	450		
53	670	13	440		
52	670	12	440		
51	660	11	430		
50	650	10	420		
49	650	9	420		
48	630	8	410		
47	630	7	410		
46	630	6	400		

PRACTICE TEST 1 ANSWER KEY

This extended answer key outlines the chapters related to all of the questions in practice test 1. For the questions you got wrong, make sure to give close attention to the related chapters as you begin reading through the book.

Part A

Question Number	Question Answer	Correct? ✎	See Chapter(s) #
1	A		8, 14
2	E		14
3	D		14
4	C		14
5	B		13
6	B		13
7	C		13
8	E		7, 9
9	D		13
10	E		13
11	C		6
12	E		12
13	B		6
14	E		10
15	B		10
16	A		10
17	B		7
18	C		7
19	D		7
20	A		8
21	B		14
22	E		8, 9
23	C		5

Part B

Question Number	Question Answer	Correct? ✎	See Chapter(s) #
101	T, T		7
102	F, T		7
103	F, F		8
104	T, T, CE		7
105	T, T, CE		5
106	T, T, CE		6, 7
107	T, T		12
108	F, T		11
109	F, F		7, 8
110	T, F		6
111	T, T, CE		8
112	T, F		8, 9
113	T, T		10
114	T, F		7, 11
115	T, T, CE		7

PRACTICE TEST 1 ANSWER KEY—CONTINUED

Part C

Question Number	Question Answer	Correct? ✎	See Chapter(s) #
24	D		6, 7
25	C		5
26	C		4
27	D		5
28	E		7
29	B		8
30	D		5, 12
31	B		11
32	D		8
33	B		9
34	C		8
35	C		6
36	A		6
37	C		5
38	A		5
39	E		5
40	B		11
41	C		7
42	C		5
43	E		9
44	D		4, 7
45	C		5
46	E		14
47	D		4

Question Number	Question Answer	Correct? ✎	See Chapter(s) #
48	B		8
49	D		9
50	D		6
51	A		7, 11
52	C		11
53	A		6
54	B		11, 13
55	E		8
56	A		8
57	C		8
58	B		7
59	A		11
60	A		10, 11
61	E		4, 7
62	A		5
63	D		11
64	E		10
65	C		10
66	B		5
67	E		8, 14
68	A		7
69	D		10
70	D		6, 7

Part III
Subject Review

Chapter 4
Atoms: The Building Blocks of Matter

Atoms are the building blocks of matter. Understanding the structure of atoms and how atoms of different elements and isotopes differ from one another is critical to success on the SAT Subject Test in Chemistry. Atoms and elements are the focus of this chapter.

Small Particle, Big History
The concept of an atom has been kicking around since ancient Greece, but it wasn't until the early 1800s that the English scientist John Dalton supported these theories with measurements. His proposal was that all elements were made up of atoms and, furthermore, that all atoms of a given element were identical to one another. He also stated that atoms of different elements therefore had different masses and that a chemical reaction would involve the rearrangement of atoms.

ATOMS AND ELEMENTS

An **element** is any substance that cannot be broken down into a simpler substance by a chemical reaction.

Now, what exactly is an **atom**? Suppose you have a spoonful of some element—carbon, for instance. The smallest, tiniest, teeniest "piece" of carbon in the spoonful is one atom of carbon. Technically, an atom is the smallest particle of an element that still retains the chemical properties of that element.

How an Atom Is Made: Protons, Neutrons, and Electrons

At the center of every atom is a nucleus. What makes up the nucleus of an atom? Two things: **protons** and **neutrons**. Protons have a charge of +1, and neutrons have no charge at all—they are neutral. Because protons and neutrons comprise the nucleus of an atom, they are sometimes referred to as **nucleons.** What's outside the nucleus? **Electrons**; electrons have a charge of –1.

In an electrically neutral atom, the number of electrons is equal to the number of protons; the charges inside and outside the nucleus are balanced.

Sometimes it happens that an atom loses or gains one or more electrons. When that happens, the number of electrons outside the nucleus is not equal to the number of protons inside. The atom isn't electrically neutral anymore and has become an **ion.** If the atom loses one or more electrons, it has fewer negative charges than positive charges, so it is a positively charged ion, or **cation**. If the atom gains one or more electrons, it has more negative charges than positive charges. This is a negatively charged ion, or **anion**.

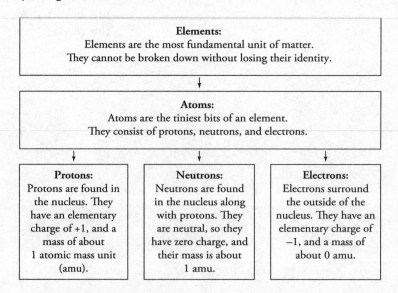

Seeing Is Believing

One of the major advances in determining atomic structure came with the creation of a cathode ray tube (CRT). A CRT is essentially an electron gun—a device capable of producing electrons and shooting them through a vacuum, along with a screen that is able to detect the electrons.

Scientists originally determined the rays created by a CRT were negatively charged, as they were attracted to positive objects and repelled from negative ones. The first scientist to determine the rays were actually made up of particles was J. J. Thomson, who also determined the relative mass and charge of the particles. These particles later came to be known as electrons.

The most famous experiment that helped shape modern atomic theory was conducted by Ernest Rutherford. Rutherford shot a beam of helium atoms at a sheet of gold foil. The vast majority of atoms passed through undeflected, which was expected—atoms were considered to be mostly empty space, a theory that is still held to be true today. However, a very small percentage (<1%) of the atoms were deflected by the foil. Rutherford theorized that this was due to the presence of a highly dense nucleus located in the center of the atom and that had sufficient mass to deflect the helium atoms.

The theory of the atom continues to evolve over time to expand beyond an understanding of the basic subatomic particles, but that will be addressed further in Chapter 6.

THE PERIODIC TABLE

When you sit down to take the SAT Subject Test in Chemistry, you will be provided with a periodic table. On the periodic table, the vertical columns are called **groups**, and the horizontal rows are called **periods**. The symbols (such as H, Li, Be, etc.) represent elements.

PERIODIC TABLE OF THE ELEMENTS

s subshell area ... *p subshell area*

B groups

d subshell area

§ Not yet named

	1A																	8A
1	1 H 1.0079	2A										3A	4A	5A	6A	7A		2 He 4.0026
2	3 Li 6.941	4 Be 9.012										5 B 10.811	6 C 12.011	7 N 14.007	8 O 16.00	9 F 19.00		10 Ne 20.179
3	11 Na 22.99	12 Mg 24.30										13 Al 26.98	14 Si 28.09	15 P 30.974	16 S 32.06	17 Cl 35.453		18 Ar 39.948
4	19 K 39.10	20 Ca 40.48	21 Sc 44.96	22 Ti 47.90	23 V 50.94	24 Cr 52.00	25 Mn 54.938	26 Fe 55.85	27 Co 58.93	28 Ni 58.69	29 Cu 63.55	30 Zn 65.39	31 Ga 69.72	32 Ge 72.59	33 As 74.92	34 Se 78.96	35 Br 79.90	36 Kr 83.80
5	37 Rb 85.47	38 Sr 87.62	39 Y 88.91	40 Zr 91.22	41 Nb 92.91	42 Mo 95.94	43 Tc (98)	44 Ru 101.1	45 Rh 102.91	46 Pd 106.42	47 Ag 107.87	48 Cd 112.41	49 In 114.82	50 Sn 118.71	51 Sb 121.75	52 Te 127.60	53 I 126.91	54 Xe 131.29
6	55 Cs 132.91	56 Ba 137.33	57 *La 138.91	72 Hf 178.49	73 Ta 180.95	74 W 183.85	75 Re 186.21	76 Os 190.2	77 Ir 192.2	78 Pt 195.08	79 Au 196.97	80 Hg 200.59	81 Tl 204.38	82 Pb 207.2	83 Bi 208.98	84 Po (209)	85 At (210)	86 Rn (222)
7	87 Fr (223)	88 Ra 226.02	89 †Ac 227.03	104 Rf (261)	105 Db (262)	106 Sg (266)	107 Bh (264)	108 Hs (277)	109 Mt (268)	110 Ds (271)	111 Rg (272)	112 § (277)						

*Lanthanide Series	58 Ce 140.12	59 Pr 140.91	60 Nd 144.24	61 Pm (145)	62 Sm 150.4	63 Eu 151.97	64 Gd 157.25	65 Tb 158.93	66 Dy 162.50	67 Ho 164.93	68 Er 167.26	69 Tm 168.93	70 Yb 173.04	71 Lu 174.97
†Actinide Series	90 Th 232.04	91 Pa 231.04	92 U 238.03	93 Np 237.05	94 Pu (244)	95 Am (243)	96 Cm (247)	97 Bk (247)	98 Cf (251)	99 Es (252)	100 Fm (257)	101 Md (258)	102 No (259)	103 Lr (262)

f subshell area

For the SAT Subject Test in Chemistry, you have to know certain things about the elements and other information you see on the periodic table.

Atomic Number

Look at any element on the periodic table. Above every element's symbol is a whole number that represents the element's atomic number. The **atomic number** of an element tells you the number of protons in the nucleus of an atom of that element. The number of protons in the nucleus of an atom gives that atom its identity. Oxygen, for instance, has the atomic number 8; an atom of oxygen has 8 protons in its nucleus. If you take a proton away from an oxygen atom, it would have only 7 protons in its nucleus, and it wouldn't be oxygen anymore; it would be a nitrogen atom. Any atom with 7 protons in its nucleus is nitrogen.

What if an oxygen atom loses an electron but not a proton? Well, as long as the atom has 8 protons in it, it's still oxygen. If it has only 7 electrons, then it's a positively charged oxygen ion, and if it has 9 electrons, then it's a negatively charged oxygen ion. But as long as the atomic number—the number of protons in the nucleus—doesn't change, the element doesn't change either: it's still oxygen.

> **Atomic number:** number of protons in nucleus; identity of element

Group Number

The group number refers to the number above each column of the periodic table, such as 1A, 2, 4, etc. Elements in the same group have the same number of electrons in their outer shells and share many properties. Carbon (C), Silicon (Si), and Germanium (Ge), for example, are all in the group 4A and have similar chemical properties.

Mass Number, Isotopes, and Atomic Weight

We said before that the nucleus of an atom is made up of two types of subatomic particles: protons and neutrons. Protons have a positive charge, and neutrons are neutral. Another important point is that both protons and neutrons have mass, while electrons have practically no mass.

Protons and neutrons each have mass of roughly 1 atomic mass unit (amu), and an atom's **mass number** is equal to the sum of its protons and its neutrons.

Now, we've said that in an electrically neutral atom, the number of protons is equal to the number of electrons. But this says nothing about neutrons. Most carbon atoms, for instance, have 6 neutrons in their nuclei. A few have 8. All have 6 protons in their nuclei, so they all have the atomic number 6, and they're all carbon. But they can differ in the number of neutrons.

If two atoms of the same element differ in the number of neutrons in their nuclei, they are said to be **isotopes**; a carbon atom that has 6 neutrons and a carbon atom that has 8 neutrons are isotopes.

Since an atom's mass number is equal to the sum of its protons and its neutrons, two different isotopes of the same element will have different mass numbers. For instance, the carbon atom that has 6 neutrons in its nucleus has a mass number of 6 protons + 6 neutrons = 12 amu. And, because its mass number is 12, we call it carbon-12. The carbon atom that has 8 neutrons in its nucleus has a mass number of 6 protons + 8 neutrons = 14 amu. And, because its mass number is 14, we call it carbon-14.

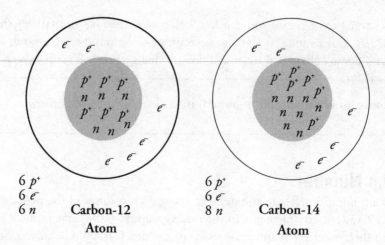

6 p^+
6 e^-
6 n

Carbon-12
Atom

6 p^+
6 e^-
8 n

Carbon-14
Atom

Let's Talk Numbers

By the way, mass number doesn't appear on the periodic table. Why not? Because for any element, there's no such thing as one mass number. As we've just learned, different isotopes of the same element have different mass numbers.

However, chemists have figured out, roughly, the degree to which each isotope of each element tends to occur on Earth. So, for each element, they've figured out an average mass number, which for each element represents the average of the mass numbers of all isotopes as they occur on Earth. This average number is called the **atomic weight** of the element. The atomic weight of each element appears on the periodic table, just below the element's symbol. When we want to know the mass of an atom of a particular element, for practical purposes, we use the atomic weight that appears on the periodic table.

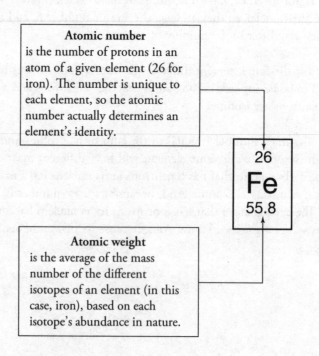

Atomic number
is the number of protons in an atom of a given element (26 for iron). The number is unique to each element, so the atomic number actually determines an element's identity.

26

Fe

55.8

Atomic weight
is the average of the mass number of the different isotopes of an element (in this case, iron), based on each isotope's abundance in nature.

Remember the following:

Neutrons:
- along with protons, make up the nucleus of an atom
- electrical neutrality
- isotopes—two atoms of the same element are isotopes if they differ in their number of neutrons

Mass number:
- number of protons plus number of neutrons;
- isotopes—two isotopes of an element have different mass numbers because they differ in the number of neutrons

Atomic weight:
- average of mass numbers for all isotopes of an element as they occur on Earth

Now try the following questions. The answers can be found in Part IV.

DRILL 1

Question Type A

Questions 4–8 refer to the following.

(A) Atom
(B) Ion
(C) Neutron
(D) Proton
(E) Electron

4. The smallest representative particle of helium

5. Its loss or gain creates a positively or negatively charged ion, respectively

6. Particle responsible for positive nuclear charge

7. Isotopes of uranium always differ in their number of this particle

8. Their number in the nucleus determines an element's atomic number

Question Type B

	I		II

105. The periodic table does not report mass numbers   BECAUSE   a mass number can be assigned to one isotope of an element but not to an element in general.

106. Addition of an electron to an atom creates a positively charged ion   BECAUSE   every electron carries a negative charge.

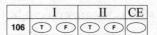

Question Type C

27. Two different sodium atoms or ions may differ in all of the following ways EXCEPT

(A) the number of electrons outside their nuclei
(B) the overall charge they carry
(C) their mass numbers
(D) the number of neutrons in their nuclei
(E) the number of protons in their nuclei

28. Two isotopes of the same element will always differ in

(A) mass number but never in atomic number
(B) atomic number but never in mass number
(C) charge outside but never inside their nuclei
(D) nuclear charge but never in overall charge
(E) the number of electrons outside their nuclei but never in the number of neutrons inside their nuclei

29. Given the following scientists and their contributions to atomic theory, which of the following concepts do we now recognize as incorrect?

    (A) Rutherford's ideas about all atoms having an extremely dense nucleus
    (B) Thomson's estimates for the mass and charge of an electron
    (C) Bohr's hypothesis that electrons orbit the nucleus at fixed distances
    (D) Planck's theory that all electromagnetic energy is quantized
    (E) De Broglie's postulate that electrons behave like electromagnetic radiation

Summary

- An atom consists of neutrons (charge = 0, mass = 1 amu) and protons (charge = +1, mass = 1 amu) in a nucleus orbited by electrons (charge = −1, mass = 0 amu).

- Atomic number is the number of protons in an atom of an element, and it defines the element.

- Mass number is the number of protons plus the number of neutrons in an atom.

- Isotopes are atoms of the same element that contain different numbers of neutrons.

- Atomic weight is the average of the masses of the different isotopes based on the frequency with which they occur in nature.

Chapter 5
Chemical Reactions and Stoichiometry

Chemistry is a science largely concerned with reactions, or how molecules of one or more substances are converted to molecules of a different substance(s). This chapter discusses formula (or molecular) weight, empirical formulas, and percent composition; moles and molar mass; balancing chemical reactions and stoichiometry; and thermodynamics, which is the role of energy in a reaction: how much energy is given off or absorbed by a reaction and what this can tell us about the reaction.

THE WORLD OF MOLECULES

As we mentioned in Chapter 4, an atom is the smallest particle of an element. Atoms of one element often attract each other or atoms of a different element. If this attraction is strong enough, a chemical bond can result. Chemical bonds join two or more atoms into units called **molecules.** (We'll talk more about bonding in Chapter 7.)

Everybody knows the formula of water—it's H_2O. This formula tells us that, in a molecule of water, 2 hydrogen atoms and 1 oxygen atom are bonded together into a unit. An individual water molecule is the smallest unit of water that exists.

Diatomic Molecules

Elements as Diatomic Molecules

One good way to remember all of the diatomic molecules is the following mnemonic:
Oh I Have Nice Closets For Brooms
O_2, I_2, H_2, N_2, Cl_2, F_2, Br_2

When a molecule consists of just two atoms (whether they are of identical or different elements), it's called a **diatomic molecule.** Some elements exist as diatomic molecules at room temperature and atmospheric pressure (1 atm). For example, oxygen in air exists in the form of O_2. There are seven important elements that exist as diatomic molecules: oxygen (O_2), iodine (I_2), hydrogen (H_2), nitrogen (N_2), chlorine (Cl_2), fluorine (F_2), and bromine (Br_2).

Formula Weights, Empirical Formulas, and Percent Composition

For the SAT Subject Test in Chemistry, you'll need to know some simple atom-molecule math.

1. **Formula Weight:** For any molecule, we calculate the formula weight by adding up the atomic weights of all the atoms in the molecule. It's easy. Take hydrogen peroxide (H_2O_2) as an example.

    - The molecule has 2 hydrogen atoms and 2 oxygen atoms. Let's start with hydrogen.
    - The atomic weight of hydrogen is 1 amu. Since there are 2 atoms, we have a total of 2×1, or 2 amu.
    - Now let's talk about the oxygen in the molecule. The atomic weight of oxygen is 16, and since there are 2 atoms, the total is 16×2, or 32 amu.
    - The total is $2 + 32 = 34$. The formula weight for H_2O_2 is 34 amu.

Here's another example. Let's figure out the weight for sulfuric acid: H_2SO_4.

    - The molecule has 2 hydrogen atoms, 1 atom of sulfur, and 4 oxygen atoms. Let's start with hydrogen.
    - The atomic weight of hydrogen is 1 amu. We have 2 hydrogens, so there are a total of 2 amu.

- The atomic weight of sulfur is 32 amu. So we have 32 amu of sulfur.
- Now let's talk about the oxygen. We know the atomic weight of oxygen is 16 and there are 4 atoms. So we have a total of 16×4, or 64 amu.
- $2 + 32 + 64 = 98$. The formula weight for H_2SO_4 is 98 amu.

2. **Empirical Formula:** An empirical formula shows the ratio of atoms within a molecule. To find an empirical formula from a molecular formula, first find the largest whole number by which all of the subscripts in the molecular formula are divisible. Then divide each subscript by that number. Let's look at a few examples.

- We talked about the molecular formula of hydrogen peroxide, which is H_2O_2. The largest number that can divide into 2 is 2. If we factor a 2 out of both subscripts, we're left with HO. So the empirical formula for hydrogen peroxide is HO.
- Ethane has the molecular formula C_2H_6. Let's find the empirical formula. What's the largest number that goes evenly into 2 and 6? It's 2. If we divide both subscripts by 2, we get an empirical formula of CH_3.
- How about water? The largest whole number that will divide evenly into 2 and 1 is 1. So the empirical formula for water is the same as its molecular formula: H_2O.

3. **Percent Composition:** This refers to the percent of a substance contained within a molecule. The test writers may ask you to determine this percent. Here is one example of a question you might see on the test.

What is the percent of oxygen by mass in hydrogen peroxide, H_2O_2?

In order to determine the percent composition of oxygen, you need to find the mass in amu of all of the oxygen atoms in the molecule and compare it with the total formula weight. As shown earlier, each of the two oxygen atoms in H_2O_2 weighs 16 amu. This means that the mass due to oxygen is 2(16) or 32 amu. The formula weight of H_2O_2 is 34 amu. So the percent of oxygen by mass in H_2O_2 is $\frac{32}{34} \times 100\%$, or roughly 94%. You can then calculate the percent of hydrogen by mass in H_2O_2, which is $100\% - 94\%$, or about 6%.

Percent by Mass
Whenever a question asks about the percent composition, the implication is the percent by mass of the substance.

THE MOLE

What's a mole? It's a number, like a dozen or a gross. Dozen, as you know, means 12. Gross means 144. **Mole** means 6.02×10^{23}. The number 6.02×10^{23} is known as **Avogadro's number.**

We said earlier that atomic mass is measured in atomic mass units (amu); 1 amu is 1/12 the mass of a carbon-12 atom, or a relative mass of 1 gram (g). Each 1 g of a substance has 6.02×10^{23} amu. Think about what that means. If, for any element, we take a sample whose mass in grams is numerically equal to its atomic weight in amu, the sample has 1 mole of atoms in it. If we take a substance whose mass in grams is numerically equal to twice its atomic weight in amu, we have 2 moles of atoms. If we take a substance whose mass in grams is numerically equal to three times its atomic weight in amu, we have 3 moles of atoms. It's as simple as that.

For example, helium's atomic weight is 4 amu, so 4 g of helium contain 1 mole (6.02×10^{23}) of helium atoms, and 8 g of helium contain 2 moles of helium atoms. Carbon's atomic weight is 12 amu, so in 12 g of carbon there is 1 mole (6.02×10^{23}) of carbon atoms, and in 36 g of carbon there are 3 moles (18.06×10^{23}) of carbon atoms. Got it?

How many moles of oxygen molecules are in 64 g of oxygen gas? Remember that oxygen is diatomic. Each O_2 molecule has a mass of roughly 2(16), or 32 amu, so 1 mole of O_2 molecules would have a mass of 32 g. Thus, in 64 g of oxygen gas, there are 2 moles of oxygen molecules. Now how many moles of oxygen atoms would be present in this 64 g sample? Each O_2 molecule is made up of 2 oxygen atoms, so if the sample contains 2 moles of oxygen molecules, it contains 4 moles of oxygen atoms.

Note that the lower the molar mass is for a given element, the more moles there will be present in 1.0 g of it. Hydrogen has a molar mass of 1.0 g/mol, and helium has a molar mass of 4.0 g/mol. 1.0 g of hydrogen atoms would thus represent one mole of hydrogen, but 1.0 g of helium atoms is only 0.25 mol of helium! This is important—moles represents the amount of substance that reacts (or is produced) during a chemical reaction, and all calculations in chemistry revolve around moles!

Converting Mass Composition to Empirical Formula

Now that you know what an empirical formula is, we'll tell you how to figure out an empirical formula from the percent composition of a molecule. For example, the test writers might tell you that some unknown substance is made up of approximately 75% mercury and 25% chlorine, and they might ask you to take this percent composition and figure out the substance's empirical formula.

Here's how you do it.

1.   Imagine, first, that you have 100 g of the substance.

2. If you have 100 g of the substance, and it's 75% mercury by mass, then you've got 75 g of mercury, right? Since the atomic weight of mercury is about 200 amu (which means that 1 mole of mercury atoms weighs 200 g), you've got $\frac{75}{200}$ mole = 0.375 moles of mercury atoms in a 100 g sample.

3. If you have 100 g of the substance, and it's 25% chlorine by mass, then you've got 25 g of chlorine. Since the atomic weight of chlorine is about 35 amu (which means that 1 mole of chlorine atoms weighs 35 g), you've got $\frac{25}{35}$ = 0.700 moles of chlorine atoms in the 100 g sample.

4. If you've got 0.375 moles of mercury atoms and 0.700 moles of chlorine atoms, then the ratio of chlorine to mercury atoms is $\frac{0.700}{0.375}$ (which is close to 2:1), which means the empirical formula is $HgCl_2$.

Now review everything we've told you about molecules and moles, and answer the following questions. The answers can be found in Part IV.

Finding Moles
When finding moles of a diatomic element such as chlorine in a compound, use its atomic weight, not its formula weight in the calculation.

DRILL 1

Question Type A

Questions 1–4 refer to the following.
(A) N_2O
(B) $C_6H_{12}O_6$
(C) SO_3
(D) NO
(E) N_2O_5

1. Is a diatomic molecule

2. Has a formula weight of approximately 108 amu

3. Has an empirical formula that is different from its molecular formula

4. Composition is approximately 60% oxygen by mass

Question Type B

	I		II

101.   Chlorine is an element   BECAUSE   chlorine exists as unbonded atoms at room temperature and atmospheric pressure.

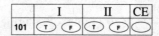

102.   One mole of HBr has greater mass than one mole of NO_2 BECAUSE   the mass of a molecule of HBr is greater than the mass of a molecule of NO_2.

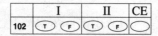

Question Type C

24.   The formula for calcium nitrate is $Ca(NO_3)_2$. What is its approximate formula weight?

(A)   64 amu
(B)   164 amu
(C)   240 amu
(D)   310 amu
(E)   380 amu

25.   An unknown substance is found to have a composition of 9% magnesium and 91% iodine by weight. The empirical formula for the substance is

(A)   MgI
(B) Mg_2I_2
(C) Mg_2I
(D) MgI_2
(E) Mg_3I_2

26. What is the percent by mass of silicon in a sample of silicon dioxide?

(A) 21%
(B) 33%
(C) 47%
(D) 54%
(E) 78%

27. $4Fe + 3O_2 \rightarrow 2Fe_2O_3$

4.0 moles of iron react with 4.0 moles of oxygen to create iron(III) oxide via the reaction above. If 1.5 moles of Fe_2O_3 are created, what is the percent yield for the reaction?

(A) 20%
(B) 33%
(C) 50%
(D) 75%
(E) 100%

CHEMICAL REACTIONS—HOW MOLECULES ARE FORMED, BROKEN DOWN, AND REFORMED

In the course of a chemical reaction, the bonds that hold together the atoms that make up the reactants break. The free atoms then form new bonds with one another to form new molecules—the products of the reaction. Take a look at the chemical reaction below:

$$C_3H_8(g) + 5O_2(g) \rightarrow 4H_2O(l) + 3CO_2(g)$$

What does this equation tell us? Well, two things. On a molecular level, this equation says that 1 molecule of propane (C_3H_8) and 5 molecules of oxygen react to form 4 molecules of water and 3 molecules of carbon dioxide. It also tells us that 1 mole of C_3H_8 reacts with 5 moles of O_2 to form 4 moles of H_2O and 3 moles of CO_2. This equation also indicates the state of each reactant and product: (*s*) means solid, (*l*) means liquid, and (*g*) means gas.

Note that when a substance is dissolved in water to create a solution, it is in the aqueous phase, represented with (*aq*). This is not the same thing as the liquid phase. If you were to take table salt (NaCl (*s*)) and heat it until it melted, it would become NaCl (*l*). However, if you took that table salt and dissolved it into a glass of water, it would create NaCl (*aq*). Much of chemistry is solution-based, and compounds will frequently be dissolved in water to form aqueous solutions before any reactions take place.

Chemical Equations Must Be Balanced

Look again at the chemical equation we just presented:

$$C_3H_8(g) + 5O_2(g) \rightarrow 4H_2O(l) + 3CO_2(g)$$

This is a balanced equation. How can you tell? For each element on the left side of the equation, multiply the molecular coefficient by the element's subscript. (Any number that doesn't appear is assumed to be 1.) For oxygen, in $5O_2$, there are $5 \times 2 = 10$ oxygen atoms. Now do the same for the right side of the equation. In $4H_2O$, there are $4 \times 1 = 4$ oxygen atoms. In $3CO_2$, there are $3 \times 2 = 6$ oxygen atoms. So there are $4 + 6 = 10$ oxygen atoms on the right side, and since there are also 10 oxygen atoms on the left side, oxygen is balanced. Now check to see that carbon and hydrogen are also balanced. They are. There are 3 carbons on the left and 3 carbons on the right. There are 8 hydrogens on the left and 8 hydrogens on the right. For each element in a balanced equation, the total number of atoms on the left must equal the total number of atoms on the right.

Balancing Equation Steps:

1. First, start with the smallest answer choice, and plug it in front of what you want to solve for.

2. Next, turn to the other side of the equation and fill in coefficients based on what you started with.

3. If you can't find whole number coefficients so all the atoms on either side of the equation add up, turn to the next smallest answer choice and repeat.

4. If you can balance the equation, check to make sure there is no common factor for all of the coefficients. For example, 4, 6, and 10 have a common factor of 2. If there is a common factor, divide the coefficients, and you have your answer. If there isn't, you already have your answer.

On the SAT Subject Test in Chemistry, you may see up to five questions that will show you unbalanced equations and ask you to balance them. Here's what those will look like.

29. $\ldots C_2H_4(g) + \ldots O_2(g) \rightarrow \ldots CO_2(g) + \ldots H_2O(l)$

When the equation above is balanced and all coefficients are reduced to lowest whole-number terms, which of the following would be the coefficient for CO_2 ?

(A) 1
(B) 2
(C) 4
(D) 5
(E) 6

Fortunately, these questions are easy to answer if you use the "plug-in" balancing strategy. Start with (A), and put the number 1 in front of CO_2. (Don't be afraid to write in your test booklet as much as you want. Your test booklet belongs to you, and nobody cares what you write in it; only your answer sheet is scored.) By adding a 1 in front of CO_2, we end up with 1 carbon on the right. Yet, we have at least 2 carbons on the left, so we know that 1 is not the answer.

Let's try (B). Put a 2 in front of CO_2, and see what happens. We have 2 carbons on the right and 2 on the left. Good. We have 4 hydrogens on the left, so let's try putting a 2 in front of the H_2O. That gives us a total of 6 oxygens on the right and 2 on the left. Let's put a 3 in front of O_2 on the left, so we have a total of 6 oxygens on the left.

Now we have 2 carbons on the right and the left, 4 hydrogens on the right and the left, and 6 oxygens on the right and the left. The equation is balanced, and (B) is correct. So, every time a question asks you to balance an equation, use the plugging-in strategy. It can't fail.

STOICHIOMETRY

Sometimes SAT Chemistry questions will ask you to determine how much product is formed or reactant is consumed in the course of a chemical reaction. These are stoichiometry questions. When you begin a stoichiometry problem, always remember to work from a balanced equation. The coefficients in front of each species indicate the molar ratio between the species. Consider the reaction between ammonia gas and oxygen, which yields nitrogen monoxide and water.

$$4NH_3(g) + 5O_2(g) \rightarrow 4NO(g) + 6H_2O(l)$$

This equation tells us that

- For every 4 moles of ammonia consumed, 5 moles of oxygen are also consumed.
- For every 5 moles of oxygen consumed, 6 moles of water are produced.
- For every 4 moles of ammonia consumed, 4 moles of nitrogen monoxide are produced. In other words, the molar ratio of ammonia consumption to nitrogen monoxide production is 1:1.

How do you put these molar ratios to use? Take a look: if 2 moles of ammonia are consumed, how many moles of water are produced?

The best way to figure this problem out is to use unit conversions. The number of moles in our conversion comes from the coefficients of the balanced equation.

$$2 \text{ moles NH}_3 \times \frac{6 \text{ moles H}_2\text{O}}{4 \text{ moles NH}_3} = 3 \text{ mol H}_2\text{O}$$

We know the moles of NH_3 cancel because they appear in both the numerator and denominator, leaving us with moles of H_2O.

It can get a bit more complicated; we can only use the coefficients in the balanced equation to determine the mole ratio, not the mass ratio. So, if we start with mass, we have to convert to moles first. After we get our moles of product, we can then convert those to the mass of product. Consider this: if 34 g of NH_3 gas reacts, how many grams of NO(g) are created?

This time we have three necessary conversions:

$$34 \text{ g NH}_3 \times \frac{1 \text{ mol NH}_3}{17 \text{ g NH}_3} \times \frac{4 \text{ mol NO}}{4 \text{ mol NH}_3} \times \frac{30 \text{ g NO}}{1 \text{ mol NO}} = 60 \text{ g NO}$$

Note that when converting from grams to moles, we use the molar mass of each compound, which is always equivalent to the mass of one mole of that compound. The coefficients from the balanced equation only appear in the mole ratio step, and never in the moles to grams step.

The last thing that you need to know about stoichiometry (for now!) is that if you start with the amount of both reactants, inevitably, one of them will run out first. Once one of the reactants is gone, the reaction will stop. The reactant that runs out first is called the limiting reactant, and the reactant which does not run out is called the excess reactant.

You can mathematically determine which reactant is limiting by seeing which would produce LESS product. Whichever reactant is able to produce less product will always run out first and thus be limiting. When 3 mol of NH_3 is mixed with 3 mol of O_2, the limiting reactant can be determined as follows:

$$3 \text{ mol NH}_3 \times \frac{4 \text{ mol NO}}{4 \text{ mol NH}_3} = 3 \text{ mol NO}$$

$$3 \text{ mol O}_2 \times \frac{4 \text{ mol NO}}{5 \text{ mol O}_2} = 2.4 \text{ mol NO}$$

In this case, the oxygen would be the limiting reactant (and 2.4 moles of NO would be produced). We could have gone to moles of H_2O instead of NO if we wanted to; it doesn't matter which product we choose as long as we're consistent. It's important to realize that it's not always the reactant which is present in lower amounts that will limit. The limiting reactant depends on a number of variables, including the molar mass of each reactant and the mole ratio between the reactants and the products.

THERMODYNAMICS

Entropy

One of the most important things to remember about thermodynamics is that low-energy states are more stable than high-energy states. That's such a fundamental principle that we'll ask you to repeat it. Fill in the blank lines:

_____ energy states are more stable than _____ energy states.

The State of Things

Entropy is a measure of randomness, or disorder. To get an idea of what this means, consider the two boxes below. Which one has greater entropy, or disorder? It's the one on the right.

 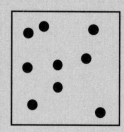

Fundamentally, the universe prefers low-energy states, and also fundamentally, it tends toward disorder. When we talk about disorder, we use the term **entropy**, which is symbolized by S. Everything tends toward maximum entropy. When we talk about a chemical reaction and the difference between entropy of the products and entropy of the reactants, we use the symbol ΔS. If ΔS is negative, the reaction has lost entropy; the products are more "orderly" than the reactants. If ΔS is positive, the reaction has gained entropy; the products are less "orderly" than the reactants.

The universe, it turns out, likes disorder. Systems move toward increasing disorder. They also tend to move toward states of lower energy. For the SAT Subject Test in Chemistry, when you see the word *entropy*, think "disorder," and realize that, because the universe is lazy, it tends toward maximum entropy. All things in the universe are more stable when they're in (1) states of low energy, and (2) states of high entropy.

Higher Entropy + Lower Energy → More Stability

Lower Entropy + Higher Energy → Less Stability

Enthalpy

Because the universe tends toward lower energy, chemical reactions that release energy—reactions that set energy free—are favored in the universe. When we talk about the energy states of reactants or products, we use the term **enthalpy,** which is symbolized by H. High enthalpy means high-energy state, and low enthalpy means low-energy state. So, the universe likes reactions in which the enthalpy decreases—reactions in which ΔH (the change in enthalpy that occurs in the course of a reaction) is negative. These reactions are said to be **exothermic,** and they result in the release of energy in the form of heat. If, however, the enthalpy of the products is greater than the enthalpy of the reactants, then ΔH is positive and the reaction is said to be **endothermic.** Endothermic reactions require the input of energy in order to take place.

Energetic Bonds

When we say that the products are at a higher or lower energy than the reactants, we mean the bonds in the products are at a higher or lower energy. If energy is released in a reaction, that energy comes from the potential energy stored in the bonds of the reactants. If the bonds of the products have more potential energy than the bonds of the reactants, we have to supply the difference, and energy is absorbed in the reaction.

Exothermic reaction → energy is released → $\Delta H < 0$ → enthalpy decreases

Endothermic reaction → energy is absorbed → $\Delta H > 0$ → enthalpy increases

Enthalpy is often represented graphically by a diagram usually called a reaction coordinate. The reaction coordinate for an exothermic reaction looks like this:

Exothermic Reaction

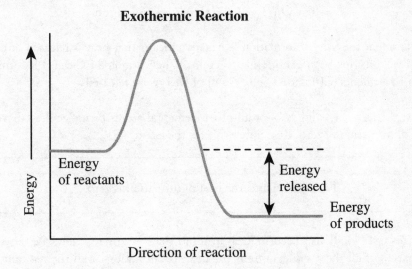

And an endothermic reaction would look like this:

Endothermic Reaction

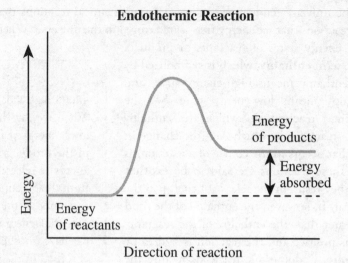

Note that all that matters here is the energy difference between the reactants and the products. The "hump" in between them is related to the reaction's speed, something that we'll take a look at in a later chapter.

Heat of Formation

Another term you should be familiar with for the test is **heat of formation**—that is, the amount of heat that's released or absorbed when 1 mole of a compound is formed from its elements. When we talk about heat of formation, we use the same symbol we use for enthalpy change, but we put a subscript "f" on it: ΔH_f. Let's consider the heat of formation of gaseous carbon dioxide, CO_2.

$$C(s) + O_2(g) \rightarrow CO_2(g); \Delta H_f = -393 \text{ kJ/mol}$$

The fact that the heat of formation is negative means that heat is released during this reaction; this is an exothermic reaction. When 1 mole of $CO_2(g)$ is formed from its elements ($C(s)$ and $O_2(g)$), 393 kJ of energy are released.

C, Ni, Cl_2, O_2, H_2, and N_2—or all other elemental atoms or molecules—have a heat of formation of zero. Remember this for the exam.

> For all elements, the heat of formation is zero.

For this test, you'll also need to keep in mind that for any reaction, the heats of formation of all the products minus the heats of formation of all the reactants is equal to ΔH_f *for the whole reaction*. The test writers might show you a reaction and give you heats of formation for all of the reactants and products. Then they'll ask you to figure out ΔH_f for the whole reaction.

That's simple to do; you just add up the heats of formation for all of the products and then all of the reactants, multiplying each by its coefficient from the balanced equation, and you've got ΔH_f for the reaction. Remember that ΔH_f (reaction) = ΔH_f (products) $-$ ΔH_f (reactants) and that the heats of formation of all elements are zero. Look at this reaction:

$$C_6H_{12}O_6(s) + 6O_2(g) \rightarrow 6CO_2(g) + 6H_2O(l)$$

Suppose you're told that the heat of formation for

- $C_6H_{12}O_6(s)$ is $-1,273$ kJ/mol
- $H_2O(l)$ is -286 kJ/mol
- $CO_2(g)$ is -393 kJ/mol

(ΔH_f for $O_2(g)$, of course, is 0.)

ΔH_f for the whole reaction is equal to

$$\Delta H_f(\text{products}) - \Delta H_f(\text{reactants})$$

So

$$\Delta H_f(\text{products}) = 6 \text{ mol}(-393 \text{ kJ/mol}) + 6 \text{ mol}(-286 \text{ kJ/mol}) = -4,074 \text{ kJ}$$
$$\Delta H_f(\text{reactants}) = -1,273 \text{ kJ} + 0 \text{ kJ} = -1,273 \text{ kJ}$$

So, ΔH for the whole reaction = $(-4,074) - (-1,273) = -2,801$ kJ. ΔH for the whole reaction is negative, which means the reaction is exothermic.

We can also combine stoichiometry with thermochemistry in order to figure out how much heat is given off or released when a certain amount of reactants are used up. Let's use the reaction we just looked at to show you how.

If 18.0 g of $C_6H_{12}O_6$ were to be reacted, how much energy would be released?

$$18.0 \text{ g } C_6H_{12}O_6 \times \frac{1 \text{ mol } C_6H_{12}O_6}{180 \text{ g}} \times \frac{-2,801 \text{ kJ}}{1 \text{ mol } C_6H_{12}O_6} = -280 \text{ kJ}$$

Note that the $-2,801$ kJ goes with 1 mole of $C_6H_{12}O_6$ because that is the coefficient on the $C_6H_{12}O_6$ in the balanced reaction. If you were to instead start with 32.0 g of oxygen, the math would look like this:

$$32.0 \text{ g } O_2 \times \frac{1 \text{ mol } O_2}{32.00 \text{ g}} \times \frac{-2,801 \text{ kJ}}{6 \text{ mol } O_2} = -467 \text{ kJ}$$

Remember, without a calculator, any math you would be asked to do should be fairly straightforward, as it is above.

Hess's Law

If you have to manipulate any reaction, then there are rules in place for how the enthalpy of that reaction changes as well. There are three rules you should know:

1. If you multiply (or divide) all of the species in that reaction by a coefficient, the enthalpy change must be multiplied (or divided) by the same coefficient.
2. If you flip a reaction, you must also flip the sign on the enthalpy.
3. If a reaction is the sum of several component reactions, the enthalpy for that reaction will be the sum of the enthalpies of the various components.

These rules combined are often called Hess's Law. What Hess's Law essentially tells us is that ΔH for a reaction is independent of the number of steps or the pathway the reaction follows.

Take a look at the following example.

Given:

$$C(s) + O_2(g) \rightarrow CO_2(g) \qquad \Delta H = x$$

$$H_2O(l) \rightarrow H_2(g) + \tfrac{1}{2} O_2(g) \qquad \Delta H = y$$

$$C_3H_8(g) \rightarrow 3C(s) + 4 H_2(g) \qquad \Delta H = z$$

Find the enthalpy change for $C_3H_8(g) + 5 O_2(g) \rightarrow 3 CO_2(g) + 4 H_2O(l)$ in terms of the defined variables.

To solve this, we need to manipulate the given reactions so that when they are added together, we get our target reaction. The first step in doing this is to flip the middle reaction—the H_2O (l) has to be on the right side when we finish. While we're at it, we'll also multiply it by four so the coefficient on the H_2O (l) is correct. That gives us:

$$4H_2(g) + 2O_2(g) \rightarrow 4 H_2O(l) \qquad \Delta H = y \times -4 = -4y$$

We also need to multiple the top reaction by 3, so the coefficient on the $CO_2(g)$ is correct.

$$3C(s) + 3O_2(g) \rightarrow 3CO_2(g) \qquad \Delta H = x \times 3 = 3x$$

If we add all three equations together:

$$4H_2(g) + 2O_2(g) + 3C(s) + 3O_2(g) + C_3H_8(g) \rightarrow 4H_2O\ (l) + 3CO_2(g) + 3C(s) + 4H_2(g)$$

Anything that appears on both sides of the arrow cancels out and any identical substances on the same side of the arrow combine, leaving us with our target equation:

$$4H_2(g) + 2O_2(g) + 3C(s) + 3O_2(g) + C_3H_8(g) \rightarrow 4H_2O(l) + 3CO_2(g) + 3C(s) + 4H_2(g)$$

$$C_3H_8(g) + 5O_2(g) \rightarrow 3CO_2(g) + 4H_2O(l)$$

To determine the enthalpy for that equation, all we have to do is add the enthalpies for all three reactions. So, the enthalpy in terms of the given variables would be $3x - 4y + z$.

Spontaneity and Gibbs Free Energy

A **spontaneous reaction** is one that will occur at a given temperature without the input of energy. Strangely enough, however, sometimes endothermic reactions (which require the input of energy in order to take place) occur spontaneously. Why? Because, as we said, the universe likes entropy—disorder. If a particular reaction is endothermic (ΔH is positive) but creates greater disorder (ΔS is also positive), and the disorder the reaction creates exceeds the energy it requires, then the reaction may occur spontaneously although it's endothermic. Similarly, if a reaction creates order instead of disorder, it may occur spontaneously as long as it's exothermic and the negative enthalpy change exceeds the negative entropy change.

What determines whether a reaction will or won't occur spontaneously? The combination of ΔH and ΔS. This combination of ΔH and ΔS is called Gibbs free energy, and is symbolized by ΔG. The actual formula for determining ΔG is $\Delta G = \Delta H - T\Delta S$ (where T is temperature, measured in degrees Kelvin). Remember the following points about Gibbs free energy:

- If ΔG for the reaction is negative, then that reaction occurs spontaneously in the forward direction.
- If ΔG for the reaction is positive, then that reaction occurs spontaneously in the reverse direction.
- If ΔG for the reaction is zero, then the reaction is in equilibrium. (We'll discuss equilibrium later.)

Important Facts About Gibbs Free Energy

$\Delta G = \Delta H - T\Delta S$

If $\Delta G < 0$, then the reaction is spontaneous in the forward direction.

If $\Delta G > 0$, then the reaction is spontaneous in the reverse direction.

Review everything we've talked about in this chapter, and then answer the following set of questions. The answers can be found in Part IV.

DRILL 2

Question Type A

Questions 5–7 refer to the following.

(A) Gibbs free energy
(B) Heat of formation
(C) Enthalpy change
(D) Entropy
(E) Kinetic energy

5. Value that determines whether a reaction is spontaneous

6. Quantity that determines whether a reaction is exothermic or endothermic

7. Indicates the degree of disorder of a system

Question Type B

I		II

103. If a reaction is exothermic, it always proceeds spontaneously   BECAUSE   the universe favors a negative enthalpy change.

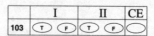

104. Ice melting is an endothermic process   BECAUSE   heat must be absorbed by ice if it is to melt.

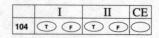

Question Type C

26. $\ldots C_2H_4(g) + \ldots O_2(g) \rightarrow \ldots CO_2(g) + \ldots H_2O(l)$

If the equation for the reaction above is balanced using the smallest possible whole-number coefficients, then the coefficient for oxygen gas is

(A) 1
(B) 2
(C) 3
(D) 4
(E) 5

27. $2Na(s) + Cl_2(g) \rightarrow 2NaCl(s) + 822$ kJ

How much heat is released by the above reaction if 0.5 mole of sodium reacts completely with chlorine?

(A) 205 kJ
(B) 411 kJ
(C) 822 kJ
(D) 1,644 kJ
(E) 3,288 kJ

28. $2Al(s) + Fe_2O_3(s) \rightarrow Al_2O_3(s) + 2Fe(s)$

If 80 grams of Al and 80 grams of Fe_2O_3 are combined, what is the maximum number of moles of Fe that can be produced?

(A) 0.5
(B) 1
(C) 2
(D) 3
(E) 4

29. $CH_4(g) + 2O_2(g) \rightarrow CO_2(g) + 2H_2O(g) + 800$ kJ

If 1 mole of $O_2(g)$ is consumed in the reaction given above, how much energy is produced?

(A) 200 kJ
(B) 400 kJ
(C) 800 kJ
(D) 1,200 kJ
(E) 1,600 kJ

30. ....PH_3 + ...O_2 → ...P_2O_5 + ...H_2O

When the equation above is balanced and the coefficients are reduced to the lowest whole numbers, the coefficient for H_2O is

(A) 1
(B) 2
(C) 3
(D) 4
(E) 5

Summary

o   A molecule is a unit consisting of two or more atoms.

o   The elements that exist as diatomic molecules are: O_2, I_2, H_2, N_2, Cl_2, F_2, Br_2.

o   The formula weight of a molecule is the sum of the weights of the atoms making up that molecule.

o   The empirical formula is the smallest whole number ratio of the numbers of atoms of different elements within a molecule.

o   The percent composition of an element in a molecule is the mass of all the atoms of that element within the molecule, divided by the formula weight, times 100.

o   A mole is 6.02×10^{23} molecules. 1 mole of atomic mass units is 1 gram (1/12 the mass of a carbon-12 atom), so the atomic weight of a molecule equals the mass of 1 mole of that molecule in grams.

o   To convert mass composition to empirical formula, first calculate the number of moles of each element in a 100-gram sample, dividing the percent composition of each element by that element's atomic weight. The whole number ratio of moles of each element gives the empirical formula.

o   To balance chemical equations on the SAT Subject Test in Chemistry, plug in each answer choice as the coefficient of the molecule being asked about. If the equation can be balanced so that the numbers of each type of atom are the same on the right and left, and that the resulting coefficients don't have any common factor, then you've found the right answer.

o   To solve limiting reactant problems, use stoichiometry to determine which reactant would create less of a given product. The reactant which creates less product is limiting, and the other reactant is excess.

o   If we manipulate a chemical reaction by flipping it or multiplying it by a coefficient, the enthalpy of that reaction will also change in the manner outlined using Hess's Law.

o   Entropy, S, is a measure of the randomness of a system. The higher the entropy and lower the energy, the more stable the system.

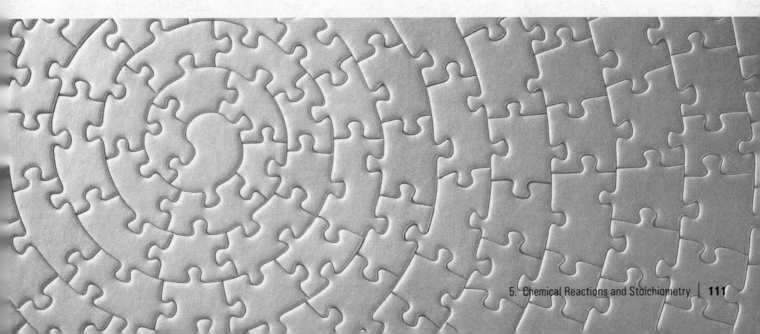

o The energy given off or absorbed by a reaction is the enthalpy change, ΔH.
- Enthalpy change is the difference in potential energy between the bonds in the reactants and the bonds in the products.

- A reaction with a negative enthalpy is exothermic, or produces heat, while a reaction with a positive enthalpy is endothermic, or absorbs heat.

- Heat of formation is the energy released or absorbed when a molecule is created from its constituent elements.

- The enthalpy change for a reaction is the heat of formation of the products minus the heat of formation of the reactants.

o Gibbs free energy is given by

$$\Delta G = \Delta H - T\Delta S$$

If the Gibbs free energy is positive, the reaction is non-spontaneous; if the Gibbs free energy is negative, the reaction is spontaneous.

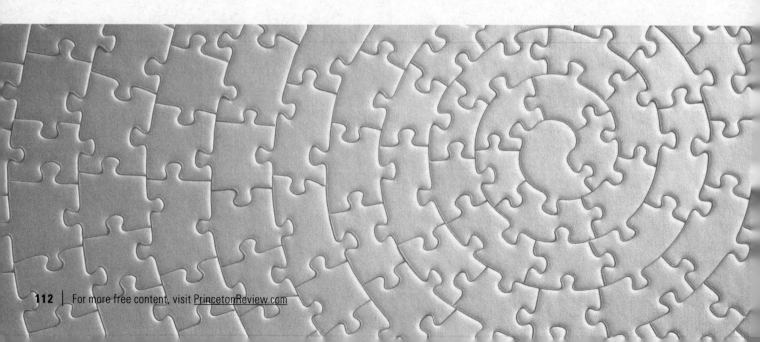

Chapter 6
Electron Configurations and Radioactivity

Chemical reactions involve interactions between the electrons of atoms. To understand how and why atoms react, we need to know something about electron configuration—the arrangement of electrons in atoms. Radioactivity involves changes that occur within an atom's nucleus. In this chapter, we will go over electron orbitals, electron configurations, the stable octet, and radioactivity.

ORBITALS

Quantum Mechanics

With the advent of **quantum mechanics,** our understanding of the atom has changed dramatically. An important precursor to the field of quantum mechanics was the atomic theory of Max Planck. He figured out that electromagnetic energy is quantized. That is, for a given frequency of radiation (or light), all possible energies are multiples of a certain unit of energy, called a quantum. So, energy changes do not occur smoothly but rather in small but specific steps. Neils Bohr took this quantum theory and predicted that in atoms the electrons orbit the nucleus just as planets orbit the Sun. He proposed the Bohr model of the atom, which was later proved to be incorrect. For the SAT Subject Test in Chemistry, you have to know that electrons do *not* circle the nucleus as planets circle the Sun. Electrons do not orbit. Instead, they exist in things called **orbitals.**

Just as a room is a region in a house in which a person may be found, an orbital is a region in an atom where an electron may be found. Rooms come in a variety of sizes and shapes and so do orbitals. A collection of orbitals with roughly similar sizes constitutes an **energy shell**. Electrons that are farther from the nucleus have greater energy than those that are closer, so electrons in the orbitals of larger energy shells have greater energy than those in the orbitals of smaller energy shells. Each energy shell is designated by a whole number, so we have the 1st (smallest energy shell), 2nd, 3rd, and so on.

Shape is another important characteristic of orbitals. There are four significant types of orbital shapes. Orbitals that have the same shape in a given energy shell comprise a **subshell**. An *s* subshell always consists of one spherical orbital; a *p* subshell always consists of three dumbbell-shaped orbitals; and the *d* and *f* subshells contain five and seven oddly shaped orbitals, respectively. Any orbital, regardless of size and shape, can hold a maximum of two electrons.

Quantum Numbers

To find the location of an electron around an atom utilizing quantum theory, a set of numbers is assigned to each electron of an atom. These numbers, called the **quantum numbers** for that electron, are essentially an electron address—they give us an idea of approximately where the electron is located relative to the nucleus of the atom. Each electron has four primary quantum numbers:

1. Principal quantum number (n)
   The first quantum number describes how far an electron is from the nucleus. This is consistent with previous models of the atoms, with the first energy shell ($n = 1$) being the one closest to the nucleus.

2. Azimuthal quantum number (l)
    Each of the subshells is assigned a different quantum number. An
    s-subshell = 0, p-subshell = 1, d-subshell = 2, and f-subshell = 3. The
    subshell describes the shape of the orbital within which the electron
    can be found.

3. Magnetic quantum number (ml)
    Each of the subshell types has a different number of orbitals, and each
    of those orbitals is represented with a different quantum number.
    An s-subshell has one orbital that is always represented with a 0. The
    three orbitals in a p-subshell are represented with –1, 0, and +1. The
    five d-orbitals are represented with –2, –1, 0, +1, and +2. Finally, the
    seven f-orbitals are represented with –3, –2, –1, 0, +1, +2, and +3.

4. Spin projection quantum number (ms)
    Every orbital can contain exactly two electrons, and these two elec-
    trons must have opposing spins. One will spin clockwise, and the
    other will spin counterclockwise. These two spins are represented by
    $+\frac{1}{2}$ and $-\frac{1}{2}$.

Putting it all together, if you were asked to assign a set of quantum numbers to
an electron in a 3p subshell, you have the following six sets of quantum numbers
(written as n, l, ml, ms):

$$(3, 1, -1, +\frac{1}{2}) \qquad (3, 1, -1, -\frac{1}{2}) \qquad (3, 1, 0, +\frac{1}{2})$$

$$(3, 1, 0, -\frac{1}{2}) \qquad (3, 1, +1, +\frac{1}{2}) \qquad (3, 1, +1, -\frac{1}{2})$$

A total of six electrons can fit in the 3p subshell, and those six quantum number sets each represent one possibility. The s-subshells contain a maximum of two
electrons and thus would have two potential sets of quantum numbers, d-orbitals
would have ten potential sets, and f-orbitals would have fourteen potential sets.

Bohr Model

The Bohr Model of the atom states that the electrons surrounding the nucleus orbit at fixed distances, much like planets around the Sun. (Setting aside for now that the orbit of the planets around the Sun is not, in fact, a circle!). The Bohr model for a magnesium atom would look like this:

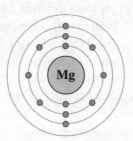

The number of electrons that can be found on each energy level can be determined by looking at how many elements are in that row of the periodic table. The first row has only two elements, and thus, the first energy level can only hold two electrons. The second row has eight, and thus can hold eight electrons. The third row also has eight, but notice that magnesium only has twelve total electrons. The first ten electrons went into the first two energy levels, leaving just two left to partially fill the third level.

The Bohr model of magnesium above shows a magnesium atom in its **ground state**. The ground state is the configuration of the electrons in an atom under standard conditions. If the magnesium atom were exposed to an energy source, that energy could cause an electron to jump from a lower energy level to a higher energy level. When this occurs, we say the atom is in an **excited state** (just like you are right now reading this!) An excited magnesium atom might look like this:

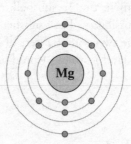

Notice that one of the electrons that was originally in the third energy level jumped to the fourth. Electrons can jump up more than one energy level, so there are many possible excited configurations for magnesium. When in an excited state, the electrons are not stable, and they will eventually fall back to their ground state. When they do, they will emit a specific wavelength of energy that corresponds to the distance they fell between energy levels. That energy is often in the visible light range. If you were to look at all the light given off by all the various possible distances that excited electrons can fall in a magnesium atom, you would get what is called the emission spectrum of magnesium.

Every element has a different emission spectrum, and the emission spectrum of an element is one of the things that can be used to help identify it.

The Bohr model of the atom can also be looked at as a diagram. When looking at individual electrons, the amount of energy they have is measured in a unit called an electron volt (eV). 1 eV is an incredibly small unit of energy. The Bohr diagram for magnesium would look like this:

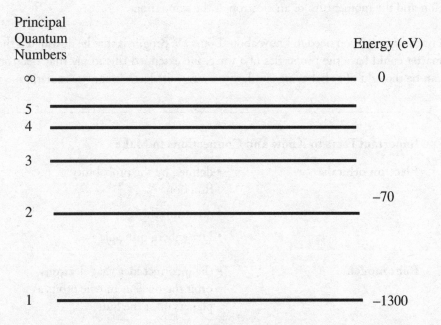

Notice that even though there are only electrons in the first three energy levels, there are still lines for the fourth and fifth energy level there. Just because the energy levels are empty does not mean they don't exist, it just means there are no electrons present in them. Notice that as the energy levels increase, there is a smaller and smaller distance between them. Energy levels 4 and 5 and much closer than energy levels 1 and 2, and this trend would continue.

The infinity symbol at the top represents the amount of energy that would be needed to remove an electron from the magnesium atom. To remove an electron from the first energy level would require a lot more energy than removing an electron from the third energy level; this is represented by the greater distance between level 1 and infinity. The energy needed to remove an electron from an atom is called the ionization energy, and we'll look at that in more detail next chapter.

One last caveat. The Bohr model is an excellent model when it comes to figuring out various chemical properties of elements, and you should be familiar with the principles described above utilizing it. However, the Bohr model is not perfect. Electrons do not actually orbit at fixed distances from the nucleus. Instead, an electron's position is better defined using probability, so it's time to discuss how the definition of "orbital" has changed over time.

The Heisenberg Principle and De Broglie's Hypothesis

But what's an orbital? The test writers expect you to associate the word *orbital* with something called a "probability function." An orbital describes the "likelihood that an electron will be found in a particular location." Another important concept to know for the test is the **Heisenberg principle**. What's the Heisenberg principle? Well, simply put, it means this: it is impossible to know both the position and the momentum of an electron at the same time.

For this test, all you need to know about Louis De Broglie is that he postulated that matter could have the properties of a wave. He extended this to say that electrons can be thought of as behaving similarly to waves of electromagnetic radiation.

Check Your Work
Add the superscripts from fluorine's electron configuration: 2 + 2 + 5 = 9. This can serve as a check of your work or as a quick way to eliminate incorrect choices on an electron configuration question.

Important Facts to Know and Connections to Make

Electron orbitals:	• defined by the probability function
	• quantum theory
	• Heisenberg principle
Bohr model:	• the incorrect idea that electrons orbit the nucleus in true orbits as planets orbit the Sun
Heisenberg principle:	• electrons are located in orbitals, not orbits
	• one cannot know an electron's position and momentum at the same time
De Broglie's hypothesis:	• matter (including electrons) can be thought of as having properties of both a particle and a wave

ELECTRON CONFIGURATIONS

For the SAT Subject Test in Chemistry, you'll have to be able to figure out electron configurations. Here's how:

1. The test will give you a periodic table. First, draw these brackets on it.

Where Does Helium Go?

Notice that, although Helium looks like it should be in the *p* subshell area, it's actually a member of the *s* subshell. Make sure you memorize that as well as your general *s*, *p*, *d*, and *f* subshells.

PERIODIC TABLE OF THE ELEMENTS

s subshell area

p subshell area

	1A	2A											3A	4A	5A	6A	7A	8A
1	1 **H** 1.0079																	2 **He** 4.0026
2	3 **Li** 6.941	4 **Be** 9.012											5 **B** 10.811	6 **C** 12.011	7 **N** 14.007	8 **O** 16.00	9 **F** 19.00	10 **Ne** 20.179
3	11 **Na** 22.99	12 **Mg** 24.30											13 **Al** 26.98	14 **Si** 28.09	15 **P** 30.974	16 **S** 32.06	17 **Cl** 35.453	18 **Ar** 39.948
4	19 **K** 39.10	20 **Ca** 40.48	21 **Sc** 44.96	22 **Ti** 47.90	23 **V** 50.94	24 **Cr** 52.00	25 **Mn** 54.938	26 **Fe** 55.85	27 **Co** 58.93	28 **Ni** 58.69	29 **Cu** 63.55	30 **Zn** 65.39	31 **Ga** 69.72	32 **Ge** 72.59	33 **As** 74.92	34 **Se** 78.96	35 **Br** 79.90	36 **Kr** 83.80
5	37 **Rb** 85.47	38 **Sr** 87.62	39 **Y** 88.91	40 **Zr** 91.22	41 **Nb** 92.91	42 **Mo** 95.94	43 **Tc** (98)	44 **Ru** 101.1	45 **Rh** 102.91	46 **Pd** 106.42	47 **Ag** 107.87	48 **Cd** 112.41	49 **In** 114.82	50 **Sn** 118.71	51 **Sb** 121.75	52 **Te** 127.60	53 **I** 126.91	54 **Xe** 131.29
6	55 **Cs** 132.91	56 **Ba** 137.33	57 ***La** 138.91	72 **Hf** 178.49	73 **Ta** 180.95	74 **W** 183.85	75 **Re** 186.21	76 **Os** 190.2	77 **Ir** 192.2	78 **Pt** 195.08	79 **Au** 196.97	80 **Hg** 200.59	81 **Tl** 204.38	82 **Pb** 207.2	83 **Bi** 208.98	84 **Po** (209)	85 **At** (210)	86 **Rn** (222)
7	87 **Fr** (223)	88 **Ra** 226.02	89 **†Ac** 227.03	104 **Rf** (261)	105 **Db** (262)	106 **Sg** (266)	107 **Bh** (264)	108 **Hs** (277)	109 **Mt** (268)	110 **Ds** (271)	111 **Rg** (272)	112 **§** (277)						

B groups

d subshell area

§ Not yet named

*Lanthanide Series	58 **Ce** 140.12	59 **Pr** 140.91	60 **Nd** 144.24	61 **Pm** (145)	62 **Sm** 150.4	63 **Eu** 151.97	64 **Gd** 157.25	65 **Tb** 158.93	66 **Dy** 162.50	67 **Ho** 164.93	68 **Er** 167.26	69 **Tm** 168.93	70 **Yb** 173.04	71 **Lu** 174.97
†Actinide Series	90 **Th** 232.04	91 **Pa** 231.04	92 **U** 238.03	93 **Np** 237.05	94 **Pu** (244)	95 **Am** (243)	96 **Cm** (247)	97 **Bk** (247)	98 **Cf** (251)	99 **Es** (252)	100 **Fm** (257)	101 **Md** (258)	102 **No** (259)	103 **Lr** (262)

f subshell area

2. Each period (horizontal row) of the periodic table corresponds to an energy shell. For example, atoms of carbon, C, (row **2**) have outer electrons in the **2nd** energy shell; atoms of sodium, Na, (row **3**) have outer electrons in the **3rd** energy shell, and so on.

3. When writing electron configurations, and determining which subshells to fill, be aware of what area and row the element is in. Then remember the following points:
   - An element in the *s* area of row **n** has outer electrons in the **n***s* subshell.
   - An element in the *p* area of row **n** has outer electrons in the **n***p* subshell.
   - An element in the *d* area of row **n** has outer electrons in the (**n** − 1)*d* subshell.
   - An element in the *f* area of row **n** has outer electrons in the (**n** − 2)*f* subshell.

Let's put it all together and try writing the electron configuration for an atom of fluorine.

How Does This Work?

Consider an atom of phosphorus, P, (row 3). It's in the p area, so its outer electrons are in the $3p$ sub-shell. What about an atom of nickel, Ni, (row 4)? It's in the d area. That means its outer electrons go into the $(4-1)d$ or $3d$ subshell.

Step 1. Where do we start? At hydrogen, of course. It's in the s area of row 1. Hydrogen (H) has an electron in its $1s$ subshell. Remember that although helium looks like it is in the p area, it is actually part of the $1s$ area.

Step 2. Now we have 2 electrons in the lone orbital of the $1s$ subshell. Since no orbital can hold 3 electrons, we need to go to a different (higher energy) subshell for the next addition.

Step 3. Follow the numbers to lithium (Li) and then beryllium (Be); they're in the s area of row 2 and fill the $2s$ subshell and keep going. Starting with boron (B) and continuing through fluorine (F), we are in the p area of row 2. Boron atoms have 1 electron in the $2p$ subshell, carbon atoms have 2, and so on—up to fluorine, which has 5 electrons in its $2p$ subshell.

Step 4. This makes the electron configuration of a fluorine atom $1s^2 2s^2 2p^5$. The superscripts indicate the number of electrons occupying a particular subshell. Adding these superscripts gives the total number of electrons in a species. Since fluorine has the atomic number 9, we expect fluorine atoms to have 9 electrons.

Finding the electron configuration of ions follows the same rules as those for atoms but with one additional step. Suppose we need the electron configuration of the fluoride ion, F^-. First, find the electron configuration for the atom. That would be $1s^2 2s^2 2p^5$. Now, how does F^- differ from the neutral F atom? It has 1 extra electron. So add 1 electron to the electron configuration. Thus, the electron configuration of F^- is $1s^2 2s^2 2p^6$ (the same as that of a neon atom). If we were dealing with positive ions, we would find the atomic electron configuration and then remove one or more electrons.

Now, what about the f subshell, which you might remember learning about in school? For the test you don't have to know much about it. Just remember this: if an element has an atomic number greater than 57, some of its electrons are in the f subshell, which is another way of saying they're in f orbitals. So, element number 76, osmium (Os), has electrons in the f subshell, as do gold (Au), samarium (Sm), and terbium (Tb).

One more thing: the **Aufbau principle** states that a subshell is completely filled before electrons are placed in the next higher subshell. But there are some exceptions to this principle that are worth mentioning. First, since completely filled and half-filled d subshells give extra stability to an atom, chromium (Cr) and copper

(Cu) violate the Aufbau principle and promote a $4s$ electron to the $3d$ orbital. Second, hybrid orbitals, which we will talk about in the next chapter, also violate the Aufbau principle by mixing orbitals of different energy levels.

The Stable Octet

Look at element 10, neon (Ne). Its electron configuration is $1s^2 2s^2 2p^6$. Neon's configuration has one 1 subshell and two 2 subshells. It has no 3 subshells or 4 subshells, so the two 2 subshells (indicating the 2nd subshell) constitute its outermost shell.

Now take a look at neon's outermost shell: $1s^2 2s^2 2p^6$. Count the electrons in this shell: 2 + 6 = 8. The fact that neon has 8 electrons in its outermost shell means that it has a stable octet: 8 electrons.

Examine element number 18, argon (Ar), and look especially at its outermost shell, which is the 3rd shell: $1s^2 2s^2 2p^6\ 3s^2 3p^6$. Argon, too, has a stable octet. That is, it has 8 electrons in its outermost shell. The same is true for the following:

> krypton (Kr): $1s^2 2s^2 2p^6 3s^2 3p^6 4s^2 3d^{10} 4p^6$
> xenon (Xe): $1s^2 2s^2 2p^6 3s^2 3p^6 4s^2 3d^{10} 4p^6 5s^2 4d^{10} 5p^6$
> radon (Rn): $1s^2 2s^2 2p^6 3s^2 3p^6 4s^2 3d^{10} 4p^6 5s^2 4d^{10} 5p^6 6s^2 4f^{14} 5d^{10} 6p^6$

All of the elements with stable octets are called **noble gases** or **inert gases**. They're very stable. They don't like to react with anything or change themselves in any way. They're very happy the way they are. Why? Because atoms are happiest with 8 electrons in their outermost shell. Helium (He, atomic number 2) is also very stable. It, too, is an inert gas although it has only 2 electrons in its outermost shell.

The electrons in an atom's outermost shell are called **valence electrons**. So another way of saying "stable octet" is to say "8 valence electrons." All of the noble gases have 8 valence electrons. Beryllium, however, (Be, atomic number 4)—$1s^2 2s^2$— has 2 valence electrons. Oxygen—$1s^2 2s^2 2p^4$—has 6 valence electrons.

> Remember:
>
> - Valence electrons are the electrons in the outermost energy shell.
> - Atoms with 8 valence electrons have a stable octet. They're very stable and are often referred to as the noble gases.

Now review the material on electrons, electron configurations, and the stable octet, and try these questions. The answers can be found in Part IV.

DRILL 1

Question Type A

Questions 1–3 refer to the following.

(A) Bohr model
(B) De Broglie's hypothesis
(C) Heisenberg principle
(D) Quantum theory
(E) Atomic theory

1. Provides that all matter may be considered as a wave

2. Views electrons in true orbits around the nucleus

3. Considers that one cannot know the position and velocity of an electron at the same moment

Questions 4–7 refer to the following.

(A) $1s^2 2s^2 2p^6 3s^1$
(B) $1s^2 2s^2 2p^6 3s^2$
(C) $1s^2 2s^2 2p^6 3s^2 3p^3$
(D) $1s^2 2s^2 2p^6 3s^2 3p^5$
(E) $1s^2 2s^2 2p^6 3s^2 3p^6$

4. The electron configuration of an element usually found as a single atom of gas at STP

5. The electron configuration of an element with the largest first ionization energy

6. The electron configuration of the element whose atoms are most likely to form 3 covalent bonds

7. The electron configuration of an element that is diamagnetic, but not a noble gas

Question Type B

<table>
<tr><td></td><td>I</td><td>BECAUSE</td><td>II</td></tr>
</table>

	I		II
101.	The Bohr model of the atom is inaccurate	BECAUSE	an element may exist as several isotopes, each with a different number of neutrons in the nucleus.

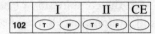

	I		II	CE
101	T F		T F	⬭

	I		II
102.	Krypton is an extremely unstable atom	BECAUSE	an atom with 8 electrons in its outermost shell tends toward great stability.

	I		II	CE
102	T F		T F	⬭

Question Type C

24. The electron configuration $1s^22s^22p^63s^23p^64s^23d^7$ represents an atom of the element

   (A) Br
   (B) Co
   (C) Cd
   (D) Ga
   (E) Mg

25. The electron configuration for an atom of the element Tc is

   (A) $1s^22s^22p^63s^23p^63d^{10}4s^24p^55s^25p^6$
   (B) $1s^22s^22p^63s^23p^63d^{10}4s^24p^35s^24d^5$
   (C) $1s^22s^22p^63s^23p^63d^{10}4s^24p^3$
   (D) $1s^22s^22p^63s^23p^63d^{15}$
   (E) $1s^22s^22p^63s^23p^63d^{10}4s^24p^65s^24d^5$

26. A neutral species whose electron configuration is $1s^22s^22p^63s^23p^63d^{10}4s^24p^65s^24d^{10}5p^6$ is

   (A) highly reactive
   (B) a positively charged ion
   (C) a noble gas
   (D) a transition metal
   (E) a lanthanide element

RADIOACTIVITY AND HALF-LIVES

Atomic nuclei, as you know, are made of protons and neutrons. In some atoms, the combination of protons and neutrons makes the nucleus unstable. These atoms will decay—on their own—spontaneously. As they decay, they emit high-energy radioactive particles. Radioactive particles include alpha (α) particles, beta (β) particles, and gamma (γ) rays. If you think about it, the process of radioactive decay makes sense: a radioactive nucleus is trying to become more stable; greater stability means lower energy, so the radioactive nucleus wants to lose energy.

As a radioactive atom decays—emitting α or β particles and γ rays—its identity changes, and it becomes either (1) another isotope of the element it originally was or (2) another element entirely. Some nuclei are stable, and some are unstable; the unstable ones have a tendency to break apart, and they are said to be **radioactive.**

Why are some nuclei unstable? For this test, you have to know only that the instability has something to do with the combination of neutrons and protons. Some combinations of neutrons and protons just don't get along well, and they try to solve this problem by undergoing nuclear decay. When you think of radioactivity, think this: when an unstable nucleus undergoes nuclear decay, it's radioactive, and it gives off radioactivity. A **Geiger counter** is used to detect and measure radioactive particles.

You should know about four kinds of radioactive decay.

Radioactive Decay Type 1: Alpha Decay

An alpha particle is made up of 2 protons and 2 neutrons. When a nucleus gives off an alpha particle, its atomic number is reduced by 2 and its mass number is reduced by 4. Since the atomic number changes, it actually turns into a different element. After all, the atomic number is the basis of an atom's identity.

Another thing about alpha particles: since an alpha particle consists of 2 protons and 2 neutrons, it's actually the same thing as a helium-4 nucleus, and it's often symbolized that way—^4_2He. The 4 represents the mass number, and the 2 represents the atomic number (number of protons).

> To sum up alpha decay:
>
> - An alpha particle is emitted.
> - The atomic number decreases by 2; the mass number decreases by 4.

Radioactive Decay Type 2: Beta Decay

Sometimes a nucleus becomes more stable through beta decay, in which it reduces its neutron-to-proton ratio by taking a neutron and turning it into a proton. In these cases, the atomic number goes up by 1, since there's an extra proton, but the mass number remains the same. (It lost a neutron, but it gained a proton, so there is no net change in the mass number.) When an atom undergoes beta decay, it emits a beta particle; a beta particle is identical to an electron and is symbolized as $_{+1}^{0}e$.

To sum up beta decay:

- A neutron is converted to a proton.
- A beta particle (an electron) is emitted.
- The atomic number increases by 1, but the mass number stays the same.

Radioactive Decay Type 3: Positron Emission (Positive Beta Decay)

Sometimes, when a nucleus can become more stable by increasing its neutron-to-proton ratio, it takes a proton and converts it to a neutron. The result of this is that the atomic number decreases by 1, and the mass number remains the same; this type of radioactive decay is known as positron emission. When a nucleus undergoes positron emission, it emits a positron. What is a positron? Well, it's a positively charged particle, but it isn't a proton. It has the same mass as an electron, but it carries a positive charge. A positron is symbolized as $_{+1}^{0}e$.

To sum up positron emission:
- A proton is converted to a neutron.
- A positron is emitted.
- The atomic number decreases by 1, and mass number stays the same.

Radioactive Decay Type 4: Gamma Decay

We should also mention gamma rays, which are a form of electromagnetic radiation. Radioactive nuclei often emit gamma rays; these are high-energy particles with the symbol $_0^0\gamma$, together with alpha particles, beta particles, or positrons. When nuclei emit alpha or beta particles, they are sometimes left in a high-energy state, but when they emit gamma rays, they become stable.

Summary of Radioactive (or Nuclear) Decay

Type of Decay	Problem with Nucleus	Conversion	Emitted Particle	Nuclear Change
Alpha Decay	Nucleus is too heavy	Two protons and two neutrons split off of the nucleus.	Alpha particle or helium nucleus	Atomic number decreases by 2; mass number decreases by 4.
Beta Decay	Too many neutrons, too few protons	An electron is pulled off of a neutron, which turns into a proton.	Beta particle or electron	Atomic number increases by 1; mass number is unchanged.
Positron Emission	Too many protons, too few neutrons	A positron, or positive electron, is pulled off a proton, which turns into a neutron.	Positron	Atomic number decreases by 1; mass number is unchanged.
Gamma Decay	Too much energy	A nucleus releases energy in the form of high-energy radiation.	Gamma photon	Nucleus becomes more stable, but is otherwise unchanged.

Half-Life

For the SAT Subject Test in Chemistry, you should know everything we just said about radioactive decay, and you should also know about the *rate* of radioactive decay. The rate of radioactive decay of a substance is called its **half-life.** For example, if we start with 1,000 g of a radioactive substance, and its half-life is 1 year, then after 1 year we'll have 500 g of the original sample left. After another year we'll have 250 g of the original sample left, and so on. That's how half-lives work. Let's take a look at the rate of decay, illustrated on the following page.

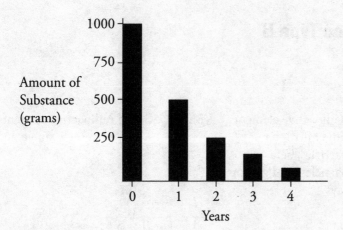

Now review everything we've said about radioactive decay and half-lives, and try the following questions. The answers can be found in Part IV.

DRILL 2

Question Type A

Questions 4–6 refer to the following.

    (A) Alpha decay
    (B) Beta decay
    (C) Positron emission
    (D) Gamma decay
    (E) Electron capture

4. Often accompanies other radioactive processes

5. Causes an atom to reduce its atomic number by 2 and its mass number by 4

6. Occurs when a neutron is converted into a proton in a nucleus

Question Type B

	I		II
	<u>I</u>		<u>II</u>

103. Radioactive elements can emit alpha particles, beta particles, and gamma rays

BECAUSE

radioactive elements have extremely stable nuclei.

104. If a radioactive sample with a half-life of 40 years decays for 80 years, 25% of the original sample will remain

BECAUSE

one half of 100% is 50%, and one half of 50% is 25%.

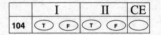

Question Type C

$$^{222}_{86}Rn \rightarrow \,^{218}_{84}Po + \,^4_2He$$

27. The radioactive decay shown above is an example of

(A) positron emission
(B) gamma ray emission
(C) alpha decay
(D) beta decay
(E) ionization

$$^{131}_{53}I \rightarrow {}^{131}_{54}Xe + {}^{0}_{-1}e$$

28. The radioactive decay shown above is an example of

    (A) positron emission
    (B) gamma ray emission
    (C) alpha decay
    (D) beta decay
    (E) ionization

29. For the radioactive atom ^{99}Tc, what is the correct number of protons and neutrons?

    (A) 43 protons and 56 neutrons
    (B) 43 protons and 99 neutrons
    (C) 56 protons and 43 neutrons
    (D) 56 protons and 99 neutrons
    (E) Cannot be determined

Summary

○ The Bohr Model is the incorrect idea that electrons orbit the nucleus like planets orbit the Sun.

○ Electrons exist in orbitals. Their location and movement can never be known with exactitude, and can only be approximated to a degree of certainty with probability functions.

○ Electrons have properties of both particles and waves, as given by the De Broglie hypothesis.

○ Electron configurations tell us the energy levels and orbitals that the electrons in a certain atom inhabit.

○ Valence electrons are electrons in the outermost shell. Atoms with 8 valence electrons are very stable.

○ Radioactivity is a spontaneous change in the nucleus resulting from nuclear instability.
  • There are four types of radioactive decay:
    alpha, beta, positron emission, and gamma. Each results from a different "problem" with the nucleus.
  • Half-life describes the amount of time it takes until exactly half of a radioactive sample has decayed.

○ When atoms are exposed to an outside source of energy, they change from their ground state to their excited state, where some of their electrons have jumped to a higher energy level.

○ Each element has a unique emission spectra that is based of the distances between its various energy levels.

Chapter 7
The Periodic Table and Bonding

When you sit down to take the SAT Subject Test in Chemistry, the periodic table may well be your best friend. Why? Well, first, it is one of the few tools you'll be allowed to use on test day. Second, it can help you answer quite a few different types of test questions. We just saw how to use the periodic table to figure out an atom's electron configuration, and we'll now take a look at how it can help you predict how atoms will bond. This chapter will discuss the chemical families, periodic trends, different types of bonds, and molecular shapes.

THE PERIODIC TABLE

PERIODIC TABLE OF THE ELEMENTS

s subshell area

p subshell area

1A																	8A
1																	2
H	2A												3A	4A	5A	6A	7A	**He**
1.0079																	4.0026

$s \longrightarrow$

B groups
d subshell area

	1A	2A											3A	4A	5A	6A	7A	8A
1	1 **H** 1.0079																	2 **He** 4.0026
2	3 **Li** 6.941	4 **Be** 9.012											5 **B** 10.811	6 **C** 12.011	7 **N** 14.007	8 **O** 16.00	9 **F** 19.00	10 **Ne** 20.179
3	11 **Na** 22.99	12 **Mg** 24.30											13 **Al** 26.98	14 **Si** 28.09	15 **P** 30.974	16 **S** 32.06	17 **Cl** 35.453	18 **Ar** 39.948
4	19 **K** 39.10	20 **Ca** 40.48	21 **Sc** 44.96	22 **Ti** 47.90	23 **V** 50.94	24 **Cr** 52.00	25 **Mn** 54.938	26 **Fe** 55.85	27 **Co** 58.93	28 **Ni** 58.69	29 **Cu** 63.55	30 **Zn** 65.39	31 **Ga** 69.72	32 **Ge** 72.59	33 **As** 74.92	34 **Se** 78.96	35 **Br** 79.90	36 **Kr** 83.80
5	37 **Rb** 85.47	38 **Sr** 87.62	39 **Y** 88.91	40 **Zr** 91.22	41 **Nb** 92.91	42 **Mo** 95.94	43 **Tc** (98)	44 **Ru** 101.1	45 **Rh** 102.91	46 **Pd** 106.42	47 **Ag** 107.87	48 **Cd** 112.41	49 **In** 114.82	50 **Sn** 118.71	51 **Sb** 121.75	52 **Te** 127.60	53 **I** 126.91	54 **Xe** 131.29
6	55 **Cs** 132.91	56 **Ba** 137.33	57 *****La** 138.91	72 **Hf** 178.49	73 **Ta** 180.95	74 **W** 183.85	75 **Re** 186.21	76 **Os** 190.2	77 **Ir** 192.2	78 **Pt** 195.08	79 **Au** 196.97	80 **Hg** 200.59	81 **Tl** 204.38	82 **Pb** 207.2	83 **Bi** 208.98	84 **Po** (209)	85 **At** (210)	86 **Rn** (222)
7	87 **Fr** (223)	88 **Ra** 226.02	89 †**Ac** 227.03	104 **Rf** (261)	105 **Db** (262)	106 **Sg** (266)	107 **Bh** (264)	108 **Hs** (277)	109 **Mt** (268)	110 **Ds** (271)	111 **Rg** (272)	112 **§** (277)						

§ Not yet named

	58	59	60	61	62	63	64	65	66	67	68	69	70	71
*****Lanthanide Series**	**Ce** 140.12	**Pr** 140.91	**Nd** 144.24	**Pm** (145)	**Sm** 150.4	**Eu** 151.97	**Gd** 157.25	**Tb** 158.93	**Dy** 162.50	**Ho** 164.93	**Er** 167.26	**Tm** 168.93	**Yb** 173.04	**Lu** 174.97
	90	91	92	93	94	95	96	97	98	99	100	101	102	103
†**Actinide Series**	**Th** 232.04	**Pa** 231.04	**U** 238.03	**Np** 237.05	**Pu** (244)	**Am** (243)	**Cm** (247)	**Bk** (247)	**Cf** (251)	**Es** (252)	**Fm** (257)	**Md** (258)	**No** (259)	**Lr** (262)

f subshell area

We've already seen that elements are arranged on the periodic table from left to right in order of increasing atomic number (except, of course, for the *f* area elements, which are alone at the bottom). We've also noted that the periodic table can be divided into four regions: the *s*, *p*, *d*, and *f* areas. By arranging elements in both of these ways, two important themes emerge.

1. Elements in the same period (horizontal row) have electrons in the same energy shells.
2. Elements in the same group (vertical column) generally have similar chemical and physical properties.

Let's look at these ideas a little more closely, one at a time.

The first period on the table consists of just hydrogen and helium. Both of these elements have electrons in the 1st energy shell. Since the 1st energy shell consists of one 1*s* orbital, it can hold only 2 electrons, so the third element, lithium (Li) has an electron in the 2nd energy shell. So do Be, B, C, N, O, F, and Ne. These elements make up the 2nd period, and their 2nd energy shells are filled. Third-period elements from sodium (Na) to argon (Ar) fill up the 3rd energy shell. Now, you may ask: what about elements in the *d* area, such as iron (Fe)? Doesn't iron have valence electrons in the *3d* subshell of the *third* energy shell? Well, it does, but iron also has 2 electrons in the *4s* subshell. It's an element in the 4th period, and it has electrons in its 4th energy shell.

Chemical Families

Valence electrons are the most important electrons in an atom because they can participate in chemical bonds. Since chemical reactions involve bond breaking and bond making, the behavior of valence electrons is responsible for all the chemical reactions you see, from the souring of milk to the burning of rocket fuel. Thus, it makes sense that if two elements have atoms with the same number of valence electrons, they will react similarly. And in general, this is true. We mentioned that all of the atoms of elements (except helium) in the extreme right-hand column of the periodic table (the noble gases) have 8 valence electrons. Do they have similar reactivities? Yes. These elements (including helium) are all very unreactive and are said to be part of the noble gas *family*. A **family** is a collection of elements from the same vertical group that have similar chemical properties. Not surprisingly, all of the members of a particular family have the same number of valence electrons.

There are other important families of elements. All of the atoms of elements in the extreme left-hand group on the periodic table have 1 valence electron (in an *s* subshell). With the exception of hydrogen, these elements—from lithium (Li) to francium (Fr)—also have much in common. Chemically, all are extremely reactive. (A piece of potassium, for example, will produce a violent reaction if placed into water.) Physically, they are shiny, grayish-white metals. However, they melt more easily than the metals you're used to seeing, such as iron or copper. They also tend to have lower densities than the more common metals. The elements in the first column, from lithium (Li) to francium (Fr), are placed in the family of **alkali metals.**

The elements of the group to the right of the alkali metals, from beryllium (Be) to radium (Ra), constitute another family—the **alkaline earth metals**. The alkaline earth metals have 2 valence electrons. They are less reactive than the alkali metals but more reactive than common metals such as iron and copper. They look a lot like alkali metals. Because of their highly reactive nature, elements of the alkali and alkaline earth families are collectively known as the **active metals**.

The group of elements alongside the noble gases make up another important family of elements—the **halogens**. All of the halogens are very reactive. These elements are quite physically distinct from one another: fluorine (F) and chlorine (Cl) are greenish-yellow, toxic gases; bromine (Br) is a brown liquid at room temperature; and iodine (I) is a grayish-purple solid. So what makes these elements a family? All have 7 valence electrons, so they have similar chemical properties.

All of the groups on the periodic table are indicated by a combination of a number and a letter. For instance, the alkali metals group is designated 1A. The alkaline

Valence Electrons
Remember that these are the electrons in an atom's outermost shell.

earth metals group is 2A. All of the groups in the *d* area have a designation that ends in a B. To the right of the *d* area, designations ending in A resume. The group containing aluminum is 3A, and so on up to 7A (the halogens) and 8A (the noble gases). Notice that for the A groups, the number represents the number of valence electrons possessed by elements in that group. So a lithium atom (1A) has 1 valence electron, a carbon atom (4A) has 4 valence electrons, and an iodine atom (7A) has 7 valence electrons.

Some Important Element Groups

Group	Common Name	# of Valence Electrons	Reactivity	Elements Included
Group 1	Alkali metals	1	Very reactive	Li, Na, K, Rb, Cs, Fr
Group 2	Alkaline earth metals	2	Reactive	Be, Mg, Ca, Sr, Ba, Ra
Group 7	Halogens	7	Very reactive	F, Cl, Br, I, At
Group 8	Noble gases	8 (Exception: **He** only has 2)	Inert	He, Ne, Ar, Kr, Xe, Rn

Metals, Nonmetals, and Semimetals

All elements can be classified as being a **metal, nonmetal,** or **semimetal** (also referred to as a **metalloid).** Let's start by talking about metals. **Metals** share certain physical characteristics. They are usually shiny and are good conductors of heat and electricity. Many metals are **malleable,** which means they can be hammered into thin sheets such as aluminum foil. Metals are also often **ductile,** which means that they can form wires. (Copper, for example, is ductile.) With the exception of mercury (a liquid), all metals are solid at room temperature. While these characteristics are noteworthy, there is one chemical characteristic that, above all else, makes an element a metal. Metals tend to give up electrons when they bond.

Nonmetals are elements that tend to *gain* or *share* electrons when they bond. This distinguishes them from metals. Nonmetals are usually poor conductors of heat and electricity, and some such as sulfur (S) and phosphorus (P) are solids at room temperature. Unlike metals, they are dull, brittle, and

Transition Metals

Roughly 75 percent of the elements are considered to be metals, and metals can be further divided into **active** and **transition metals.** The reactive metals of the *s* area are classified as active, while the rest are classified as transition metals. Transition metals are quite different from active metals. They are generally harder, more difficult to melt, and less reactive than active metals. Transition metals include those elements in the *d* and *f* areas. Many of the elements that come to mind when we think of metals are transition metals such as iron, copper, gold, and silver. Many compounds that contain a transition metal are intensely colored. For instance, many copper compounds (but not the element itself) are blue.

melt easily (although diamond, which is composed of the nonmetal carbon, is an exception to these rules). A few nonmetals, such as oxygen (O) and fluorine (F), are gases. The nonmetal bromine (Br) is a liquid at room temperature. As you can see, the physical properties of nonmetals vary considerably.

Semimetals, or **metalloids**, have some of the physical characteristics of both metals and nonmetals. For instance, silicon (Si) is shiny like a metal but brittle like a nonmetal. Appropriately enough, semimetals lie between metals and non-metals on the periodic table.

Let's break it down.

	Physical Characteristics	**Bonding Behavior**
Metals	Shiny, good conductors, malleable, ductile	Tend to give up electrons when they form a bond
Nonmetals	Poor conductors, brittle, low melting point	Tend to gain electrons in an ionic bond or share electrons in a covalent bond
Semimetals	Possess characteristics of metals and nonmetals	Can either gain, lose, or share electrons in a bond

The diagram below summarizes key families and regions on the periodic table.

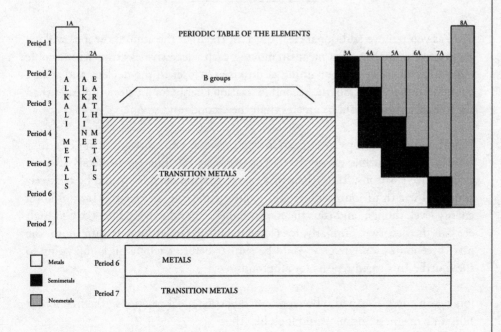

SOME IMPORTANT PERIODIC TRENDS

For the SAT Subject Test in Chemistry, you'll need to know about five important trends seen in the periodic table.

Ionization Energy

Because the atomic nucleus contains protons, nuclei are positively charged; the attraction between opposite charges is what keeps the negatively charged electrons in their orbitals. In order for an electron to be extracted from an atom (which creates a positively charged ion), energy must be expended. For any atom, the amount of energy required to remove an electron from an atom is called the ionization energy. As you move from left to right across the periodic table, ionization energy generally increases; it gets much harder to remove an electron from the atom. As you move from top to bottom through a column (group), ionization energy decreases. For the exam, remember that **ionization energy increases from left to right across the periodic table as you move up through a group.** Ionization energy increases as you move towards fluorine.

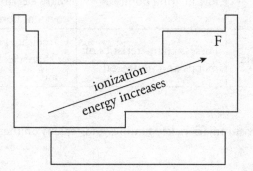

Also, as you remove additional electrons past the first, the atom (now ion) will get progressively smaller. This means removing each successive electron will become more difficult, since the remaining electrons are closer to the nucleus and attracted more strongly to it. So, the second ionization energy for an atom is greater than the first, the third would be greater than the second, and so on.

You also get BIG jumps in ionization energy when you start removing electrons from a lower principle energy level. For instance, alkaline earth metals all have two valence electrons. Thus, their first two ionization energies would be relatively similar. Their third ionization would require removing an electron from a lower energy level, though, and thus the ionization energy value would be MUCH higher than the first two. Similarly, for elements in the same group as aluminum, the first three ionization energies would be similar before seeing a big jump going to the fourth. This trend repeats for all groups.

Ionization energies can also be represented via chemical reactions. The first ionization for a magnesium ion would look like this:

$$Mg(g) \rightarrow Mg^+ + e^-$$

And the second would look like this:

$$Mg^+ \rightarrow Mg^{2+} + e^-$$

Electronegativity

An atom's electronegativity value refers to the amount of "pull" that an atom's nucleus exerts on another atom's electrons when it is involved in a bond. Atoms of different elements typically have different electronegativities. **As you move across the periodic table from left to right, electronegativity increases. As you move down a column (group) on the periodic table, electronegativity decreases. Electronegativity increases as you move towards fluorine.**

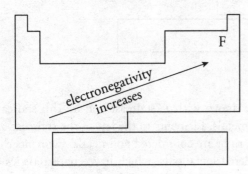

Atomic Radius

We can think of an atom as being roughly spherical, with the nucleus at the center of the sphere. Electrons move about in orbitals within the sphere. Every atomic sphere has a radius, which is known as atomic radius—the distance from its center to the edge. The larger the atom, the greater its radius. **As you move across the periodic table from left to right, atomic radius decreases. As you move down a group (toward francium), atomic radius increases.**

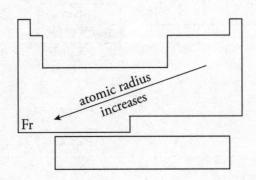

How Does This Work?		
	Definition	**Periodic Behavior**
Ionization Energy	Energy required to remove an electron from an atom	Increases across the table; decreases down the table
Electro-negativity	How much an atom "pulls" on electrons in a bond	Increases across the table; decreases down the table
Atomic Radius	Distance from the center of an atom to the edge	Decreases across the table; increases down the table
Metallic Character	How easily an atom gives up an electron in a bond	Decreases across the table; increases down the table
Reactivity	How easily an atom gains or loses electrons	Increases up and right and down and left (except for noble gases)

Metallic Character

Metallic character is a measure of how easily an atom gives up electrons to form a positive ion. **As you move from left to right across a period, metallic character decreases. As you move from top to bottom down a group (toward francium), metallic character increases.**

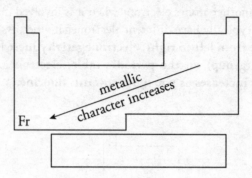

Often, you will see a periodic table drawn with a "staircase" on it. This staircase delineates the metals from the nonmetals. Elements to the left of the staircase are considered metals, and those to the right are considered nonmetals. Elements that touch the staircase itself are considered metalloids, which have characteristics of both metals and nonmetals.

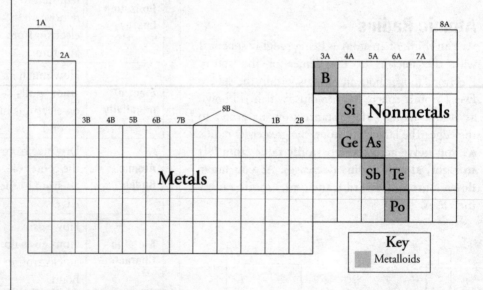

Reactivity

Chemical reactions often involve the movement of electrons between various elements. Elements are most stable when they have a full valence shell of electrons, and the way they get that is by either losing or gaining electrons. An alkali metal, with only one valence electron in its outermost shell, is most likely to lose that electron, leaving it with the full outer shell at the lower energy level. Halogens, being only one valence electron away from a full energy level, are most likely to gain a single electron to complete their outermost shell.

The closer elements are to completing a full valence shell by either gaining or losing electrons, the more likely they are to react chemically. Reactivity increases going up and right (more likely to gain electrons) or down and left (more likely to lose electrons) on the periodic table. Elements in the middle of the table, like the transition metals, are thus fairly unreactive. Note that noble gases are the exception to this trend; all noble gases have full valence shells and are thus very unreactive.

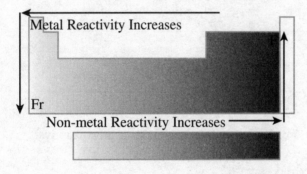

Review what we've said about the periodic table, and tackle the following questions. The answers can be found in Part IV.

DRILL 1

Question Type A

Questions 1–3 refer to the following.

(A) Na
(B) Ca
(C) Mn
(D) F
(E) Ne

1. Is an alkaline earth metal

2. Regularly forms bonds by receiving electrons

3. Has the greatest difference between its first and second ionization energies

Question Type B

	I		II
101.	Only an atom's valence electrons can participate in bonding	BECAUSE	an atom's inner shell electrons are held too tightly to be shared or transferred.

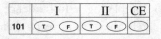

	I	II	CE
101	T F	T F	

	I		II
102.	Potassium has greater metallic character than iron	BECAUSE	potassium has a higher melting point than iron.

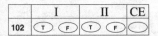

	I	II	CE
102	T F	T F	

Question Type C

24. Which of the following metals is most reactive?

   (A) Sodium, Na
   (B) Magnesium, Mg
   (C) Copper, Cu
   (D) Gold, Au
   (E) Chlorine, Cl

25. Which one of the following is NOT true regarding nickel, Ni ?

   (A) It is malleable.
   (B) It is ductile.
   (C) It is lustrous.
   (D) It is an insulator.
   (E) It forms colored compounds.

26. Which of the following represents an ordering of the period 4 elements bromine (Br), calcium (Ca), krypton (Kr), and potassium (K) by increasing atomic size?

   (A) K, Kr, Ca, Br
   (B) K, Ca, Br, Kr
   (C) Kr, Br, Ca, K
   (D) Ca, K, Br, Kr
   (E) Br, Kr, Ca, K

27. Which of the following is NOT true of the element sodium?

    (A) It takes the oxidation state +1.
    (B) It reacts with water to form a basic solution.
    (C) It forms metallic bonds in its solid uncombined form.
    (D) It is found in nature as a diatomic gas.
    (E) It reacts with a halogen to form an ionic salt.

CHEMICAL BONDING

Not surprisingly, the SAT Subject Test in Chemistry will want you to know something about bonding—that is, the way atoms join to form molecular or ionic compounds.

You'll need to remember, first of all, that bonding usually occurs because every atom in the bond would like to end up with 8 electrons (a stable octet) in its outermost shell.

There are three main types of bonds: ionic, covalent (nonpolar covalent and polar covalent), and metallic.

The Ionic Bond

When an atom in a bond gives up 1 or more electrons to the atom it bonds with, an ionic bond is formed. Ionic bonds generally form between atoms that differ significantly in their electronegativity values. The atom that gives up the electron becomes a positively charged ion, and the one that accepts the electron becomes a negatively charged ion. The positively charged atom attracts the negatively charged atom, and this draws the two atoms together and results in the release of energy.

Now let's look at an example of an ionic bond. When sodium (Na) bonds with chlorine (Cl), the sodium atom gives up its outermost electron to become Na^+ and the chlorine atom receives it to become Cl^-. The Na^+ ion has 8 electrons in its outermost shell. (Its electron configuration looks like neon's.)

One term you should be familiar with for the test is **lattice energy**—the lattice (binding) energy of an ionic solid is a measure of the energy required to completely separate a mole of a solid ionic compound into its separate ions. So, the higher the lattice energy, the stronger the ionic bond.

Substances that are held together by ionic bonds are solids at room temperature and atmospheric pressure. Ionic solids are characterized by their hardness, brittleness, and high melting points. Although ions are charge carriers, ionic solids cannot conduct electricity because their ions have very restricted movement. However, if an ionic solid is melted, its ions are freer to move, and the substance can conduct electricity.

But what about chlorine? Having *gained* an electron, chlorine also ends up with 8 electrons in its outermost shell. Its electron configuration looks like argon's. The bond that results creates sodium chloride: NaCl. The attraction between a positive charge and a negative charge is called an **electrostatic force**; this force is very strong. The strength of an ionic bond gives ionic compounds their high melting points, hardness, and other physical properties.

For this test, think as follows:

> When a metal and nonmetal bond, the result is an ionic bond, in which the atoms are held together by an electrostatic attraction between a positive and a negative ion.

Coulomb's Law

Coulomb's Law allows us to determine how much energy is present in any ionic bond.

$$E = \frac{kq_1q_2}{r}$$

E	is the amount of energy
k	is a constant
q_1 and q_2	are the charges on each ion
r	is the length of the bond

When dealing with ionic bonds, the greater the charge on the ions, the greater the bond energy. The bond energy present in an ionic compound is also known as the lattice energy. In magnesium oxide, the charges on the ions are +2 (Mg) and –2 (O). In sodium chloride, the ion charges are +1 (Na) and –1 (Cl). Thus, there is a greater lattice energy in MgO than there is in NaCl. This is quantified by the melting point of each substance. The greater the lattice energy present in an ionic substance, the higher the melting point of that substance will be. So, MgO has a higher melting point than NaCl.

If the charge profile is the same in two ionic substances, the other factor which comes into play is the bond length. If we compare NaF vs. KCl, we can see that the charge profiles are the same: +1 and –1. However, Na and F are smaller than K and Cl, meaning the length of the NaF bond is shorter. As bond length appears in the denominator of Coluomb's Law, a shorter bond length leads to a greater bond energy. Therefore, NaF has a greater lattice energy and a higher melting point than KCl.

Coulomb's Law can also be used to think about the ionization energy of electrons. The more protons there are in the nucleus of an atom, the greater the charge (q_1) is. Also, the closer the electrons are to the nucleus, the shorter the distance is. (Remember, the lower the energy level is the closer the electrons are to the nucleus) Both greater charge and shorter distance lead to greater energy. In this case, we're talking about the amount of energy needed to remove an electron from an atom and not the amount of energy necessary to break a bond, but the underlying concept is nevertheless the same.

Ionic Formulas

It is possible to use the periodic table to predict the charges of many common ions. As we discussed in Chapter 6, elements are most stable when they have a full valence octet. So, a neutral atom will either gain or lose sufficient electrons to create an ion that has a full octet, no more and no less.

Let's take sulfur as an example. Sulfur has six valence electrons, and can either gain two electrons to fill the third energy shell, or lose six electrons to leave behind a full second energy shell. It is easier for a sulfur atom to gain two electrons than it is for it to lose six, so sulfur forms negative anions with a charge of negative two, represented by S^{2-}. Every other element in the same group as sulfur (like oxygen and selenium) will also form ions with a charge of negative two.

The halogens are one group to the right. The easiest way for the halogens to achieve a full octet is by gaining one electron. So, a fluorine ion would have a charge of negative one, represented by F^-. Going in the other direction, the elements in the nitrogen group (such as phosphorous) typically form ions with a charge of negative three.

If we take an element like magnesium, we see that it has two valence electrons. It is going to be easier for a magnesium atom to lose those two electrons, leaving behind a full octet in the second shell, than it would be for that atom to gain the six electrons that would be necessary to fill the octet in the third shell. So, magnesium atoms form ions with a charge of positive 2, or Mg^{2+}. The same would be true for all other alkaline earth elements (such as Be or Ca). Alkali metals (such as Li or Na) form ions with a charge of positive one, and the metals in aluminum's group form ions with a charge of positive 3.

The elements in the carbon group all have four valence electrons, and it would be equally easy for them to lose all four or gain an additional four to complete the nearest octet. However, carbon and silicon in particular do not like to form ions—they are much more inclined to share their four valence electrons with other elements, forming covalent bonds (discussed in the next section). However, the metals in carbon's group (notably, lead and tin) typically form ions with a charge of +4.

Looking at the transition metals in the *d* and *f* blocks, there is no fast and easy way to determine the charge of those ions. It is possible to determine that they will lose electrons to form cations, as is the case with all metals. However, the number of electrons they will lose can vary, and these transition metals often form ions with multiple possible charges. Copper atoms are typically +1 or +2, iron atoms are +2 or +3, and so on. There is no easy way to determine the charge on transition ions using the periodic table.

To determine the formula of an ionic compound, the important rule to remember is that the total charge on any stable compound must be zero. When sodium forms an ion, it loses an electron to become Na^+. When sulfur forms an ion, it gains two electrons to become S^{2-}. In order to balance the charge, two sodium ions must be present to neutralize the charge on one sulfur ion, creating a compound with a formula of Na_2S.

When an oxygen anion (O^{2-}) bonds with a magnesium cation (Mg^{2+}), the charges balance each other already, and only one of each ion is needed—thus the formula is MgO. When nitrogen ions (N^{3-}) bond with barium ions (Ba^{2+}), in order to zero out the total charge, two nitrogen ($-3 \times 2 = -6$) and three barium ($+2 \times 3 = +6$) ions are necessary, creating a compound with the formula Ba_3N_2. Notice the cation <u>always</u> comes first in the formula of an ionic compound.

Polyatomic Ions

There are some ions that are created of multiple elements that stay bonded together and act as a single unit when forming ionic compounds. These ions are called **polyatomic ions**. There are dozens of different polyatomic ions, but your best bet is to memorize the names, formulas, and charges of the following six, which are by far the most common.

NO_3^-: Nitrate	SO_4^{2-}: Sulfate	CO_3^{2-}: Carbonate
OH^-: Hydroxide	PO_4^{3-}: Phosphate	NH_4^+: Ammonium

To determine the formula of a compound containing a polyatomic ion, the same rules are applied. When a potassium ion (K^+) bonds with a sulfate ion, two potassium ions must be present to balance out the charge, creating a compound with the formula K_2SO_4.

The only catch here is that if there are multiple polyatomic ions present in a compound, parentheses must be used to show that. When an aluminum ion (Al^{3+}) bonds with a nitrate ion, to represent the three nitrate ions that are necessary to balance the charge, the formula would be $Al(NO_3)_3$, *not* $AlNO_{33}$ (which would imply 33 oxygen atoms!).

Other polyatomic ions may appear on the test, but if they do, the formula and charges will be provided for you, so you just need to apply the above rules to determine the formula of any compound they might create.

Ionic Nomenclature

It can sometimes seem like chemistry has its own language. (To an extent, it does.) The study of naming chemical compounds is called **nomenclature**. Nomenclature is based on the type of bonding, and each type of bonding has different nomenclature rules.

If you are looking at a binary ionic compound (one containing only two elements), the cation in that compound keeps its name, and the anion changes its ending to -ide. So, NaF is sodium fluoride, and Li_3P would be lithium phosphide. The number of each ion is irrelevant when it comes to naming the compound. When a polyatomic ion is present as part of the compound, it keeps its name. $Sr(OH)_2$ would be strontium hydroxide, $BeCO_3$ would be beryllium carbonate, and $(NH_4)_2S$ would be ammonium sulfide.

Things get a little more complicated when we have to name compounds containing transition metals. Because transition metals can form cations with multiple charges, the charge of the cation must be specified in the name of the compound. This is done by using Roman numerals. So, copper (I) sulfate indicates a copper cation with a charge of positive one, so Cu^+. Two of those copper ions would be needed to balance the negative two charge on the sulfate ion, making the compound formula Cu_2SO_4. However, copper (II) sulfate would have Cu^{2+} ions in it, meaning only one copper cation is needed for every sulfate, creating a compound with a formula of $CuSO_4$. **Keep in mind that the Roman numeral represents the charge on the ion, not how many there are.** This is a very common mistake to make!

You should also be able to work backward from the formula of an ionic compound to its name. MgS would just be magnesium sulfide, and K_3PO_4 is potassium phosphate. However, when dealing with a compound containing a transition metal, this requires you to deduce the charge on the cation. $Fe(OH)_2$ and $Fe(OH)_3$ have different names. The hydroxide anion has a charge of negative one, so in the first compound, the charge of the iron cation must be positive two to balance out the two hydroxide anions. Thus, the name of the first compound is iron (II) hydroxide. The second compound, with three hydroxide ions, requires an iron cation with a charge of positive three, yielding a name of iron (III) hydroxide.

A compound like $Ti_2(CO_3)_3$ is a bit harder to figure out, but it still can be done by keeping the rule in mind that the entire compound must have a charge of zero. Each carbonate ion has a charge of negative two, and with three of them, there is a total charge of negative six. There are two titanium ions present, and each of those must carry a charge of positive three in order to have a total charge of positive six to balance the compound. The name of the compound is titanium (III) carbonate.

The Covalent Bond

When two nonmetals bond, the result is a covalent bond. In a covalent bond, two atoms *share* electrons. By sharing electrons, each atom can achieve a stable octet. In fact, atoms form covalent bonds simply because it's a way for them to obtain a stable octet.

Lewis Diagrams

The easiest way to determine how the electrons are shared in a covalent molecule is to draw a Lewis diagram (also called an electron dot diagram) for the molecule. To draw a Lewis diagram, use the following steps:

1) Count the number of valence electrons in each atom and add them up.
2) Draw a skeletal structure of the molecule with the least electronegative atom in the center.
3) Create a single bond (shared electron pair) connecting the central atom to each terminal atom.
4) Add lone pairs around each terminal and central atom until each atom has eight total electrons (except hydrogen, which only needs two).
5) Count up the total number of electrons in the structure. If they equal the total number of valence electrons available (calculated in step 1), your structure is correct. If you have more assigned electrons than valence electrons, you need to shift some lone pairs over and create double or triple bonds.

Two examples:

Draw the Lewis diagram for PF_3.

1) P + F(3)

   5 + 7(3) = 26 valence e^-

2)

        F

      P

  F   F

3)

4)

5) 26 assigned e^- =

   26 valence e^- ✔

Draw the Lewis diagram for CO_2.

1) $C + O(2)$
$4 + 6(2) = 16$ valence e^-

2) $O \quad C \quad O$

3) $O-C-O$

4) $:\ddot{O}-\ddot{C}-\ddot{O}:$

5) 20 assigned $e^- \neq$
16 valence e^-

50

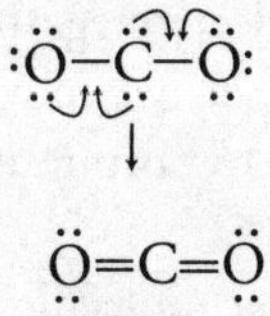

$:\ddot{O}-\ddot{C}-\ddot{O}:$

$\downarrow$

$\ddot{O}=C=\ddot{O}$

16 assigned $e^- =$
16 valence e^- ✔

Lewis diagrams can get considerably more complex than the examples that are shown here, but as long as you understand these fundamentals, you should be ready for the test.

The Nonpolar Covalent Bond

When two nonmetals share electrons equally, they are said to be nonpolar covalent. Because this can only occur between atoms with identical electronegativity values, this means that the only truly nonpolar covalent bonds are those present in molecules made up of one type of atom. For example, both oxygen atoms in O_2 have the same "pull" on electrons, which means the electrons in the shared bond between them are shared equally, with neither atom gaining a negative charge. Look how two oxygen atoms bond to form a molecule of O_2. The dots signify oxygen's 6 valence electrons.

$$\ddot{O}: \quad :\ddot{O}$$

Now, if each atom could somehow acquire two more electrons, it would have a stable octet. So what happens?

Each atom donates a pair of electrons, and the shared pairs are attracted to the nuclei of both atoms. In a sense, each atom has 8 valence electrons instead of 6. Each atom is happy. The sharing keeps the atoms together because each atom now has a stable octet.

$$\ddot{O}::\ddot{O}$$

The Polar Covalent Bond

The two oxygen atoms that we just looked at form a bond and share their electrons equally. But sometimes in a covalent bond, one atom tends to hog the electrons. It still shares them with the other atom, but it tends to keep the electrons for more than its fair share of the time. This hogging of the electrons is a result of one atom having a greater electronegativity value than the other. (Remember that electronegativity increases as we move from left to right across a period and decreases as we move from top to bottom in a column.)

Think about a water molecule. It's made of 2 hydrogen atoms and 1 oxygen atom. Each hydrogen atom has 1 valence electron, which it shares with oxygen. The oxygen atom donates 2 electrons to be shared with the hydrogen atoms. Then what happens? Basically, each hydrogen atom acquires an electron and has a configuration like helium's (which is very stable), and the oxygen atom acquires 2 electrons and has an electron configuration like neon's (an octet).

So a water molecule can be represented as follows:

$$H \!:\! \overset{\displaystyle ..}{\underset{\displaystyle ..}{O}} \!:\! H$$

But oxygen's electronegativity is greater than hydrogen's. Oxygen "hogs" the electrons it shares with hydrogen, and the shared electrons spend more time around the oxygen than they do around the hydrogen. The result? Each hydrogen atom has a partial positive charge, while the oxygen atom has a partial negative charge.

When, in a covalent bond, certain atoms have a partial positive charge and others have a partial negative charge, we say that the covalent bond is polar.

Covalent Nomenclature

Covalent nomenclature is significantly less complicated than ionic nomenclature. When naming binary covalent compounds, you should be familiar with the following prefixes:

One: Mono-	Two: Di-	Three: Tri-	Four: Tetra-
Five: Penta-	Six: Hexa-	Seven: Hepta-	Eight: Octa-

When naming the compound, how many of each atom present is represented by the appropriate prefix. Si_3N_6 would be trisilicon hexanitride, and C_4F_8 would be tetracarbon octafluoride. The only exception to this rule is that if the first element has only one atom present, you do not use the mono prefix. CO would be carbon monoxide, not monocarbon monoxide.

The easiest way to determine whether you are using ionic nomenclature rules or covalent nomenclature rules is by determining the type of bond first. Metals and nonmetals combine to form ionic bonds, while two nonmetals combine to form covalent bonds.

The Metallic Bond

As you've probably guessed, a metallic bond results when two metals bond. For example, the copper atoms that make up a copper wire are joined by metallic bonds. In metallic bonding, the metal atoms donate valence electrons to become cations. These valence electrons are not directly transferred to another atom as they are in ionic bonding. Instead, they move about freely throughout the sample, producing an attractive force that keeps the metal cations in place. Often the behavior of these free electrons is referred to as a "sea of mobile electrons." Because of the motions of the free electrons, metals are characteristically good conductors of electricity and heat.

Bond Type	Description	Types of Elements Involved	Example
Ionic Bond	Atoms gain or lose electrons to form a stable octet—ions held together by electrostatic attraction	Bond formed between metal and nonmetal	$NaCl$, CaF_2, Fe_2O_3
Nonpolar Covalent Bond	Equal sharing of electrons to form a stable octet	Bond formed between two same nonmetals or two nonmetals with the same electronegativities	Cl_2, O_2, N_2
Polar Covalent Bond	Unequal sharing of electrons to form stable octet	Bond formed between nonmetals with different electronegativities	H_2O, NH_3
Metallic Bond	Sea of mobile electrons	Bond formed between metals	Cu, Ag, Fe

Single, Double, and Triple Bonds

So far, we've considered covalent bonds in which one pair of electrons is shared between two atoms; these types of bonds are also called **single bonds.** In the structural formula of a compound, a single bond is represented by a single line. For example, water has two single bonds.

ΔH

Remember that ΔH is the change in enthalpy that occurs in the course of a reaction. A positive ΔH indicates a net absorbance of energy.

But more than one pair of electrons can be shared between atoms in a covalent bond. If two pairs of electrons are shared, the bond is called a **double bond.** If three pairs of electrons are shared, it is a **triple bond.** In general, as more pairs of electrons are shared between atoms, the bond gets stronger and the distance between bonded nuclei gets shorter. The oxygen molecule we looked at earlier contains a double bond. It is represented by a double line, as follows:

As you might expect, a triple bond, such as the one that's present in hydrogen cyanide (HCN), is represented by a triple line. Take a look:

$$H - C \equiv N:$$

Bond Energies

We can make some rough generalizations about the strength of covalent bonds by applying Coulomb's Law here as well. As neither atom involved in a covalent bond obtains a full charge, the only variable that affects covalent bond strength is the length of the bond. A short bond length will lead to greater energy, and can be examined in one of two ways.

First and foremost, the more bonds there are between two atoms, the shorter the bond length is going to be. A triple bond will always be shorter than a double bond, and a double bond will always be shorter than a single bond. Thus, triple bonds are the strongest type of covalent bond, and single bonds are the weakest.

Second, if the number of bonds is identical, we can also look at the size of the atoms involved in the bond to determine the bond length. Let's compare a H–O bond to a H–F bond. A fluorine atom is smaller than an oxygen atom, and so the length of the H–F bond will be shorter than the H–O bond. The H–F bond thus has greater energy and is stronger.

Chemical reactions involve the breaking of bonds in the reactants (which requires energy) and the formation of new bonds to make products (which releases energy). If we know which bonds are to be made and which are to be broken, and we know their respective bond energies, we can estimate ΔH for the reaction.

Suppose we need to estimate ΔH for the reaction $H_2 + Br_2 \rightarrow 2HBr$, given the following bond energies:

H–H bond: 436 kJ/mol
Br–Br bond: 193 kJ/mol
H–Br bond: 366 kJ/mol

In converting H_2 and Br_2 to products, we must break 1 mole of H–H bonds and 1 mole of Br–Br bonds. This will require (1 mole) (436 kJ/mol) + (1 mole) (193 kJ/mol) = 629 kJ of energy. Since we form 2 moles of H–Br bonds, this releases (2 moles) (366 kJ/mol) = 732 kJ of energy. The enthalpy change for the reaction, ΔH, is equal to the net energy change, which is 629 kJ – 732 kJ = –103 kJ. If 1 mole of H_2 and 1 mole of Br_2 react to form 2 moles of HBr, the reaction should gain 103 kJ. (A negative ΔH indicates a net release of energy.)

One thing that's important to understand at this point is that when a covalent substance undergoes a phase change, bonds are NOT breaking as they would in an ionic substance. We will look at what happens when covalent substances change phase in more detail in the next chapter.

MOLECULAR SHAPES

Some questions on the SAT Subject Test in Chemistry might ask you about the shapes of molecules. Although we can represent molecules in two dimensions on paper, they are actually three-dimensional. If you are given a molecular formula and asked to determine its shape, follow these preliminary steps:

Step 1:   Assume the first atom in the formula is the central atom of the structure (unless it is hydrogen, which is never a central atom).

Step 2:   Using dots to indicate the valence electrons of each atom, surround the central atom with the others, trying to give each atom an octet. Remember hydrogen needs only 2, not 8, valence electrons to be satisfied. It is important to realize that electrons shared between two atoms count toward the total for both.

Completing steps 1 and 2 will give you the structural formula of a molecule. To determine the *shape* of the molecule, you must consider the number of sites in which valence electron pairs surround the central atom. Since all electrons have the same negative charge, they repel each other. The valence electron sites will arrange themselves around the central atom to be as far from each other as possible. There are two types of electron pair sites: those that contain electron pairs in a bond and those that contain unbonded electron pairs (also called **lone pairs**). The number of total electron pair sites and number of lone pairs will dictate the molecule's shape.

Suppose we have a molecule of carbon tetrachloride, CCl_4. The structural formula of CCl_4 is as follows:

$$\overset{\displaystyle ..}{:}\overset{\displaystyle \textrm{Cl}}{:}$$

Focus on the central carbon atom. It has four sites at which it is surrounded by electron pairs. How can these four sites be situated as far from each other as possible around the central carbon atom? You might be tempted to say that they should be 90° apart from each other, as the structural formula shows. But that's thinking in two dimensions, not three.

The four sites can actually be 109° apart if they arrange themselves in a tetrahedron (a symmetrical, four-sided figure):

A slightly different situation arises in a molecule of ammonia, NH_3. Ammonia's structural formula is as follows:

$$\textrm{H}-\overset{\displaystyle ..}{\textrm{N}}-\textrm{H}$$
$$\underset{\displaystyle \textrm{H}}{|}$$

In ammonia, there are four distinct electron pair sites around the central atom of nitrogen. Three of these sites involve bonded pairs of electrons, and one involves a lone pair. These four sites arrange themselves in a tetrahedral geometry around nitrogen. *However, when you attempt to determine molecular shape, look only at the central atom and its surrounding atoms.*

Ammonia looks as follows:

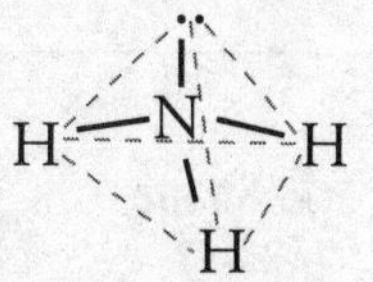

The molecular shape you see is not exactly a tetrahedron; it's more of a pyramid. This molecular geometry is known as a **trigonal pyramidal**. See why? The shape is a pyramid, so it's pyramidal; the base is a triangle, so it's trigonal. Now look at water's molecular structure.

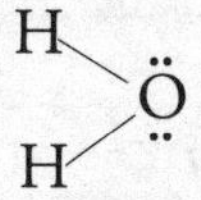

Water has four electron pair sites around the central oxygen atom. However, two of them are lone pairs, so water's molecular geometry is as follows:

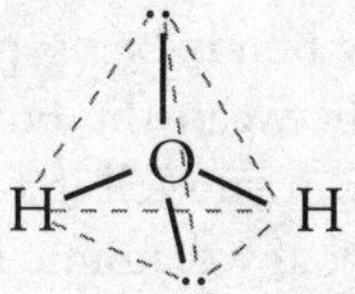

It's another variant of the tetrahedron, but with two corners occupied by electron pairs. This molecular geometry is known as **bent.** The angle between O–H bonds is about 105°.

The central molecule need not have four electron pair sites. If it has two, the molecular geometry will be **linear,** with 180° between bonds. If it has three electron pair sites (and no lone pairs), the sites will be 120° apart and the molecular geometry is **trigonal planar. Planar** means that the molecule is flat or two-dimensional. If there are three sites and one is a lone pair, the shape resembles that of the water molecule and is also called bent.

You should also be aware of two elements that violate the octet rule. Beryllium (Be) atoms are stable with 4 valence electrons. When beryllium is the central atom, the molecule is linear. Boron (B) atoms strive to gain 6 valence electrons. When boron acts as the central atom in a molecule, the shape is generally trigonal planar.

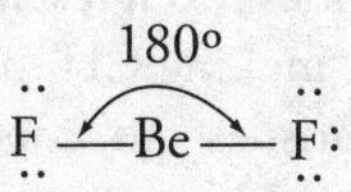

beryllium difluoride
(linear)

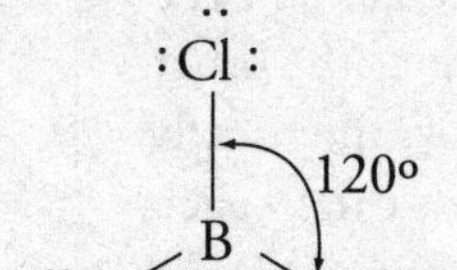

boron trichloride
(trigonal planar)

Summary of Molecular Shapes

Number of Electron Pair Sites Around Central Atom	Number of Lone Pairs Around Central Atom	Shape	Bond Angles with Central Atom*	Example
4	0	Tetrahedral	109.5°	CCl_4
4	1	Trigonal Pyramidal	approximately 107°	NH_3
4	2	Bent	approximately 107°	H_2O
3	0	Trigonal Planar	120°	NO_3^-
3	1	Bent	approximately 116°	SO_2
2	0	Linear	180°	CO_2

*assuming atoms of the same element surround the central atom

Molecules Can Also Be Polar or Nonpolar

We talked earlier about covalent bonds being polar or nonpolar, depending on the electronegativity difference between the bonded atoms. Well, *molecules* can also be polar or nonpolar. How can you tell if a molecule is polar or nonpolar? If the molecule is diatomic, it's easy: any diatomic molecule that has a polar bond is polar, for example, CO. Any diatomic molecule that has a nonpolar bond is nonpolar. For example, all elemental diametric molecules, such as Cl_2, N_2, and O_2, are nonpolar. Otherwise there will be some electronegativity difference that makes the bond, and thus the molecule, polar. Molecules that consist of three or more atoms are generally polar unless the following condition is met: if the central atom has no lone pairs and is surrounded by atoms of one element, then the molecule will be nonpolar, for example, CO_2. In these cases, the individual bond polarities cancel each other out. So it's possible for a molecule to contain polar bonds but, itself, be nonpolar. Methane is an example of this:

Becoming Polar

In order for a molecule to be polar, polar bonds must line up so that the more electronegative atom or atoms are at one end of the molecule, and the less electronegative atom or atoms are at the other. Whenever polar bonds are arranged symmetrically around a central atom, the polar bonds cancel each other out, and there is no positive or negative end.

The individual polarities from each C–H bond cancel each other out, making CH_4 nonpolar. Also note that methane satisfies our condition for being nonpolar: the carbon central atom has no lone pairs and is surrounded by atoms of one element (in this case, hydrogen).

Look back over what we've discussed since the last question set, and then try to answer the following questions. Answers can be found in Part IV.

DRILL 2

Question Type A

Questions 4–6 refer to the following.

(A) Hydrogen gas, H_2
(B) Carbon monoxide, CO
(C) Potassium, K
(D) Aluminum oxide, Al_2O_3
(E) Bromine, Br_2

4. Substance held together by metallic bonds

5. Substance held together by ionic bonds

6. Consists of polar molecules

Question Type B

	I		II

103. Some covalent bonds are polar in nature   BECAUSE   atoms of different electronegativities are unequal in the degree to which they attract electrons.

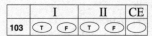

104. Most atoms are less stable in the bonded state than in the unbonded state   BECAUSE   both ionic and covalent bonds fail to provide the participating atoms with a stable electron configuration.

Question Type C

27. How many single bonds are in a molecule of carbon dioxide, CO_2 ?

    (A) None
    (B) One
    (C) Two
    (D) Three
    (E) Four

28. The geometry of a molecule of SO_2 is

    (A) linear
    (B) bent
    (C) trigonal planar
    (D) trigonal pyramidal
    (E) tetrahedral

29. What is the approximate ΔH for the reaction $CH_4 + Cl_2 \rightarrow CH_3Cl + HCl$ given the following bond energies:
    C–H bond = 410 kJ/mol
    C–Cl bond = 330 kJ/mol
    Cl–Cl bond = 240 kJ/mol
    H–Cl bond = 430 kJ/mol

    (A) +270 kJ
    (B) +110 kJ
    (C) +70 kJ
    (D) –70 kJ
    (E) –110 kJ

30. Choose the answer below that accurately describes the correct molecular shape for the molecule $XeOF_4$.

    (A) Tetrahedral
    (B) Trigonal pyramidal
    (C) Trigonal bipyramidal
    (D) Square pyramidal
    (E) Flat

Summary

o   The rows of the periodic table are called periods; the columns are called groups.
   •   Elements in the same period have the same number of electron energy shells.

   •   Elements in the same group have the same valence configuration and similar chemical properties.

o   The periodic table is arranged to keep together different groups and their qualities.

o   Elements in Group 1, the Alkali Metals, have one valence electron, and are very reactive.

o   Group 2 is the Alkaline Metals, which have two valence electrons and are also very reactive.

o   Group 7 consists of the Halogens, which range from gas to solid, have 7 valence electrons, and are very reactive.

o   Chemical reactivity increases towards the "edges" of the periodic table, specifically going down and left as well as up and right. Noble gases are the exception, and have no real reactivity.

o   Coulomb's Law describes the effects of charge and atomic radius when it comes to determining the amount of energy in an ionic bond. The greater the amount of energy, the higher the melting point of that compound will be.

o   For covalent bonds, Coulomb's Law dictates that the higher the bond order and smaller the atomic radii of the atoms, the greater the bond energy will be.

o   The middle section of the periodic table contains the transition metals, which have electrons in the f and/or d subshells.

o   All metals share certain physical properties, and all tend to give up electrons when they bond.

o   The upper-right section of the periodic table holds the nonmetals, which have valence electrons in the p subshell, and tend to gain or share electrons in bonds. They do not conduct heat or electricity well, and have low boiling points.

o   Semimetals have physical properties of both metals and nonmetals, and form the boundary between the two on the periodic table.

o   Ionization energy, or the energy required to pull an electron off an atom, increases from left to right across the periodic table, and as you move up a given group.

o   Electronegativity is a measure of how strongly an atom pulls on electrons in a bond. It increases from left to right across the periodic table, and as you move up the table.

o   Atomic radius increases down and to the left on the periodic table.

o   When a metal and a nonmetal combine, the metal completely loses an electron or electrons, and the nonmetal completely gains them. The two ions are held together by force of attraction between opposite charges in an ionic bond.

o   A covalent bond is a bond in which electrons are shared, usually so that each atom in the molecule achieves an octet.

   •   A polar bond is a covalent bond between atoms of differing electronegativities. The more electronegative element pulls more on the electron, giving it a partial negative charge, and the less electronegative element a positive one.

   •   A nonpolar covalent bond is a covalent bond between two of the same atoms or two atoms with the same electronegativity. The atoms share electrons equally.

o   Areas that contain electrons, including bonds and nonbonding electron pairs, repulse each other. This repulsion determines molecular shape. Common molecular shapes include tetrahedral, trigonal pyramidal, trigonal planar, bent, and linear.

Chapter 8
Phases: Gases, Liquids, and Solids

Phase refers to whether a substance is a solid, liquid, or gas. Understanding what, on the molecular level, affects a substance's phase and how a substance goes about changing from one phase to the next is necessary for the SAT Subject Test in Chemistry. This chapter will deal with both the qualitative and quantitative aspects of phases and phase change, as well as the behavior of gases. It will include discussions of the ideal gas equation, partial pressures, intermolecular forces, phase change and phase change diagrams, and vapor pressure.

GASES

Theoretically, all matter becomes gaseous if its temperature exceeds its boiling point, no matter how high or low that boiling point may be. For the SAT Subject Test in Chemistry, you should be familiar with certain characteristics and properties of gases.

Let's start by looking at these gas molecules moving around in a box.

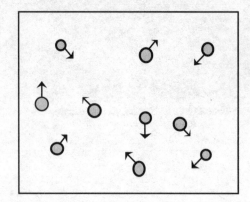

Ideal Gas Behavior

Under conditions of low pressure, gas molecules occupy very little volume relative to the volume of the container. Because ideal gases have zero volumes, gases under low pressure conform more closely to the Ideal Gas Law than gases under higher pressure. They act similarly at higher temperatures, and forces between gas molecules are negligible. Because ideal gases do not exert any forces on each other, gases at high temperatures behave more ideally than gases under cooler temperatures.

The molecules are moving, banging and bumping against one another and against the walls of the box in every which way. Because they bang into the walls of the box, they create pressure against the walls. When we talk about pressure, in relation to gases, we're talking about the amount of force the gas particles are exerting on the walls of their container, per unit area of the container. As we've said before, we measure pressure in torr or in millimeters of mercury (mmHg) or atmospheres (atm). Each of these units represents a unit of force per area, and 760 torr = 760 mmHg = 1 atm.

All of the gases you'll see on the SAT Subject Test in Chemistry are assumed to be ideal gases.

Ideal Gas Assumptions

Molecules of an ideal gas do not attract or repel each other.

Molecules of an ideal gas occupy zero volume.

No gas ever acts completely as an ideal gas. In real gases, molecules attract each other slightly, which causes them to strike the walls of their container with slightly less force than ideal gases. However, most gases (especially lighter ones such as hydrogen and helium) under typical temperatures and pressures act enough as an ideal gas to make the concept useful.

In order to succeed on this test, you've got to know the relationships that exist among the temperature, volume, and pressure of an ideal gas.

Pressure and Temperature

Suppose we start with a 3 L sample of gas at 200 K and a pressure of 900 torr. If we raise the temperature to 400 K without changing the volume of the container, what will happen? Because we doubled the temperature, the pressure will double too—to 1,800 torr. In other words, if volume doesn't change, then pressure is directly proportional to the temperature in degrees Kelvin.

Why is that? The increased temperature provides the gas molecules with more heat, which is converted to kinetic energy, which means, basically, movement. The molecules start moving faster, and if they're moving faster, they're hitting the walls of the container harder, and that increases the pressure.

The technical term for this phenomenon is **kinetic molecular theory**, which states that the kinetic energy of a gas molecule increases proportionally with temperature in degrees Kelvin. The mathematical formula that relates temperature and pressure while volume is held constant is called Gay-Lussac's Law, and it is represented as $\dfrac{P_1}{T_1} = \dfrac{P_2}{T_2}$.

While any unit of pressure can be used as long as it's consistent across both sides of the equation, temperature must be measured in Kelvins to make use of this law.

Pressure and Volume

Now suppose we start with the same 3 L sample of gas at 200 K and 900 torr. Imagine that, without changing the temperature, we suddenly increase the size of the container to 6 L. We've doubled the volume of the gas, and we haven't changed the temperature. What happens to the pressure of the system? It goes down by one-half, to 450 torr. Here's why. The gas molecules have just as much kinetic energy as they had before, but they've got twice the volume in which to move around. Thus, gas molecules will hit the container walls less often, exerting half as much pressure.

When there's no change in temperature, volume and pressure are inversely proportional. Triple the volume, and you'll cut the pressure to one-third of its original value. Cut the volume by one-half, and you'll double the pressure.

The mathematical formula which relates pressure and volume while temperature is held constant is called Boyle's Law, and it is represented by $P_1 \times V_1 = P_2 \times V_2$. The units of pressure and volume don't matter, as long as they are consistent across both sides of the equation.

Temperature and Volume

Now suppose we start with the same 3 L sample of gas at 200 K and 900 torr. If, without changing the pressure, we were to increase the temperature to 400 K, what would happen to the volume? Well, if the gas molecules are moving faster, they are going to spread out further, effectively doubling the volume of the container. You can test this yourself; if you put a balloon in the freezer (lowering the temperature of the gas inside), the balloon will shrink. If you leave the balloon outside on a hot summer day, the balloon will expand.

When there's no change in pressure, temperature and volume are directly proportional. This is mathematically represented by Charles' Law:

$$\frac{V_1}{T_1} = \frac{V_2}{T_2}$$

While the units of volume don't matter as long as they are consistent across both sides of the equation, temperature must be measured in Kelvins in order to use this law.

Making Gases Even Simpler: The Ideal Gas Equation

The relationship among pressure, volume, amount (moles), and temperature of an ideal gas is given by the **ideal gas equation**, $PV = nRT$.

$PV = nRT$		
P	=	pressure in atm (or mmHg or torr)
V	=	volume in liters
n	=	number of moles of gas particles in the container
R	=	the ideal gas constant
T	=	temperature in Kelvin

On this exam, the ideal gas equation is practically all you need to answer questions about gases. Let's start by talking about R—the ideal gas constant, which is equal to $0.082 \ \frac{L \cdot atm}{mol \cdot K}$ (you don't have to remember that number for the test).

From looking at the equation, you can see that P is inversely proportional to V. Both P and V are directly proportional to T and to n. Here's another way to look at it. When you think about the ideal gas equation, think

- Values on the *same* side of the equation are *inversely* proportional to each other when the other variables are held constant.
- Values on *opposite* sides of the equation are *directly* proportional to one another when the other variables are held constant.

The relationship between a gas' density and its molar mass can be examined using the Ideal Gas Law as well. Gas volume appears in both the density and the ideal gas equation, and through some tedious algebraic manipulation that you don't need to worry about, you can come up with the following equation:

$$MM = \frac{dRT}{P}$$

MM	=	molar mass in grams/mol
d	=	density in grams/liter
R	=	the ideal gas constant
T	=	temperature in Kelvin
P	=	pressure in atmospheres

Essentially, the higher the molar mass of a gas, the more dense it will be.

More About Gases: Partial Pressures

If you have a container filled with more than one gas, each gas exerts a pressure. The pressure of any one gas within the container is called its partial pressure, and all of the partial pressures add up to create the total pressure inside the container.

Partial Pressures

- $$\frac{\text{Moles of gas A}}{\text{Total moles in container}} = \frac{\text{Partial Pressure of gas A}}{\text{Total pressure of container}}$$
- 1 mole of gas at STP occupies 22.4 L

When the test writers tell you about a container that has different gases in it, they might ask you to figure out the partial pressure for one of them. Let's say there are 100 moles of gas in a container: 20 moles of oxygen, 30 moles of hydrogen, and 50 moles of nitrogen. Oxygen makes up 20% of the gas, which means that it will make up 20% of the total pressure. So if you're told that the total pressure within the container is 500 torr, you know that

- oxygen's partial pressure is (0.20)(500) = 100 torr,
- hydrogen's partial pressure is (0.30)(500) = 150 torr,
- nitrogen's partial pressure is (0.50)(500) = 250 torr, and
  100 + 150 + 250 = 500 torr.

Partial Volumes

In the same way that you can use the molar ratio to determine the partial pressure of a gas in a mixture, you can also determine the partial volume at standard temperature and pressure (STP). Using the ideal gas equation, $PV = nRT$, you can calculate that, at STP, 1 mole of a gas occupies a volume of 22.4 L. But this value does not apply only to ideal gases—it's also the accepted molar volume for *any* gas at STP. This is often called Avogadro's Law. This means that, at STP, the molar ratio in a gaseous mixture will be directly proportional to the volume ratio, in a total volume of 22.4 L. For example, you can use the following formula to relate the molar ratio of gas A in a mixture of many gases to its partial volume in that mixture:

$$\frac{\text{\# of moles of gas A}}{\text{\# of total moles of gas}} = \frac{\text{volume of gas A at STP}}{22.4 \text{ L}}$$

If you know the ideal gas equation ($PV = nRT$) and what you've just learned about partial pressures, you'll be in good shape when the test asks you about gases.

Maxwell-Boltzmann Diagrams

Temperature is a measure of the average kinetic energy present in a substance. Kinetic energy is based on a particle's velocity. However, just because a gas sample is at a given temperature, that does not mean ALL of its particles will have the same velocity. This is because temperature is a measure of average velocity. If you were to look at the velocity distribution for all of the molecules, it would look like this:

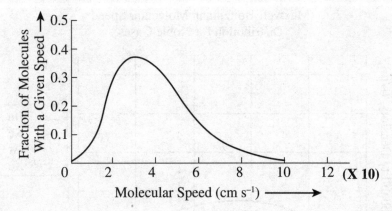

This is called a Maxwell-Boltzmann distribution. Note that the peak of the curve is the average velocity of the gas particles, and is the value that is used to calculate the temperature.

It stands to reason that if we were to change the temperature of a gas, we also change the amount of kinetic energy in that gas, and thus the velocity of the gas particles. If we were to chart the velocity distributions of a single sample of nitrogen gas at various temperatures, we'd get curves that look like this:

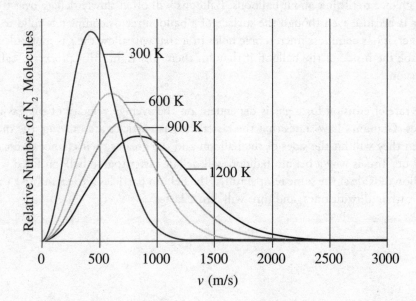

Note that the area under the curves is the same because the total number of gas molecules is the same. The curves decrease in height because as the temperature increases, the velocities at which the gas molecules can be found will cover a larger range, flattening out the distribution.

That being said, kinetic energy actually has two components: mass and velocity. If samples of two gases that have different molar masses are at the same temperature, they would have the same kinetic energy. However, because one gas has a higher molar mass, it follows that is must have a lower velocity. If you had samples of the various noble gases at the same temperature and plotted their velocity distributions it would look like this:

Maxwell-Boltzmann Molecular Speed Distribution for Noble Gases

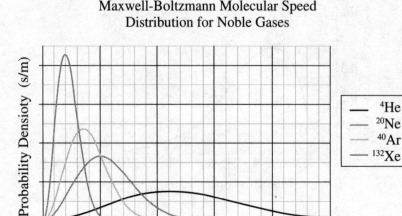

Note that the heavier the individual gas atoms are, the slower their overall average velocity is. That's why xenon has the lowest velocity, while helium has the highest.

The final application of this deals with how quickly gases can escape when given the chance to. Think about balloons. Balloons will often slowly deflate over time. This is because even though the surface of a balloon seems completely solid to us, in fact, it has countless microscopic holes in it that will allow the gas molecules to escape the inside of the balloon if they hit them just right. This process is called effusion.

The rate of effusion for a gas is dependent on the average velocity of the gas particles. Graham's Law states that the faster the gas particles are moving, the more often they will hit the sides of the balloon and the greater their chance to escape will be. This is why a helium balloon will deflate faster than a balloon filled with carbon dioxide at the same temperature. The helium particles are less massive than the carbon dioxide ones, and thus will effuse faster.

Now try these. Answers can be found in Part IV.

DRILL 1

Question Type A

Questions 1–3 refer to the following.
(A) Ideal gas constant
(B) Celsius temperature
(C) Kelvin temperature
(D) Partial pressure
(E) Volume

1. Is inversely proportional to moles of gas, when other variables are held constant

2. Sum for each gas in a mixture yields total for that mixture

3. Is a measure of average kinetic energy of gas molecules in a closed container used in the ideal gas equation

Question Type B

	I		II

101. If an ideal gas is located in a closed container and temperature is increased, the average speed of the molecules will always increase as well   BECAUSE   for an ideal gas, temperature and moles of gas are inversely proportional.

	I	II	CE
101	T F	T F	⬭

102. For an ideal gas, pressure and volume have no relationship   BECAUSE   according to the Ideal Gas Law, temperature and volume are directly proportional when other variables are held constant.

	I	II	CE
102	T F	T F	⬭

Question Type C

24. Four grams of helium are in a sealed 2 L container. If helium were a true ideal gas, how would its behavior differ from its actual behavior?

    (A) Its molecules would attract each other.
    (B) Its molecules would repel one another.
    (C) Its molecules would be in continuous motion.
    (D) It would exert more pressure on the container walls.
    (E) It would exert less pressure on the container walls.

25. A closed mixture of helium, hydrogen, and carbon dioxide gases are at a pressure of 1,200 torr in a 4 L container. There are a total of 24 moles of gas molecules in the container. If the helium concentration is 2 moles/L and the hydrogen concentration is 1.5 moles/L, which of the following expresses the approximate partial pressure of the carbon dioxide in torr?

    (A) $\frac{1}{24} \times 1,200$ torr

    (B) $\frac{2}{24} \times 1,200$ torr

    (C) $\frac{3}{24} \times 1,200$ torr

    (D) $\frac{10}{24} \times 1,200$ torr

    (E) $\frac{14}{24} \times 1,200$ torr

INTERMOLECULAR FORCES

At this point in our study of the states of matter, we will stop to look more closely at the attractive forces that exist between molecules. These **intermolecular forces** (IMF) are responsible for many of the physical properties of matter, such as boiling point. Intermolecular forces are typically due to the attraction between the positively charged portion of one molecule and the negatively charged portion of a nearby molecule. The positively and negatively charged parts of a molecule are called **dipoles**, and are symbolized by ($\delta-$) and ($\delta+$). While all intermolecular forces are caused by dipole attraction, they can be further divided into three specific categories.

1)   Hydrogen Bonding

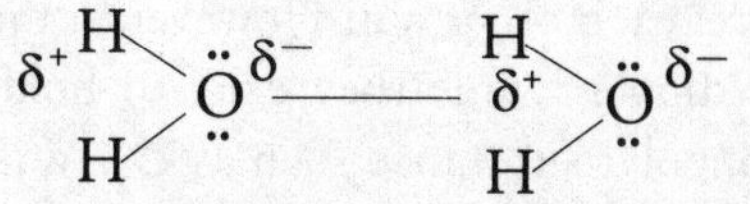

The attractive forces that exist between water molecules (shown above) are a special type of intermolecular force called hydrogen bonds. Hydrogen bonds occur whenever hydrogen is bonded to F, O, or N. These are the three most electronegative elements, and as such, they "hog" electrons so much that the hydrogen bonded to them are essentially naked protons, unshielded on the side facing away from the bond. This positive, naked proton is attracted to the negative charge around an F, O, or N in a hydrogen bond.

Hydrogen bonds are stronger than any other form of intermolecular attraction, yet they are far weaker than any covalent or ionic bond.

2)   Permanent Dipole

Another type of intermolecular force arises between two polar molecules of an atom where there is no hydrogen bonding. An example of this would be PF_3.

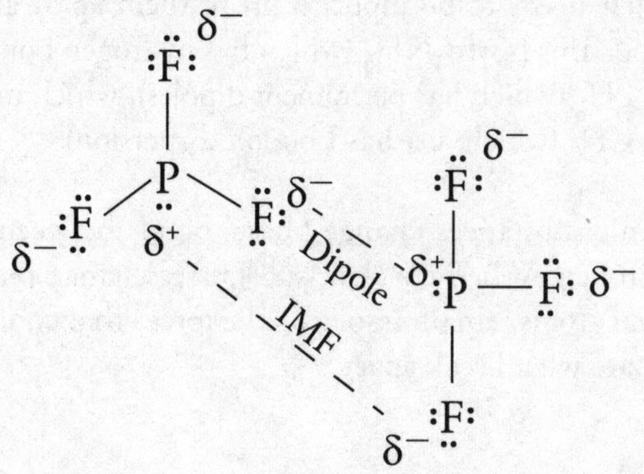

Forces of Attraction
These forces of attraction are present between molecules throughout the water sample, holding it together.

As with hydrogen bonding, the positive and negative dipoles between different molecules attract each other. However, the attraction is not as strong as that of a hydrogen bond.

3) London Dispersion (aka Temporary Dipole)

Every type of covalent compound exhibits the final type of intermolecular force, known as London dispersion forces. For all molecules, the electrons are in constant motion around the molecules. At any given moment in time, the electron density will be greatest around one part of the molecule. That place where the electron density is the highest will have a negative dipole, and the place where the electron density is the lowest will have a positive dipole.

Over time, as the electrons keep moving around, these dipoles will shift position and ultimately will cancel each other out. However, sufficient attraction exists between these temporary dipoles while they exist to hold the molecules together, even in a completely nonpolar substance such as O_2. Without London dispersion forces, nonpolar molecules would not be attracted to each other in any way.

Boiling Points

The most common way to quantitatively measure the strength of intermolecular forces within a covalent compound is to measure the boiling point of the compound. A substance boils when the intermolecular forces holding the molecules together in a liquid phase are broken and the molecules move into a gaseous phase. When water boils, you are NOT breaking the covalent bonds that hold the hydrogen and oxygen atoms together within the molecule. If you were to do so, the H_2O would break down into H_2 and O_2, both highly flammable gases that would make cooking your dinner very interesting! Instead, when you boil water, you are simply changing the phase of the water by increasing the kinetic energy of the water molecules, to that point that they are energetic enough to overcome the intermolecular forces between separate H_2O molecules (the boiling point).

Between compounds of similar mass, the stronger the intermolecular forces are, the more energy that needs to be input to break them apart and the higher the boiling point will be. This is why NH_3 (which has hydrogen bonding) has a higher boiling point than PH_3 (which has permanent dipoles), which in turn has a higher boiling point than CH_4 (which just has London dispersion).

Note that when ionic substances change phase, bonds between the individual atoms are actually broken. When covalent substances change phase, the bonds between the individual atoms remain in place. The forces that connect the molecules to other molecules are what break apart.

Solids, Liquids, and Gases

The relationship between a substance's average kinetic energy and the strength of its intermolecular forces is responsible for determining if the substance will be a solid, a liquid, or a gas. In a solid, a substance's intermolecular forces are much stronger than the average kinetic energy of its molecules. As a result, molecules are restricted in their ability to move about. These strong intermolecular forces permit molecules to merely vibrate in place. This gives a solid its definite size and shape.

In a liquid, intermolecular forces are still more significant than the kinetic energy of molecules. However, molecules in a liquid have enough kinetic energy to move past each other. This allows for the liquid's ability to flow. Despite being able to move about, molecules in a liquid are still confined within the sample.

The relationship between intermolecular forces and molecular kinetic energies is vastly different in a gas. Molecules in a gas are so energetic that they easily overcome intermolecular attraction. Gas molecules spread about to fill the volume of whatever container they are in.

What's a Network Solid?

For the SAT Subject Test in Chemistry, you may need to know about something called a network solid. No, it has nothing to do with television. **Network solids** are covalently bonded substances that do not consist of individual molecules. Instead they consist of atoms joined to form molecules that attract each other through intermolecular forces. So, in a sense, the substance is one giant molecule. For this reason, network solids are sometimes called macromolecular substances. Since covalent bonds are much stronger than intermolecular forces, network solids are extremely hard to melt. Diamond (pure carbon network) and quartz (SiO_2 network) are examples of network solids.

Properties of Crystalline Solids

Keep in mind that not all solids are network solids. There are actually four types of crystalline solids: ionic, network, molecular, and metallic solids. Each type of crystalline solid is held together in a different way, which means each has unique properties. The table on the next page summarizes some aspects of these solids that you should know for the SAT Subject Test in Chemistry.

Crystal Type	Force Holding Units Together	Examples	Melting Point	Hardness	Electrical Conductivity
Ionic	Electrostatic attraction	LiF, NaCl	High	Hard, brittle	Only molten or aqueous solution
Covalent Network	Shared electrons	Diamond	Very high	Very hard	None
Molecular	H-bonding, dipole-dipole, dispersion forces	H_2O, HCl, He	Low	Soft	None
Metallic	Electrostatic attraction between cations and sea of electrons	Na, Fe, Cu	Variable	Malleable	High

Allotropes

Allotropes are multiple states of the same element that are bonded in different ways. Due to its ability to share electrons easily, carbon in particular is an element that forms many different allotropes. One common allotrope of carbon, graphite, is found pencil lead. In graphite, the carbon atoms are bonded in two-dimensional "sheets" that can easily slide over each other.

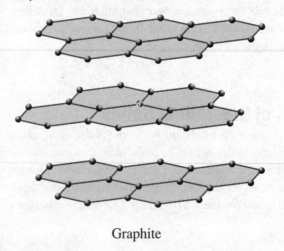

Graphite

When you write with a pencil, the carbon sheets slide onto the paper and stick there. On the other end of the spectrum, another allotrope of carbon is diamond. Diamonds are pure carbon, just like graphite is, but they are bonded very differently. In diamond, carbon experiences a three-dimensional covalent network bond, which makes the diamond very hard and difficult to chip.

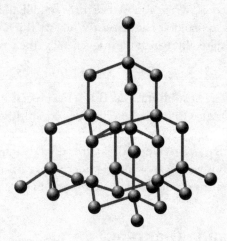

Diamond

In fact, diamond is one of the hardest known naturally occurring substances on Earth, and is often used in the tip of industrial drills due to its ability to cut through just about anything.

Do I Need to Know About Hydrates?

Yes, but they're nothing you can't handle. A **hydrate** (or hydrated salt) is an ionic substance in which water molecules bond to the ions in a fixed ratio. For example, in copper sulfate pentahydrate, the ratio is given by the formula $CuSO_4 \cdot 5H_2O$. Anytime you see "$\cdot H_2O$" in a formula, you're looking at a hydrate. You might need to determine the percent composition of water in the hydrate (called its **water of hydration**). If you do, you simply multiply the molecular weight of water (18 amu) by the coefficient that precedes H_2O in the formula. For example, for a unit of $CuSO_4 \cdot 5H_2O$, the formula weight is approximately $64 + 32 + (4)(16) + 5(18) = 250$ amu. The percentage of water in the hydrate is about $\frac{90}{250} \times 100\%$, or 36%.

PHASE CHANGES

We refer to the condition of being a solid, liquid, or gas as being in a particular **state** or **phase**. Whether a substance is in one phase or another depends on temperature and pressure. H_2O, for instance, turns from solid to liquid or from liquid to solid at 0°C and 1 atm. It turns from liquid to gas or gas to liquid at 100°C and 1 atm.

When a substance turns from solid to liquid, we say it **melts.** When it moves in the reverse direction—from liquid to solid—we say it **freezes.** So when we think of H_2O at 1 atm, we say 0°C is the **melting point** or **freezing point**: the temperature at which it melts or freezes. When a substance turns from liquid to gas, it **vaporizes;** when it goes from gas to liquid, it **condenses.** When we think of H_2O at 1 atm, we say 100°C is the boiling point, which means, generally, the temperature at which it vaporizes or condenses.

You should also be aware of **sublimation.** This is the process in which a solid turns directly into a gas. Dry ice (solid carbon dioxide) does this when it is exposed to room temperature. The opposite of sublimation is **deposition**, which is the name of the phase change that occurs when a gas turns directly into a solid. A common example of deposition is water vapor in the atmosphere turning directly into solid ice; this is how frost forms on the ground after a cold night.

The Phase Change Diagram

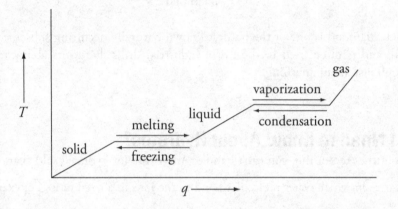

Above, we've shown the phase change diagram for some substance at some pressure. You might very well see a phase change diagram on the SAT Subject Test in Chemistry, so you should understand what information they might give you. Starting from the lower left, we see that, as heat is added to the substance, its temperature rises. Moving left to right, we reach the first plateau; that's the substance's freezing/melting point. Notice that the line is flat for a little while as the substance passes its melting point. In other words, to move from a solid to liquid phase, we add heat—but for a while, the temperature of the substance doesn't change. The heat energy absorbed is used to move the substance from one phase to the next. The amount of heat that it takes a substance to just move from solid to liquid phase—to just pass through its melting point—is called the **heat of fusion.** For H_2O at 1 atm, the heat of fusion is 80 cal/g; this means that it takes 80 calories to change 1 g of H_2O from 0°C in the solid phase (ice) to 0°C in the liquid phase (water).

After the substance melts, if we continue to add heat, the temperature increases until the substance reaches its boiling point. At the boiling point, the substance doesn't change temperature despite the continued addition of heat. The absorbed heat is used to move the substance from the liquid phase to the gaseous phase. The amount of energy that must be added to move the substance from liquid to gaseous phase is called the substance's **heat of vaporization**. For H_2O at 1 atm, the heat of vaporization is 540 cal/g; it takes 540 calories to change 1 g of H_2O from 100°C in the liquid phase (water) to 100°C in the gaseous phase (steam).

Golden Rule of Phase Change

Adding heat to a substance can change kinetic energy or potential energy, but never both.

Phase Change and Pressure

You know that if we add heat to a solid, the temperature of the solid moves toward the melting point. If we add heat to a liquid, the temperature of the liquid increases until it reaches the boiling point. One interesting phenomenon that you should be aware of for the SAT Subject Test in Chemistry is that, under higher pressure, it's harder for solids to melt, and it's harder for liquids to vaporize. However, if we reduce the pressure of the surrounding environment, we lower a substance's melting and boiling points. Reduced pressure makes it easier for solids to melt and liquids to vaporize.

How come? Just imagine pressure as something that's pushing down on the solid or liquid, tending to prevent its molecules from moving around. If we increase that downward push, melting and boiling are harder to achieve; melting and boiling points, therefore, increase. If we reduce that downward push, melting and boiling are easier to achieve; melting and boiling points, therefore, decrease.

> ### An Exception to the Rule
> The exception to this rule is water. Increasing pressure on ice or water lowers the freezing or melting point. One commonly cited example illustrating the relationship between pressure and the freezing point of water is ice-skating. The pressure of the blade of the skate pushing down on the ice causes the ice to melt. The layer of water that results under the blade allows the blade to slide along with little friction. Most substances tend to want to freeze under greater pressure. Skating is really possible then only on the few substances which share water's property of tending to melt under greater pressure.

Another Type of Phase Diagram

We mentioned that whether a particular substance is a solid, liquid, or gas depends on both its pressure and temperature. The relationship among pressure, temperature, and phase can be neatly shown in the following type of phase diagram, which is a graph of pressure versus temperature:

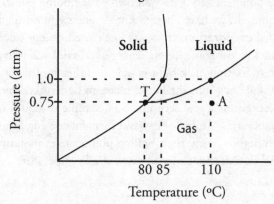

Phase Diagram for Substance X

In this diagram, each region—solid, liquid, and gas—represents the phase that will exist for substance X at a given set of pressures and temperatures. For example, at a pressure of 0.75 atm and 110°C (point A), substance X is a gas. The normal freezing point (at 1 atm) for substance X is 85°C, and the normal boiling point (at 1 atm) is 110°C. Any point that lies on a line on the phase diagram represents a temperature and pressure at which the substance can exist in both phases. For instance, substance X can be a solid or a liquid at 1 atm and 85°C. Point T is a special combination of pressure and temperature called the **triple point.** At this particular pressure and temperature, the substance can exist as a solid, liquid, or a gas. For substance X, the triple point is at 0.75 atm and 80°C.

In general, when a substance is at relatively low pressure and high temperature, it exists as a gas. When it is at relatively high pressure and low temperature, it is a solid. The liquid phase dominates at moderate pressures and temperatures. Keeping these relationships in mind can help you to predict how a change in pressure or temperature will affect the phase of a substance. For instance, if substance X, at 0.75 atm and 110°C (point A) is put under increasing pressure but its temperature is maintained, what phase change will eventually occur? Look at the phase diagram for substance X. Follow the dotted line up from point A (in the direction of increasing pressure). You'll see that beyond 1 atm (at 110° C), substance X will become a liquid. So an increase in pressure at constant temperature will cause substance X to condense.

Vapor Pressure

Even if a solid is well below its melting point, a small number of its molecules will always have enough kinetic energy to enter the liquid phase. So when you have a block of ice stored in a freezer, a little bit of it is always melting to form liquid. The molecules of that liquid immediately lose kinetic energy and form a solid again, but right away, a few other molecules gain enough kinetic energy to become liquid. They, too, become solid again after a few seconds. But a few other molecules take their place, becoming liquid, and then solid again. In other words, every solid is always melting—on the molecular level—and the molecules that melt are always refreezing.

The same goes for liquids. Even if it's well below the boiling point, a few molecules of a particular liquid always have enough kinetic energy to escape into the gaseous phase. This is called **evaporation.** If they're in a closed system (such as a pot with a lid on it), they quickly lose some kinetic energy and fall back into the liquid phase, only to be replaced continuously by a couple of other molecules that manage to escape. They, too, fall back into the liquid phase to be replaced by other molecules that manage to escape for a few seconds. So a sample of liquid below its boiling point is always evaporating—a little bit—and then condensing again (if the liquid is contained). When liquids below their boiling points are evaporating, a **vapor pressure** is created. All liquids in a closed system, at all temperatures, exert some vapor pressure.

But what if the liquid is *not* in a closed system but is out in the open environment? Here's what happens. A little bit evaporates and is blown away. Then a little more evaporates and is blown or drifts away. Ultimately the whole sample evaporates. If you put a pot of water outside, even at a temperature of 10°C, it will eventually evaporate, although it will take some time.

Factors Affecting Vapor Pressure

Different liquids differ in their volatility; for instance, if you leave a bucket of gasoline and a bucket of water outside on a cold day—at a temperature well below the boiling point of either substance—both will eventually evaporate. But the gasoline will evaporate much more quickly than the water. This is because the **intermolecular forces** that attract gasoline molecules to each other are weaker than the hydrogen bonds that attract water molecules. Gasoline molecules need less kinetic energy than water molecules do to overcome the intermolecular forces that hold them in the liquid state. Because gasoline evaporates more readily than water, we can say that its *vapor pressure is higher,* and *it is more volatile* than water.

What other factors besides intermolecular force will affect a substance's vapor pressure? Well for one, **temperature**: the higher the temperature, the higher the average kinetic energy of the molecules. This means more molecules have enough energy to escape into the gas phase, so there will be more vapor particles and more vapor pressure above the surface of the liquid. If the container is open to the environment, the total pressure above the surface of the liquid must equal atmospheric pressure. The total pressure above the surface is just the vapor pressure plus the partial pressure of the atmospheric molecules.

atmospheric pressure = vapor pressure +
partial pressure of atmospheric molecules

As the substance gets warmer, the vapor pressure increases. Because atmospheric pressure is constant, the partial pressure of atmospheric molecules must decrease. At the point when the pressure above the liquid is all vapor pressure, or when vapor pressure equals atmospheric pressure, boiling occurs.

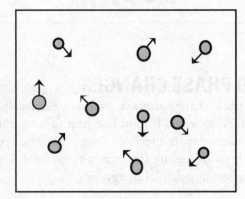

Besides intermolecular forces and temperature, molecular weight also affects vapor pressure. The heavier the molecule, the slower its average velocity at a given temperature, and the harder it is to vaporize. Think about the halogens. Fluorine and chlorine are gases at room temperature, bromine is a liquid, and iodine is a solid. They have the same valence structure and exhibit the same types of intermolecular forces. Molecular weight accounts for their respective phases.

F	A gas at room temperature
Cl	A dense green gas at room temperature
Br	A dark red liquid at room temperature
I	A solid that sublimes at room temperature

Vapor pressure:	• molecules of liquid escaping into gas phase although temperature of the liquid is below boiling point
More volatile liquid:	• liquid that has higher vapor pressure
	• evaporates more readily when temperature is below boiling point (compared to a less volatile liquid)
Less volatile liquid:	• liquid that has lower vapor pressure
	• evaporates less readily when temperature is below boiling point

ENERGY AND PHASE CHANGES

As we saw from the phase change diagram, a substance must absorb heat to change from a solid to a liquid to a gas. It must lose heat to turn from gas to liquid to solid. Heat, as you remember, is a form of energy. So, when you think of phases and energy, remember that among the three phases, solid is lowest in potential energy and gas is highest in potential energy.

One more thing: when ice melts, there is an increase in entropy, and when liquids vaporize, entropy increases even more. Under certain conditions, the increase in entropy (which the universe likes) is enough to overcome the increase in energy (which it dislikes) and make a phase change spontaneous. What are these conditions? Well, in the case of melting, if the substance is at a temperature above the melting point, the phase change will be spontaneous. In order for boiling to be spontaneous, the substance must be at a temperature above the boiling point.

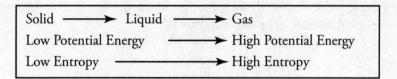

One more thing to keep in mind is that when an ionic substance is undergoing a phase change, actual bonds are being weakened or broken. When a covalent substance undergoes a phase change, it is IMFs that are broken. Students often confuse the two, but think about it this way. Water is a covalent substance. When cooking, we often boil water. The equation for that would look like this:

$$H_2O(l) \rightarrow H_2O(g)$$

It would NOT look like this:

$$2H_2O(l) \rightarrow 2H_2(g) + O_2(g)$$

If, every time we boiled water, we were breaking covalent bonds, then both hydrogen and oxygen gas would be created. Both of these gases are highly flammable, and given that many gas stoves have open flames—well, it would certainly make cooking more interesting!

Fortunately for us (and for our food!), changing the phase of a covalent substance such as water does NOT break bonds. Instead, boiling water will break the IMFs present between gas molecules, transition water form a liquid to a gaseous phase.

Review what we've discussed since the last set of questions, and then try the following set. Answers can be found in Part IV.

DRILL 2

Question Type A

Questions 4–7 refer to the following.

(A) $N_2O_4(g) + heat \rightarrow 2NO_2(g)$
(B) $I_2(s) \rightarrow I_2(g)$
(C) $CHCl_3(l) \rightarrow CHCl_3(g)$
(D) $Br_2(s) \rightarrow Br_2(l)$
(E) $O_2(g) \rightarrow O_2(l)$

4. At constant pressure, requires a decrease in heat to occur

5. Is an example of sublimation

6. Produces a decrease in system entropy

7. Enthalpy change for the process can equal heat of fusion for the process

Question Type B

	I		II
	<u>I</u>		<u>II</u>
103.	A network solid has a high melting point	BECAUSE	hydrogen bonds are more difficult to break than covalent bonds.

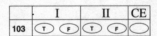

| 104. | A pot of water will boil above 100°C at high elevations | BECAUSE | the average kinetic energy of molecules must increase as the pressure on them increases. |

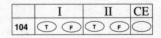

Question Type C

26. A 10-gram sample of which substance is held together by hydrogen bonding?

    (A) H_2
    (B) NH_3
    (C) C_3H_8
    (D) CaH_2
    (E) HBr

27. A substance possessing a characteristically low vapor pressure can be expected to have

    (A) extremely weak intermolecular forces
    (B) a relatively small heat of vaporization
    (C) a relatively high boiling point
    (D) a relatively high rate of evaporation
    (E) a significantly high percentage of molecules that have high kinetic energy

28. Identify the equation used to determine the amount of heat required to melt 10 grams of ice.

    (A) $Q = mC_{sp}\Delta T$

    (B) $Q = n\Delta H$

    (C) $KE = \dfrac{1}{2}mv^2$

    (D) $PE = mgh$

    (E) $PV = nRT$

Summary

o   The Ideal Gas Law is $PV = nRT$. The assumptions underlying this equation are that gas molecules do not experience any intermolecular forces, so they do not attract or repel one another, and that gas molecules occupy zero volume.

o   The ratio of the moles of a particular gas in a sample to total moles in the sample equals the ratio of the partial pressure of that gas to the total pressure of the vessel:

$$\frac{\text{moles A}}{\text{total moles}} = \frac{\text{partial pressure A}}{\text{total pressure}}$$

o   Standard Temperature Pressure (STP) is 0 degrees Celsius or 273 K, and 1 atm or 760 mmHg. One mole of an ideal gas at STP occupies 22.4 liters.

o   The strength of the intermolecular forces and atomic weight determine melting point and boiling point. The intermolecular forces, from strongest to weakest, are ionic and network covalent, metallic, hydrogen bonding, dipole-dipole, and dispersion.

o   Phase changes (melting, freezing, vaporization, condensation, sublimation, and deposition) represent a change in the potential energy of the bonds between molecules in a sample. As heat is added to a sample, either the kinetic energy of the molecules increases, or the potential energy of the bonds increases (phase change), but never both.

o   Heat of fusion and heat of vaporization are the amounts of energy needed to melt or vaporize, respectively, 1 gram of that substance.

o   The phase of a substance depends on both temperature and pressure, and the relationship between the three (temperature, pressure, and phase). Generally, increasing pressure moves a substance toward the solid phase. H_2O is an exception because ice is less dense than water.

o   Vapor pressure is the partial pressure of vapor molecules that have escaped from a liquid sample, above the surface of that sample. Vapor pressure depends, externally, on temperature alone. It also depends on the intermolecular forces and molecular weight of the substance.

o   The various particles in a gas are moving at random velocities. These velocities form a bell-shaped distribution called a Maxwell-Boltzmann diagram.

o   If the temperature of a gas increases, its velocity distribution range will increase. For samples of different gases at the same temperature, the gas with the lowest molar mass with have the greatest velocity distribution.

o   When a covalent substance changes phase, it is the intermolecular forces that are being broken apart, NOT the actual covalent bonds within the molecules.

Chapter 9
Solutions

A solution is a mixture of a solute (the substance of which there is less) and a solvent (that of which there is more). Generally, problems dealing with solutions tend to focus on a few key areas. This chapter will focus on understanding solubility, as well as what factors, both external (temperature and pressure) and internal (nature of the solute and solvent) affect it. It will also deal with some specific reactions between solutions and how addition of a solute changes the freezing point and melting point of a solution (colligative properties).

MEASURING CONCENTRATIONS

The most commonly used unit for concentration is **molarity**. Its symbol is M. Molarity is a measure of the number of moles of solute dissolved per liter of solution (volume).

$$\text{molarity } (M) = \frac{\text{number of moles solute}}{\text{number of liters solution}}$$

Molality, another fairly common unit for concentration, is a measure of the number of moles of solute dissolved per kilogram of solvent (mass). Its symbol is m.

$$\text{molality } (m) = \frac{\text{number of moles solute}}{\text{number of kilograms solvent}}$$

To help you distinguish between the two, think of molarity as moles of dissolved solute per *liter of solution* and molality as moles of dissolved solute per *kilogram of solvent*.

Another way to measure the concentration of a solute is by dividing the mass of the solute by the total mass of the solution (solute + solvent):

$$\text{percent by mass} = \left(\frac{\text{moles solute}}{\text{mass solution}} \right) \times 100\%$$

It's important to realize the denominator is not the mass of the solvent only; it represents the mass of the total solution. If you dissolve 15 g of sugar in 100 mL of water (density of water: 1.0 g/mL), the percent by mass would be calculated by dividing 15 g by 115 g, NOT dividing 15 g by 100 g.

Solubility and Saturation

Suppose you take a glass of water and add table salt to it. The table salt dissolves. Suppose you keep adding table salt to it. After a while, the table salt doesn't dissolve, it just sits at the bottom of the glass. At that point the water is **saturated** with table salt. Another way to describe this is to say that the table salt has reached the limit of its **solubility** in water.

The temperature of the solvent affects solubility. Generally, a solid solute is *more* soluble in a liquid solvent at *higher* temperatures and *less* soluble at *lower* temperatures. If we took the glass of water and heated it, some of the table salt that hadn't dissolved would dissolve. The increased temperature increases the solubility of table salt in water.

Substances that are held together by ionic bonds (such as table salt, NaCl) are generally soluble in water.

Other solutes are completely insoluble. For instance, if you place a pat of butter in a glass of water, it won't dissolve, ever, even if you heat it. This illustrates an important general principle; polar solutes such as NaCl and HCl dissolve in polar solvents such as water, and nonpolar solutes dissolve in nonpolar solvents. Butter, which is a fat, is nonpolar. Just remember: "Like dissolves like."

The solubility of gases in water is quite different from that of solids. Think about a bottle of soda; its carbonation is the result of dissolved carbon dioxide gas. Once the bottle has been opened, should you store it where it's warm or cold to prevent it from going flat? You should store it where it's cold, of course. The CO_2 gas is more soluble in water at lower temperatures, and flat soda is simply soda after its CO_2 has diffused out into the air. This is typical of the solubility of gases in water. One more thing about the solubility of gases in water: the higher the pressure, the more soluble the gas. Again consider soda, bottled under pressure. Once you open the bottle, the pressure over the soda decreases, and CO_2 starts to come out of solution.

	Increased Temperature	Decreased Temperature	Increased Pressure	Decreased Pressure
Solids	Increased solubility	Decreased solubility	N/A	N/A
Gases	Decreased solubility	Increased solubility	Increased solubility	Decreased solubility

Dissociation and Electrolytes

When an ionic substance (NaCl, KCl, $CaBr_2$, or $CuSO_4$) dissolves in water, its bonds break, and ions are released into solution. For instance, when KCl dissolves in water, K^+ ions and Cl^- ions dissociate into solution.

The dissociation of ionic compounds always creates an equal number of positive and negative charges in solution. One mole of NaCl will dissociate into 1 mole of Na^+ ions and 1 mole of Cl^- ions, and 1 mole of $CaBr_2$ will dissociate into 2 moles of Br^- ions and 1 mole of Ca^{2+} ions. Both of these solutions have equal amounts of positive and negative charges, and both are therefore neutral.

Although these solutions are neutral, the presence of charged particles—ions—enables the solution to conduct electricity. This is why ionic solutions are also called **electrolytic solutions,** and we call the ions **electrolytes.**

BOILING POINT ELEVATION AND FREEZING POINT DEPRESSION

When a solute is dissolved in a liquid solvent, the solvent's boiling point is raised, its freezing point is lowered, and its vapor pressure is lowered. By how much? The change in boiling point (ΔT_b) or freezing point (ΔT_f) is always equal to a constant (k) times the number of moles of *dissolved particles* of solute per kilogram of solvent.

$$\Delta T = kmi$$

The value k is different for different solvents; however, for all liquid solvents, the extent of boiling point elevation or freezing point depression is directly proportional to the molality of the solute. It is also directly proportional to the number of dissolved particles, which we denote by i. For example, when we dissolve NaCl in water, it dissociates into Na$^+$ ions and Cl$^-$ ions. For every mole of NaCl we dissolve, we get 1 mole of Na$^+$ and 1 mole of Cl$^-$, for a total of 2 moles of dissolved particles. For NaCl, then, $i = 2$. If we dissolve 1 mole of sucrose (table sugar), however, the sugar molecules dissolve but don't dissociate, so we get only 1 mole of dissolved particles, and $i = 1$.

Now, suppose we take the same amount of water and add 1 mole of KCl. KCl is an ionic substance; it dissociates in solution. Each unit of KCl produces two dissolved particles: 1 K$^+$ ion and 1 Cl$^-$ ion. The boiling point elevation and freezing point depression will be twice as great as they would be in the case of the dissolution of sucrose.

Again, why is this? Boiling point elevation and freezing point depression are directly proportional to the number of particles dissolved in a solution, but independent of the *type* of particle (i.e., sucrose and KCl equally affect melting point and freezing point at the same molality). Sucrose doesn't dissociate and KCl does. When 1 mole of sucrose is dissolved in water, it yields 1 mole of dissolved particles. When 1 mole of KCl is dissolved in water, it yields 2 moles of dissolved particles. If the sucrose elevated the water's boiling point by 0.5°C, the KCl would raise it by 1°C. If the sucrose depressed the water's freezing point by 2°C, the KCl would depress it by 4°C. Remember the relationship of proportionality we've just described.

There are many practical applications of boiling point elevation and freezing point depression. For example, spreading calcium chloride onto roadways during snowstorms makes it harder for ice to form on them (since the freezing point of water is made lower).

Let's Look at That Equation Again
$$\Delta T = kmi$$

k = constant that depends on solvent

m = molality = $\dfrac{\text{moles solute}}{\text{kilogram solvent}}$

i = whole number equaling the number of particles a substance dissolves into

---

Boiling Point Elevation and Freezing Point Depression
These points depend only on the type of solvent and the number of solute particles.

PRECIPITATION REACTIONS

Okay, so now you know that when ionic solids are dissolved in water, they dissociate. But what happens when soluble ions in separate solutions are mixed together, and they form an insoluble compound? Well, the product of this type of reaction will result in a solid substance that settles out of solution, called a **precipitate.** One example of this is the reaction between lead nitrate and potassium iodide.

$$2KI(aq) + Pb(NO_3)_2(aq) \rightarrow 2KNO_3(aq) + PbI(s)$$

Each of the reactants in this reaction is an ionic compound that's colorless in solution, but when they're combined, they react to form a product, lead iodide, which precipitates out of solution as a yellow solid. In this reaction, the anions and cations of the reactants are exchanged in a **double replacement reaction,** which typically results in the formation of a precipitate. But how do you know when a precipitation reaction will proceed? The **solubility rules** tell you which ionic compounds are soluble in water and which are not and enable you to make predictions about whether certain ions will react with one another to form a precipitate.

The Solubility Rules

- Most silver, lead, and mercury salts are INSOLUBLE except for their nitrates and perchlorates.
- Most hydroxides (OH^-) are INSOLUBLE except those of alkali metals and barium.
- All nitrates (NO_3^-) and perchlorates (ClO_4^-) are SOLUBLE.
- All alkali metal and ammonium (NH_4^+) compounds are SOLUBLE.

Enough said! Now review what we've said about solutions, and try the following set of questions. Answers can be found in Part IV.

DRILL 1

Question Type A

Questions 1–3 refer to the following.

(A) Nitrogen dioxide, $NO_2(g)$
(B) Iodine, $I_2(s)$
(C) Glucose, $C_6H_{12}O_6(s)$
(D) Naphthalene, $C_{10}H_8(s)$
(E) Sodium chloride, NaCl (aq)

1. Yields an electrolytic solution upon dissolution in water

2. Solubility in water increases as temperature is decreased

3. Produces the greatest boiling point elevation per mole dissolved into 1 L of water

Question Type B

	I		II

101.	Aqueous solutions with ionic solutes conduct electricity	BECAUSE	a liquid solvent becomes saturated when the solute reaches the limit of its solubility.

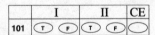

102.	Freezing point depression caused by a 2-molal aqueous solution of nonionic solute is equal to one- half the freezing point depression caused by a 2-molal aqueous solution of NaCl	BECAUSE	the constant associated with freezing point depression does not vary with the nature of the solvent.

	I	II	CE
102	T F	T F	

Question Type C

24. Which of the following will most likely increase the solubility of NaCl in water?

    (A) Reducing the temperature of the water
    (B) Raising the temperature of the water
    (C) Reducing the molality of the solution
    (D) Raising the molality of the solution
    (E) Raising the molarity of the solution

25. Which of the following would most likely give a sample of water the capacity to conduct electricity?

    (A) Reducing the temperature of the water
    (B) Raising the temperature of the water
    (C) Removing all electrolytes from the water
    (D) Dissolving a nonionic substance in the water
    (E) Dissolving $CaCl_2$ in the water

26. Aqueous solutions of barium chloride and sodium sulfate react to form -------, an insoluble white solid.

    (A) $BaSO_4(s)$
    (B) $Na_2SO_4(s)$
    (C) $BaCl_2(s)$
    (D) $NaCl(s)$
    (E) $BaNa_2SO_4(s)$

Summary

o   Molarity is a measure of concentration and is given by

$$\text{molarity} = M = \frac{\text{moles of solute}}{\text{liters of solution}}$$

o   Molality is another measure of concentration used to determine boiling point elevation and freezing point depression. It is given by

$$\text{molality} = m = \frac{\text{moles of solute}}{\text{kilograms of solvent}}$$

o   Solubility refers to the degree to which a given solute will dissolve in a given solvent.
   • Solubility of solids in water increases with increasing temperature.

   • Solubility of gases in water decreases with increasing temperature.

   • Solubility of gases in water increases with increasing pressure.

o   When ionic substances dissolve, the ionic bonds are broken and the substance dissociates into free-moving positive and negative ions. Such ions are called electrolytes; such a solution is called electrolytic and will conduct electricity.

o   Boiling point elevation and freezing point depression are given by
$$\Delta T = kmi$$
where k is a constant dependent on the solvent and m is molality.
   • Boiling point elevation and freezing point depression depend only on the type of solvent and the number of solute particles, but not the type of solute particles.

   • For different solutions with the same molality, the boiling point elevation and freezing point depression will be greatest for the solute that dissociates into the greatest number of particles.

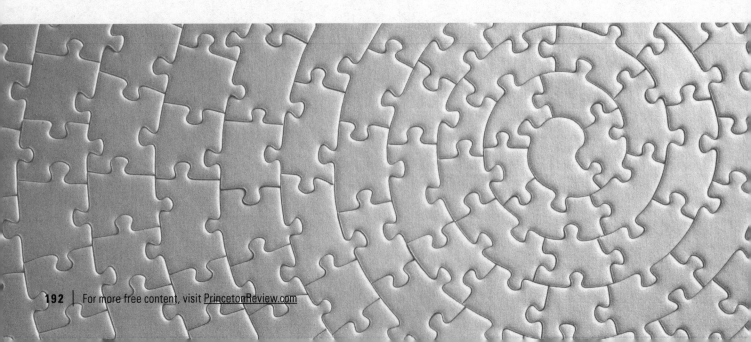

o   In a precipitation reaction, a mixture of two solutions of soluble salts results in the precipitation out of solution of an insoluble salt.

- All ammonium (NH_4^+), alkali (Li^+, Na^+, K^+, Cs^+, Rb^+), nitrate (NO_3^-), and perchlorate (ClO_4^-) salts are soluble.

- Silver, lead, and mercury salts are insoluble, except the perchlorates and nitrates.

- Most hydroxides (OH^-) are insoluble, except for the alkalis and barium.

Chapter 10
Kinetics and Equilibrium

Kinetics is the study of the rate at which reactant molecules are converted to products in a chemical reaction. Equilibrium refers to the fact that reactions are reversible; products can be converted back to reactants. As this chapter will show you, no matter how often you may see the terms used together, these are two fundamentally different concepts. Some specific topics covered in this chapter are rates of reaction, equilibrium and K_{eq}, and Le Châtelier's principle.

KINETICS

Kinetics is the study of the rates of reactions—the speed at which reactants are converted into products.

Equilibrium is defined as the point in a chemical reaction at which the concentration of all the reactants and products ceases to change. As we will show you, no matter how often you may see the terms used together, these are two fundamentally different concepts.

The rate at which reactants are converted into products in a reaction is called the **reaction rate**. Remember that chemical reactions involve breaking old bonds (in the reactants) and making new bonds (in products). In order for bond breaking and bond making to occur, reactant molecules (or atoms or ions) must collide with sufficient energy and proper orientation. Why are energy and orientation important? Well, the reactant molecules need to collide with enough kinetic energy to break their bonds, and they need to collide with the proper orientation for new bonds to form. Consider the gas phase reaction.

$$H_2(g) + I_2(g) \rightarrow 2HI(g)$$

Notice that if an H_2 and I_2 molecule collide with enough kinetic energy and in the orientation shown below, the atoms are in an ideal position to form new H–I bonds.

First: Reactant molecules H_2 and I_2 move toward each other with sufficient energy.

$$
\begin{array}{cc}
H & I \\
| \rightarrow \leftarrow | \\
H & I
\end{array}
$$

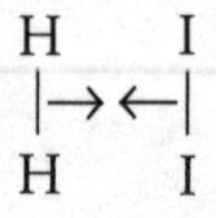

Next: The collision causes H–H and I–I bonds to begin to break. Since the reactant molecules were properly aligned, new H–I bonds also start to form.

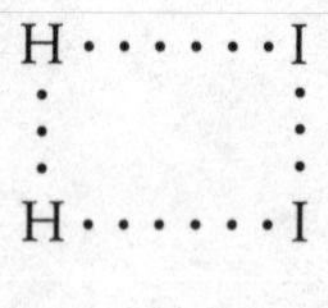

$$
\begin{array}{cc}
H \cdots\cdots I \\
\vdots \qquad \vdots \\
\vdots \qquad \vdots \\
H \cdots\cdots I
\end{array}
$$

The above species is an extremely unstable, high-energy arrangement of atoms called an **activated complex** or **transition state**. Reactants must form an activated complex before products can be made.

Finally: H–H and I–I bonds are completely broken, and H–I bonds are formed. The chemical reaction has produced hydrogen iodide.

H–I
H–I

Although this was a somewhat simplified account of what happens during a chemical reaction, the actual process does involve molecular collisions, bond breaking and making, and the formation of an activated complex.

Factors That Affect Reaction Rate

The test writers will expect you to be familiar with several key factors that influence the rate of a reaction. All of these factors impact the reaction rate by affecting the rate of molecular collisions, the energy of the collisions, or both.

Concentration of Reactants Reactant molecules must collide in order to form products. If the rate at which reactant molecules collide is increased, then the reaction rate will also increase. One way to increase the rate of reactant collisions is to increase the amount of reactant present, or in other words, to increase the concentration of reactants. For example, wood burns much faster in a pure (100 percent) oxygen environment than in air (which is only about 20 percent oxygen by mass). An increase in the concentration of the reactant oxygen causes an increase in the rate of combustion. However, this is true only of reactants that are gaseous or in solution, whose concentrations can be changed. For instance, a gas can be compressed into a smaller volume (increasing the concentration of gas molecules per volume). Since the molecules in a pure solid or liquid are relatively close together, they cannot be significantly compressed, so their concentration is essentially constant. To sum up: *If one or more reactants are gaseous or in solution, the reaction rate can be increased by increasing the concentration of those reactants.* Obviously, a decrease in reactant concentration will produce a decrease in reaction rate. If the reactants are in gaseous phase, then increasing their pressure will also increase their concentration, thereby accelerating the reaction rate.

Surface Area of Reactants The greater the surface area of the reactants, the greater the number of collisions; hence the faster reaction rate. For instance, a cube of sugar will dissolve less quickly in water than the same amount of sugar in loose form. Only the surface areas of solids and liquids can be changed: We can increase the surface area of a solid by breaking it up or grinding it into a powder, and a liquid's surface area can be increased by spraying it out as a mist of fine droplets.

Temperature The factor that has perhaps the most profound effect on reaction rate is temperature. This is because a temperature change affects both the rate of reactant collisions and the energy involved in the collisions. Remember that temperature is a measure of the average kinetic energy of molecules. As the temperature of the reactants is increased, the molecules move around faster; this results in more frequent and energetic collisions and increases the likelihood that a given collision will have sufficient energy to break bonds. A good rule of thumb says that for every 10°C increase in temperature, the reaction rate will double.

Nature of Reactants Since bond breaking is part of the reaction process, it makes sense that reactant molecules composed of weaker bonds will react more quickly than will reactant molecules held together by stronger bonds. Reactions between dissolved ions tend to be rapid, since bond breaking has already occurred, with the dissolution of the ionic substance.

Catalysts A catalyst increases the rate of a chemical reaction without being consumed by it. Enzymes are examples of catalysts. They are involved in many important biological reactions. How do catalysts accelerate reaction rates? Before we get to that, let's first consider the energy changes that occur in the course of a reaction.

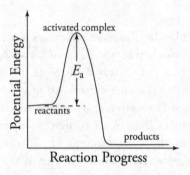

This figure is sometimes referred to as a potential energy diagram. The potential energy of the activated complex is greater than that of the reactants, and the energy difference between the two is called the activation energy (symbolized as E_a). The **activation energy** is the minimum energy that must be supplied for the activated complex to be formed. It is an energy barrier that must be overcome by reactant molecules; reactant molecules acquire the necessary activation energy by absorbing heat from the surroundings.

The size of the activation energy barrier indicates how difficult it is for the reaction to proceed. A relatively small barrier, indicating a low activation energy, means that collisions between reactant molecules need less energy to produce an activated complex. Thus, a greater percentage of reactant collisions is likely to lead to product formation, resulting in a relatively high rate of reaction.

Let's return to the question *How do catalysts work?* Catalysts increase the reaction rate by enabling the reaction to proceed through a series of different steps with a lower activation energy than they ordinarily would require. So a catalyst reduces the minimum energy requirement of the reaction. This leads to a greater percentage of product-forming collisions and thus an increased rate of reaction. Since a catalyst is not consumed by the process, a small amount of catalyst can be used to speed up a reaction with a fairly large reactant concentration.

> ### Catalyst Facts
>
> Catalysts increase the rate of a reaction by lowering the activation energy.
>
> Catalysts are not consumed in a reaction.
>
> Catalysts do not change the equilibrium of a reaction.

The rate of reaction depends on both the frequency of molecular collision and the energy of molecular collision.

Factors affecting frequency of collision	Factors affecting energy of collision
Concentration of reactants	Temperature
Surface area of reactants	Nature of reactants
Temperature	Catalysts

CHEMICAL EQUILIBRIUM

We've been talking about chemical reactions as if they occur in only one direction—from reactants to products.

$$aA + bB \rightarrow cC + dD$$

However, many reactions are reversible; as products are formed, some of them go through the reverse reaction and reform the reactants. Reversible reactions are written as follows:

$$aA + bB \rightleftharpoons cC + dD$$

What do the two arrows mean? They mean that the reaction is taking place in both directions. Reactants are forming products (the forward reaction), and products are forming reactants (the reverse reaction). Let's talk about how this works. When a reaction first starts, the concentration of the reactants is high, and the concentration of the products is very low. At this point, the rate of the forward reaction is greater than the rate of the reverse reaction. After a while, as more of the products are formed, less of the reactants are present.

Ultimately, if pressure and temperature are maintained and the system is closed (meaning no species are allowed to escape), the rate of the reverse reaction will be equal to the rate of the forward reaction. In other words, reactants are being made as rapidly as are products. When this occurs, we say that the reaction is in **equilibrium,** or dynamic equilibrium. When a reaction is in **dynamic equilibrium,** the forward and reverse reaction rates are equal, which also means that the concentrations of products and reactants are constant.

But here's what equilibrium definitely does NOT mean: *It does not mean that the concentrations of products and reactants are equal.* It just means that whatever the concentrations of products and reactants may be, they aren't changing once the reaction reaches equilibrium.

If we want to know about the relative concentrations of products and reactants of a reaction at equilibrium, we must know two things: (1) the reaction's equilibrium constant, or K_{eq}, and (2) the reaction's equilibrium expression.

For the reaction aA + bB $\leftrightharpoons$ cC + dD, the equilibrium expression is written as follows:

$$K_{eq} = \frac{[C]^c [D]^d}{[A]^a [B]^b}$$

(The symbol [ ] means "concentration of," so [A] means "the concentration of A.")

Keep in mind that the concentrations referred to in an equilibrium expression are those of the species at equilibrium; the coefficients in the balanced equation become exponents in the equilibrium expression; and only those species whose concentrations can be varied are included. So, only species that are gaseous or in solution (and not solids or pure liquids) belong in an equilibrium expression.

Thus, given the reaction

$$BF_3(g) + 3H_2O(l) \leftrightharpoons 3HF(aq) + H_3BO_3(aq)$$

(remember that the notation (*aq*) indicates a species is dissolved in water),

we get the equilibrium expression

$$A + B \leftrightharpoons C + D$$

Take a close look at the above equilibrium expression. Notice that the equilibrium constant K_{eq} is proportional to product concentrations over reactant concentrations, or $\frac{[products]}{[reactants]}$.

What's the significance of that ratio? Suppose that in a particular reaction, almost all of the reactants are converted into products and that products do not reform reactants to any great extent. How would the K_{eq} of the reaction reflect such behavior? Well, product concentrations would be much greater than reactant concentrations at equilibrium. As a result, K_{eq}, which is roughly a ratio of product concentrations to reactant concentrations, will be a relatively large number (greater than 100).

If, instead, we have a reaction in which reactants form relatively little product, then K_{eq} will be relatively small (smaller than $\frac{1}{100}$, or 1×10^{-2}). If product and reactant concentrations at equilibrium are somewhat close, then K_{eq} will be close to 1 (not particularly large or small). So the value of the equilibrium constant K_{eq} of the reaction can give us a good idea about the extent to which reactants form products.

> **Some Great K_{eq} Facts**
>
> Solvents (usually H_2O) are not included in the equilibrium expression.
>
> Each concentration is taken to the power of its coefficient in the balanced equation.

> **Equilibrium Facts**
>
> $$K_{eq} = \frac{\text{products}}{\text{reactants}}$$
>
> **Dynamic Equilibrium**—Rate of forward reaction equals rate of reverse reaction; constant but not equal concentration of products and reactants.
>
> $K_{eq} > 1$ forward reaction favored (concentration of products greater than reactants)
>
> $K_{eq} < 1$ reverse reaction favored (concentration of reactants greater than products)

Phase Change Equilibrium

The principle of equilibrium does not only apply to chemical reactions but also to any system in which one thing is transforming, reversibly, into another—such as a phase change, for instance. Remember vapor pressure? Suppose water is in a sealed container, at a temperature below water's boiling point; some molecules will still gather enough kinetic energy to escape from the liquid and become gas. Then they will lose their kinetic energy—they will cool down and fall back into the container as water. Other liquid molecules gain enough kinetic energy to escape into the gas phase, and the process continues. Some liquid is converted to gas, and some gas is converted to liquid. The process is in equilibrium.

Thing or Things?
The principle of equilibrium would also hold true if more than one thing in a system were being reversibly transformed.

Le Châtelier's Principle

The Effects of Substrate Concentration on Equilibrium

Look at this equilibrium.

$$A + B \rightleftharpoons C + D$$

On the left side of the equilibrium equation, we find A and B. On the right side, we find C and D. A and B act together to produce C and D; meanwhile, C and D act together to produce A and B.

If we add more A to the reaction system, the reaction will shift to the right, to produce *more* C and D at equilibrium.

$$A \searrow$$
$$A + B \rightleftharpoons \uparrow C + \uparrow D$$

If we add more B to the reaction, the reaction will shift to the right, to produce more C and D at equilibrium.

$$B \searrow$$
$$A + B \rightleftharpoons \uparrow C + \uparrow D$$

Adding more A *and* B, of course, will also increase the production of C and D.

$$A \searrow$$
$$B \searrow \quad A + B \rightleftharpoons \uparrow\uparrow C + \uparrow\uparrow D$$

Adding more C or more D to the system has an analogous but opposite effect.

$$\uparrow\uparrow A + \uparrow\uparrow B \rightleftharpoons C + D \quad \begin{array}{c} C \\ D \end{array}$$

Think about it this way. When you add more A to the system, you're increasing the amount of reactant available to react and form products. Similarly, if you add more C or D to the system, you're increasing the amount of product available to react and form reactants. The system will adjust by moving to the left to reestablish equilibrium.

When we increase the concentration of one species on the left side of an equation, what happens to the concentration of the *other* species on the left side of the equation? Say we add more A to the system: There will be more collisions between A particles and B particles. Since we did not add any B to the system, the increased collisions among A and B particles, along with the increased production of C and D, will tend to reduce the concentration of B at equilibrium. After equilibrium has shifted, there will be more A particles than there were before we added any more A. There will be fewer B particles than there were before we began, and there will, of course, be more C and D particles.

To give you an idea of what we mean by "driving or shifting equilibrium to the right," consider this example.

Suppose for the reaction, $2A(g) + B(g) \rightleftharpoons C(g)$, equilibrium concentrations at a particular temperature are [A] = 2 M, [B] = 6 M, and [C] = 8 M.

When we plug these into the equilibrium expression $K_{eq} = \dfrac{[C]}{[A]^2[B]}$, we get $K_{eq} = \dfrac{[8]}{[2]^2[6]} = \dfrac{1}{3}$.

Now, according to Le Châtelier's principle, if we add more A into the system at equilibrium, equilibrium will shift to the right. So once equilibrium is reestablished, the concentration of C will be greater than 8 M, and the concentration of B will be less than 6 M. Of course, the concentration of A will also be greater than before. But as long as we maintain the original temperature, K_{eq} will stay the same. So when the new equilibrium concentrations are plugged back into the equilibrium expression, it will still equal $\dfrac{1}{3}$. For instance, the new equilibrium concentrations could be [A] = 3 M, [B] = 4 M, and [C] = 12 M. The equilibrium concentrations have changed, but the K_{eq} has not.

The Effects of Heat on Equilibrium

Consider this equilibrium equation.

$$H + I + Heat \rightleftharpoons J + K$$

The reaction consumes heat in the forward direction, and it produces heat in the reverse direction. In a sense, you can think of heat as being one of the reactants in this equation. So what happens if we increase the temperature of this reaction? That is, what happens if we add heat to the system? According to Le Châtelier's principle, we drive the equilibrium to the right. What happens if we decrease the temperature of the system? We drive the equilibrium to the left.

There is one important thing to know about temperature changes: this is the only type of stress that causes an equilibrium shift *and* changes the value of K_{eq} for a given reaction. The others do *not* alter K_{eq}.

So to summarize:

Le Châtelier's Principle

If some stress is placed on a reaction at equilibrium, then the equilibrium will shift in a direction that relieves the stress.

The Effects of Pressure Changes on Equilibrium

If one or more of the species in the reaction are gaseous, then changing the system's pressure can affect equilibrium. Consider the important ammonia-producing reaction that is at the heart of what is known as the **Haber process.**

$$N_2(g) + 3H_2(g) \rightleftharpoons 2NH_3(g)$$

If the above reaction at equilibrium is stressed by a reduction of its volume (which would increase the pressure of the system), then the reaction will relieve this stress by shifting equilibrium in the direction that produces fewer moles of gas. Therefore, in the above reaction, equilibrium would shift to the right. If the reaction system was stressed by an increase in its volume (which would decrease the pressure of the system), then equilibrium would shift to the left. The equilibrium of a reaction that involved equal moles of gaseous reactants and products would not be affected by either a change in volume or a change in pressure.

The Effects of Catalysts on Equilibrium

So how does the presence of a catalyst affect equilibrium? The answer is simple: It doesn't. Catalysts change reaction rates, but they do not affect equilibrium. A catalyst can aid the reaction in achieving equilibrium more quickly, but it won't affect the concentration of product at equilibrium. This emphasizes what we said at the start of this chapter: kinetics and equilibrium address quite different aspects of a chemical reaction.

Equilibrium in Precipitation Reactions

As you learned in the last chapter, some combinations of cation and anion form ionic solids with very low water solubilities or precipitates. However, even the most insoluble ionic precipitate dissolves into ions in water to a certain degree. If pressure and temperature are maintained for a precipitate in water, equilibrium exists between the precipitate and its dissolved ions. For instance, consider the equilibrium between the precipitate lead chloride ($PbCl_2$) and its dissolved ions.

$$PbCl_2(s) \rightleftharpoons Pb^{2+}(aq) + 2Cl^-(aq)$$

The equilibrium expression for the above equilibrium is

$$K_{sys} = [Pb^{2+}][Cl^-]^2$$

Remember that solids are not included in equilibrium expressions! When we consider equilibrium between a so-called insoluble ionic solid and its dissolved ions, we call the equilibrium constant a **solubility product constant** and symbolize it as K_{sp}. As you might expect, since the forward reaction is so insignificant for these precipitates, K_{sp} values are typically very small. For $PbCl_2$ at 25°C, $K_{sp} = 1.6 \times 10^{-5}$ (or 0.000016). The smaller K_{sp} is for a given ionic solid, the more insoluble it is.

Review everything we've said about kinetics, reversible reactions, and equilibrium; then answer the following questions. Answers can be found in Part IV.

DRILL 1

Question Type A

Questions 1–3 refer to the following.

(A) $Ca^{2+}(aq) + CO_3{}^{2-}(aq) \rightleftharpoons CaCO_3(s)$
(B) $N_2(g) + 2O_2(g) \rightleftharpoons 2NO_2(g)$
(C) $4NH_3(g) + 5O_2(g) \rightleftharpoons 4NO(g) + 6H_2O(g)$
(D) $H_2(g) + I_2(g) \rightleftharpoons 2HI(g)$
(E) $Na_2O_2(s) + H_2O(l) \rightleftharpoons NaOH(aq) + H_2O_2(aq)$

1. Reaction rate can be increased by increasing the surface area of reactants

2. Increasing system pressure by decreasing reaction volume shifts equilibrium to the right

3. Impossible to increase rate of reverse reaction by increasing the concentration of reactant(s)

Question Type B

I   II

101. For any chemical   BECAUSE   a dynamic equilibrium
     reaction in dynamic   will shift in a direction that
     equilibrium,   tends to relieve a stress
     increasing the   imposed on it.
     concentration of one
     product will decrease
     the concentration of
     all reactants

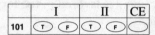

102. When a reversible   BECAUSE   on the right side of any
     chemical reaction   equilibrium expression,
     reaches equilibrium,   the numerator and
     concentrations   denominator are always
     of products and   equal.
     reactants are always
     equal

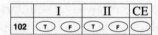

103. Increasing the   BECAUSE   the reaction rate is
     concentration of   increased as the energy
     a gaseous reactant   per molecular collision
     typically increases the   increases.
     reaction rate

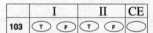

Question Type C

$$(1) \ \ N_2(g) + 3H_2(g) \leftrightharpoons 2NH_3(g), \ K_{eq} \ (472°C) = 0.105$$

$$(2) \ \ H_2(g) + I_2(g) \leftrightharpoons 2HI(g), \ K_{eq} \ (448°C) = 50$$

24. In comparing the two reactions above, performed at the indicated temperatures, which of the following is true?

    (A) Reaction 1 is favored in the forward direction, and reaction 2 is favored in the reverse direction.
    (B) Reaction 1 is favored in the reverse direction, and reaction 2 is favored in the forward direction.
    (C) Both reactions 1 and 2 are favored in the forward direction.
    (D) Both reactions 1 and 2 are favored in the reverse direction.
    (E) Neither reaction favors either the forward or reverse direction.

$$2SO_3(g) \leftrightharpoons 2SO_2(g) + O_2(g)$$

25. If the reaction given above is at equilibrium, the result of a sudden increase in the concentration of O_2 will result in

    (A) increased concentration of SO_2 and decreased concentration of SO_3
    (B) increased concentration of SO_2 and increased concentration of SO_3
    (C) decreased concentration of SO_2 and increased concentration of SO_3
    (D) decreased concentration of SO_2 and decreased concentration of SO_3
    (E) no change in concentration of any product or reactant

26. Which of the following statements is NOT true regarding the activated complex?

    (A) It represents the highest energy state achieved during the course of a reaction.
    (B) It is not consumed during the course of a reaction.
    (C) It is very unstable.
    (D) It is formed before reactant bonds are completely broken.
    (E) It is formed before product bonds are completely formed.

Summary

o   Rate of reaction is the speed at which reactants are converted into products.

o   Rate of reaction is affected by the concentration of reactants in solution, surface area of solid reactants, temperature, the type of reactants involved, and the presence of a catalyst.

o   A catalyst lowers the activation energy, or the amount of energy each reactant molecule needs to be converted to a product.

o   Catalysts are never consumed during a reaction.

o   Dynamic equilibrium refers to the fact that for a given system, reactants can be converted to products, and products can be converted back to reactants. When the concentrations of the reactants and products are such that the rate of the forward reaction (reactants to products) equals the rate of the reverse reaction, the system is in equilibrium.

o   The equilibrium constant for a given reaction defines the ratio of products to reactants. It is dependent on temperature. For the reaction

$$aA + bB \rightarrow cC + dD$$

it is given by

$$K_{eq} = \frac{[C]^c [D]^d}{[A]^a [B]^b}$$

o   Le Châtelier's principle states that stressing a system at equilibrium causes the system to shift to relieve the stress.

   • Adding more reactants or removing products shifts the equilibrium to the right. Adding products or removing reactants shifts it to the left.

   • Adding heat to an endothermic reaction shifts the equilibrium to the right. Adding heat to an exothermic reaction shifts it to the left.

   • Adding pressure by reducing the volume of a gaseous reaction shifts the equilibrium to the side with fewer moles.

o   Catalysts have no effect on equilibrium.

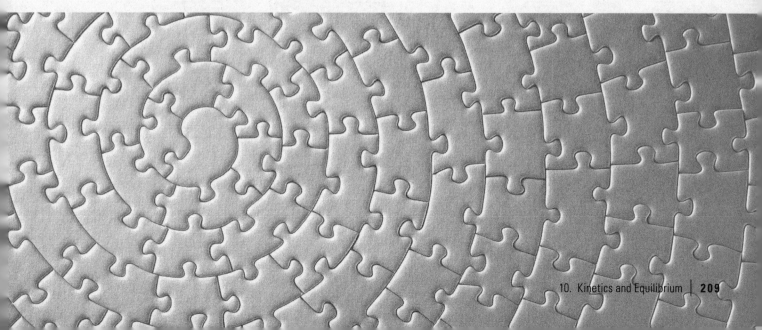

Chapter 11
Acids and Bases

In order to do well on the SAT Subject Test in Chemistry, you'll need to know a few things about acids and bases, including what they are, how they behave in water, and how they react with each other.

Sometimes water molecules split apart to form H^+ (a hydrogen ion) and OH^- (a hydroxide ion). An acid is anything that increases the H^+ concentration of the solution; a base is anything that increases the OH^- concentration. How, why, and the degree to which this happens will be the focus of this chapter.

THE AUTOIONIZATION OF H₂O

This might surprise you, but a glass of water is not entirely composed of molecules of H_2O. Small amounts of $H^+(aq)$ and $OH^-(aq)$ are also present; these are formed during the spontaneous dissociation of water, a process called **autoionization**.

$$H_2O(aq) \rightleftharpoons H^+(aq) + OH^-(aq)$$

Autoionization is reversible, and an equilibrium exists in which $[H^+]$, $[OH^-]$, and $[H_2O]$ are stable.

This equilibrium can be upset by the addition of compounds that alter $[H^+]$ or $[OH^-]$, as predicted by Le Châtelier's principle. In fact, you'll see that aqueous acid-base chemistry is nothing new; it is simply the study of how other compounds introduced into solution can disturb the autoionization equilibrium of water.

Dissociation Constant for Water, K_w

The equilibrium expression for the autoionization of water is

$$K_w = [H^+][OH^-]$$

(Remember that H_2O doesn't appear in the equilibrium expression because it is the solvent.)

For pure water at 25°C, both $[H^+]$ and $[OH^-]$ are 10^{-7} M. Therefore, in pure water

$$K_w = [H^+][OH^-]$$

$$= (10^{-7} \, M)(10^{-7} \, M)$$

$$= 10^{-14} \, M^2 \text{ at } 25°C$$

Furthermore, at constant temperature, regardless of whether more $[H^+]$ or more $[OH^-]$ is added to the solution, the K_w, or $[H^+] \times [OH^-]$, of any aqueous solution is equal to 10^{-14} M^2 at 25°C. That's because *the only way to change the value of an equilibrium constant is to change the temperature of the solution.*

What Is pH?

The $[H^+]$ of pure water at $25°C$ is 10^{-7} M. Many people find working with exponents, especially negative exponents, a bit scary. Luckily for you, the tradition of pH was conceived and created; pH and $[H^+]$ have the following relationship:

$$\text{If } [H^+] = 10^{-7} \; M$$

$$\text{then pH} = -\log(10^{-7}) = 7$$

Note that "p" is the abbreviation for the numerical operation of $-\log$; the $-\log$ is taken from whatever number follows the p. For example, given that

$$K_w = [H^+][OH^-] = 10^{-14} \; M^2$$

taking the p of every term gives

$$pK_w = p[H^+] + p[OH^-] = 14$$

Notice that we don't include units here, so after taking the $-\log$, the resulting number has no units.

Doing Log$_{10}$ in Your Head

For some people, having to figure out a base ten logarithm ($\log_{10}$) is just as daunting as working with exponents. If you are one of these people, try the following trick:

> Look at the number, and ask the question: "What's this number's exponent when it is written in scientific notation (in other words, 10 to some power)?"

For example

$$\log 10^4 = ?$$

Ask yourself, "What's the exponent of 10_4 when it's written as 10 raised to a power?" Well, it's already written as 10_4, so the answer is 4.

Try these.

$$\log 10^{-8} =$$
$$\log 1,000 =$$
$$\log 0.01 =$$
$$\log 1 =$$

The answers are −8, 3, −2, and 0, respectively.

But taking a logarithm of a number that isn't an even factor of 10 can seem tough. For example

$$\log 58 = ?$$

Well, for this test, you can just make a good guess: 58 is between 10 and 100. Since $\log 10 = 1$ and $\log 100 = 2$, $\log 58$ must be between 1 and 2.

And that's good enough for the SAT Subject Test in Chemistry.

ACIDS AND BASES

Over the years, several different definitions for acids and bases have been introduced.

For example:

Arrhenius:	Acids produce H^+ in aqueous solution. Bases produce OH^- in aqueous solution.
Lewis:	Acids are electron pair acceptors in solution. Bases are electron pair donors in solution.
Brønsted-Lowry:	Acids are proton donors; bases are proton acceptors.

The Brønsted-Lowry definition is the one that's most widely used today, although it is commonplace for chemists to flip between the Brønsted-Lowry and Arrhenius definitions.

Brønsted-Lowry Acids and Bases

The most important thing to remember about the Brønsted-Lowry definition of acids and bases is that *acids are proton donors and bases are proton acceptors*. The term *proton* is used to mean $H^+(aq)$, and $H^+(aq)$ reacts with water to form the **hydronium ion**, $H_3O^+(aq)$.

<table>
<tr><td colspan="2">

Acid Dissociation

$$HA(aq) \rightarrow H^+(aq) + A^-(aq)$$

or

$$HA(aq) + H_2O(l) \rightarrow H_3O^+(aq) + A^-(aq)$$

</td><td>

Reaction of a Base

$$A^-(aq) + H^+(aq) \rightarrow HA(aq)$$

or

$$A^-(aq) + H_2O(l) \rightarrow HA(aq) + OH^-(aq)$$

</td></tr>
</table>

Most compounds behave either just as acids or just as bases no matter what other chemical species are in a solution. However, a handful of molecules/ions can act as either acids or bases. They elect to either donate or accept $H^+(aq)$ in response to whatever else is in a solution; these are called **amphoteric** molecules/ions. One example of an amphoteric ion is the bicarbonate ion, $HCO_3^-(aq)$.

The bicarbonate ion can act as an acid via the following reaction:

$$HCO_3^-(aq) + H_2O(l) \rightarrow CO_3^{2-}(aq) + H_3O^+ (aq)$$

Or as a base via the following reaction:

$$HCO_3^-(aq) + H_2O(l) \rightarrow H_2CO_3(aq) + OH^-(aq)$$

Strong Acids and Bases

Acids and bases that dissociate completely and stay dissociated are referred to as strong acids and bases. The term *strong* is NOT used as a common adjective in acid-base chemistry; it has a very specific meaning. It means completely dissociating. For example, HCl is a strong acid, and NaOH is a strong base.

$$HCl(aq) \rightarrow H^+(aq) + Cl^-(aq)$$

$$NaOH(aq) \rightarrow Na^+(aq) + OH^-(aq)$$

In the case of strong acids and bases, dissociation is considered 100 percent and irreversible, so a one-way reaction arrow is used in reactions of strong acids and bases. (Keep this in mind when you're asked to calculate the pH of strong acid-base solutions; it makes the math simpler.)

For the test, you MUST memorize the following list of strong acids and bases:

	Strong Acids
HCl	hydrochloric acid
HBr	hydrobromic acid
HI	hydroiodic acid
HNO$_3$	nitric acid
H$_2$SO$_4$	sulfuric acid (only the first H is strong)
HClO$_4$	perchloric acid

Strong Bases
Group 1 hydroxides such as LiOH, NaOH, KOH, etc.
$Sr(OH)_2$ and $Ba(OH)_2$

Calculating pH for Strong Acid or Base Solutions

We've said that strong acids and bases completely dissociate. This means that, for strong acids, [H$^+$] equals the [STRONG ACID], and for strong bases, [OH$^-$] equals the [STRONG BASE].

Example: What is the pH of 1.0 M HNO$_3$(aq)?

Solution: First, write the balanced chemical equation.

$$HNO_3(aq) \rightarrow H^+(aq) + NO_3^-(aq)$$

Second, realize that there is really no HNO$_3$(aq) in solution; it has all dissociated. Therefore, what we really have is

$$HNO_3(aq) \rightarrow H^+(aq) + NO_3^-(aq)$$
~~1.0 M~~   1.0 M 1.0 M

Third, since pH is the $-\log$ [H$^+$], we get

$$pH = -\log [H^+]$$
$$= -\log (1.0\ M) = -\log (10^0\ M)$$
$$= 0$$

It's a good idea to remember that for a 1.0 M solution of any strong acid, pH = 0. These solutions are commonly used in the SAT Subject Test in Chemistry laboratory questions. Don't make the mistake of thinking that $-\log (1) = 1$!

Example: What is the pH of 1.0 M KOH(aq)?

Solution: First, write the balanced chemical equation.

$$KOH(aq) \rightarrow K^+(aq) + OH^-(aq)$$

Second, realize that there is really no KOH(aq) in solution. It's all dissociated. Therefore, what we really have is

$$KOH(aq) \rightarrow K^+(aq) + OH^-(aq)$$
~~1.0 M~~   1.0 M 1.0 M

Third, take the pOH since that's what we have.

$$pOH = -\log [OH^-]$$
$$= -\log (1.0\ M) = -\log (10^0\ M)$$
$$= 0$$

Fourth, recall that pH + pOH = 14 (at 25°C), and solve for pH.

$$pH = 14 - pOH$$
$$= 14 - 0 = 14$$

It is also a good idea to remember that for 1.0 M strong base, pH = 14. These solutions are also commonly used in the SAT Subject Test in Chemistry laboratory questions.

Weak Acids and Bases

Acids and bases that partially, reversibly dissociate are referred to as weak acids or bases. Again, the term *weak* is NOT used as a common adjective in acid-base chemistry. It has a very specific meaning; it means *partial* or *reversible dissociation*. For example, HF is a weak acid, and NH_3 is a weak base.

$$HF(aq) \rightleftharpoons H^+(aq) + F^-(aq)$$

$$NH_3(aq) + H_2O(l) \rightleftharpoons NH_4^+(aq) + OH^-(aq)$$

The reversible double-reaction arrow is used in weak acid-base dissociation reactions. It is important to know that weak acids dissociate less than 10% in solution. Thus, in a solution of HF, over 90% of the HF molecules stay combined, and very few of them dissociate. For weak bases there is a similar rule; there are significantly more NH_3 molecules than there are NH_4^+ ions in a solution of ammonia.

Being able to identify weak acids and bases will really help you on test day. No one memorizes the list of weak acids and weak bases because there are tens of thousands of them. The way to identify a weak acid or weak base is first to recognize whether a compound is acidic or basic, and then know that if it isn't in the set of the strong acids or strong bases, it must be weak.

One important weak acid that you should familiarize yourself with is carbonic acid, H_2CO_3. Carbonic acid is an important ingredient in soda pop. When carbonic acid is dissolved in water, the carbonic acid decomposes via the following reaction:

$$H_2CO_3(aq) \rightarrow H_2O(l) + CO_2(g)$$

The carbon dioxide gas that is produced is what gives soda its fizz. A flat soda is one in which all of the carbonic acid has fully decomposed and no more carbon dioxide is being produced.

Calculating pH for Weak Acid or Base Solutions

As weak acids and bases do not dissociate completely, calculating the pH of a weak acid or base solution is considerably more complicated than a strong acid or base. Starting with weak acids, to calculate pH we need to look at the acid dissociation constant, K_a. The acid dissociation constant is an equilibrium constant, so we use the same [products]/[reactants] idea to figure it out.

Let's look at an example. We'll calculate the pH of a 0.01 M solution of nitrous acid, HNO_2, which has a K_a value of 4.0×10^{-4}. First, let's look at the equation for the dissociation of HNO_2.

$$HNO_2(aq) \rightleftharpoons H^+(aq) + NO^{2-}(aq)$$

Then, we'll write the K_a expression for it.

$$K_a = \frac{[H^+][NO_2^-]}{[HNO_2]}$$

Finally, we'll plug in some numbers. We know the K_a value, as well as the concentration of the HNO_2. We can also see that both the H^+ and NO_2^- ions would exist in a 1:1 ratio—that is, for every molecule of HNO_2 that dissociates, we get one H^+ ion and one NO_2^- ion. Since those values will be the same, we'll replace them both with x.

$$4.0 \times 10^{-4} = \frac{(x)(x)}{0.01}$$

With a little algebra, we can then solve for x.

$$x^2 = 4.0 \times 10^{-6}$$
$$x = 2.0 \times 10^{-3}$$

At this point, since we don't have a calculator, we can't get the exact pH, but we do know it will be between 2 and 3 (since $[H^+]$ is between 1×10^{-2} and 1×10^{-3}).

The same sort of logic applies to weak bases, only this time, we'll be calculating the pH base of the hydroxide ion concentration. We will also use the base dissociation constant, K_b, but it is determined the same way as every other equilibrium constant we've seen, so no big deal. Let's calculate the pH of a 1.0 M solution of hydroxylamine, $HONH_2$, which has a K_b of 1.0×10^{-8}.

$$HONH_2(aq) + H_2O(l) \rightleftharpoons HONH_3^+(aq) + OH^-(aq)$$
$$K_b = \frac{[HONH_3^+][OH^-]}{[HONH_2]}$$

Remember, the water does not appear in the equilibrium constant expression because it is a liquid and thus has an unchangeable concentration.

$$1.0 \times 10^{-8} = \frac{(x)(x)}{1.0}$$
$$x^2 = 1.0 \times 10^{-8}$$
$$x = 1.0 \times 10^{-4}$$

In this case, x represents the hydroxide ion concentration, so the pOH is 4 ($-\log 1.0 \times 10^{-4}$), meaning the pH of this solution will be 10.

Polyprotic Acids

Some acids can donate more than one proton. These acids are called polyprotic, and acids which can only donate a single proton are called monoprotic. One common example of a polyprotic acid is phosphoric acid, H_3PO_4. Phosphoric acid can donate all three of its protons as follows:

$$H_3PO_4(aq) + H_2O(l) \rightleftharpoons H_2PO_4^-(aq) + H_3O^+(aq)$$

$$H_2PO_4^-(aq) + H_2O(l) \rightleftharpoons HPO_4^{2-}(aq) + H_3O^+(aq)$$

$$HPO_4^{2-}(aq) + H_2O(l) \rightleftharpoons PO_4^{3-}(aq) + H_3O^+(aq)$$

One thing to understand about polyprotic acids is that each dissociation is weaker than the one before it. Phosphoric acid is a weak acid, so in a solution of phosphoric acid, there are far more dissociated H_3PO_4 molecules than any of the dissociated ions. In a similar vein, there would also be a lot more $H_2PO_4^-$ ions than HPO_4^{2-} ions, and in turn a lot more HPO_4^{2-} ions than PO_4^{3-} ions. As for the hydronium (H_3O^+) ion, even though it appears as a product multiple times, there would still be very little of it compared to the undissociated H_3PO_4 molecules, simply because so few of the various acid molecules donate protons.

Na⁺ and NaOH
$Na^+(aq)$ can also be thought of as $Na(H_2O)^+$, or simply remember that aqueous metal ions are the conjugates of their metal hydroxides.

Conjugate Acid/Base Pairs

A **conjugate pair** of molecules refers to two molecules that have identical molecular formulas except that one of them has an additional H^+.

Some examples of conjugate pairs are

HCl and Cl⁻
H_2O and OH⁻
$H_2PO_4^-$ and HPO_4^{2-}
Na⁺ and NaOH

Some molecules/ions that are often *mistaken* for conjugate pairs are

H_3O^+/OH⁻, H_2SO_4/SO_4^{2-}, H_2CO_3/CO_3^{2-}

Since all of these differ by more than 1 H^+, they do NOT qualify as conjugate pairs. Now, the member of a conjugate pair that has an extra H^+ is called the conjugate acid, and the member that has one fewer H^+ is the conjugate base.

When looking at conjugate acids and bases, one useful value to understand is the pK_a (or pK_b) value of an acid or a base. The "p" term still means $-\log_{10}$ here, so the pK_a of lactic acid ($HC_3H_8O_3$), which has a K_a of 1.0×10^{-4}, would simply be 4.

The reason this is important here is that for any conjugate acid/base pair, the pK_a of the acid plus the pK_b of its conjugate base is equal to 14. So, in this case, we know that the pK_b of the lactate ion, $C_3H_8O_3^-$, would be 10.

Using the above, we can see that the stronger an acid is, the lower its pK_a value is. Think about pH; a lower pH means a stronger acid. The same logic applies here to pK_a (and for bases, pK_b) values.

Strong acids, which dissociate completely, are not given pK_a values, but because they do dissociate completely, that means their conjugate bases are not at all likely to accept protons and are thus very weak indeed. Looking at the list of strong acids on page 215, we can see that their conjugate bases are:

$$Cl^-, Br^-, I^-, NO_3^-, ClO_4^-, \text{ and } HSO_4^-$$

All six of those ions do not act as conjugate bases, and it's worth knowing that list. Although, if you have memorized the list of the six strong acids, all you have to do to each of them is remove a proton to get to their conjugate bases!

Buffers

Buffers are solutions used to minimize (not prevent) a change in pH when an additional acid or base is introduced into solution. Buffers are made out of conjugate weak acids and bases—the acid/base pair must be conjugates because if they weren't, they would immediately react, neutralize one another, and fail to establish a reversible reaction. Therefore, a **buffer** consists of a conjugate pair of a weak acid and weak base.

One example of a buffer is a mixture of acetic acid, $HC_2H_3O_2$, and sodium acetate, $NaC_2H_3O_2$. The acetate ion, $C_2H_3O_2^-$, is the conjugate base of acetic acid. Thus, if you were to dissolve some sodium acetate into acetic acid, you would create a buffer. The pH of the buffer would be close to the pK_a of acetic acid.

If you were to add more sodium acetate, the pH of the buffer would increase, since you are adding more base. If you were to increase the concentration of the acetic acid, the pH would decrease since you'd be making the buffer more acidic.

It's worth noting here that because the conjugate bases of strong acids are not effective bases, you cannot make a buffer out of any of the strong acids or their conjugates.

ACID-BASE TITRATIONS

An acid-base titration is an experimental technique used to acquire information about a solution containing an acid or base. Specifically, an acid-base titration can be used to figure out the following:

1. concentration of an acid or base
2. whether an unknown acid or base is strong or weak
3. pK_a of an unknown acid or pK_b of unknown base

All titration experiments are carried out in the same way. The procedure consists of adding a strong acid or base of known identity and concentration, called the **titrant,** to the unknown acid or base solution. The titrant is carefully added stepwise, and changes in pH are monitored and recorded. With each small sample of titrant, a fraction of the unknown base or acid molecules is neutralized and converted into its conjugates.

This procedure continues until either the pH of the solution starts to level off or a color change is observed using a pH indicator.

Analyzing a **titration curve**—a curve obtained by plotting pH as a function of the volume of added titrant—provides information about the unknown solution's concentration.

The Equivalence Point

The most important feature of any titration curve is the **equivalence point.** This is the point during the titration where just enough titrant (in moles) has been added to completely neutralize the subject acid or base. At the equivalence point, no unreacted titrant or unknown base/acid remains in solution. Keep in mind that conjugate acids and bases need not be neutral (recall the conjugate rules). Therefore, do not make the mistake of automatically associating the equivalence point with pH 7.

You can locate the equivalence point by eyeballing the titration curve: it is the point at which the curve is the steepest.

Different Ways to Say It
The equivalence point is also called the *inflection* and the *end point.*

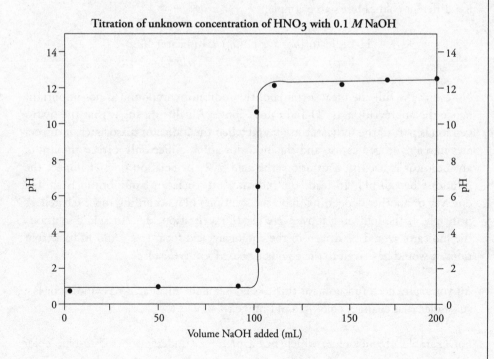

Titration of unknown concentration of HNO$_3$ with 0.1 M NaOH

Determining Concentration

As we said earlier, the equivalence point is that point in the titration where just enough titrant has been added to completely neutralize the unknown acid or base. Therefore, since the number of moles must be equal at the equivalence point, if we know the concentration of the titrant, and the amount of the titrant we've added, we can calculate the concentration of the unknown solution, using an adaptation of the dilution equation, $M_i V_i = M_f V_f$.

$$\text{Molarity}_{(\text{subject})} \times \text{Volume}_{(\text{subject})} = \text{Molarity}_{(\text{titrant})} \times \text{Volume}_{(\text{titrant})}$$

Rearranging this to solve for Molarity$_{(\text{subject})}$ gives

$$\text{Molarity}_{(\text{subject})} = (\text{Molarity}_{(\text{titrant})} \times \text{Volume}_{(\text{titrant})})/\text{Volume}_{(\text{subject})}$$

Therefore, for the titration curve we just saw

$$\text{Molarity}_{(\text{HNO}_3)} = (0.1\ M \times 100\ \text{mL})/100\ \text{mL}$$

$$= 0.1\ M$$

The concentration of HNO_3 was 0.1 M.

Acid-Base Indicators

An indicator is just the conjugate pair of a weak acid or base, where each conjugate is a different color. Here's an example:

$$\text{H-Indicator}(aq) \rightleftharpoons \text{H}^+(aq) + \text{Indicator}^-(aq)$$
$$(red) \qquad\qquad\qquad (yellow)$$

Note that the full chemical formula of the indicator compound is not important, hence the abbreviation as "H-Indicator" above. All this means is that the hydrogen ion is part of the indicator itself, and when the indicator dissociates, it dissociates into a hydrogen cation and the indicator anion. Since only a trace amount of an indicator is used in a titration, the acid-base dissociation doesn't impact the solution's overall pH. Instead, the indicator's dissociation equilibrium is shifted one way or another depending upon the solution's pH, according to Le Châtelier's principle. If the indicator above were used in a titration, then in acidic solutions, the indicator would be driven to the conjugate acid form (*red*), and in basic solutions, it would be driven to the conjugate base form (*yellow*).

All you really need to know for this test is that a chemical acid-base indicator is a substance that changes color in a pH range ±1 of its pK_a.

For example, thymol blue, which has a pK_a = 2, undergoes a red-to-blue color change in the pH range 1 to 3. Also, litmus paper changes color at about pH 7. At pH's lower than 7, the paper is red, while at pH's greater than 7, the paper is blue. Keep these things in mind when selecting an appropriate chemical indicator.

Incidentally, the test writers will want you to know how we add acid to base or base to acid, and the answer is to use a buret. A **buret** is a little measuring device that allows us to drop small, known amounts of liquid into a container.

Review this section on acids and bases, and then try the following questions. Answers can be found in Part IV.

DRILL 1

Question Type A

Questions 1–4 refer to the following.

(A) $HBr(aq)$
(B) $NH_3(aq)$
(C) $H_2O(l)$
(D) $HF(aq)$
(E) $H_2CO_3(aq)$

1. A strip of litmus paper will appear blue in it

2. At 25°C, it has a pH > 7

3. Is essentially a nonelectrolyte

4. Its aqueous ionization goes virtually to completion

Question Type B

	I		II

101. If an acid is added to water with an original pH of 7, the concentration of hydroxide ions will increase   BECAUSE   the product of hydroxide ions and protons is equal to 1.0×10^{-14} in all aqueous solutions at 25°C.

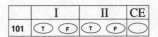

102. An aqueous solution of HI is considered to be a Brønsted-Lowry base   BECAUSE   HI(aq) can accept an H^+ ion from another species

	I	II	CE
102	T F	T F	

Question Type C

24. $HNO_3(aq) + OH^-(aq) \rightleftharpoons H_2O(l) + NO_3^-(aq)$

In the reaction above, which species is the conjugate acid?

(A) $HNO_3(aq)$
(B) $OH^-(aq)$
(C) $H_2O(l)$
(D) $NO_3^-(aq)$
(E) There is no conjugate acid in the above reaction.

25. A titration experiment is conducted in which 15 milliliters of a 0.015 M Ba(OH)$_2$ solution is added to 30 milliliters of an HCl solution of unknown concentration and titration is complete. What is the approximate concentration of the HCl solution?

(A) 0.015 M
(B) 0.03 M
(C) 1.5 M
(D) 2.5 M
(E) 3.0 M

26. Which is true regarding an aqueous solution of H_3PO_4 at 25°C ?

    (A) It has a very large acid ionization constant.
    (B) It has a bitter taste.
    (C) The concentration of $[OH^-] > 1.0 \times 10^{-7}$ M.
    (D) It is a weak electrolyte.
    (E) It can be formed by the reaction of a metal oxide and water.

27. What volume of a 0.200-molar solution of sodium hydroxide is required to neutralize 40 liters of a 0.300-molar hydrochloric acid solution?

    (A) 10 liters
    (B) 20 liters
    (C) 40 liters
    (D) 60 liters
    (E) 120 liters

28. Which one of the following acids is NOT strong?

    (A) HCl
    (B) HBr
    (C) HNO_3
    (D) H_3PO_4
    (E) H_2SO_4

Summary

- In any aqueous solution, the product of the H$^+$ and OH$^-$ concentrations will equal 1×10^{-14} at 25 degrees Celsius.

- The pH and pOH of a solution are given by

  pH= –log ([H$^+$])
  pOH = –log ([OH$^-$])

- pH + pOH = 14

- An Arrhenius acid is anything that produces H$^+$, and an Arrhenius base is anything that produces OH$^-$.

- A Lewis acid accepts a pair of electrons in solution, and a Lewis base donates a pair of electrons.

- A Brønsted-Lowry acid is a proton donor, and a Brønsted-Lowry base is a proton acceptor.

- Amphoteric substances can act as either acids or bases.

- The conjugate base of a strong acid is an ineffective base.

- Strong acids and strong bases completely and irreversibly dissociate.

- To calculate the pH of a strong acid, simply calculate the molarity of the solution. Because every acid molecule produces 1 H$^+$, the molarity equals the H$^+$ concentration, and can be used to find pH.

- Weak acids and weak bases partially and reversibly dissociate.

- To calculate pH for a weak acid, use the equation

$$K_a = \frac{(x)(x)}{M}$$

where x is the H$^+$ concentration, and M is the molarity of the solution. Solve for x, and then convert to pH.

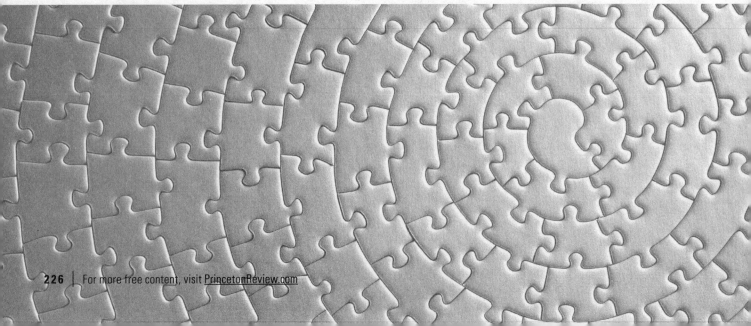

o   After one H⁺ has been removed from an acid molecule, the molecule that remains is the conjugate base.

- For any conjugate acid base pair:
  $pK_a + pK_b = 14$.

o   A buffer is a solution of a weak acid/base conjugate pair that resists changes in pH when other acids or bases are added.

o   In a titration, $\text{molarity}_{(acid)} \times \text{volume}_{(acid)} = \text{molarity}_{(base)} \times \text{volume}_{(base)}$.

o   The equivalence point in the titration of a strong acid or base is always at a pH of 7.

o   The equivalence point in a titration is above 7 for a weak acid and below 7 for a weak base.

o   Polyprotic acids can donate multiple protons. The first dissociation is always the strongest, and each ensuing dissociation becomes progressively weaker.

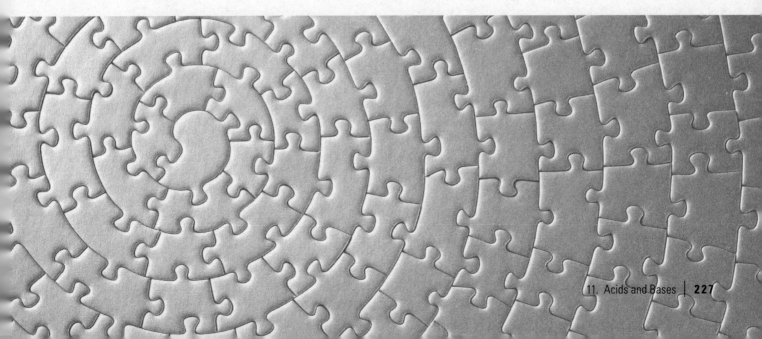

Chapter 12
Oxidation and Reduction

When dealing with molecules, we use oxidation numbers to indicate how many electrons an atom in a molecule tends to gain or lose. Any change in the oxidation numbers from one side of a reaction to the other is an oxidation-reduction, or "redox" reaction. Such movement involves a change in energy of the electrons. In this chapter, we will focus on oxidation states, balancing oxidation-reduction reactions, as well as reviewing some common oxidations-reduction reaction types.

OXIDATION AND REDUCTION

When an atom becomes involved in a bond, the atom is either oxidized or reduced. But what do these terms mean? Well, any chemistry teacher will tell you that an atom that loses electrons is **oxidized**; an atom that gains electrons is **reduced.** They'll tell you to recite "LEO says GER," which means **L**ose **E**lectrons **O**xidized and **G**ain **E**lectrons **R**educed. You should definitely remember that sentence for this exam.

> Losing electrons = oxidation (LEO)
>
> Gaining electrons = reduction (GER)

The only kind of reaction in which an atom truly loses an electron and another truly gains one is one that results in an ionic bond. But, as a way of keeping track of electrons, chemists assign each term in a compound a positive or a negative charge based upon the relative electronegativities of the atoms. For example, take HF. H—F has a covalent bond; F has a higher electronegativity value than does H. Although this isn't an ionic bond, chemists will assign the H a +1 charge and the F a –1 charge. These charges are called oxidation numbers and are always whole numbers.

The following are some important points to remember about oxidation states:

> - The atoms in any compound can be assigned oxidation states. The charges given to the atoms are formal charges that reflect their electronegativities.
> - For any compound, the total number of electrons given up by atoms is the same as the number gained. Thus, the oxidation states of all of the atoms in a neutral compound always add up to zero.

Oxidation States and Oxidation Numbers

Each atom in a compound can also be assigned what's called an oxidation state. The **oxidation state** is positive if the atom is likely to lose electrons and negative if the atom is likely to gain electrons.

If, for instance, we imagine that some atom has gained two electrons, its oxidation state is –2, and if it has lost one electron, its oxidation state would be +1. Since total reduction has to equal total oxidation for all compounds, the sum of all oxidation numbers of a compound is always zero. It is important to remember that we assign oxidation states to atoms only when they aren't in their elemental forms. For example, each atom of H_2, O_2, Cl_2, N_2, Na, or Fe has an oxidation state of zero. Atoms in all other compounds, such as those in H_2CO_3, CaO, or N_2O, can be assigned an oxidation number that is not zero.

On the SAT Subject Test in Chemistry, the writers might show you a compound and ask you to calculate the oxidation states of its atoms. If you remember a few simple rules, you'll always be able to answer these questions.

For some elements, the oxidation state is almost always the same, no matter what compound they're sitting in, while for other elements, the oxidation state varies depending on the compound. Here are the important points to remember.

1. When oxygen is in a compound, its oxidation state is usually –2 (it has been reduced). One important exception is oxygen in a peroxide such as hydrogen peroxide (H_2O_2). In a peroxide, oxygen has an oxidation state of –1.
2. When an alkali metal (Li, Na, etc.) is involved in a compound, its oxidation state is always +1 (it's been oxidized).
3. When an alkaline earth metal (Be, Mg, etc.) is involved in a compound, its oxidation state is +2.
4. When a halogen (F, Cl, etc.) is involved in a compound, its oxidation state is often –1. The oxidation state of fluorine in a compound is always –1.
5. When hydrogen is combined with a nonmetal, its oxidation state is +1. When hydrogen is combined with a metal, its oxidation state is –1.
6. In any compound, the sum of all oxidation states is zero.

> **Oxidation States**
>
> Oxygen: –2
>
> Alkali Metals: +1
>
> Alkaline Earth Metals: +2
>
> Halogens: –1
>
> Hydrogen: ±1

Remember those six simple rules, and you'll be able to answer the questions about oxidation state on the exam. Here's an example.

> What is the oxidation state for nitrogen in the compound nitrogen monoxide (NO)?

Oxygen's oxidation number is –2; there's 1 oxygen atom in the molecule, so oxygen contributes a total reduction of –2.

Since the total reduction (gain of electrons) must equal the total oxidation (loss of electrons), nitrogen must have an oxidation state of +2 (which means it has been oxidized, having lost two electrons).

Try another one.

> What is the oxidation number of carbon in
> iron(III) carbonate, $Fe_2(CO_3)_3$?

If Fe's subscript is 2 and CO_3's is 3, that means the charge on Fe must be +3, and the charge on CO_3 must be –2. The oxidation state of an ion is equal to its charge. So the oxidation state of Fe is +3. The total oxidation state of CO_3 is –2. The oxidation state of oxygen is –2. Since there are 3 oxygen atoms in CO_3, the total contribution by oxygen is –6. This means that carbon's oxidation state must be +4 so that CO_3's total oxidation state is $(+4) + 3(–2) = –2$.

Now let's consider how these oxidation states add to give the total oxidation state of $Fe_2(CO_3)_3$.

- Oxygen contributes total reduction of $(3)(3)(–2) = –18$.
- Carbon contributes total oxidation of $3(+4) = +12$.
- Iron contributes total oxidation of $2(+3) = +6$.

So the oxidation state of $Fe_2(CO_3)_3$ is $(–18) + (+12) + (+6) = 0$. This is just what we would expect. Each iron atom has lost 3 electrons, each oxygen atom has gained 2 electrons, and each carbon atom has lost 4 electrons. The losses equal the gains; total oxidation equals total reduction.

BALANCING REDOX REACTIONS

In **oxidation reduction** or **redox reactions,** as reactants form products, one or more atoms are reduced while one or more other atoms are oxidized. If reduction occurs in a reaction, then oxidation must also take place. If one species gains electrons, another must have lost them. If we want to represent just the reduction or just the oxidation in a redox reaction, we write something called a **half-reaction.**

With redox reactions, it's important to make sure that the electrons are balanced. The number of electrons lost by one species must be gained by another species, and even though electrons don't appear in the actual reaction (as they cancel out), they must still be balanced. This makes balancing redox reactions potentially trickier than other reaction types.

For instance, when a copper bar is submerged in a solution of silver nitrate, the silver ions will reduce to solid silver and the copper bar will be oxidized into copper ions via the following half-reactions.

$$\text{Reduction: } Ag^+ + e^- \rightarrow Ag(s)$$

$$\text{Oxidation: } Cu(s) \rightarrow Cu^{2+} + 2e^-$$

Putting them together, you might think the final balanced equation would look like this:

$$Ag^+ + Cu(s) \rightarrow Ag(s) + Cu^{2+}$$

However, that would be wrong! Even though the silver and copper appear to be balanced at first glance, the problem is the electrons are not. Notice that every time copper is oxidized, it loses two electrons. However, every time silver is reduced, it only gains one. Therefore, twice as much silver must be reduced in order for all of those electrons being lost by copper to have someplace to go. The correctly balanced equation would be:

$$2Ag^+ + Cu(s) \rightarrow 2Ag(s) + Cu^{2+}$$

The "2" coefficient is there to ensure that the charge is balanced and the correct number of electrons are being transferred.

Let's look at a full redox reaction and work backwards to the original half reactions.

$$Fe + 2HCl \rightarrow FeCl_2 + H_2$$

On the left side of the equation, iron's oxidation state is 0 and hydrogen's is +1. On the right side of the equation, iron's oxidation state is +2 and hydrogen's is 0. So iron has been oxidized (each atom has gone from an oxidation state of 0 to +2, so each has lost two electrons), and hydrogen has been reduced (each atom has gone from an oxidation state of +1 to 0, so each has gained one electron). We can write two half-reactions, one showing the oxidation of iron and the other showing the reduction of hydrogen. Here they are.

Oxidation: $Fe \rightarrow Fe^{+2} + 2e^-$
1 iron atom loses 2 electrons and takes on an oxidation state of +2.

Reduction: $2H^+ + 2e^- \rightarrow H_2$
2 hydrogen atoms each gain 1 electron to yield 2 hydrogen atoms with an oxidation state of 0.

Notice that if we take the two half-reactions together, oxidation equals reduction: in the oxidation half-reaction, iron loses 2 electrons. In the reduction half-reaction, 2 hydrogen atoms each gain 1 electron; the total electron gain is 2.

Oxidizing and Reducing Agents

There are two other terms that you should be familiar with: oxidizing agent (or oxidant) and reducing agent (or reductant). An **oxidizing agent** causes another species to be oxidized by undergoing reduction. A **reducing agent**—by itself being oxidized—causes another substance to be reduced. Consider the two redox reactions we examined earlier.

- $Fe + 2HCl \rightarrow FeCl_2 + H_2$
- $4NH_3 + 5O_2 \rightarrow 4NO + 6H_2O$

In the first reaction, Fe (which is oxidized) is the reducing agent, and HCl (which contains the species being reduced, H) is the oxidizing agent.

In the second reaction, NH_3 (which contains the species being oxidized, N) is the reducing agent and O_2 (which is reduced) is the oxidizing agent. Note that oxygen (O_2) is an excellent oxidizing agent, and fluorine (F_2) is also a powerful oxidizing agent. The active metals make strong reducing agents.

Different substances will have different reactivity levels based on how easily they can be oxidized when placed in water or acid. For instance, lithium will very easily lose an electron to form Li^+, and thus is a strong reducing agent. On the other hand, a transition metal like copper does not give up its electrons nearly as readily, and it is a very weak reducing agent that cannot be oxidized by water (but can still be oxidized by some strong acids).

The **activity series** is a qualitative series that compares the reactivity of the various metals with water or acids. The higher the metal is on the activity series, the more vigorously it will react with water/acid. The metals at the top are thus very strong reducing agents, while those at the bottom are much weaker reducing agents. You do not need to memorize the activity series, but you should understand the general chemical principles underlying it.

Reactivites of Metals	Elements	
Most reactive	K	Potassium
	Na	Sodium
	Ca	Calcium
	Mg	Magnesium
	Al	Aluminium
Reactivity decreases	Zn	Zinc
	Fe	Iron
	Pb	Lead
	H	Hydrogen
	Cu	Copper
	Hg	Mercury
	Ag	Silver
Least reactive	Au	Gold

Common Redox Reactions

Let's look at some common redox reactions that frequently appear on the test.

1. **Rusting**
    As noted above, oxygen is a pretty good oxidizing agent. It is able to take electrons from most metals, and in doing so, will combine with those metals to form an oxide. When iron is left exposed to oxygen for a long enough time, the following reaction will occur:

$$2Fe(s) + 3O_2(g) \rightarrow Fe_2O_3(s)$$

The iron oxide that forms above has a much more common name—rust! Most metals can rust when exposed to air. There are a few metals, however, that resist this. If you look at the table above, you can see silver and gold are at the bottom of it. Those are two metals that resist the chemical attack of oxygen, and cannot rust. That is one of the reasons gold and silver are so valuable! Other valuable metals, such as copper and platinum, also have very low reactivity and will not rust.

2.   **Dissolving**

You probably know that acids are pretty good at dissolving things. However, do you know what that means chemically? When a metal dissolves, what's actually going on is a type of redox reaction in which the solid metal loses electrons and converts into an aqueous state. This occurs because acids (particularly strong acids) have a lot of H^+ ions floating around. H^+ is a pretty good oxidizing agent, and many substances will lose electrons when submerged in an acid and thus start to dissolve. When some lead is added to a concentrated solution of hydrochloric acid, the following reaction occurs:

$$Pb(s) + 2H^+ \rightarrow H_2(g) + Pb_2^+$$

The lead still exists, it's just gone from being a solid to being dissolved into an aqueous form.

Note that while H^+ is a good oxidizing agent, those metals low on the activity series, such as silver and gold, will resist being oxidized, just as they do when exposed to oxygen gas. Oxygen gas is actually a much better oxidizing agent than a strong acid, however, there are very few oxygen molecules in contact with a metal surface at any given time due to the diffuse nature of a gas. In liquid or aqueous form, a lot more H^+ ions will come into contact with a metal surface, which is why dissolving tends to be a faster process than rusting. It's not only acids that can dissolve things, though.

There are some metals that actually dissolve in water too. Water is not a particularly strong oxidizing agent, however, it is strong enough that the most reactive metals (the alkali and some alkali earth) will still be oxidized when they come into contact with water. If you were to drop a chunk of pure sodium into water, it would dissolve as follows:

$$2H_2O(g) + 2Na(s) \rightarrow 2Na^+ + H_2(g) + 2OH^-$$

In both types of dissolutions we've discussed, hydrogen is reduced from a state of +1 to a state of 0 in the hydrogen gas which is produced.

3. **Nitric Acid Dissolution**

The final common reaction type you should become familiar with involves nitric acid. Even though nitric acid is a strong acid, unlike the other five acids it will not dissolve a metal in the same type of reaction. This is because the nitrate ion, NO_3^-, is a stronger oxidizing agent than the H^+ ion present in all strong acids. If you were to dissolve lead into a solution of concentrated nitric acid, you'd get one of the following:

$$Pb(s) + 4H^+(aq) + 2NO_3^-(aq) \rightarrow Pb_2^+(aq) + 2NO_2(g) + 2H_2O(l)$$

You don't need to know that exact reaction, however, you should know that the nitrogen dioxide gas produced is a brownish-yellow toxic gas that is poisonous when inhaled.

Review what we've said about oxidation-reduction and electrochemistry, and try the following questions. The answers can be found in Part IV.

DRILL 1

Question Type A

Questions 1–4 refer to the following.

(A) $Al^{3+} + 3e^- \rightarrow Al(s)$
(B) $Na(s) \rightarrow Na^+ + e^-$
(C) $Cu^{2+} + Mg(s) \rightarrow Cu(s) + Mg^{2+}$
(D) $CH_4(g) + 2O_2(g) \rightarrow CO_2(g) + 2H_2O(l)$
(E) $Ag^+ + Cl^- \rightarrow AgCl(s)$

1. An example of a reduction half-reaction

2. Is not a redox reaction

3. Does not contain any atoms with an oxidation state of 0

4. Exactly two moles of electrons transfer during the reaction

Question Type B

<u>I</u>   <u>II</u>

101.   Any reaction in which   BECAUSE   if one species donates
       one atom is oxidized   electrons, another must
       requires that another   acquire them.
       atom be reduced

	I		II		CE
101	T	F	T	F	

102.   Nickel would be   BECAUSE   nickel is a stronger
       higher than cesium on   oxidizing agent than
       the activity series   cesium.

	I		II		CE
102	T	F	T	F	

Question Type C

24. $2Na + Cl_2 \rightarrow 2NaCl$

      Which of the following is true of the reaction
      given by the equation above?

      (A) Chlorine is oxidized.
      (B) Sodium is oxidized.
      (C) Sodium is the oxidizing agent.
      (D) Both sodium and chlorine are oxidized.
      (E) Neither sodium nor chlorine is oxidized
            nor reduced.

25.   The oxidation state of manganese (Mn) in the
      compound potassium permanganate ($KMnO_4$) is

      (A) +7
      (B) +4
      (C) 0
      (D) −4
      (E) −7

26. $2Al + 6HCl \rightarrow 2AlCl_3 + 3H_2$

    If 2 moles of Al and 6 moles of HCl react according to the above equation, then how many moles of electrons are transferred during the redox reaction?

    (A) 1
    (B) 2
    (C) 3
    (D) 5
    (E) 6

27. What is the oxidation state of bromine in $HBrO_3$?

    (A) −3
    (B) −1
    (C) +1
    (D) +3
    (E) +5

28. How many electrons does a ^{37}Cl ion with a charge of −1 contain?

    (A) 16
    (B) 17
    (C) 18
    (D) 37
    (E) 38

Summary

o An oxidation-reduction, or redox reaction, is one in which electrons are transferred.

o Oxidation state, or oxidation number, tells how many electrons an atom in a compound has gained or lost.

o The following is a list of the most common oxidation states for various elements and groups of elements:
oxygen: –2
alkali metals: +1
alkaline earth metals: +2
halogens: –1
hydrogen: +1 or –1

o Whenever atoms in a reaction undergo a change in oxidation state, a redox reaction has occurred.

o The atoms that lose electrons are oxidized and are called reducing agents; those that gain electrons are reduced and are called oxidizing agents.

o The electron transfer must be balanced in a redox reaction. The same number of electrons that are lost in the oxidation process must also be gained in the reduction process. This concept is sometimes called the conservation of charge.

o Some common oxidizing agents are oxygen gas, which can cause metals to rust, and the H^+ ion, which is present in acids and can cause metals to dissolve.

Chapter 13
Organic Chemistry and Environmental Chemistry

Organic chemistry is the study of carbon-based compounds. It's one of those things that send shivers down some people's spines. However, for the SAT Subject Test in Chemistry, we need to worry only about the relatively minor tasks of identifying organic compounds by their names and structural formulas, understanding some organic reactions on a basic level, and being familiar with the four families of biomolecules. Some topics discussed in this chapter are hydrocarbon chains, functional groups, organic reactions, biomolecules, and environmental chemistry.

ORGANIC CHEMISTRY

Carbon compounds are especially important because all living things on Earth are made up of carbon (in addition to a few other elements). Each carbon atom can form up to four bonds with other atoms; this enables carbon to form long chains with itself and certain other atoms, which is what makes it such an important biomolecule. Organic molecules almost always contain nonpolar covalent bonds. Here are some other properties of organic compounds that you should know.

- Organic compounds are much more soluble in nonpolar solvents than in polar solvents. Remember, like dissolves like, so since carbon compounds are generally nonpolar, they will be soluble in nonpolar solvents. That means that organic substances are not very soluble in water, which is a highly polar solvent.

- Organic compounds don't dissociate in solution; since organic compounds do not contain ionic bonds, they will not dissociate into ions. That means that organic solutions are poor conductors of electricity, and organic compounds do not behave as electrolytes in solution.

There is an infinite variety of organic molecules. Sometimes two organic molecules may have the same chemical make-up with identical constituent elements, but these elements are arranged in a different geometrical arrangement. In these cases, the two compounds have completely different chemical properties and are said to be **isomers.**

An example of two isomers is below:

CH_3CH_2OH, Ethanol CH_3OCH_3, Dimethyl Ether

Ethanol and dimethyl ether have very different chemical properties. Treated properly, ethanol is the active ingredient in drinking alcohol, while dimethyl ether is currently being investigated for use in automotive engines.

Hydrocarbons

The simplest organic compounds are hydrocarbons, compounds that contain only carbon and hydrogen. Hydrocarbons can be grouped into three categories: **alkanes,** which contain only single carbon-carbon bonds; **alkenes,** which contain carbon-carbon double bonds; and **alkynes,** which contain carbon-carbon triple bonds.

Alkanes

Alkanes are hydrocarbons that contain only single bonds. They are also known as **saturated hydrocarbons** because each carbon atom is bonded to as many other atoms as possible.

Alkane (C_nH_{2n+2}) Formula

Methane	CH_4
Ethane	C_2H_6
Propane	C_3H_8
Butane	C_4H_{10}
Pentane	C_5H_{12}

The prefixes (*meth-*, *eth-*, *prop-*, *etc.*) indicate the number of carbons in the hydrocarbon chain.

Prefixes

Prefixes indicate the number of carbon atoms in the longest chain of a hydrocarbon as follows:

meth-	1
eth-	2
prop-	3
but-	4
pent-	5
hex-	6

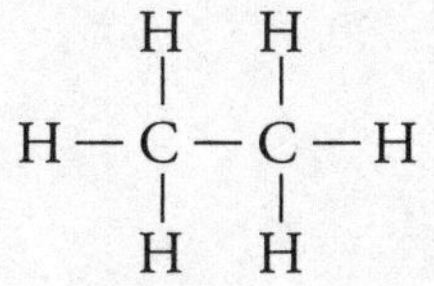

Ethane 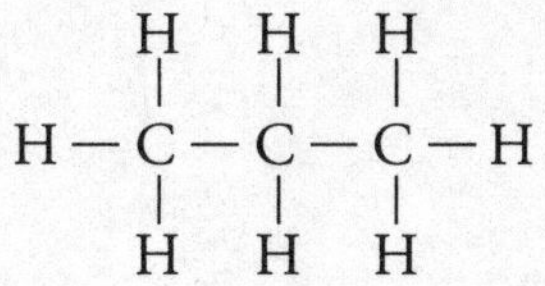   Propane

Alkenes

Alkenes are hydrocarbons that contain at least one double bond. They are said to be unsaturated hydrocarbons because each carbon atom is not bonded to as many atoms as possible—the two or more carbons double bonded to one another could theoretically instead bond to other H atoms, for example.

Alkene (C_nH_{2n}) Formula

Ethylene	C_2H_4
Propene	C_3H_6
Butene	C_4H_8
Pentene	C_5H_{10}

Suffixes

Suffixes of hydrocarbons indicate what types of carbon-carbon bonds are present as follows:

-ane	all single bonds
-ene	at least 1 double bond
-yne	at least 1 triple bond

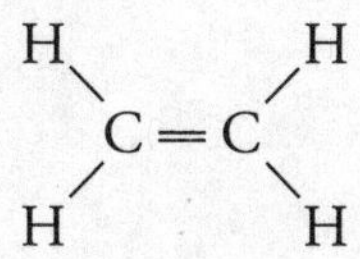

Ethylene 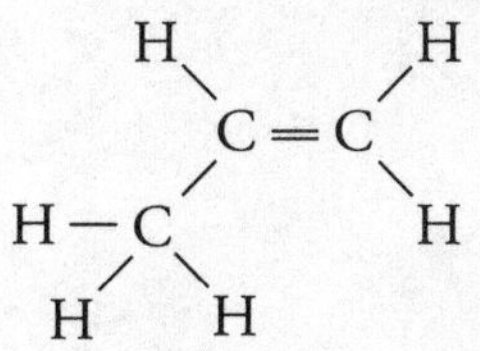   Propene

Alkynes

Alkynes are hydrocarbons that contain triple bonds; they are also unsaturated hydrocarbons.

Alkyne (C_nH_{2n-2}) Formula

Ethyne C_2H_2
Propyne C_3H_4
Butyne C_4H_6
Pentyne C_5H_8

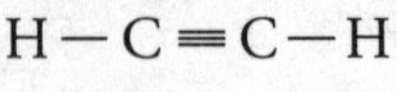

$$H-C \equiv C-H \qquad H-C \equiv C-\overset{\displaystyle H}{\underset{\displaystyle H}{C}}-H$$

Ethyne 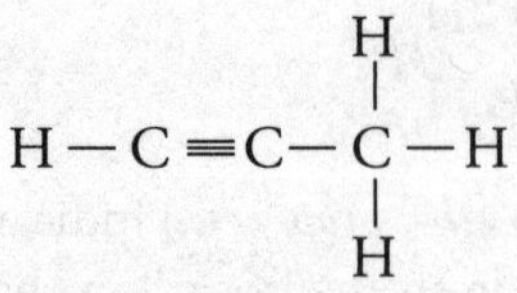   **Propyne**

Hydrocarbon Rings

Many hydrocarbons form rings instead of chains. One of the most important classes of these compounds is the **aromatic hydrocarbons,** the simplest of which is benzene, C_6H_6.

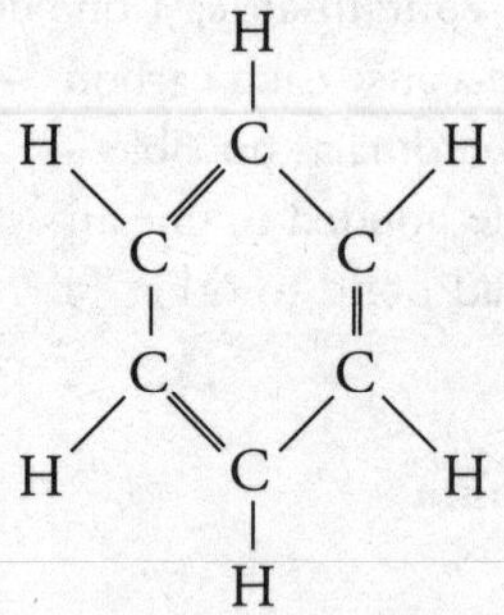

Benzene

Functional Groups

The presence of certain groups of atoms, called functional groups, in organic compounds can give the compounds specific chemical properties.

Name	Description	Naming	Example
Alcohol	An O–H bonded to a carbon atom. Because of hydroxyl (–OH) group, alcohols are polar	-ol e.g., methanol (1 carbon) ethanol (2 carbons)	Methanol $$\begin{array}{c} H \\ | \\ H-C-O-H \\ | \\ H \end{array}$$
Halides	Halogen bonded to a carbon atom	Can be named by suffixes: fluoride, chloride, bromide, iodide—or prefixes: fluoro, chloro, bromo e.g., fluoromethane, carbon tetrachloride	Chloromethane $$\begin{array}{c} H \\ | \\ H-C-Cl \\ | \\ H \end{array}$$
Organic acids, or carboxylic acids	A carboxyl group (COOH) bonded to a carbon chain; the H dissociates, making these molecules acidic	-ic acid e.g., formic acid, acetic acid	Acetic acid $$\begin{array}{ccc} H & & O \\ | & & \| \\ H-C-&C& \\ | & & \diagdown \\ H & & O-H \end{array}$$
Amines	An amine (NH_2) bonded to a carbon atom; the amine group is similar to ammonia (NH_3), and thus these molecules are basic	-amine e.g., methylamine, ethylamine	Methylamine $$\begin{array}{ccc} H & & H \\ | & & \diagup \\ H-C-&N& \\ | & & \diagdown \\ H & & H \end{array}$$
Aldehydes	A carbonyl (C=O) group bonded to a terminal carbon, or a carbon that is at the end of the carbon chain	-aldehyde e.g., formaldehyde (1 carbon), acetaldehyde (2 carbons)	Acetaldehye $$\begin{array}{ccc} H & O \\ | & \| \\ H-C-C-H \\ | \\ H \end{array}$$
Ketones	A carbonyl (C=O) group that is bonded to a nonterminal carbon, or one that is not at the end of the carbon chain	-one e.g., acetone (2-propanone), hexanone	Acetone $$\begin{array}{ccccc} H & O & H \\ | & \| & | \\ H-C-C-C-H \\ | & & | \\ H & & H \end{array}$$

Ethers	An oxygen atom links two hydrocarbon chains	ether e.g., dimethyl ether, diethyl ether	Dimethyl ether
Esters	An ester is essentially a ketone and an ether put together	-ate e.g., methyl formate	Methyl formate

Organic Reactions

You should be familiar with a handful of organic reactions, so study the reactions below carefully.

Addition—In an addition reaction, a carbon-carbon double bond is converted into a single bond, freeing each of the two carbons to bond with another element. Also in an addition reaction, a triple bond can be converted into a double bond.

Substitution—In a substitution reaction, one atom or group in a compound is replaced with another atom or group. Chemically, this very rarely happens (i.e., direct replacement of H).

Polymerization—In polymerization, two smaller compounds, called *monomers,* are joined to form a larger third compound. In condensation polymerization, two monomers are joined in a reaction that produces water.

Cracking—In cracking, a larger compound is broken down into smaller compounds.

Combustion—When a hydrocarbon is exposed to oxygen and a spark is provided, a combustion reaction will occur. The spark is necessary in order to make sure the reactants can overcome the activation energy barrier. As combustion reactions are always exothermic, once the reaction begins, enough heat is generated to ensure the remaining reactants have enough energy to overcome that barrier.

The products of a combustion reaction are always carbon dioxide and water. One example is the combustion of butane, C_4H_{10}:

$$C_4H_{10}(l) + \frac{13}{2}O_2(g) \rightarrow 4CO_2(g) + 5H_2O(g)$$

When looking at some of the stoichiometry here, it's important to understand that in a combustion reaction, the hydrocarbon will always be the limiting reactant. After all, there's plenty of oxygen in our atmosphere!

Thus, all of the carbon originally present in the hydrocarbon ends up in the CO_2, in a 1:1 ratio. So, for every mole of carbon present in the hydrocarbon one mole of CO_2 will be produced. In the above example, every mole of butane contains four moles of carbon, and so four moles of CO_2 are produced. All of the hydrogen present in the original hydrocarbon will be in a 2:1 ratio with the water. For every two moles of hydrogen that are produced, one mole of water (which itself contains two moles of hydrogen) will be produced.

One way this concept could be tested is in the following example:

A hydrocarbon is combusted, producing 88 g of carbon dioxide and 54 g of water. What is the original formula of the hydrocarbon?

The way to solve this is to figure out how many moles of carbon and hydrogen are present in the products. Carbon dioxide has a molar mass of 44 g/mol, so 88 g of it represents two moles of carbon dioxide, and thus two moles of carbon. Water's molar mass of 18 g/mol means that 54 g of it represent six moles of hydrogen (remember, there are two moles of hydrogen in every mole of water). Thus, the original formula of the hydrocarbon is C_2H_6.

Esterification—In esterification, an organic acid reacts with an alcohol to produce an ester and water.

The Four Major Groups of Biomolecules

Four important types of organic molecules that you'll hear a lot about if you go into the fields of biochemistry (for instance, if you're planning on being pre-med in college) or biology are lipids, carbohydrates, nucleic acids, and proteins. All of these biomolecules are carbon compounds, and each of them is characterized by different functional groups, which gives them different functions in the human body.

Lipids

Lipids are made up of carbon, hydrogen, and oxygen atoms, connected in long branching chains. The most common examples of lipids are fats and oils. One group of lipids commonly talked about in biology is the **triglycerides**. Triglycerides are made up of three long fatty acid chains (long hydrocarbon chains) attached to a head group that consists of a molecule of glycerol. (No need to know the structure of glycerol for the test.) The molecules that make up cell walls are a type of lipid, specifically known as phospholipids. And one final note about lipids: lipids are not water-soluble and tend to aggregate to form droplets when placed in water.

Carbohydrates

Carbohydrates are also known as sugars; they are organic compounds that contain carbon, hydrogen, and oxygen, usually in a ratio of 1:2:1. They are polymers made up of sugar monomers. Some simple types of carbohydrates are glucose and fructose, for example. Both of these are examples of monosaccharides, carbohydrates made up of just one unit of sugar. Larger sugars, called polysaccharides, are the energy storage units in both plants and animals—the storage carbohydrate of animals is glycogen, and the storage carbohydrate of plants is cellulose. Carbohydrates can be straight chains of these sugar monomers, or they can be extensively branched.

Nucleic Acids

Nucleic acids contain carbon, hydrogen, oxygen, nitrogen, and phosphorus. They are polymers made up of monomers known as nucleotides. There are two major nucleic acids: DNA (which you've probably heard of, stands for deoxyribonucleic acid) and RNA (you might have heard of this type of nucleic acid too—ribonucleic acid). **DNA** is the genetic material of all living things; it contains the blueprints for all life.

Proteins

Proteins are polymers that are made up of amino acid monomers. All amino acids have two functional groups in common—an amino group (remember, $-NH_2$) and a carboxyl group ($-COOH$). This means that they are amphoteric and can act as either an acid or a base. All of the 20 different amino acid monomers that make up proteins differ in their side chain or R group. Chains of linked amino acids are known as **polypeptides**, and proteins are formed by the folding of the polypeptide chains (and oftentimes the association of one or more polypeptide chains). Recall our discussion of catalysts: all **enzymes**, which are biological catalysts that speed up the rate of nearly all cellular reactions, are proteins.

Okay, that's it for organic chemistry—let's briefly review what you'll need to know about environmental chemistry and then wrap up this chapter!

ENVIRONMENTAL CHEMISTRY

Here we'll cover three main topics that fall under the broad category of environmental chemistry: Earth's atmosphere, the greenhouse effect, and the causes and effects of acid rain.

The Chemistry of Earth's Atmosphere

For this test, you should remember that Earth's atmosphere is about 78% nitrogen, 20% oxygen, less than 1% argon, and then contains a trace amount of the following other elements: carbon dioxide, neon, helium, methane, krypton, hydrogen, nitrous oxide, and xenon. While the test won't ask you about the trace elements of the atmosphere, it could ask you about its major components. The atmosphere is divided into four regions: the **troposphere,** which is the layer of the atmosphere that's closest to the Earth; the **stratosphere,** which is the layer above the troposphere; the **mesosphere,** which is further out; and then the **thermosphere,** which is the furthest out of all.

Atmospheric Composition	
Nitrogen (N_2)	78%
Oxygen (O_2)	20%
Argon (Ar)	< 1%
Water Vapor	variable
Other	< 1%

One molecular component of the atmosphere that you should be aware of is **ozone,** O_3, which you've probably heard about before in conjunction with global warming. Ozone is the result of the collision of elemental oxygen, O, and diatomic oxygen, O_2. But how come oxygen can exist in the atmosphere in elemental form, if it's supposed to be one of those diatomic molecules? Well, O is produced in the atmosphere in the following reaction:

$$O_2(g) + h\gamma = 2O(g)$$

This type of reaction is called **photodissociation**—in photodissociation, a bond is broken as a molecule absorbs a photon of light energy.

In the next step in the production of ozone, elemental oxygen and diatomic oxygen collide.

$$O(g) + O_2(g) \rightarrow O_3(g)$$

Atmospheric ozone absorbs solar radiation and decomposes back to elemental and diatomic oxygen. If ozone didn't absorb this high-energy radiation, the damaging rays would reach the planet and destroy much of its plant and animal life. Certain chemicals produced by humans are thought to be responsible for the gradual degradation of the ozone layer. The primary culprits in ozone layer destruction are chlorofluorocarbons, also known as CFCs, which have been created for use as propellants in spray cans and car air conditioners. Chlorofluorocarbons react with light energy to form, among other compounds, free chlorine. This chlorine reacts with ozone to form chlorine monoxide, ClO, and oxygen. The fact that ozone is a reactant in this chemical reaction means that it is slowly being consumed; Earth's atmosphere is slowly being robbed of its protective ozone layer.

The Greenhouse Effect

Another environmental topic that's hotly debated in the news is the greenhouse effect. In short, the **greenhouse effect** refers to the buildup of carbon dioxide, CO_2, and other greenhouse gases in the atmosphere. Greenhouse gases are the result of the combustion of fossil fuels such as coal and oil; they absorb infrared radiation that reflects off the Earth from the Sun, effectively trapping it in the atmosphere and creating an effect much like that in a greenhouse (hence the name).

Acid Rain

More Fascinating Facts
Many nonmetal oxides, e.g., SO_3, N_2O_2, CO_2, produce acids when dissolved in water. The dilution (addition of water) of concentrated sulfuric acid, H_2SO_4, is a highly exothermic reaction.

The SAT Subject Test in Chemistry might also expect you to know a little something about what acid rain is and how it's formed. By definition, **acid rain** is rain that has an abnormally low pH due to the presence of certain oxides, which are pollutants produced by human activities. One of the most prevalent classes of oxide pollutants is the sulfur oxides, in the form SO_2. SO_2 is produced when coal and oil are combusted and can react with either ozone or diatomic oxygen to form SO_3. In turn, SO_3 reacts with rainwater to produce sulfuric acid, in the following reaction:

$$SO_3(g) + H_2O(l) \rightarrow H_2SO_4(aq)$$

Other oxides that also contribute to the production of acid rain are the nitrogen oxides, which combine with water to form nitric acid.

Acid rain is harmful to buildings and other structures because it reacts with metals and is corrosive. It's also harmful for organisms that live in ponds and lakes; most natural ponds and lakes have a pH of about 7, which is neutral, and a drop in pH has many negative effects on the inhabitants of these bodies of water. In fact, the fall of acid rain has significantly reduced the number of fish and other aquatic organisms in many polluted areas of the world.

Carbon Monoxide

The last air pollutant that you'll need to know about for this test is carbon monoxide, CO. Carbon monoxide is found in car exhaust and cigarette smoke and can be dangerous for humans because it binds irreversibly to hemoglobin, the biomolecule that is responsible for transporting oxygen around the body through the bloodstream.

Okay, we're done with environmental chemistry—now read through the laboratory chapter, and you'll be all set to take the practice exams at the back of the book.

DRILL 1

Question Type A

Questions 1–4 refer to the following.

(A) Esters
(B) Alkenes
(C) Ketones
(D) Halides
(E) Amines

1. Contain no atoms with lone pairs

2. In solution, have a pH greater than 7

3. Contain a nonterminal carbonyl group

4. Can contain fluorine atoms

Question Type B

<u>I</u>   <u>II</u>

101.   The depletion of ozone   BECAUSE   elemental chlorine reacts
       in our atmosphere   with ozone to create
       is caused by   chlorine monoxide.
       photodissociation

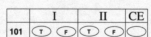

102.   Enzymes speed up   BECAUSE   polysaccharides can store
       the rate of biological   large amounts of energy.
       reactions

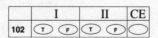

Question Type C

24. $C_6H_{12}O_6 \rightarrow 2C_2H_5OH + 2CO_2$

    The above is an example of which type of reaction?

    (A) Addition
    (B) Polymerization
    (C) Esterification
    (D) Fermentation
    (E) Substitution

25. Which of the following chemicals leads to the production of acid rain?

    (A) CO
    (B) CO_2
    (C) SO
    (D) SO_2
    (E) Cl_2

26. Choose the option that correctly lists the layers of Earth's atmosphere from lowest in altitude (nearest to Earth's surface) to highest:

    (A) Troposphere < Stratosphere < Mesosphere < Thermosphere
    (B) Stratosphere < Mesosphere < Troposphere < Thermosphere
    (C) Thermosphere < Troposphere < Mesosphere < Stratosphere
    (D) Troposphere < Mesosphere < Thermosphere < Stratosphere
    (E) Thermosphere > Mesosphere < Stratosphere < Troposphere

Summary

o Organic chemistry is the study of carbon compounds, and environmental chemistry is chemistry of the environment.

o Organic compounds are nonpolar so they don't dissolve in water.

o Isomers are compounds that have the same chemical formula (same number and ratios of atoms) but a different geometrical arrangement of atoms.

o A hydrocarbon is a compound made of hydrogen and carbon.
  - Alkanes are hydrocarbons with only single bonds, alkenes are hydrocarbons with at least one double bond, and alkynes are hydrocarbons with at least one triple bond.
  - Aromatic hydrocarbons are six carbon rings with alternating double bonds. The most common is benzene.

o Functional groups are groups of certain atoms that give organic compounds certain chemical properties.

o The name of an organic compound is given by a prefix that determines the number of carbon atoms and a suffix that gives the functional group.

o The most common functional groups are alcohol (–OH), amine (–NH$_2$), halides (–F/Cl/Br/I), carboxylic acids (COOH), aldehydes and ketones (C=O), ethers (C-O-C), and esters (COO).

o The major types of organic reactions are addition, substitution, polymerization, cracking, combustion, esterification, and fermentation.

o The four major types of biomolecules are lipids, carbohydrates, nucleic acids, and proteins.

o Earth's atmosphere is about 78% nitrogen, 20% oxygen, and less than 1% argon. Carbon dioxide, neon, helium, methane, krypton, hydrogen, nitrous oxide, and xenon are also present in trace amounts.

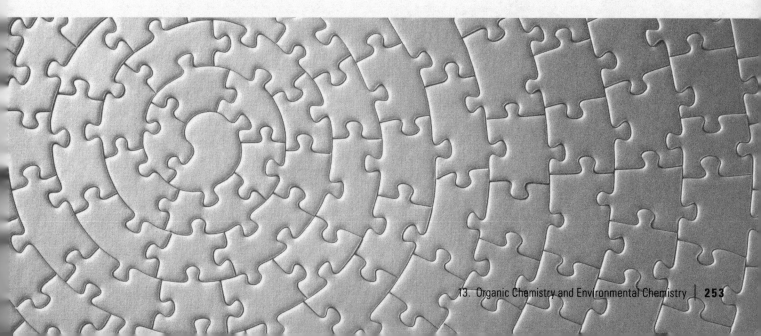

o   Ozone, O_3, protects Earth by absorbing high-energy radiation from the Sun. It is destroyed by chlorofluorocarbons released into the atmosphere by spray cans and car air conditioners.

o   The greenhouse effect refers to the buildup of CO_2 and other carbon gases in the atmosphere. As Earth's surface absorbs solar radiation, it warms and radiates infrared radiation back into the atmosphere. The extra CO_2 reflects and traps this radiation, causing Earth to warm.

o   Nitrogen and sulfur oxides produced by pollution interact with water in the atmosphere to produce acid rain, which is harmful to organisms and human-made structures.

o   The products of a hydrocarbon combustion are carbon dioxide and water, and they can be stoichiometrically linked to the formula of the hydrocarbon.

Chapter 14
Laboratory

Laboratory procedures make up a relatively small part of the test. Among the things you should know are how to ensure accuracy, how to calculate significant figures, some basic methods of separation, and some of the more common experimental apparatuses and set-ups.

SAFETY RULES

- Always wear safety goggles in the laboratory.
- Always work with good ventilation; many common chemicals are toxic.
- Take extra care when working with an open flame.
- When diluting an acid, always add the acid to the water to avoid spattering the acid solution.
- When heating substances, do it slowly. When you heat things too quickly, they can spatter, burn, or explode.

ACCURACY

- When titrating, rinse the buret not with water but with the solution to be used in the titration. If you rinse the buret with water, you might dilute the solution, which will cause the volume added from the buret to be too large.
- Allow hot objects to return to room temperature before weighing them. Hot objects on a scale create convection currents that may make the object seem lighter than it is.
- Don't weigh reagents directly on a scale. Use a glass or porcelain container to prevent corrosion of the balance pan.
- Don't contaminate your chemicals. Never insert another piece of equipment into a bottle containing a chemical. Instead you should always pour the chemical into another clean container. Also, don't let the inside of the stopper for a bottle containing a chemical touch another surface.
- When mixing chemicals, stir slowly to ensure even distribution.
- Be conscious of significant figures when you record your results. The number of significant figures that you use should indicate the accuracy of your results.

SIGNIFICANT FIGURES

When you do calculations based on measurements that you take in the lab, your answers can be only as precise as the measurements that you took. The way to make sure all your calculations reflect the precision of your measurements is to be aware of significant figures (or significant digits). The more significant figures in the numbers you use, the more precise your answer will be. The number of significant figures you use will be determined by the precision of your measuring device.

The following are rules for recognizing and calculating with significant figures.

- Nonzero digits and zeros between nonzero digits are significant.

    362   3 significant figures

    4.609   4 significant figures

    103.06   5 significant figures

- Zeros to the left of the first nonzero digit in a number are not significant.

    0.004   1 significant figure

    0.0802   3 significant figures

- Zeros at the end of a number to the right of the decimal point are significant.

    67.000   5 significant figures

    0.030   2 significant figures

    2.0   2 significant figures

- Zeros at the end of a number greater than 1 are not significant, unless their significance is indicated by the presence of a decimal point.

    2,600   2 significant figures

    2,600.   4 significant figures

    50   1 significant figure

    50.   2 significant figures

- The coefficients of a balanced equation and numbers obtained by counting objects are infinitely significant. So if a balanced equation calls for 3 moles of carbon, we can think of it as 3.00 moles of carbon.

When multiplying and dividing, the result should have the same number of significant figures as the number in the calculation that has the smallest number of significant figures.

$$0.352 \times 0.90876 = 0.320$$

$$864 \times 12 = 1.0 \times 10^4$$

$$7.0 \times 0.567 = 12$$

When adding and subtracting, the result should have the same number of decimal places as the number in the calculation that has the smallest number of decimal places.

$$26 + 45.88 + 0.09534 = 72$$

$$780 + 35 + 4 = 819$$

Remember: *The result of a calculation cannot be more accurate than the least accurate number in the calculation.*

And one more thing to remember for test day. Accurate and precise do NOT mean the same thing! **Accuracy** is a measure of how correct a measurement is, compared to some standard, while **precision** is a measure of how exact a measurement is, compared to the real value of the measurement.

LAB PROCEDURES

Methods of Separation

Filtration—In filtration, solids are separated from liquids as the mixture is passed through a filter. Typically, porous paper is used as the filter. To find the amount of solid that is filtered out of a mixture, the filter paper containing the solid is allowed to dry and is then weighed. The initial weight of the clean, dry filter is then subtracted from the weight of the dried filter paper and solid.

Distillation—In distillation, the differences in the boiling points of liquids can be used to separate them. The temperature of the mixture is raised to a temperature that is greater than the boiling point of the more volatile substance and lower than the boiling point of the less volatile substance. The more volatile substance will vaporize, leaving the less volatile substance as a liquid.

Chromatography—In chromatography, substances are separated by the differences in the degree to which they are adsorbed onto a surface. The substances are passed over the adsorbing surface, and the ones that stick to the surface with greater attraction will move more slowly than the substances that are less attracted to the surface. This difference in speeds is what separates the substances.

How much a substance moves depends on the similarity of its intermolecular forces to those of the adsorbing surface. The more similar the IMFs are between the substance and surface, the slower they will move. This is the "like dissolves like" concept all over again. If a polar substance is passed over a polar adsorbing surface, it won't move far, as it will be very attracted to the surface. However, a nonpolar substance would travel much further over a polar adsorbing surface, due to the lack of attraction between the substance and the surface.

Titration

Titration is one of the most important laboratory procedures. In titration, an acid-base neutralization reaction is used to find the concentration of an unknown acid or base. It takes exactly 1 mole of hydroxide ions (base) to neutralize 1 mole of hydrogen ions (acid), so the concentration of an unknown acid solution can be found by finding out how much of a known basic solution is required to neutralize a sample of given volume. The most important formula in titration experiments is derived from the definition of molarity.

At the equivalence point,

$$\text{moles}_{(\text{acid})} = \text{moles}_{(\text{base})}$$

which means that

$$\text{molarity}_{(\text{acid})} \times \text{volume}_{(\text{acid})} = \text{molarity}_{(\text{base})} \times \text{volume}_{(\text{base})}$$

The moment when exactly enough base has been added to the sample to neutralize the acid present is called the equivalence point. In the lab, an indicator is used to tell when the equivalence point has been reached. An indicator is a substance that is one color in acid solution and a different color in basic solution. Two popular indicators are **phenolphthalein,** which is clear in acidic solution and pink in basic solution; and **litmus,** which is pink in acidic solution and blue in basic solution.

Identifying Chemicals

Precipitation—Unknown ions in solution can be identified by precipitation. If you know which salts are soluble and which are insoluble, you can use POE to identify unknown ions in solution. For instance, nearly all salts containing chlorine are soluble, but silver chloride is not; if you put chloride ions into a solution and a precipitate is formed, silver ions were probably present in the solution.

Conduction—You can tell whether a solution contains ions or not by checking to see if the solution conducts electricity. Ionic solutes conduct electricity in solution; nonionic solutes do not.

Flame Tests—Certain chemicals burn with distinctly colored flames. This is especially true of the alkali metals and the alkaline earth metals. It's a good idea to know which colors salts of certain metals burn.

Red	Lithium, Strontium
Orange	Calcium
Yellow	Sodium
Green	Barium
Violet	Potassium

Colored Solutions—The color of a solution will sometimes indicate which chemicals are present. For instance, the colors of solutions containing transition metals will vary depending on the element present. Some common solution colors for transition metal ions that may be useful to know are:

Copper (Cu^{2+})	Blue
Nickel (Ni^{2+})	Green
Cobalt (Co^{2+})	Pink
Iron (Fe^{3+})	Yellow
Chromate (CrO_4^-)	Yellow
Dichromate ($Cr_2O_7^{2-}$)	Orange
Permanganate (MnO_4^-)	Deep Purple

Gas Evolution—When we want to measure the amount of gas that is evolved in a reaction, we use a device called a manometer. The reaction takes place in an Erlenmeyer flask, which is hooked up to a U-shaped tube filled partially with mercury. As the reaction proceeds and the gas is produced, the pressure increases. This causes the mercury in the tube to rise. We can tell what the change in pressure inside the flask is by how much the mercury in the tube rises. In the diagram of the manometer below, you can see the difference between the mercury level in each end of the tube is 760 mm. Thus, the pressure would be read as 760 mmHg. Note that the use of mercury in manometers has become considerably more rare over time due to mercury's toxicity. However, even if another liquid is used to fill the tube, the concept remains the same.

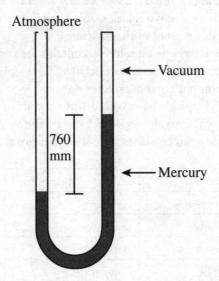

Another way to test for the evolution of flammable gases in particular is through the splint test. If you light the end of a wooden splint and place it over the end of a test tube where a flammable gas is being produced, the splint will combust and make a popping sound. This type of test is particularly useful for determining the presence of hydrogen or oxygen gas, as both are flammable.

Calorimetry—This is how we determine how much heat is produced by or absorbed by a reaction, i.e., ΔH. A calorimeter consists of a very well insulated container in which the reaction of known amounts of reactants occurs. A thermometer measures the temperature change of either the compounds involved in the reaction, or some other substance, which absorbs/provides the heat for the reaction. The temperature change of this substance, along with its mass and specific heat, allows us to calculate the amount of heat produced or absorbed by the reaction:

$$Q = mc\Delta T$$

See pages 31–32 for examples.

LABORATORY EQUIPMENT

The pictures below show some standard chemistry lab equipment.

Beaker	Used to hold and pour liquids—also your favorite muppet.
Buret	Used to add small but precisely measured volumes of liquid to a solution, used frequently in titration experiments.
Burner	Used to apply heat and to wake up sleeping AP Chemistry students.
Crucible tongs	Used to handle objects that are too hot to touch (careful though, they can break test tubes!).
Dropper pipette	Used to add small amounts of liquid to a solution, but only when a precise volume is not needed because the drops themselves should be consistent only for one particular dropper (i.e., adding an indicator, comparing the amount of drops of strong acid or base needed for a pH change in different solutions).

	Erlenmeyer flask	A flask used for heating liquids. The conic shape allows stirring.
	Evaporating dish	Used to hold liquids for evaporation. The wide mouth allows vapor to escape.
	Florence flask	Used for boiling liquids. The small neck prevents excessive evaporation and splashing.
	Forceps	A fancy name for tweezers.
	Funnel	Used to get liquids into a smaller container. Doubles as a cute hat when inverted.
	Graduated cylinder	Used for precisely measuring a volume of liquid to be poured all at once (rather than dripped from a buret).

Metal spatula	Used to scoop and transport powders.
Mortar and pestle	Used to grind solids into powders suitable for dissolving or mixing.
Pipette bulb	Rubber bulb used to draw liquid into pipette. In a pinch could be used as a miniature clown nose.
Platform balance (triple beam)	A very precise scale operated by moving a set of three weights (typically corresponding to 100, 10, and 1 gram increments). A measurement will proceed like this: Rear weight is in the notch reading 30 g Middle weight is in the notch reading 200 g Front beam weight reads 3.86 g The sample weighs 200 + 30 + 3.86 = 233.86 g
Ring clamp	Used to hold funnels or other vessels in conjunction with a stand.
Rubber policeman	A hard-tipped rubber scraper used to transfer precipitate.
Safety goggles	Used by chemists worldwide to protect their eyes during all laboratory experiments.

Test tube	Used to contain samples, especially when heating.
Thermometer	Measures temperature of a solution (don't use these to measure your body temperature, you don't know where they've been).
Volumetric Flask 100 ml	This is a flask that is used to measure an exact volume of liquid. They generally come in sizes that are very round numbers—100 mL, 250 mL, 500 mL, etc.
Volumetric pipette	A volumetric pipette, like a volumetric flask, is used to measure out an exact volume of liquid. The primary difference between the pipette and the flask is the pipette is usually used to measure out smaller volumes (such as 10 mL or 25 mL).

Measuring Liquids

As you can see from the table above, there are a lot of different types of glassware that can be used to read fluid volumes, and it's important to know when to use each type.

For measuring an exact volume (25 mL, 50 mL, 100 mL, etc.) of a solution, it's best to use either a volumetric pipet or a volumetric flask. Both of these pieces of glassware are considered to be infinitely accurate when it comes to measuring out the volume they are calibrated to. The downside is that they can only measure out one specific volume.

For an accurate reading of a volume that is not a common volumetric flask or pipet size (say, 11.7 mL), you would use a buret. These are not as accurate as volumetric glassware, but are still considered to be the most accurate way to measure non-specific volumes.

For a fairly accurate reading of a volume, a graduated cylinder is also a good choice. While graduated cylinders are not as accurate as burets, they are much easier and faster to use. They also cost quite a bit less than a typical buret!

Finally, normal (non-volumetric) flasks and beakers should never be used to measure volumes. If you have a 250 mL beaker and there appears to be 50 mL of liquid in there, that reading can be as off by as much as 10 mL. Beakers and flasks are great for storing solutions, but their graduations should never be trusted to give accurate volume readings.

YOU'RE READY!

If you've gone through this whole book, answered our questions (don't forget the ones at the end of this chapter!), and read our explanations along the way, you're going to do well on the SAT Subject Test in Chemistry. Next, take our practice tests. If you like, you can also take assorted practice questions from actual SAT Subject Tests in Chemistry that the College Board has released.

Will there be some questions you can't answer? Of course—but that's okay. Use our elimination strategies and guess from among the choices that remain, and there will be so many questions that you can answer, you won't be bothered by the few that you have to guess. We've taught you all the chemistry you need, so go to it, and good luck! Now here's your final drill before the practice tests.

DRILL 1

Question Type A

Questions 1–4 refer to the following:

(A) Ethanol
(B) Phenolphthalein
(C) Ba(NO$_3$)$_2$
(D) Litmus
(E) U-tube manometer

1. Will glow green when flamed

2. Commonly isolated by distillation

3. Can be used to demonstrate that gasses pressurize when heated

4. Blue in basic solution

Question Type B

I		II
_I_		_II_

101. In an acidic solution being titrated with NaOH, equivalence has been passed when the phenolphthalein indicator turns slightly pink   BECAUSE   a nearly equal volume of NaOH solution and acid has been added.

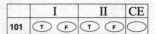

102. When distilled, hexane will evaporate before pentane   BECAUSE   pentane has more vapor pressure than hexane.

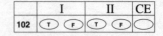

Question Type C

24. To the correct number of significant figures, what is the mass of 2.5 moles deuterium gas (isotope mass = 2.014 amu)?

   (A) 5.035 g
   (B) 5.0 g
   (C) 5.04 g
   (D) 1.241 g
   (E) 1.3 g

25. A NaOH solution is titrated with HCl. The resulting neutral solution is evaporated over a burner and the resulting crystalline solid is burned in a strong flame. The flame will likely be

   (A) extinguished
   (B) yellow
   (C) orange
   (D) green
   (E) clear

Summary

- Be sure to exercise proper safety procedures at all times.

- Make sure that all measurements are made carefully, that all equipment is clean, and that all chemicals are uncontaminated.

- When recording measurements, make sure to use the proper number of significant figures.

- Filtration, distillation, and chromatography are common methods of separation.

- In a titration, an indicator is used to determine when the equivalence point has been reached.

- Precipitation reactions, conduction, flame tests, and colored solutions can all indicate what chemicals are present in a solution or reaction.

- A manometer is used to measure gases in a gaseous reaction.

- A calorimeter is used to measure heat produced by a reaction.

- Different types of glassware can be used to measure volume. From most precise to least precise they are: volumetric glassware (flasks and pipets) > burets > graduated cylinders > beakers and Earlenmeyer flasks.

Part IV
Drill
Answers and
Explanations

CHAPTER 3: SOME BASIC STUFF

Drill 1 (Pages 34–36)

1. **A** If you chose "mass" or "density" just because those words appeared in the question, you fell for the temptation trap. The test writers wanted you to do this. To answer this question correctly, you have to think carefully about what the words mean, and you must not rush to an answer simply because an answer choice contains a word that reminds you of something.

   Let's work through this. If you're given a sample of some substance, and you know the density of the substance, what additional information would allow you to calculate the mass? If you know its density, then you know the ratio of mass/volume. Therefore, if you were also provided with the sample's volume, you could figure out its mass. That's why (A) is right.

2. **E** You're asked to determine which quantity or property always varies with the number of molecules in a given sample of a substance. You have the knowledge to answer this question, so don't let the wording throw you.

   Think about what you know; mass is a measure of the quantity of matter. This means that for any sample of a particular substance, mass always varies with the number of molecules in the sample. More molecules of substance X have a greater mass than fewer molecules of substance X.

   What about volume, temperature, density, and pressure? Volume, (A), is a measure of the space a sample occupies. The volume of a substance might vary as the number of molecules of that substance is varied; however, it does not *have* to change with the number of molecules. This is certainly true in the case of gases: a rigid container (with a fixed volume) may hold vastly different amounts of the same gas because gases are expandable and compressible.

   Changing the amount of a substance will not raise its temperature, (B). By remembering the formula for density, (C), *(d = m/v)*, we see that the density of a substance will remain the same despite an increase or decrease in the mass of a substance, if the volume is changed in direct proportion to the change in mass. The pressure, (D), exerted on a solid or liquid will remain the same, regardless of the number of molecules of the substance. The pressure of a gas in a closed container will change with an increase or decrease in mass, but if the volume of the container holding the gas is increased or decreased as the mass changes, the pressure will not change.

3. **C** Kilograms are used to represent mass, and liters are used to represent volume. Mass/volume = density, so (C) is correct.

4. **B** If you remembered to associate temperature with average kinetic energy, you knew that (B) was correct.

101. **T, F** Divide and conquer! First, examine each statement separately, and determine whether it's true or false.

Is the first statement true? Yes, it is, although you might not realize at first. But because

$$density = \frac{mass}{volume}$$

simple algebra allows you to calculate mass, if you know density and volume.

mass = (density)(volume)

Now look at statement II, and decide whether it's true or false. What does the statement mean? For a bigger piece of some substance, the relationship between mass and volume is different than it is for a smaller piece of that same substance. That's false. For any substance, the relationship between mass and volume is given by the density of the substance. For solids and liquids, density does not change with sample size.

102. **F, T** Again, divide and conquer. Look at the first statement. Is it true? For solids and liquids, volume can increase somewhat by heating the substance, even while the mass remains constant. The volume of a constant amount of gas can also be increased by heating or cooling the gas, or by simply placing the gas in a larger container. Therefore, the statement is false.

Look at the second statement. Does density represent mass per volume? Yes, it does. The second statement is true. Since one of the statements is false, you leave the CE oval blank.

103. **F, F** Divide and conquer. Since you do not know the temperature of X or Y, you cannot say which 10-g sample has more heat content, so statement I is false.

Consider statement II. A substance with a relatively low specific heat will undergo a relatively large temperature change upon the addition of heat, so statement II is false. Don't fill in the CE oval.

24. **E** Don't even look at the answer options until you really understand the situation that's being described. You've got two objects. They occupy the same volume, but one has half the density of the other. Since

$$density = \frac{mass}{volume}$$

you know that this means that the object with less density has one-half the mass of the object with greater density.

Object A has twice the density, so it should have twice the mass of an equal volume of object B. That's why (E) is right.

25. **C** Remember $q = mc\Delta T$? Substituting the values into it gives

$$30 \text{ cal} = (15 \text{ g})(0.5 \text{ cal/g} \cdot °C) \Delta T$$

Solve for ΔT, and you'll get 4°C. This is the increase in temperature. So if the substance was at 30°C, it's now at 34°C. That's (C).

26. **E** Adding more oxygen gas will certainly increase the mass of the gas sample; therefore, statement I is true.

Since density is the ratio of mass per volume, increasing the mass while maintaining the same volume will increase the density of the gas, so statement II is also true.

Pressure is a measure of the force per unit area with which gas molecules collide with the walls of the vessel. More gas occupying the same volume will mean more collisions and, therefore, greater pressure. So statements I, II, and III are true, and (E) is the answer.

Notice that even if you don't know if all of the statements are true, you can make a really good guess with just a little knowledge. Just knowing that statement I is true allows you to eliminate (B) and (D), and by knowing that statement II is also true, you can rule out (A). At this point, you have a 50 percent chance of choosing the right answer even if you know nothing about pressure!

CHAPTER 4: ATOMS: THE BUILDING BLOCKS OF MATTER

Drill 1 (Pages 87–89)

4. **A** Helium is an element, and the smallest piece of an element is an atom. That's why (A) is correct. An atom is the smallest particle of an element that still retains the properties of that element.

5. **E** You know that every electron carries a charge of –1, and that an atom becomes a positively charged ion when it loses an electron(s), and a negatively charged ion when it gains an electron. That's why (E) is correct.

6. **D** Which of the components of the nucleus—protons or neutrons—have a positive charge? Protons have a positive charge, while neutrons have no charge—they are electrically neutral. The answer is (D).

7. **C** Don't be fooled by the mention of uranium; it's just another element. You know that isotopes of the same element do not differ in their number of protons, may differ in their number of electrons, but *must* differ in their number of neutrons. That's why (C) is correct.

8. **D** The atomic number of an element depends on the number of protons in that element's atoms, so the answer must be (D).

105.   **T, T, CE**

Divide and conquer! Evaluate the first statement without looking at the second, and decide whether it's true or false. It's true. The periodic table reports atomic weights but not mass numbers.

Now see if the second statement is true or false. Is it true that a mass number can be assigned only to a single isotope of an element but not to an element in general? Yes. Mass number = number of protons + number of neutrons. Different atoms of the same element may vary as to the number of neutrons they contain. That's what makes them isotopes.

Both statements are true. Now see if this sentence makes sense: "The periodic table does not report mass numbers because a mass number can be assigned to one isotope of an element but not to an element in general." It does, so fill in the oval marked CE.

106. **F, T** Divide and conquer. Look at the first statement on its own, and decide whether it's true or false. Electrons are negatively charged, so if you add an electron to an atom, it becomes a negatively charged ion. This statement is false. Now look at the second statement; is it true? Yes. Electrons are negatively charged. The first statement is false, and the second is true. Do not fill in the CE oval.

27.   **E**   You know the answer, so don't fall into the camouflage trap. The atomic number represents the number of protons in the nucleus, and it gives the atom its identity. Any sodium atom or ion must have, in its nucleus, the same number of protons as any other sodium atom; otherwise it isn't sodium. Both (A) and (B) are wrong because sodium ions can carry different charges, depending on how many electrons they've gained or lost. Choices (C) and (D) are wrong because different isotopes of sodium will differ in the number of neutrons in the nucleus. That means their mass number will differ. But all sodium atoms or ions must have 11 protons in their nuclei. That's why (E) is correct.

28.   **A**   You know what isotopes are—atoms of the same element that differ in their number of neutrons. Isotopes may also differ in their number of electrons. They must differ in their mass numbers since they have different numbers of neutrons. They can't differ in their number of protons, or they wouldn't be atoms of the same element. Choices (B), (C), (D), and (E) are incorrect, and (A) is correct.

29.   **C**   Electrons don't actually orbit the nucleus at fixed distances, although many textbooks use the graphical representation of the Bohr atom because it is difficult to draw the true electron orbitals (first proposed by Heisenberg) as a two-dimensional representation.

CHAPTER 5: CHEMICAL REACTIONS AND STOICHIOMETRY

Drill 1 (Pages 95–97)

1. **D** A diatomic molecule consists of two atoms that are bonded. Among the choices, only nitrogen monoxide (NO) contains just two atoms. Never mind that the atoms are from different elements; it's still a diatomic molecule. The correct answer is (D).

2. **E** First, eliminate the obvious wrong choices: by inspection, you know that N_2O and NO are nowhere near 108 amu, so cross them out. Then you'll need to do some math. Use the periodic table to find the atomic weight of each element in the compounds. Then multiply this mass by the number of that kind of atom in the molecule. Add the mass contributions from each element to get the formula weight. When you do this for (E), you'll get 2(14 amu) + 5(16 amu) = 28 amu + 80 amu = 108 amu. Choice (E) is your answer.

3. **B** Look at the ratios between different types of atoms. If the ratio can be put in terms of smaller whole numbers, then the formula is *not* an empirical formula. Check out (B). In this molecule, the ratio of carbon to hydrogen to oxygen is 6:12:6. If you divide this ratio by 6, you'll get the simpler (though still equivalent) ratio of 1:2:1. So the empirical formula of $C_6H_{12}O_6$ is CH_2O. Since the molecular and empirical formulas differ, this must be the answer.

4. **C** Proceed as you did in question 2. If you are comfortable with your intuitive sense of relative molecular weights, you should be able to eliminate (A) and (E) without doing any calculations. After you get the formula weight for each choice, compare it with the weight contributed by oxygen. Look at (C). The formula weight of SO_3 is 32 amu + 3(16 amu) = 80 amu. Oxygen's percent, by mass, is $\frac{48}{80} \times 100\%$ or 60%. Choice (C) is correct.

101. **T, F** Divide and conquer! Look at the first statement. Is it true or false? Of course it's true. Chlorine is an element. What about statement II? It's false. Remember that chlorine exists in diatomic form at room temperature and atmospheric pressure.

102.   **T, T, CE**

Divide and conquer. Consider statement I. One mole of HBr contains the same number of molecules as one mole of NO_2—6.02×10^{23} molecules—but this doesn't necessarily mean that 6.02×10^{23} HBr molecules weigh the same as 6.02×10^{23} NO_2 molecules. Do ten paper clips weigh the same as ten elephants? Certainly not. Use the periodic table. One molecule of HBr has a mass of about 1 amu + 80 amu, or 81 amu. One molecule of NO_2 has a mass of about 14 amu + 2(16 amu), or 46 amu, so one molecule of HBr has greater mass than one molecule of NO_2. And one mole of HBr would thus have greater mass than one mole of NO_2. Statement I is true.

What about statement II? Well, we've already determined that it's also true.

Now does this sentence make sense? "One mole of HBr has greater mass than one mole of NO_2 because the mass of a molecule of HBr is greater than the mass of a molecule of NO_2." It sure does, so fill in the oval marked CE.

24.   **B**   Remember that to calculate the formula weight of $Ca(NO_3)_2$, all you need to do is add up the weights of its constituent atoms. Calcium's atomic weight is 40 amu, nitrogen's is 14 amu, and oxygen's is 16 amu. That means the formula weight = 40 + 2(14 + 3(16)) = 40 + 2(14 + 48) = 40 + 28 + 96 = 164 amu. Choice (B) is correct.

25.   **D**   You're given a substance's mass composition, and you need to determine its empirical formula. So imagine that you have 100 g of the substance.

- You've got 9 g of magnesium, and magnesium's atomic weight is 24 amu, so you have $\frac{9}{24}$ = 0.375 mole of magnesium atoms.

- You've got 91 g of iodine, and iodine's atomic weight is 127 amu, so you have $\frac{91}{127}$ = 0.717 mole of iodine.

- The ratio of iodine atoms to magnesium atoms is $\frac{0.717}{0.375}$, which is very close to 2:1.

This means that the empirical formula of the substance is MgI_2, and that's why (D) is correct.

26.   **C**   The molecular formula of silicon dioxide is SiO_2, so the molecular weight is (28) + (2)(16) = (28) + (32) = 60. The percent by mass of silicon is equal to 28/60 x 100, which is slightly less than 50 percent, or 46 percent to be exact.

27.   **D**   Using the coefficients, you can determine that 4.0 moles of Fe would only require 3.0 moles of oxygen to react fully, so there is excess oxygen, making iron the limiting reactant. The theoretical yield of the Fe_2O_3 for the reaction would then be 2.0 moles, and $\frac{1.5}{2.0} \times 100\%$ = 75%.

Drill 2 (Pages 108–110)

5. **A** You know to associate Gibbs free energy with the spontaneity of reactions—that alone is enough to tell you which answer choice is correct. But if you want to take it further, remember that a reaction is spontaneous if the overall combination of enthalpy change—energy change—and entropy change is energetically adequate. Even an endothermic reaction—a reaction in which energy is consumed—can proceed spontaneously if it's accompanied by a large enough increase in entropy.

6. **C** You should associate enthalpy with the words "exothermic" and "endothermic." Exothermic reactions release energy (which the universe tends to like), while endothermic reactions consume energy (which the universe tends to dislike). If, in the course of the reaction, the enthalpy change is negative, the reaction is exothermic. If it's positive, the reaction is endothermic. That's why (C) is correct.

7. **D** Remember to always associate entropy with disorder. That's what it measures, and that's why (D) is correct.

103. **F, T** Divide and conquer! Look at the first statement on its own. Is it true? No. The fact that a reaction is exothermic does not necessarily mean that it's spontaneous. The first statement is false.

   Does the universe favor a negative enthalpy change? Yes. Generally speaking, it likes exothermic reactions. So the first statement is false, and the second is true.

104. **T, T, CE**

   Divide and conquer. Evaluate the first statement by itself. Is it true or false? It's true! In order for ice to melt, it must absorb heat. Melting involves a net absorption of heat energy because bonds between water molecules must be broken in order for melting to occur; it is an endothermic process.

   What about statement II? Your own experience tells you that this is true. Ice must absorb heat in order to melt. Now put both statements together: "Ice melting is an endothermic process because heat must be absorbed by ice if it is to melt." Does it make sense? Absolutely. So fill in the CE oval.

26. **C** Starting with (A), plug in choices. If the coefficient for O_2 is 1, then there are two oxygen atoms on the left. Since you are starting with 3 oxygen atoms on the right, this number is too small. Try (B). If the coefficient for O_2 is 2, you get 4 oxygen atoms on the left. Putting a 2 in front of H_2O gives 4 oxygen atoms on the right. However, now you cannot balance carbon without upsetting the oxygen balance. So (B) is also wrong. What about (C)? If the coefficient for O_2 is 3, then you have 6 oxygen atoms on the left. Putting a 2 in front of CO_2 and H_2O gives 6 oxygen atoms on the right. So far, so good. Notice that putting a "1" in front of C_2H_4 puts carbon and hydrogen in balance, so the answer is (C).

27. **A** Notice that the consumption of 2 moles of Na releases 822 kJ of heat. What happens if only 0.5 mole of Na is consumed? Since 0.5 is only 25% of 2, only 25% of 822 kJ of heat will be released. As you can see, (A) is about one-quarter of 822 kJ, so the correct answer is (A).

28. **B** Since you are given information about both reactants, this is a limiting reactant problem.

$$80 \text{ g Al} \times \frac{1 \text{ mol Al}}{27 \text{ g Al}} \times \frac{2 \text{ mol Fe}}{2 \text{ mol Al}} = 3 \text{ mol Fe}$$

$$80 \text{ g Fe}_2\text{O}_3 \times \frac{1 \text{ mol Fe}_2\text{O}_3}{160 \text{ g Fe}_2\text{O}_3} \times \frac{2 \text{ mol Fe}}{1 \text{ mol Fe}_2\text{O}_3} = 1 \text{ mol Fe}$$

The Fe_2O_3 creates less product and is thus the limiting reacting, creating 1 mol of Fe.

29. **B** From the balanced equation, you can see that when 2 moles of $O_2(g)$ are consumed, 800 kJ of energy are produced. So when half that number of moles of $O_2(g)$ (1 mole) is consumed, half as much energy is produced (400 kJ).

30. **C** Plug the answers into the equation. If the coefficient for H_2O is 3, then there are 6 hydrogens and the coefficient for PH_3 must be 2. That makes 1 the coefficient for P_2O_5. Now you have 8 oxygens on the right, so the coefficient for O_2 on the left must be 4. Since you have 1 as a coefficient for one of the species in the reaction, these must be the lowest whole number coefficients, and (C) is correct.

CHAPTER 6: ELECTRON CONFIGURATIONS AND RADIOACTIVITY

Drill 1 (Pages 122–123)

1. **B** You may be tempted to pick (E), but don't. Atomic theory is associated with a fellow named Dalton and says that all elements are composed of atoms. For this test, you're not expected to fully understand the De Broglie hypothesis; you're just supposed to associate it with the idea that matter can be conceived of as waves, and waves can be conceived of as matter. So (B) is correct.

2. **A** You learned that Bohr incorrectly believed that electrons circled the nucleus in orbits, the way planets circle the Sun. So (A) is correct.

3. **C** For this test, you need not completely understand the Heisenberg principle; you only need to associate it with the idea that one cannot, at any one moment, know both an electron's position and momentum. So (C) is correct.

4. **E** For this question, you need to look for a noble gas configuration with a full octet because noble gases do not interact with other gas molecules. Choice (E) is correct.

5. **E** Similar to the previous question, look for the electron configuration of a noble gas because they have a full octet and do not want to lose any electrons. They are also the most stable elements, so it takes a lot of energy to remove one electron from their shell.

6. **C**   Look for an element that needs 3 electrons to fill its octet. Since (C) has only 3 more electrons necessary to fill its p shell and its octet, that would be the correct answer.

7. **B**   Diamagnetic elements have all of their electrons paired (no unpaired electrons). Most of us immediately look to the column of noble gases since we know that all of their electrons are paired since their octets are full, but this question specifically stated that the element is not a noble gas. The other place we look for all electrons paired is column 2, alkaline earth metals. Even though they do not have a full final orbital or octet ($n = 3$ in this case, so their $3p$ orbital does not have any electrons in it), the element has a full $3s$ orbital, which are paired electrons.

101. **T, T**   Divide and conquer! Evaluate the first statement on its own, and decide whether it's true or false. Is it true that according to the Bohr model electrons circle the nucleus in true orbits? Yes, it is.

   Now, look at the second statement by itself. Is it true? Yes. Now let's find out if the sentence makes sense. "The Bohr model of the atom is inaccurate because an element may exist as several isotopes each with a different number of neutrons in the nucleus." The second part of the statement has nothing to do with the first. Both statements are true, but they have nothing to do with each other, so do not fill in the CE oval.

102. **F, T**   Evaluate the first statement by itself, and decide whether it's true or false. Is it true that krypton is an unstable atom? No, that isn't true. Krypton is a very stable atom. Why? Because it has a full octet in its outermost shell.

   Now look at the second statement. Is it true or false? It's true: atoms with 8 electrons in their outermost shell are stable. The first statement is false, and the second is true.

24. **B**   Here you're given the configuration and asked to identify the element. The easiest way to solve this problem is to add up the electrons in the configuration; you'll find that their sum is 27. Since the question asks about an *atom*, and not an *ion*, this means the answer is Co, which has the atomic number 27. The correct answer is (B).

25. **E**   Here you're given the element and asked to identify the electron configuration. Follow the steps we showed you for writing electron configurations, and you'll see that (E) is correct. If you had trouble writing the electron configuration, you could also have arrived at the answer by testing each answer choice. See which answer choices have superscripts that add up to the atomic number of Tc, which is 43. Then eliminate the other answer choices, and take your best guess.

26. **C**   Do it the easy way: count up the superscripts. They add up to 54. Look on the periodic table, and you'll see that element 54 is xenon. Xenon, as you can see from the table, is a noble gas.

Drill 2 (Pages 127–129)

4. **D** As we said earlier, the emission of gamma rays generally accompanies other forms of radioactive decay. So (D) is right.

5. **A** In order for its atomic number to be reduced by 2, an atom must lose 2 protons. In order for its mass to be reduced by 4, it must also lose a total of 4 nucleons (protons or neutrons). The atom loses 2 protons and 2 neutrons. That's the description of alpha decay, so (A) is correct.

6. **B** Beta decay—which involves the emission of an electron—converts a neutron into a proton. Positron emission and electron capture (a decay process that you don't need to know for the test) convert a proton into a neutron. Beta decay is the correct answer; that's (B).

103. **T, F** The first statement correctly lists three types of radioactive decay. However, radioactive nuclei do not emit these particles because they are stable. Instead, they emit them in an effort to bring an unstable nucleus to a lower energy level, so the second statement is false.

104. **T, T, CE**

     Divide and conquer. The first statement is true: if an element decays for one half-life, half of the original sample remains. If it decays for two half-lives, one-quarter of the original sample remains. The second statement is also true. Does the whole sentence make sense? Yes. So fill in the CE oval.

27. **C** In this problem, an atom of Rn (radon) with an atomic number of 86 and a mass number of 222 undergoes a change. What happens to it? All of a sudden it's a different element, Po (polonium), with an atomic number of 84 and a mass number of 218. It lost 2 protons and 2 neutrons. The Rn atom has undergone alpha decay. In fact, you can see that an alpha particle—helium-4 nucleus—has been emitted as a part of the whole process. This is alpha decay, so (C) is correct.

28. **D** To begin with, you can see that an electron has been emitted, so that's one way to know, right away, that this is beta decay. You can also see that the atom of I (iodine) has turned into something else—xenon—because its atomic number increased from 53 to 54. But its mass number stayed the same, so it looks as if a neutron was turned into a proton. That's beta decay, and (D) is correct.

29. **A** After examining the periodic table, realize that the full atomic symbol for this isotope of technicium is $^{99}_{43}\text{Tc}$

     Remembering that the superscript (the mass number) represents the total number of protons and neutrons, and the subscript (the atomic number) represents just the number of protons, $^{99}_{43}\text{Tc}$ has 43 protons and 99 − 43 = 56 neutrons—(A).

CHAPTER 7: THE PERIODIC TABLE AND BONDING

Drill 1 (Pages 139–141)

1. **B** Remember that the group 2A elements are alkaline earth metals. Calcium (Ca) is in this family, so (B) is correct.

2. **D** Metals bond by *losing* valence electrons, so eliminate (A), (B), and (C). This leaves fluorine and neon.

    They're both nonmetals; however, neon is a noble gas, so it generally does not form bonds. Fluorine does. Choice (D) is the answer.

3. **A** The first ionization of an element refers to the amount of energy needed to remove one electron from an atom. The second ionization energy refers to the removal of a second electron. What kind of electrons are hardest to remove from an atom? Inner shell electrons. So the correct answer should be an element whose atoms have only 1 valence electron. Why? Because removing a second electron from such an atom would involve removing an inner shell electron and thus take an enormous amount of energy. So which of the choices has atoms with 1 valence electron? Think group 1A elements. Sodium is one of those, and (A) is correct.

101. **T, T, CE**

    Time to divide and conquer. Is the first statement true or false? It's true. What about statement II? It's also true. Inner shell electrons are held more closely to the positive nucleus than valence electrons; inner shell electrons are held too strongly to be useful in bonding.

    See if the whole sentence makes sense: "Only an atom's valence electrons can participate in bonding because an atom's inner shell electrons are held too tightly to be shared or transferred." It certainly does, so fill in the CE oval.

102. **T, F** Consider statement I. Does potassium have greater metallic character than iron? Remember that metallic character involves the ease with which an element's atoms can give up electrons. Potassium is much more reactive than iron and thus can be expected to give up its electrons much more readily, so potassium does have greater metallic character, and statement I is true.

    Look at the second statement. Is it true or false? It's false. Potassium is an active metal, and active metals tend to have lower melting points than transition metals such as iron.

24. **A** Don't be fooled by (E). Chlorine is very reactive, but it isn't a metal. Recall that the alkali metals are the most reactive metals. Sodium is a member of the alkali metal family, so (A) is correct.

25. **D** Nickel is a transition metal, so you can expect it to be malleable, ductile, and lustrous (shiny). As is true of many transition metals, nickel compounds are intensely colored (usually a bright green), so eliminate (A), (B), (C), and (E). That leaves (D). Nickel is a conductor of heat (and electricity), not an insulator. Pick (D).

26. **C** Remember the periodic table trends. As you move from left to right within a period, atoms get smaller. So the smallest atom of a period 4 element is krypton (Kr). Eliminate any choice that does not start with Kr; that makes (C) the correct answer.

27. **D** All of the statements are true except (D). Sodium is not found in nature as a diatomic gas; it is usually seen in nature in ionic salts.

Drill 2 (Pages 155–156)

4. **C** Metals are held together by metallic bonds. Potassium is the only pure metal listed; therefore, (C) is the correct answer.

5. **D** Ionic compounds possess ionic bonds. How can you spot an ionic compound by looking at formulas? Easily; just find a compound composed of a metal and a nonmetal. Choices (A), (B), and (E) are substances composed solely of nonmetals. Choice (C) represents a purely metallic substance. Aluminum oxide consists of Al^{3+} ions from the metal aluminum and O^{2-} ions from the nonmetal oxygen, so (D) is the correct answer.

6. **B** A polar molecule must contain polar covalent bonds. Of the choices, only (A), (B), and (E) involve covalent bonding. However, (A) and (E) involve diatomic molecules consisting of one element; these molecules will contain nonpolar covalent bonds, since their atoms won't differ in electronegativity. Carbon monoxide molecules contain different nonmetals, and thus form polar covalent bonds. That's why (B) is correct.

103. **T, T, CE**

    Divide and conquer! Look at the first statement on its own and decide whether it's true or false. It's true. Look at the second statement by itself. It's true; atoms have different electronegativities.

    See if the whole sentence makes sense. "Some covalent bonds are polar in nature because atoms of different electronegativities are unequal in the degree to which they attract electrons." Does that make sense? What makes a polar covalent bond polar? One of the atoms in the bond hogs the shared electrons; one atom has a higher electronegativity than the other. The sentence makes sense, so fill in oval CE.

104. **F, F** Divide and conquer. Look at the first statement by itself. Is it true? No! Most atoms form bonds because they would like to achieve a stable octet.

What about the second statement? It's false. Ionic and covalent bonding *do* provide atoms with a stable configuration—the configuration that resembles a stable octet.

27. **A** A carbon atom has 4 valence electrons, and an oxygen atom has 6. Using carbon as the central atom and arranging the atoms to give them octets yields

$$\ddot{O}::C::\ddot{O} \quad \text{or} \quad \ddot{O} = C = \ddot{O}$$

Notice that the carbon dioxide molecule consists of 2 double bonds, but no single bonds. The answer is (A).

28. **B** Determine the structure of SO_2. Sulfur is the central atom, and each atom has 6 valence electrons. Arranging them all so that they have octets gives you

$$\ddot{O}::\ddot{S}:\ddot{O} \qquad$$

Notice that there are three electron pair sites around the central sulfur atom (a double or triple bond counts as only one site), one of which is a lone pair. This will result in a bent shape, so (B) is correct.

29. **E** In the course of this reaction, 4 moles of C–H bonds and 1 mole of Cl–Cl bonds are broken. So 4(410 kJ) + 240 kJ, or 1,880 kJ, are needed to break these bonds. The reaction produces 1 mole of C–Cl bonds, 1 mole of H–Cl bonds, and 3 moles of C–H bonds. So 330 kJ + 430 kJ + 3(410 kJ), or 1,990 kJ, of energy is released by bond making. The net change, which is roughly equal to ΔH, is 1,880 kJ – 1,990 kJ = –110 kJ. Therefore, this reaction is exothermic, and the correct answer is (E).

30. **D** First, draw the Lewis dot structure for $XeOF_4$

Now, count the groups of electrons around the central atom (Xe), keeping in mind that every pair of nonbonding electrons, every single bond, every double bond, and every triple bond counts as one group. So here, Xe is surrounded by six groups of electrons. Any atom that is surrounded by six groups of electrons has an sp^3d^2 hybridization and an octahedral geometry. However, because the question asks about the molecular shape (as opposed to the geometry), look at the arrangement of the surrounding atoms. In this case, the F would make a flat square around the Xe with the oxygen atom lying directly above. This traces out a square pyramid, (D).

CHAPTER 8: PHASES: GASES, LIQUIDS, AND SOLIDS

Drill 1 (Pages 167–168)

1. **C** Remember that values that are on the same side of the ideal gas equation are inversely proportional. In $PV = nRT$, both R and T (Kelvin temperature) are on the same side as n (moles of gas). Since R (ideal gas constant) cannot change with a change in moles, the answer must be (C).

2. **D** In a mixture of gases, each fills the container, so (E) cannot be right. It doesn't make sense to add the gases' temperatures to get a total temperature, so (B) and (C) are eliminated. That leaves (A) and (D). The ideal gas constant is not something that could be summed up for each gas either, so the answer is (D). Remember that adding the partial pressures of a mixture gives you the total pressure of the system.

3. **C** Don't forget that temperature is a measure of average kinetic energy and that for ideal gases, Kelvin temperature increases in proportion to changes in kinetic energy. Choice (C) is correct.

101. **T, T** It's time to divide and conquer. What do you think of the first statement by itself? It's true; it describes kinetic molecular theory.

   The second statement is also true; you know this from the ideal gas law: $PV = nRT$. Temperature and moles of gas are on the same side of the equation, so they're inversely proportional when other variables are constant.

   See if the whole sentence makes sense. "If an ideal gas is located in a closed container and temperature is increased, the average speed of the molecules will always increase as well because for an ideal gas, temperature and moles of gas are inversely proportional."

   The sentence does not make sense. Both halves are true, but when they're put together the statement makes no sense. Do not fill in the CE oval.

102. **F, T** Divide and conquer. The first statement is false. Pressure and volume do have a relationship: $PV = nRT$.

   Now, what about the second statement? It's true. Look at the ideal gas law: $PV = nRT$. Temperature and volume are on opposite sides of the equation, so they're directly proportional when other variables are constant. The first statement is false, and the second is true.

24. **D** Don't fall into the temptation trap. In an ideal gas there is no attraction or repulsion between molecules, so eliminate (A) and (B). Gas molecules are in continuous motion in both ideal and nonideal gases, so eliminate (C). In a real gas, molecules will slightly attract each other. As a result, gas molecules strike the container walls with less force. Less force means lower pressure. So pressure is less in the real situation as compared to the ideal. That's why (D) is correct.

25. **D** This is a partial pressure question. You know that the total pressure of the system is 1,200 torr, and you know that each gas contributes to the total pressure by exerting a partial pressure.

There are a total of 24 moles of gases in the container. The helium concentration is 2 moles/L. There are 4 L total and thus 2 × 4 = 8 moles of helium molecules in the mixture. Hydrogen's concentration is 1.5 moles/L, so there are 1.5 × 4 = 6 moles of hydrogen molecules, and 8 + 6 = 14. Since the total number of moles of molecules—for all 3 gases—is 24, there must be 10 moles of carbon dioxide molecules in the mixture.

If there are 10 moles of carbon dioxide molecules and 24 moles of molecules total, carbon dioxide's mole fraction $= \dfrac{10}{24}$. Total pressure = 1,200 torr, and carbon dioxide's pressure is therefore $\dfrac{10}{24} \times$ 1,200 torr. Choice (D) is correct.

Drill 2 (Pages 180–181)

4. **E** Think back to the first phase change diagram. As heat was removed from the system, the substance moved from gas phase to liquid phase to solid phase. Which process is clearly doing that here? In (E), a gas is condensing into a liquid, so (E) is the correct answer.

5. **B** Remember that sublimation is the direct conversion of a solid into a gas, so (B) is correct.

6. **E** A decrease in entropy means an increase in order. There is an increase in order (and restriction in molecular motion) as a gas condenses to a liquid. Choice (E) is correct.

7. **D** Heat of fusion is associated with the process of melting or freezing. Do any choices involve one of these? Yes; in (D), solid bromine melts. If this change took place solely at the melting point, then the heat of fusion of bromine would equal the enthalpy change for the process. Choice (D) is the correct answer.

103. **T, F** You know what to do with this question type by now. Is statement I true or false? It's true. What about statement II? It's false. Hydrogen bonds are stronger than most intermolecular forces but far weaker than covalent or ionic bonds.

104. **F, F** As you go up into higher elevations, the atmosphere exerts less pressure. As the pressure over a substance decreases, the boiling point of the substance will also decrease. Since water boils at 100°C at sea-level (1 atm), it will boil below 100°C at higher elevations. So statement I is false. Statement II is also false. Average kinetic energy is a measure of temperature, not pressure. So even if the pressure on a sample increases, if its temperature remains constant, so will its average kinetic energy.

26. **B** Molecules that exhibit hydrogen bonding contain one or more hydrogen atoms (H) bonded to either N, O, or F. The partial positive end of one molecule (the H end) will become attracted to the partial negative end of a nearby molecule (in this case, the N end), creating a hydrogen bond. Choice (B) is correct.

27. **C** A substance with a low vapor pressure doesn't evaporate readily because it possesses relatively strong intermolecular attractions, so eliminate (A) and (D). What would be the result of strong intermolecular forces? Recall that these must be overcome for a substance to boil. If they are strong, boiling will occur only at relatively high temperatures. Choice (C) is correct.

28. **B** First, the correct abbreviation for heat is Q. So you can eliminate (C), (D), and (E). During a phase change, the temperature of a substance remains constant. Therefore, (A) must be wrong because it has a term for changing temperature, ΔT. In fact, (A) is the equation used to determine the change in temperature when heat is added or removed from a substance that isn't undergoing a phase change. Choice (B) is the correct choice, where Q is the heat added or removed, n is the number of moles of substance, and ΔH is the heat of phase change, a quantity that is unique for every substance.

CHAPTER 9: SOLUTIONS

Drill 1 (Pages 190–191)

1. **E** When ionic solutes dissolve in water, an electrolytic solution is produced. Are there any ionic solutes among the choices? Look for the combination of a metal and a nonmetal. Sodium chloride is ionic, and (E) is the correct answer.

2. **A** When you are told that solubility increases as temperature decreases, think of dissolving a gas in aqueous solution. Are there any gases in the answer choices? Yes: NO_2. The correct answer is (A).

3. **E** Remember that the degree of boiling point elevation is proportional to the moles of dissolved particles. Choices (A) through (D) are substances composed solely of nonmetals. They are molecular compounds. In general, molecular compounds don't dissociate (acids, which we'll look at later, are an important exception), so 1 mole of the substances in (A) through (D) gives 1 mole of dissolved particles. Sodium chloride is different. As it dissolves, NaCl dissociates into Na^+ and Cl^- ions, so 1 mole of NaCl yields 2 moles of dissolved particles. NaCl is the solute that will most raise water's boiling point; the correct answer is (E).

101. **T, T** Divide and conquer. Look at the first statement by itself. Is it true? Yes; you should associate "ions dissolved in solution" with the idea of conducting electricity.

The second statement is true. When a solvent can't dissolve any more solute, it's saturated—the solute has reached the limit of its solubility. See whether the whole sentence makes sense. "Aqueous solutions with ionic solutes conduct electricity because a liquid solvent becomes saturated when the solute reaches the limit of its solubility." The sentence is nonsense—do not fill in the CE oval.

102. **T, F** Again, divide and conquer. Is the first statement true or false? It's tricky but true. For each mole of original solute, a nonionic solute produces only 1 mole of particles in solution. One mole of NaCl, however, dissociates into 2 moles of particles. So the number of particles floating around in the NaCl solution will be twice the number of moles in the nonionic solution. The freezing point depression for the nonionic solution will be one half what it is for the NaCl solution.

   What about the second statement? It's false. The freezing point depression constant does vary with the solvent.

24. **B** You've learned to associate increased temperature with increased solubility of solids in water. This question is simple, and (B) is correct.

25. **E** The question is about solutions that are capable of conducting electricity. Think of electrolytes, and remember that you should associate them with "ions in solution." Which of the answer choices lists an ionic compound capable of dissociating in solution? Choice (E) does. Ca is a metal and Cl is a non-metal, which tells you that $CaCl_2$ is most likely an ionic substance. Choice (E) is the correct answer.

26. **A** This question asks you to look for the insoluble product of this precipitation reaction. Because precipitations occur through double replacement reactions, the two products formed will be $NaCl(aq)$ and $BaSO_4(s)$. If you look back at the solubility rules, you can see that sodium chloride will be soluble; this means that you can eliminate this answer choice, which leaves you with the correct answer, (A).

CHAPTER 10: KINETICS AND EQUILIBRIUM

Drill 1 (Pages 206–208)

1. **E** While the surface area of solids and liquids can be increased (through crushing a solid or spraying a liquid), the surface area of gases cannot. Which answer choice has solid or liquid reactants? Choice (E) does, and it's the correct answer.

2. **B** When the volume of a system is decreased, equilibrium will shift in the direction that produces fewer moles of gas. Eliminate (A) and (E)—neither reaction involves a gaseous species, so pressure changes will not affect their equilibrium. Now, look at the other three choices: which reaction involves fewer moles of gas on the right than on the left? Choice (B) does (3 moles on the left, and 2 on the right). So the correct answer is (B).

3. **A** You're asked about reverse reactions, so read (A) to (E) from right to left. Recall that only gaseous and aqueous species can have their concentration increased. Choices (B), (C), (D), and (E) have either a gaseous or aqueous species on the right side (this is a bit tricky—these would be the reactants of the reverse reaction). That leaves (A), which has a single solid reactant for its reverse reaction. The concentration of pure solids cannot be changed, so (A) is correct.

101. **F, T** Divide and conquer! Assess the first statement by itself. Is it true or false? If you increase the concentration of a product, equilibrium shifts in the direction that creates more reactant, so in this case, to the left. This means that we will see an increase, not a decrease, in the concentration of reactants. The statement is false.

What about the second statement? It is a statement of Le Châtelier's principle, so it's true. The first statement is false, and the second is true.

102. **F, F** Divide and conquer. Is the first statement true or false? Don't be tricked! At equilibrium, the rates of forward and reverse reactions are equal, but the concentrations of products and reactants are usually not. This statement is false.

Look at the second statement. What do they mean by the "right side of any equilibrium expression"? Equilibrium expressions, remember, look like this:

$$K_{eq} = \frac{[\text{products}]}{[\text{reactants}]}$$

What's on the right side? The fraction showing product concentrations and reactant concentrations. As you know, those are not usually equal at equilibrium, so both statements are false.

103. **T, T** As concentrations of reactants increase, so do molecular collisions, and this produces a higher reaction rate. Statement I is true.

What about statement II? It's also true. As collisions become more energetic, they are more likely to lead to product formation.

Now put the sentences together. Does it make sense? It sounds good, but don't fall into the temptation trap: only a temperature change, not a concentration change, can change the *energy* of molecular collisions. Don't fill in the CE oval.

24. **B** Remember what we said about the size of K_{eq}:

An equilibrium constant > 1 a reaction that favors the forward direction

An equilibrium constant < 1 a reaction that favors the reverse direction

The K_{eq} is less than 1 for the first reaction and greater than 1 for the second, which means that the reverse direction is favored in the first reaction, and the forward direction is favored in the second reaction. Choice (B) is correct.

25. **C** Think of Le Châtelier's principle, and look at what's happening here. Someone increases the concentration of the product O_2 in a reaction at equilibrium. This means that the concentration of the other product, SO_2, will decrease, and the concentration of the reactant(s) will increase. Choice (C) is the correct answer.

26. **B** Don't fall into the temptation trap. You've probably heard the phrase "not consumed by the reaction" in connection with catalysts, in kinetics. But here they're asking about an activated complex. An activated complex is quickly broken down to form the products of a reaction. Choice (B) is the correct answer.

CHAPTER 11: ACIDS AND BASES

Drill 1 (Pages 223–225)

1. **B** Litmus is an indicator that is blue in basic solutions. Since NH_3 is the most obvious base among the choices, the answer is (B).

2. **B** At 25°C, a pH greater than 7 indicates a basic solution. Choice (B) is correct.

3. **C** A nonelectrolyte does not dissociate into ions in water. Soluble ionic compounds, strong acids, and strong bases are all strong electrolytes, so eliminate (A), (a strong acid). Weak acids and bases ionize to a slight extent, and, therefore, are weak electrolytes. So eliminate (B), (weak base), and (D) and (E), (both weak acids). What's left? Water. But doesn't water ionize to a slight extent? Yes, but check out how slightly: K_w (equilibrium constant for the ionization of water) at 25°C is 1.0×10^{-14}. That's so small that you can consider water to be a nonelectrolyte. Choice (C) is correct.

4. **A** The same species that makes strong electrolytes (soluble ionic compounds, strong acids, and strong bases) has an ionization reaction that essentially goes to completion. Are any of these answer choices strong acids or bases? Yes. HBr is a strong acid. It completely ionizes into H^+ and Br^- ions in water, so (A) is correct.

101. **F, T** Divide and conquer! Look at statement I by itself, and decide if it's true or false. It's false. If you add an acid to neutral water, you *increase* the hydrogen ion concentration and *decrease* the hydroxide ion concentration.

Is the second statement true or false? This is a true statement about water's ion product. So, statement I is false, and statement II is true.

102. **F, F** Remember the six common strong acids? HI is one of them, so statement I is false.

What about the second statement? Because HI is a strong acid it will donate, not accept, H^+ ions. Both statements are false.

24. **C** Conjugate acids and bases appear on the right side of the equation, so eliminate (A) and (B). A conjugate acid donates an H^+ ion. Does either H_2O or NO_3^- do that? Yes: H_2O donates an H^+ ion to NO_3^- to re-form the reactants HNO_3 and OH^-. So H_2O is the conjugate acid, and the answer is (C).

25. **A** If you fully titrate an acid, you need equal amounts of H^+ and OH^- ions. There are 2 moles of OH^- ion for each mole of $Ba(OH)_2$, and you're dealing with 0.015 L of a 0.015 M solution, so

$$(2)(0.015)(0.015) = 0.00045 \text{ moles OH}^-$$

You need 0.00045 moles of H^+ ion too. You have 0.03 L of the HCl solution, and there's just 1 mole of H^+ ion per mole of HCl, so

$$(1)(0.03)(x) = 0.00045 \text{ moles OH}^-$$

$$x = 0.015 \ M$$

Choice (A) is the correct answer.

26. **D** H_3PO_4 looks like the formula of an acid, and it is—phosphoric acid. Choices (B), (C), and (E) are properties of bases, so eliminate them. Is H_3PO_4 on our list of strong acids? No; so it must be a weak acid. Would a weak acid have a large K_a? No; so eliminate (A). A weak acid is a weak electrolyte. Choice (D) is the correct answer.

27. **D** To neutralize the HCl solution, add as many moles of hydroxide ions as there are moles of hydrogen ions in the solution. Use the relationship moles = (molarity)(liters). You have a strong acid and a strong base that will dissociate completely in solution, and 1 unit of HCl gives 1 hydrogen ion and 1 unit of NaOH gives 1 hydroxide ion upon dissociation. So, just set moles of hydroxide ion equal to moles of hydrogen ion, and use the following equation:

$$(M \text{ HCl})(L \text{ HCl}) = (M \text{ NaOH})(L \text{ NaOH})$$
$$(0.300 \ M)(40.0 \ L) = (0.200 \ M)(x)$$
$$x = 60.0 \ L$$

28. **D** Recall that the six strong acids are HCl, HBr, HI, HNO_3, $HClO_4$, and H_2SO_4. Phosphoric acid, H_3PO_4, is a weak acid.

CHAPTER 12: OXIDATION AND REDUCTION

Drill 1 (Pages 236–238)

1. **A** During a reduction half-reaction, electrons are gained.

2. **E** The oxidation number on Ag is +1 on both sides, and the oxidation number of Cl is –1 on both sides. Thus, no electrons are transferred.

3. **E** All of the other options have an element in its pure form, which always has an oxidation state of 0.

4. **C** Two moles of electrons are needed to turn Cu^{2+} into Cu (and to turn Mg into Mg^{2+}). Reaction (A) has 3 moles, (B) has 1 mole, (D) has 4 moles (two oxygen atoms changing oxidation state from 0 to –2), and (E) has no electron transfer.

101. **T, T, CE**

Divide and conquer. Look at the first statement, and evaluate it on its own. Is it true? Yes. Wherever there's oxidation, there must be reduction.

Look at the second statement by itself. Is it true? Yes. If one species gives up electrons, something else must accept them. Now see whether the whole sentence makes sense: "Any reaction in which one atom is oxidized requires that another atom be reduced because if one species donates electrons, another must acquire them." Does it? Absolutely. Oxidation means losing electrons, and reduction means gaining electrons. Oxidation must accompany reduction because if electrons are lost from one place, they must be gained by another. The second statement explains the first, so fill in oval CE.

102. **F, T** Cesium, being an alkali metal, will lose an electron much more easily than a transition metal like nickel would and so would be higher on the activity series. This also means that cesium is a stronger reducing agent than nickel; therefore, nickel must be a stronger oxidizing agent than cesium is.

24. **B** Do some simple oxidation/reduction arithmetic. Sodium starts with an oxidation state of 0 because it isn't in a compound. When Cl is in a compound, its oxidation state is usually –1. In NaCl, Cl has an oxidation state of –1, and Na has an oxidation state of +1. The oxidation state of Na was 0 and is now +1; Na has lost electrons—it has been oxidized. Choice (B) is the correct answer.

25. **A** Again, some simple oxidation/reduction arithmetic is necessary. Oxygen's oxidation state here is –2. Since there are 4 oxygen atoms in the formula, oxygen contributes a total oxidation of $(-2)(4) = -8$. Potassium's oxidation state is +1. The oxidation state of the overall compound is 0. So $1 + (-8) + x = 0$. $x = +7$. That's why (A) is correct.

26. **E** Begin by applying the rules for assigning oxidation states to the given reaction.

$$2Al^0 + 6H^{+1}Cl^{-1} \rightarrow 2Al^{+3}Cl^{-1}_3 + 3H^0_2$$

Notice that each mole of Al that's oxidized to Al^{+3} loses 3 moles of electrons, so 2 moles of Al lose 6 moles of electrons during oxidation. The 6 moles of electrons that are given up by Al are acquired by H^+ ions to form H_2. Choice (E) is the correct answer.

27. **E** The oxidation states of all of the atoms in a neutral molecule must add up to zero. Oxygen almost always takes the oxidation state –2, and hydrogen is almost always +1, so $(+1) + (Br) + (3)(-2) = 0$. This makes the oxidation state of bromine +5.

28. **C** The number of electrons in a chloride ion with a –1 charge will be one greater than the number of its protons. A chlorine atom or ion always contains 17 protons, so a chloride ion with a –1 charge will possess 18 electrons.

CHAPTER 13: ORGANIC CHEMISTRY AND ENVIRONMENTAL CHEMISTRY

Drill 1 (Pages 251–252)

1. **B** In organic molecules, oxygen atoms will have two lone pairs and nitrogen atoms will have one lone pair. The only type of organic molecule from the list that has neither oxygen nor nitrogen atoms are the alkenes, which consist entirely of carbon and hydrogen atoms, neither of which have lone pairs in organic molecules.

2. **E** Amines have an NH_2 group, which will readily accept additional protons. It thus acts as a Brønsted-Lowry base, making the pH of the resultant solution greater than 7.

3. **C** A carbonyl group (C=O) is only bonded to a terminal carbon in ketones. Aldehydes also have a carbonyl group, but in that case they are not bonded to a terminal carbon.

4. **D** Fluorine is a member of the halogens, making any organic molecule containing it a halide.

101. **F, T** Divide and conquer! Photodissociation describes the process of breaking down a diatomic oxygen molecule into elemental oxygen atoms. This is part of the creation of an ozone molecule, not the depletion of one, so the first statement is false. Regardless of that first part, elemental chlorine will still react with ozone to create chlorine monoxide (a reaction that is part of the depletion of the ozone layer) and so the second statement is true.

102. **T, T** Both statements are true: Enzymes do act as catalysts in biological reactions, and polysaccharides do contain large amounts of energy. However, are the statements connected to one another? Enzymes are always proteins, and additionally, they speed up the reaction rate by lowering the overall activation energy of the reaction. The amount of energy stored in a molecule has no effect on reaction rate.

24. **D** Fermentation involves an organic molecule breaking down to form an alcohol and carbon dioxide in the absence of oxygen, so (D) is correct.

25. **D** SO_2 reacts with ozone to form SO_3, which in turn reacts with water to form H_2SO_4, sulfuric acid.

26. **A** Only (A) correctly lists the layers of the atmosphere from lowest to highest.

CHAPTER 14: LABORATORY

Drill 1 (Pages 266–267)

1. **C** According to the chart on page 259, barium salts will burn with a green color. There is no information about the burning characteristics of (A), (B), or (D).

2. **A** Due to its relative volatility, ethyl alcohol will evaporate at a lower temperature than water. This is a common procedure for the concentration of this substance. Although phenolphthalein, (B), may also be separated by distillation, this is not a common procedure.

3. **E** A U-tube manometer will show a rising mercury level as a heated gas pushes with a greater force per unit area (pressure).

4. **D** Of our common indicators, only litmus is red in acid and blue in basic solution. Phenolphthalein is clear in acid and pink in basic solution.

101. **T, F** The indicator will change colors as soon as the solution becomes slightly basic, which will occur after equivalence, so statement I is true.

   This is a deceptive statement because, although a neutral solution will have an equal molar amount of H^+ and OH^- ions, the actual volumes of solution required to achieve this depend on the concentrations, so statement II is false.

102. **F, T** Hexane (C_6H_8) has a higher molar mass, and is of the same class of molecule as pentane (C_5H_7) and therefore will have a higher boiling point, so statement I is false.

   Vapor pressure is a measure of a substance's propensity to vaporize, and due to its lower mass, pentane's vapor pressure will be higher than hexane's, so statement II is true.

24. **B** To find mass in grams, you need only multiply the isotope mass by the number of moles present: 2.5 mol × 2.014 g/mol = 5.035 g. Only (B) reflects both the proper calculation AND the right number of significant figures.

25. **B** When NaOH and HCl neutralize, water and NaCl salt are produced. After evaporation, the solid will burn yellow, (B), in a flame test. Choices (C) and (D) are the colors for different metallic salts, while (A) and (E) are very unlikely in a standard flame test procedure.

Part V
Additional
Practice Tests

Chapter 15
Practice Test 2

PRACTICE SAT SUBJECT TEST IN CHEMISTRY–TEST 2

You are about to take the second practice SAT Subject Test in Chemistry. The bubble sheet can be found near the back of the book; feel free to tear it out for use. (Just don't lose it!)

After answering questions 1–23, which constitute Part A, you'll be directed to answer questions 101–116, which constitute Part B. Then, begin again at question 24. Questions 24–70 constitute Part C.

When you're ready to score yourself, refer to the answer key and scoring instructions on pages 314 and 326. Full explanations regarding the correct answers to all questions start on page 315.

SAT SUBJECT TEST IN CHEMISTRY

MATERIAL IN THE FOLLOWING TABLE MAY BE USEFUL IN ANSWERING THE QUESTIONS IN THIS EXAMINATION.

DO NOT DETACH FROM BOOK.

PERIODIC TABLE OF THE ELEMENTS

1 H 1.0079																	2 He 4.0026
3 Li 6.941	4 Be 9.012											5 B 10.811	6 C 12.011	7 N 14.007	8 O 16.00	9 F 19.00	10 Ne 20.179
11 Na 22.99	12 Mg 24.30											13 Al 26.98	14 Si 28.09	15 P 30.974	16 S 32.06	17 Cl 35.453	18 Ar 39.948
19 K 39.10	20 Ca 40.48	21 Sc 44.96	22 Ti 47.90	23 V 50.94	24 Cr 52.00	25 Mn 54.938	26 Fe 55.85	27 Co 58.93	28 Ni 58.69	29 Cu 63.55	30 Zn 65.39	31 Ga 69.72	32 Ge 72.59	33 As 74.92	34 Se 78.96	35 Br 79.90	36 Kr 83.80
37 Rb 85.47	38 Sr 87.62	39 Y 88.91	40 Zr 91.22	41 Nb 92.91	42 Mo 95.94	43 Tc (98)	44 Ru 101.1	45 Rh 102.91	46 Pd 106.42	47 Ag 107.87	48 Cd 112.41	49 In 114.82	50 Sn 118.71	51 Sb 121.75	52 Te 127.60	53 I 126.91	54 Xe 131.29
55 Cs 132.91	56 Ba 137.33	57 *La 138.91	72 Hf 178.49	73 Ta 180.95	74 W 183.85	75 Re 186.21	76 Os 190.2	77 Ir 192.2	78 Pt 195.08	79 Au 196.97	80 Hg 200.59	81 Tl 204.38	82 Pb 207.2	83 Bi 208.98	84 Po (209)	85 At (210)	86 Rn (222)
87 Fr (223)	88 Ra 226.02	89 †Ac 227.03	104 Rf (261)	105 Db (262)	106 Sg (266)	107 Bh (264)	108 Hs (277)	109 Mt (268)	110 Ds (271)	111 Rg (272)	112 § (277)						

§ Not yet named

*Lanthanide Series	58 Ce 140.12	59 Pr 140.91	60 Nd 144.24	61 Pm (145)	62 Sm 150.4	63 Eu 151.97	64 Gd 157.25	65 Tb 158.93	66 Dy 162.50	67 Ho 164.93	68 Er 167.26	69 Tm 168.93	70 Yb 173.04	71 Lu 174.97
†Actinide Series	90 Th 232.04	91 Pa 231.04	92 U 238.03	93 Np 237.05	94 Pu (244)	95 Am (243)	96 Cm (247)	97 Bk (247)	98 Cf (251)	99 Es (252)	100 Fm (257)	101 Md (258)	102 No (259)	103 Lr (262)

GO ON TO THE NEXT PAGE

SAT SUBJECT TEST IN CHEMISTRY–TEST 2—*Continued*

<u>Note:</u> For all questions involving solutions and/or chemical equations, assume that the system is in pure water unless otherwise stated.

Part A

Directions: Each set of lettered choices below refers to the numbered statements or questions immediately following it. Select the one lettered choice that best fits each statement or answers each question, and then fill in the corresponding oval on the answer sheet. A choice may be used once, more than once, or not at all in each set.

Questions 1–4 refer to the following.

(A) Molarity
(B) Molality
(C) Mole fraction
(D) Density
(E) Partial pressure

1. Is measured in units of atmospheres or millimeters of mercury

2. Is measured in units of moles/kilogram

3. Is a measure of mass per unit volume

4. Is the quantity used in the calculation of boiling point elevation

Questions 5–9 refer to the following.

(A) Hydrogen bonding
(B) Ionic bonding
(C) Network bonding
(D) London dispersion force
(E) Metallic bonding

5. Chiefly responsible for the relatively high boiling point of water

6. Is present in liquid oxygen

7. Is primarily responsible for the hardness of diamond

8. Allows copper to conduct electricity

9. Is present in solid KCl

GO ON TO THE NEXT PAGE

Questions 10–13 refer to the following.

   (A) Na^+
   (B) Al
   (C) F
   (D) Ti
   (E) Br^-

10. Has 7 valence electrons

11. Has the electron configuration $1s^22s^22p^63s^23p^1$

12. Has the same electron configuration as a neon atom

13. Has valence electrons in *d* orbitals

Questions 14–17 refer to the following.

   (A) A 0.01-molar solution of HNO_3
   (B) A 0.01-molar solution of $HC_2H_3O_2$
   (C) A 0.01-molar solution of $Cu(NO_3)_2$
   (D) A 0.01-molar solution of $NaNO_3$
   (E) A 0.01-molar solution of NaOH

14. Will be colored blue

15. Will have a pH of 2

16. Will have the lowest freezing point

17. Will contain undissociated aqueous particles

GO ON TO THE NEXT PAGE

Questions 18–20 refer to the following.

(A) Enthalpy change
(B) Entropy change
(C) Gibbs free energy change
(D) Activation energy
(E) Specific heat capacity

18. Is the amount of energy that must be added to raise the temperature of 1 gram of a substance 1°C

19. Its value indicates the spontaneity of a reaction

20. Its value indicates whether a reaction is endothermic or exothermic

Questions 21–23 refer to the following.

(A) Ionization energy
(B) Electronegativity
(C) Atomic radius
(D) Atomic number
(E) Mass number

21. Is the measure of the pull of the nucleus of an atom on the electrons of other atoms bonded to it

22. Is the energy required to remove an electron from an atom

23. Is equal to the number of protons in an atom

GO ON TO THE NEXT PAGE

SAT SUBJECT TEST IN CHEMISTRY–TEST 2—*Continued*

PLEASE GO TO THE SPECIAL SECTION LABELED CHEMISTRY AT THE LOWER RIGHT-HAND CORNER OF THE ANSWER SHEET YOU ARE WORKING ON AND ANSWER QUESTIONS 101-116 ACCORDING TO THE FOLLOWING DIRECTIONS.

Part B

Directions: Each question below consists of two statements, I in the left-hand column and II in the right-hand column. For each question, determine whether statement I is true or false and whether statement II is true or false, and fill in the corresponding T or F ovals on your answer sheet. <u>Fill in oval CE only if statement II is a correct explanation of statement I.</u>

EXAMPLES:

I		II
EX 1. H_2SO_4 is a strong acid	BECAUSE	H_2SO_4 contains sulfur.
EX 2. An atom of oxygen is electrically neutral	BECAUSE	an oxygen atom contains an equal number of protons and electrons.

SAMPLE ANSWERS

	I		II		CE
EX 1	●	F	●	F	
EX 2	●	F	●	F	●

	I		II
101.	An ionic solid is a good conductor of electricity	BECAUSE	an ionic solid is composed of positive and negative ions joined together in a lattice structure held together by electrostatic forces.
102.	The bond in an O_2 molecule is nonpolar	BECAUSE	the oxygen atoms in an O_2 molecule share the bonding electrons equally.
103.	When a sample of water freezes, the process is exothermic	BECAUSE	ice is at a lower potential energy state than water.
104.	At 25°C, an aqueous solution with a pH of 5 will have a pOH of 9	BECAUSE	the pH of a buffered solution is not greatly affected by the addition of a relatively small amount of acid or base.
105.	When a chlorine atom gains an electron, it becomes a positively charged ion	BECAUSE	a neutral atom has equal numbers of protons and electrons.

GO ON TO THE NEXT PAGE

I   II

106.   Lithium has a larger first ionization   BECAUSE   oxygen atoms have larger atomic radii
        energy than oxygen   than lithium atoms.

107.   Potassium chloride dissolves readily   BECAUSE   water is a polar solvent.
        in water

108.   Ammonia is a Lewis base   BECAUSE   ammonia can donate an electron pair to
                                                                     a bond.

109.   Elemental fluorine is more reactive   BECAUSE   neon has a larger atomic weight
        than elemental neon   than fluorine.

110.   The addition of a catalyst will decrease   BECAUSE   a catalyst provides an alternate reaction
        the ΔH for a reaction   pathway with a lower activation energy.

111.   The oxygen atom in a water molecule   BECAUSE   water molecules exhibit hydrogen
        has a –2 oxidation state   bonding.

112.   When a salt sample dissolves in water,   BECAUSE   for a salt sample, aqueous ions have
        ΔS for the process is positive   greater entropy than ions in a solid.

113.   When the temperature of a reaction at   BECAUSE   at equilibrium, all reactants have
        equilibrium is increased, the   been converted into products.
        equilibrium will shift to favor the
        endothermic direction

114.   An atom of ^{12}C contains 12 protons   BECAUSE   the identity of an element is determined
                                                                     by the number of protons in the
                                                                     nuclei of its atoms.

115.   Water boils at a lower temperature at   BECAUSE   the vapor pressure of water is lower
        high altitude than at low altitude   at higher altitude.

116.   Elemental sodium is a strong   BECAUSE   an atom of elemental sodium gives
        reducing agent   up its valence electron readily.

RETURN TO THE SECTION OF YOUR ANSWER SHEET YOU STARTED FOR **CHEMISTRY** AND

ANSWER QUESTIONS 24–70.

GO ON TO THE NEXT PAGE

Part C

Directions: Each of the questions or incomplete statements below is followed by five suggested answers or completions. Select the one that is best in each case and then fill in the corresponding oval on the answer sheet.

24. Identify the molar mass of a gas that effuses two times faster than methane (CH_4).

    (A) 2 grams
    (B) 4 grams
    (C) 8 grams
    (D) 16 grams
    (E) 32 grams

25. Which of the following was a phrase used to describe the Rutherford experiment?

    (A) Plum pudding model
    (B) Gold foil experiment
    (C) Bohr model
    (D) Absorption of light energy spectrum
    (E) Cathode ray tube experiment

26. A mixture of 1 mole of H_2 gas, 2 moles of NH_3 gas, 3 moles of CO_2 gas, and 6 moles of N_2 gas exerts a total pressure of 600 torr. What is the partial pressure of the NH_3 gas?

    (A) 50 torr
    (B) 100 torr
    (C) 150 torr
    (D) 300 torr
    (E) 600 torr

27. When a given number of moles of water are heated at a constant rate, the change of phase from liquid to gas takes longer than the change of phase from solid to liquid because

    (A) The heat of fusion is greater than the heat of vaporization
    (B) The heat of vaporization is greater than the heat of fusion
    (C) The specific heat of liquid water is greater than the specific heat of ice
    (D) The average kinetic energy of water vapor is greater than the average kinetic energy of liquid water at the same temperature
    (E) The average kinetic energy of water vapor is less than the average kinetic energy of liquid water at the same temperature

28. Assuming constant pressure, if chlorine gas occupies a volume of 25 ml at 25 degrees C, what volume will it occupy at 327 degrees C?

    (A) 12.5 ml
    (B) 25 ml
    (C) 50 ml
    (D) 100 ml
    (E) 200 ml

29. If an ideal gas occupies a volume of 300 ml at a pressure of 280 torr and a temperature of 298K, what will the temperature be at a volume of 150 ml and 560 torr?

    (A) 149K
    (B) 273K
    (C) 298K
    (D) 398K
    (E) 596K

GO ON TO THE NEXT PAGE

30. A sample of copper (Cu) is 100 grams and heated to 80 degrees C, and then added to 5 grams of water at 20 degrees C. What is the final temperature of the copper – water mixture? Assume the specific heat of Copper to be approximately 0.4 J/gC and the specific heat of water to be 4 J/gC.

    (A) 20 degrees C
    (B) 40 degrees C
    (C) 60 degrees C
    (D) 70 degrees C
    (E) 80 degrees C

$$H_2SO_4(aq) + Ba(OH)_2(aq) \rightarrow$$

31. Which of the following are products of the reaction shown above?

    I. $O_2(g)$
    II. $H_2O(l)$
    III. $BaSO_4(s)$

    (A) I only
    (B) III only
    (C) I and II only
    (D) I and III only
    (E) II and III only

$$2Mg(s) + O_2(g) \rightarrow 2MgO(s)$$

32. If 48.6 grams of magnesium are placed in a container with 64 grams of oxygen gas and the reaction above proceeds to completion, what is the mass of $MgO(s)$ produced?

    (A) 15.4 grams
    (B) 32.0 grams
    (C) 80.6 grams
    (D) 96.3 grams
    (E) 112 grams

33. An ideal gas in a closed inflexible container has a pressure of 6 atmospheres and a temperature of 27°C. What will be the new pressure of the gas if the temperature is decreased to –73°C ?

    (A) 2 atm
    (B) 3 atm
    (C) 4 atm
    (D) 8 atm
    (E) 9 atm

34. Equal molar quantities of hydrogen gas and oxygen gas are present in a closed container at a constant temperature. Which of the following quantities will be the same for the two gases?

    I.   Partial pressure
    II. Average kinetic energy
    III. Average molecular velocity

    (A) I only
    (B) I and II only
    (C) I and III only
    (D) II and III only
    (E) I, II, and III

35. Which of the following is a nonpolar molecule?

    (A) CO_2
    (B) H_2O
    (C) NH_3
    (D) NO
    (E) HI

36. What is the molar concentration of a 500-milliliter solution that contains 20 grams of $CaBr_2$ (formula weight = 200) ?

    (A) 0.1 molar
    (B) 0.2 molar
    (C) 0.5 molar
    (D) 1 molar
    (E) 5 molar

GO ON TO THE NEXT PAGE

37. The structure of $BeCl_2$ can best be described as

    (A) linear
    (B) bent
    (C) trigonal
    (D) tetrahedral
    (E) square

    $$2NO(g) + 2H_2(g) \rightarrow N_2(g) + 2H_2O(g)$$

38. Which of the following statements is true regarding the reaction given above?

    (A) If 1 mole of H_2 is consumed, 0.5 mole of N_2 is produced.
    (B) If 1 mole of H_2 is consumed, 0.5 mole of H_2O is produced.
    (C) If 0.5 mole of H_2 is consumed, 1 mole of N_2 is produced.
    (D) If 0.5 mole of H_2 is consumed, 1 mole of NO is consumed.
    (E) If 0.5 mole of H_2 is consumed, 1 mole of H_2O is produced.

Questions 39 and 40 pertain to the reaction represented by the following equation.

$$\ldots Cu(s) + \ldots NO_3^-(aq) + \ldots H^+(aq) \rightarrow \ldots$$
$$Cu^{2+}(aq) + \ldots NO_2(g) + \ldots H_2O(l)$$

39. When the equation above is balanced with lowest whole number coefficients, the coefficient for $H^+(aq)$ will be

    (A) 1
    (B) 2
    (C) 3
    (D) 4
    (E) 5

40. Which of the following takes place during the reaction above?

    (A) $Cu(s)$ is oxidized.
    (B) $Cu(s)$ is reduced.
    (C) $H^+(aq)$ is oxidized.
    (D) $H^+(aq)$ is reduced.
    (E) $NO_3^-(aq)$ is oxidized.

41. Which of the following could be the molecular formula for a molecule with an empirical formula of CH_2 ?

    (A) CH
    (B) CH_4
    (C) C_2H_2
    (D) C_2H_6
    (E) C_3H_6

42. When CO_2 is bubbled through distilled water at 25°C, which of the following is most likely to occur?

    (A) Solid carbon will precipitate.
    (B) An electrical current will be produced in an oxidation-reduction reaction.
    (C) The pH of the solution will be reduced.
    (D) The water will boil.
    (E) Methane (CH_4) gas will be formed.

43. In which of the following processes is entropy increasing?

    (A) $N_2(g) + 3Cl_2(g) \rightarrow 2NCl_3(g)$
    (B) $H_2O(g) \rightarrow H_2O(l)$
    (C) $2H_2O(l) \rightarrow 2H_2(g) + O_2(g)$
    (D) $CO(g) + 2H_2(g) \rightarrow CH_3OH(l)$
    (E) $2NO_2(g) \rightarrow N_2O_4(g)$

GO ON TO THE NEXT PAGE

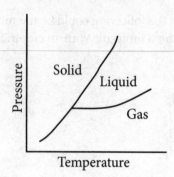

44. Based on the phase diagram above, which series of phase changes could take place as pressure is decreased at a constant temperature?

(A) Solid to liquid to gas
(B) Solid to gas to liquid
(C) Gas to liquid to solid
(D) Gas to solid to liquid
(E) Liquid to gas to solid

45. Which of the following forms of radioactive decay has (have) no electrical charge?

  I. Alpha decay
  II. Beta decay
  III. Gamma decay

(A) II only
(B) III only
(C) I and II only
(D) I and III only
(E) II and III only

46. Based on the solubility products given below, which of the following salts is the most soluble?

(A) $BaCO_3$ $K_{sp} = 5.1 \times 10^{-9}$
(B) $PbCrO_4$ $K_{sp} = 2.8 \times 10^{-13}$
(C) $AgCl$ $K_{sp} = 1.8 \times 10^{-10}$
(D) $CaSO_4$ $K_{sp} = 9.1 \times 10^{-6}$
(E) ZnC_2O_4 $K_{sp} = 2.7 \times 10^{-8}$

$$HCN(aq) \rightarrow H^+(aq) + CN^-(aq)$$

47. Hydrocyanic acid dissociates according to the reaction given above. Which of the following expressions is equal to the acid dissociation constant for HCN?

(A) $[H^+][CN^-]$

(B) $[H^+][CN^-][HCN]$

(C) $\dfrac{[HCN]}{[H^+][CN^-]}$

(D) $\dfrac{[H^+][CN^-]}{[HCN]}$

(E) $\dfrac{1}{[H^+][CN^-][HCN]}$

48. The reaction progress diagram of an uncatalyzed reaction is shown by the solid line. Which dotted line presents the same reaction in the presence of a catalyst?

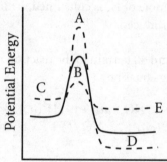

49. In a hydrogen atom, when an electron jumps from an excited energy state to a more stable energy state,

(A) electromagnetic radiation is emitted by the atom
(B) electromagnetic radiation is absorbed by the atom
(C) the atom becomes a positively charged ion
(D) the atom becomes a negatively charged ion
(E) the atom undergoes nuclear decay

GO ON TO THE NEXT PAGE

Questions 50–52 pertain to the following situation.

A closed 5-liter vessel contains a sample of neon gas. The temperature inside the container is 25°C, and the pressure is 1.5 atmospheres. (The gas constant, R, is equal to 0.08 L•atm/mol•K.)

50. Which of the following expressions is equal to the molar quantity of gas in the sample?

(A) $\dfrac{(1.5)(5.0)}{(0.08)(25)}$ moles

(B) $\dfrac{(0.08)(25)}{(1.5)(5.0)}$ moles

(C) $\dfrac{(1.5)(25)}{(0.08)(5.0)}$ moles

(D) $\dfrac{(0.08)(298)}{(1.5)(5.0)}$ moles

(E) $\dfrac{(1.5)(5.0)}{(0.08)(298)}$ moles

51. If the neon gas in the vessel is replaced with an equal molar quantity of helium gas, which of the following properties of the gas in the container will be changed?

    I. Pressure
    II. Temperature
    III. Density

(A) I only
(B) II only
(C) III only
(D) I and II only
(E) II and III only

52. The volume of the vessel was gradually changed while temperature was held constant until the pressure was measured at 1.6 atmospheres. Which of the following expressions is equal to the new volume?

(A) $5.0 \times \dfrac{1.5}{1.6}$ liters

(B) $5.0 \times \dfrac{1.6}{1.5}$ liters

(C) $25 \times \dfrac{1.5}{1.6}$ liters

(D) $0.08 \times \dfrac{1.6}{1.5}$ liters

(E) $0.08 \times \dfrac{1.5}{1.6}$ liters

53. Which of the following list of atoms is ranked from greatest to least in terms of chemical reactivity?

(A) Ne > S > Co > Fr
(B) Fr > S > Co > Ne
(C) Co > Fr > S > Ne
(D) S > Ne > Fr > Co
(E) Fr > Co > Ne > S

54. A solution containing which of the following pairs of species could be a buffer?

(A) H^+ and Cl^-
(B) H_2CO_3 and HCO_3^-
(C) Na^+ and NO_3^-
(D) Na^+ and OH^-
(E) HNO_3 and NO_3^-

GO ON TO THE NEXT PAGE

55. Which of the following species is the conjugate acid of ammonia (NH_3) ?

    (A) N_2
    (B) H_2
    (C) NH^{2-}
    (D) NH_2^-
    (E) NH_4^+

56. A solution of H_2SO_3 is found to have a hydrogen ion concentration of 1×10^{-3} molar at 25°C. What is the hydroxide ion concentration in the solution?

    (A) 1×10^{-13} molar
    (B) 1×10^{-11} molar
    (C) 1×10^{-7} molar
    (D) 1×10^{-4} molar
    (E) 1×10^{-3} molar

57. Which of the following expressions is equal to the number of iron (Fe) atoms present in a pure sample of solid iron with a mass of 10 grams? (The atomic mass of iron is 55.9.)

    (A) $(10.0)(55.9)(6.02 \times 10^{23})$ atoms

    (B) $\dfrac{(6.02 \times 10^{23})}{(10.0)(55.9)}$ atoms

    (C) $\dfrac{(10.0)(6.02 \times 10^{23})}{(55.9)}$ atoms

    (D) $\dfrac{(55.9)}{(10.0)(6.02 \times 10^{23})}$ atoms

    (E) $\dfrac{(10.0)}{(55.9)(6.02 \times 10^{23})}$ atoms

58. A radioactive material is undergoing nuclear decay. After 40 minutes, 25 percent of the sample remains. What is the half-life of the sample?

    (A) 10 minutes
    (B) 20 minutes
    (C) 40 minutes
    (D) 80 minutes
    (E) 160 minutes

Element	First Ionization Energy (kJ/mol)
Lithium	520
Sodium	496
Rubidium	403
Cesium	376

59. Based on the table above, which of the following is most likely to be the first ionization energy for potassium?

    (A) 536 kJ/mol
    (B) 504 kJ/mol
    (C) 419 kJ/mol
    (D) 391 kJ/mol
    (E) 358 kJ/mol

GO ON TO THE NEXT PAGE

Questions 60–62 pertain to the reaction represented by the following equation.

$$2NOCl(g) \leftrightharpoons 2NO(g) + Cl_2(g)$$

60. Which of the following expressions gives the equilibrium constant for the reaction above?

(A) $\dfrac{[NOCl]}{[NO][Cl_2]}$

(B) $\dfrac{[NO][Cl_2]}{[NOCl]}$

(C) $\dfrac{[NOCl]^2}{[NO]^2[Cl_2]}$

(D) $\dfrac{[NO]^2[Cl_2]}{[NOCl]^2}$

(E) $\dfrac{[NOCl]^2}{[NO]^2[Cl_2]^2}$

61. Which of the following changes to the equilibrium above would serve to decrease the concentration of Cl_2?

   I. The addition of $NOCl(g)$ to the reaction vessel
   II. The addition of $NO(g)$ to the reaction vessel
   III. A decrease in the volume of the reaction vessel

(A) I only
(B) II only
(C) I and II only
(D) I and III only
(E) II and III only

62. Which of the following is true of the reaction above as it proceeds in the forward direction?

(A) $NO(g)$ is produced at the same rate that $NOCl(g)$ is consumed.
(B) $NO(g)$ is produced at half the rate that $NOCl(g)$ is consumed.
(C) $NO(g)$ is produced at twice the rate that $NOCl(g)$ is consumed.
(D) $Cl_2(g)$ is produced at the same rate that $NOCl(g)$ is consumed.
(E) $Cl_2(g)$ is produced at twice the rate that $NOCl(g)$ is consumed.

63. Which of the following is an organic molecule?

(A) SiO_2
(B) NH_3
(C) H_2O
(D) CH_4
(E) BeF_2

GO ON TO THE NEXT PAGE

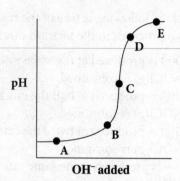

OH⁻ added

64. The graph above represents the titration of a strong acid with a strong base. Which of the points shown on the graph indicates the equivalence point in the titration?

    (A) A
    (B) B
    (C) C
    (D) D
    (E) E

65. Which of the following statements about fluorine is NOT true?

    (A) It is the most electronegative element.
    (B) It contains 19 protons in its nucleus.
    (C) Its compounds can engage in hydrogen bonding.
    (D) It takes the oxidation state –1.
    (E) It is found in nature as a diatomic gas.

66. The reactivity and chemical behavior of an atom is governed by many factors. The most important factor is

    (A) the number of protons in the atom's nucleus
    (B) the number of neutrons in the atom's nucleus
    (C) the number of protons and neutrons in the atom's nucleus
    (D) the ratio of protons to neutrons in the atom's nucleus
    (E) the number of electrons in the atom's valence shell

67. A beaker contains a saturated solution of copper(I) chloride, a slightly soluble salt with a solubility product of 1.2×10^{-6}. The addition of which of the salts listed below to the solution would cause the precipitation of copper(I) chloride?

    (A) Sodium chloride
    (B) Potassium bromide
    (C) Silver(I) nitrate
    (D) Lead(II) acetate
    (E) Magnesium iodide

68. Bromothymol blue is an acid/base indicator with a pK_a of 6.8. Therefore, at approximately what pH will bromothymol blue undergo a color change during an acid/base titration?

    (A)   1
    (B)   3
    (C)   5
    (D)   7
    (E)   13

69. Which of the following is necessarily true of a nonionic substance with a high boiling point?

    (A) It has a large vapor pressure.
    (B) It has strong intermolecular attractive forces.
    (C) It has a low freezing point.
    (D) It has a low heat of vaporization.
    (E) It will be present in gas phase at very low temperatures.

70. Which of the following substances would have the highest melting point?

    (A) CF_4
    (B) BaS
    (C) $MgCl_2$
    (D) CaO
    (E) NH_3

STOP

If you finish before time is called, you may check your work on this section only.
Do not turn to any other section in the test.

Chapter 16
Practice Test 2:
Answers and
Explanations

PRACTICE TEST 2 ANSWER KEY

Question Number	Correct Answer	Right	Wrong
Part A			
1.	E	____	____
2.	B	____	____
3.	D	____	____
4.	B	____	____
5.	A	____	____
6.	D	____	____
7.	C	____	____
8.	E	____	____
9.	B	____	____
10.	C	____	____
11.	B	____	____
12.	A	____	____
13.	D	____	____
14.	C	____	____
15.	A	____	____
16.	C	____	____
17.	B	____	____
18.	E	____	____
19.	C	____	____
20.	A	____	____
21.	B	____	____
22.	A	____	____
23.	D		____
Part B			
101.	F, T		
102.	T, T, CE		
103.	T, T, CE		
104.	T, T		
105.	F, T		
106.	F, F		
107.	T, T, CE		
108.	T, T, CE		
109.	T, T		
110.	F, T		
111.	T, T		
112.	T, T, CE		
113.	T, F		
114.	F, T		
115.	T, F		
116.	T, T, CE		

Question Number	Correct Answer	Right	Wrong
Part C			
24.	B	____	____
25.	B	____	____
26.	B	____	____
27.	B	____	____
28.	C	____	____
29.	C	____	____
30.	C	____	____
31.	E	____	____
32.	C	____	____
33.	C	____	____
34.	B	____	____
35.	A	____	____
36.	B	____	____
37.	A	____	____
38.	A	____	____
39.	D	____	____
40.	A	____	____
41.	E	____	____
42.	C	____	____
43.	C	____	____
44.	A	____	____
45.	B	____	____
46.	D	____	____
47.	D	____	____
48.	B	____	____
49.	A	____	____
50.	E	____	____
51.	C	____	____
52.	A	____	____
53.	B	____	____
54.	B	____	____
55.	E	____	____
56.	B	____	____
57.	C	____	____
58.	B	____	____
59.	C	____	____
60.	D	____	____
61.	E	____	____
62.	A	____	____
63.	D	____	____
64.	C	____	____
65.	B	____	____
66.	E	____	____
67.	A	____	____
68.	D	____	____
69.	B	____	____
70.	D	____	____

PRACTICE TEST 2 EXPLANATIONS

Part A

1. **E** Atmospheres and millimeters of mercury (also written as mmHg or torr) are units of pressure used in the measurement of gas properties. Partial pressure is the only property listed that is measured in units of pressure.

2. **B** Molality (*m*) is the measure of moles of solute present per kilogram of solvent. It is the only answer choice that measures moles per kilogram. Molality differs from molarity (*M*) in that molarity is the measure of moles of solute per liter of solution.

3. **D** Density is the measure of the mass of gas, liquid, or solid within a given volume. The densities of liquids and solids are relatively independent of their surroundings, while the density of a gas depends on the size of the container in which it is confined.

4. **B** Molality (*m*) is used in the calculation of boiling point elevation according to the formula: $\Delta T = k_b mi$, where k_b is the boiling point elevation constant for a solvent, *m* is the molality of the solution, and *i* is the van't Hoff factor, which tells how many particles 1 unit of the solute will create when it dissociates. Molality is also used in the calculation of freezing point depression.

5. **A** Liquid water (H_2O) contains hydrogen bonds between the hydrogen atoms of each molecule and the oxygen atoms of neighboring molecules. Many of water's distinctive properties, such as the fact that it has a lower density as a solid than as a liquid and that it has a relatively high boiling point, are due to hydrogen bonding.

6. **D** Liquid oxygen is held together by London dispersion forces, which are very weak attractions between molecules. London dispersion forces are the only type of intermolecular attractions that exist in nonpolar molecules, such as O_2. London dispersion forces occur because of instantaneous charge imbalances in molecules. Most substances that experience only London dispersion forces are gases at room temperature.

7. **C** Diamond owes its great strength to the fact that its carbon atoms are bonded together in a tetrahedral network of covalent bonds. This tetrahedral structure means that diamonds have no natural breaking points and are thus very difficult to shatter.

8. **E** Solid copper is held together by metallic bonding. When elements are held together by metallic bonds, positively charged nuclei float in a sea of mobile electrons. The electrons move freely from nucleus to nucleus. This electron mobility is responsible for the distinctive properties of metals such as conductivity and malleability.

9. **B** Solid KCl (potassium chloride) salt is held together by ionic bonds. The positively charged potassium ions and the negatively charged chloride ions are held together by the electrostatic force between

them. Remember that the electrostatic force comes from the attraction between two atoms that differ very significantly in electronegativity and is very strong.

10. **C** Fluorine (F) has 7 electrons in its second shell, 1 short of a complete stable octet.

11. **B** Aluminum (Al) has 3 electrons in its third shell, 2 in the s subshell, and 1 in the p subshell.

12. **A** A positively charged sodium ion (Na^+) has given up the 1 electron from its third shell, so it has the same electron configuration as a neon atom, which has a completed second shell.

13. **D** Choice (D) is correct. Titanium (Ti) is a transition metal and has 2 electrons in its $3d$ subshell.

14. **C** The solution containing Cu^{2+} ion will be blue. Most solutions containing salts of transition metals are distinctly colored because the d subshell electrons of transition metals absorb and emit electromagnetic radiation in the visible spectrum.

15. **A** HNO_3 is a strong acid, so it will dissociate completely in solution. That means that a 0.01-molar solution of HNO_3 will have a hydrogen ion concentration of 0.01-molar. pH is $-\log$ [H], and $-\log (0.01) = 2$, so the pH of the solution will be 2.

16. **C** Freezing point depression is a colligative property, which means that it depends only on the number of particles in a solution, not on their identities. For every unit of $Cu(NO_3)_2$ in a solution, 3 particles are produced: 1 Cu^{2+} and 2 NO_3^-. For all of the other choices, each unit in solution produces only 2 particles.

17. **B** $HC_2H_3O_2$ (acetic acid) is a weak acid, which means that it does not dissociate significantly in solution. That means that most of the particles present in the acetic acid solution will be undissociated $HC_2H_3O_2$. All of the other solutions listed contain solutes that dissociate completely.

18. **E** The specific heat capacity is the amount of energy that must be added to raise the temperature of 1 gram of a substance 1°C. If a substance has a large specific heat capacity, it can absorb a large amount of heat while undergoing a small temperature change.

19. **C** The value of the Gibbs free energy change (ΔG) for a reaction indicates the spontaneity of the reaction. If ΔG is negative, then the forward reaction is spontaneous. If ΔG is positive, then the reaction is not spontaneous. If ΔG is zero, then the forward reaction is at equilibrium.

20. **A** The value of the enthalpy change (ΔH) for a reaction indicates whether the reaction is endothermic or exothermic. If ΔH is positive, energy is absorbed over the course of the reaction, and the reaction is endothermic. If ΔH is negative, energy is released over the course of the reaction, and the reaction is exothermic.

21. **B** Electronegativity indicates how strongly an atom will attract the electrons of another atom in a bond. The larger the electronegativity difference between two atoms in a bond, the more polar the bond will be.

22. **A** Ionization energy is the energy required to remove an electron from an atom or ion. The larger the ionization energy, the more difficult it is to remove the electron.

23. **D** The atomic number, which determines the identity of an element, is equal to the number of protons in the atom's nucleus. The mass number is equal to the sum of the protons and neutrons in an atom's nucleus. Atoms with the same atomic number and different mass numbers are isotopes.

Part B

101. **F, T** Divide and conquer. The first statement is false. Neither the electrons nor the ions in an ionic solid are free to move about, so an ionic solid will not conduct electricity. The second statement is true. An ionic solid is composed of positive and negative ions joined in a lattice structure by electrostatic forces. The first statement is false and the second statement is true.

102. **T, T, CE**

Divide and conquer. Both statements are true. Since the oxygen atoms are identical to each other, they will have equal attraction for the bonding electrons. The second statement is a correct explanation for the first statement, so fill in the CE oval.

103. **T, T, CE**

Divide and conquer. Both statements are true. Ice has stronger intermolecular forces and more stability than water, so when water freezes, energy is released. The second statement is a correct explanation of the first statement, so fill in the CE oval.

104. **T, T** Divide and conquer. The first statement is true. For an aqueous solution at 25°C, pH + pOH = 14. The second statement is also true. The definition of a buffer is *a solution whose pH is not easily changed by the addition of an acid or base.* Now, ask yourself if the word "because" relates the two statements. The second statement does not explain the first statement, so do not fill in the CE oval.

105. **F, T** Divide and conquer. The first statement is false. When an atom gains an electron, it becomes a negatively charged ion. The second statement is true. Protons are positively charged and electrons are negatively charged, so an atom that has equal numbers of protons and electrons will be electrically neutral. The first statement is false and the second statement is true.

106. **F, F** Divide and conquer. The first statement is false. As you travel across a period on the periodic table, from left to right, ionization energy increases. That's because as you move across a period, protons are added to the nucleus, which increases the pull of the nucleus on the valence electrons, making them more difficult to remove. The second statement is also false. The same reasoning applies here; oxygen's nucleus has more protons, so oxygen exerts a greater pull on its electrons. As a result, oxygen's valence electrons will be closer to the nucleus than lithium's, making its atomic radius smaller. Both statements are false.

107.   **T, T, CE**

Divide and conquer. The first statement is true; potassium chloride (KCl) is a soluble salt. The second statement is also true. The second statement is a correct explanation of the first statement because you know that like dissolves like, so ionic solids are best dissolved by polar solvents. Both statements are true, and fill in the CE oval.

108.   **T, T, CE**

Divide and conquer. Both statements are true; we know that ammonia (NH_3) is a Lewis base and that a Lewis base is an electron pair donor. The second statement is a correct explanation of the first statement—the statements together give us the definition of a Lewis base. We fill in the CE oval.

109. **T, T** Divide and conquer. The first statement is true. Fluorine is more reactive than neon because it needs 1 electron to complete its valence shell, while neon has a complete stable octet of electrons in its valence shell. The second statement is true. Neon has an atomic weight of 20.2 g/mol, while fluorine has an atomic weight of 19.0 g/mol. Now see if the second statement explains the first. Fluorine is more reactive than neon for the reason given above, not because of its atomic weight, so the second statement does not explain the first. Both statements are true, and do not fill in the CE oval.

110. **F, T** Divide and conquer. The first statement is false. The enthalpy change (ΔH) for a reaction is unaffected by the addition of a catalyst. The second statement is true: a catalyst increases the rate of a reaction by decreasing the activation energy of the reaction. The first statement is false and the second statement is true.

111. **T, T** Divide and conquer. The first statement is true. In water (H_2O), the oxygen atom gains 2 electrons and takes the −2 oxidation state, while each of the 2 hydrogen atoms gives up an electron and takes the +1 oxidation state. The second statement is also true. Water does exhibit hydrogen bonding. Now, ask yourself whether the second statement is an explanation of the first. The two statements are not related. Both statements are true, and do not fill in the CE oval.

112.   **T, T, CE**

Divide and conquer. Entropy is a measure of disorder, and aqueous ions have greater disorder than ions in a solid, so both statements are true. The second statement is a good explanation of the first statement because knowing that aqueous ions have greater entropy than ions in a solid, we can see why entropy increases in solution. Both statements are true, and fill in the CE oval.

113. **T, F** Divide and conquer. The first statement is true. From Le Châtelier's principle, when temperature is increased, an equilibrium will move in the direction that will absorb the excess heat; that's the endothermic direction. The second statement is false. A reaction reaches equilibrium when the rate of the forward reaction is equal to the rate of the reverse reaction, not when all the reactants have been converted to products. The first statement is true and the second statement is false.

114. **F, T** Divide and conquer. The first statement is false. A carbon atom always contains 6 protons. The number 12 is the mass number, which is the sum of the protons and neutrons in the nucleus. The second statement is true. The number of protons in an atom is the atomic number and gives the element its identity. The first statement is false and the second statement is true.

115. **T, F** Divide and conquer. The first statement is true. Water's vapor pressure increases when heat is added, and water boils when its vapor pressure is equal to the atmospheric pressure. At high altitudes, atmospheric pressure is decreased, so water will boil at a lower temperature. The second statement is false. The vapor pressure of water is unaffected by altitude. The first statement is true and the second statement is false.

116. **T, T, CE**

Divide and conquer. Both statements are true. A strong reducing agent is readily oxidized. Remember LEO says GER: when something is oxidized, it loses electrons. A sodium atom has only 1 valence electron, which it gives up readily, so it is easily oxidized. Therefore, elemental sodium is a strong reducing agent. The second statement is a good explanation of the first statement. Both statements are true, so fill in the CE oval.

Part C

24. **B** Graham's Law of Effusion states that $\dfrac{\text{rate } 1}{\text{rate } 2} = \dfrac{\sqrt{(\text{molar mass gas } 2)}}{\sqrt{(\text{molar mass gas } 1)}}$

So, if gas 1 is the unknown, and gas 2 is methane, the equation above becomes,

$$2 = \frac{\sqrt{16}}{\sqrt{\text{molar mass gas } 1}}$$

which simplifies to

$$2 = \frac{4}{\sqrt{\text{molar mass gas } 1}}$$

Therefore, the square root of the molar mass of the unknown must be 2, so the molar mass must be 4.

25. **B** Ernest Rutherford, Hans Geiger, and Ernest Marsden conducted the gold foil experiment to prove the existence of a small center of mass to atoms, which was later called the nucleus. J.J. Thompson's experiments with cathode ray tubes were used to prove the existence of the electron. His plum pudding model of the atom has negatively charged electrons placed inside a positively charged "soup." Bohr's model of hydrogen assumed that electrons travel around a central nucleus in orbits arranged like concentric circles. An absorption of light energy spectrum occurs when a gas absorbs energy (usually in the form of photons of light).

26. **B** Partial pressures for gases are determined by what fraction of the total number of moles of gas that a particular gas occupies. In this example, NH_3 is 2 of the 12 total moles, so its partial pressure is $\frac{2}{12}$ or $\frac{1}{6}$ of 600 torr, which is 100 torr. H_2 is 1 of the 12 total moles, so its partial pressure is $\frac{1}{12}$ of 600 torr, or 50 torr. CO_2 is $\frac{3}{12}$ or $\frac{1}{4}$ of the total pressure, or 150 torr. Lastly, N_2 is $\frac{6}{12}$ or $\frac{1}{2}$ the total pressure, or 300 torr.

27. **B** When changing phase, the amount of heat necessary is determined by the formula q = n (number of moles) × heat of fusion or vaporization, depending on which phase change is occurring. The change of phase from liquid to gas uses the heat of vaporization, and the change of phase from ice (water as a solid) to liquid water uses the heat of fusion. If a phase change takes longer, that means that it requires more heat (q), and since the moles are not changing, the longer time will have the higher heat, which in this case is the heat of vaporization. The specific heat of liquid water is greater than the specific heat of ice, but specific heat is only used when changing temperatures, not phases. Average kinetic energy is proportional to temperature and will be higher at higher temperatures.

28. **C** $\frac{P_1 V_1}{T_1} = \frac{P_2 V_2}{T_2}$, but at constant pressure, $\frac{V_1}{T_1} = \frac{V_2}{T_2}$, so $\frac{25\text{ml}}{300\text{K}} = \frac{V_2}{600\text{K}}$.

    Since the temperature has doubled, the volume will double to 50ml.

29. **C** $\frac{P_1 V_1}{T_1} = \frac{P_2 V_2}{T_2}$ so $\frac{280 \text{ torr} \times 300 \text{ ml}}{298\text{K}} = \frac{560 \text{ torr} \times 150 \text{ ml}}{\text{x}}$

    Since the pressure has doubled and the volume has halved, the numerator of both fractions are equal, so there is no change in temperature. The correct answer is (C), $P_2 = 298$K

30. **C** The heat lost by the copper must equal the heat gained by the water. The heat lost by the copper = (100 g)(0.4)(80 – T), where T is the final temperature of the mixture. The heat gained by the water = (5 g) (4)(T – 20). So, 40(80 – T) = 20(T – 20). 3200 – 40T = 20T – 400. If we add 40T and 400 to both sides of the equation we get 3600 = 60T, so T = 60 degrees C.

31. **E** First, look at your reactants: you have an acid and a base, so you know that they will neutralize one another. Now write out the products.

    $H_2SO_4(aq) + Ba(OH)_2(aq) \rightarrow BaSO_4 + H_2O$

    Note that in this problem, you don't need to balance anything; just figure out the type of reaction and the products. The products of an acid-base neutralization (when the base is a metal hydroxide) are water and salt. In this case, the salt is barium sulfate.

32. **C** You need to determine the limiting reagent. Magnesium has an atomic weight of about 24 g/mol, so 48 grams of magnesium is 2 moles. O_2 has a molecular weight of 32 g/mol, so 64 grams of O_2 is about 2 moles. You need twice as much Mg for the reaction, so you'll run out of it first; magnesium is the limiting reagent. Two moles of Mg will produce 2 moles of MgO, which has a molecular weight of 40.3 g/mol, so you end up with 80.6 grams of MgO.

33. **C** The pressure and temperature of an ideal gas are related by the following equation (when the amount of gas and volume are held constant): $\dfrac{P_1}{T_1} = \dfrac{P_2}{T_2}$. You need to convert Celsius to Kelvin, so 27°C = 300 K and –73°C = 200 K. Now you can calculate:

$$\frac{(6\,\text{atm})}{(300\,\text{K})} = \frac{x}{(200\,\text{K})}$$

$x = 4$ atm

34. **B** The partial pressures of the two gases will be the same because partial pressure of a gas is directly proportional to the number of moles of the gas present, and you have equal numbers of moles of the two gases. The average kinetic energies of the two gases will be the same because the average kinetic energy of a gas is directly proportional to absolute temperature and the two gases are at the same temperature. The average molecular velocities will differ because when two gases have equal kinetic energies, the molecules of the gas with lower molecular weight must be moving faster on average.

35. **A** CO_2 is a nonpolar molecule although it contains polar bonds. That's because carbon dioxide has its 3 atoms arranged in linear fashion, with its negatively charged oxygen atoms on the ends. There is a partial positive charge on the carbon atom. Due to the symmetrical arrangement of 2 equivalent polar bonds, the overall molecule has no net charge.

O=C=O

$\delta^- \quad \delta^+ \quad \delta^-$

36. **B** Knowing that moles = $\dfrac{\text{grams}}{\text{formula weight}}$, calculate the number of moles of $CaBr_2$ in the solution.

Moles of $CaBr_2$ = $\dfrac{(20\,\text{g})}{(200\,\text{g/mol})}$ 0.1 mole.

Now calculate the molarity of the solution (don't forget to convert milliliters to liters):

Molarity = $\dfrac{\text{moles}}{\text{liters}} = \dfrac{(0.1\,\text{mol})}{(0.5\,\text{L})}$ = 0.2 molar.

37.   **A**   Be has 2 valence electrons to give up to Cl, so the 2 Cl atoms align themselves opposite each other and the molecule is linear. [Cl–Be–Cl]

38.   **A**   From the balanced equation, you can see that there will be twice as much H_2 consumed as there is N_2 produced.

39.   **D**   Plug the answers into the reaction, and see which one works. Start at choice (C) because it's in the middle. If there are 3 H^+, then there can't be a whole number coefficient for H_2O, so the answer can't be an odd number. So the answer must be (B) or (D). Try (D). If there are 4 H^+, then there are 2 H_2O. The coppers are in balance if each has a coefficient of 1. Notice that this makes the net charge on the right side +2. With 4 H^+, the charge on the left is +4, but the negative charge on the nitrate balances it out. The equation is now balanced with the lowest whole number terms.

40.   **A**   In the course of this reaction, Cu^0 is converted to Cu^{2+}. Remember LEO says GER; Cu has lost electrons, so it has been oxidized. By the way, NO_3^- is reduced in the reaction, and the oxidation state of H^+ is not changed.

41.   **E**   A molecule's empirical formula is its molecular formula with numbers reduced to lowest whole numbers, so if the empirical formula is CH_2, then its molecular formula must be C_3H_6.

42.   **C** CO_2 combines with water to form carbonic acid (H_2CO_3).

$$CO_2 + H_2O \leftrightharpoons H_2CO_3 \leftrightharpoons H^+ + HCO_3^-$$

Carbonic acid is a weak acid, so it will release H^+ ions into the solution. When the concentration of H^+ increases, the pH decreases.

43.   **C**   Entropy is the measure of a system's randomness, and gases are more random than liquids. Also, the more molecules, the greater the randomness. In (C), a liquid is converted into two gases, and the number of molecules is increasing, so entropy must be increasing.

44.   **A**   As pressure is decreased at constant temperature, phase changes could occur as shown in the diagram below:

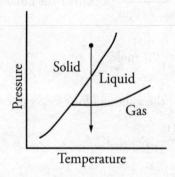

45. **B** Gamma decay involves the release of electromagnetic radiation, which has no electrical charge. Alpha particles are positively charged, and beta particles are negatively charged.

46. **D** The solubility product (K_{sp}) of a molecule is a measure of the concentrations of the particles into which it dissociates in solution at equilibrium. Since all of these salts will ionize into two ions per unit, the salt with the largest value of K_{sp} will be the most soluble.

47. **D** The acid dissociation constant (K_a) is an equilibrium constant, with the concentrations of the products in the numerator and the concentrations of the reactants in the denominator.

48. **B** A catalyst lowers the activation energy of a reaction but does not change the potential energy of the starting materials or products. Choice (A) actually raises the activation energy, and (C), (D), and (E) change the energies of the reactant or product. Choice (B) is correct.

49. **A** When an electron jumps from an excited state to a more stable state, energy is released by the atom. This energy is released in the form of electromagnetic radiation. In the reverse process, an atom may absorb electromagnetic radiation, and its electrons may jump to excited energy levels.

50. **E** Use the ideal gas equation, $PV = nRT$, and solve for n, the number of moles of gas. Don't forget to convert 25°C to 298 K.

$$n = \frac{PV}{RT} = \frac{(1.5)(5.0)}{(0.08)(298)} \text{ moles}$$

51. **C** Pressure and temperature will not be changed as long as the number of moles of gas in the vessel doesn't change. The density of the gas will decrease because equal numbers of moles of helium and neon will have different masses, and density is the measure of mass per unit volume.

52. **A** From the ideal gas equation, volume is related to pressure by the following relationship (when n and T are kept constant):

$$P_1 V_1 = P_2 V_2$$

and, by solving for the new volume, V_2, you get

$$V_2 = V_1 \frac{P_1}{P_2} = 5.0 \times \frac{1.5}{1.6} \text{ L}$$

53. **B** Elements get more reactive going towards the top left or bottom right of the periodic table. Francium is in the far bottom right and is the most reactive. The noble gases are the exception to the trend because they have full octets, and so neon would be the least reactive.

54. **B** A buffered solution is made up of a weak acid and its conjugate base (or weak base and its conjugate acid). Carbonic acid (H_2CO_3) and bicarbonate ion (HCO_3^-) are the only examples of this type of pairing in the answer choices. Choices (A) and (E) represent strong acids and their conjugates, (C) represents a salt, and (D) represents a strong base.

55. **E** Ammonia (NH_3) is a base, which means it can accept a proton or H^+ ion. NH_3 accepts a proton to become NH_4^+.

56. **B** You know that pH + pOH = 14 and that $[H^+][OH^-] = 1 \times 10^{-14}$ at 25°C.

So, $\left[OH^- \right] = \dfrac{\left(1 \times 10^{-14} \right)}{\left[H^+ \right]} M = \dfrac{\left(1 \times 10^{-14} \right)}{1 \times 10^{-3}} M = 1 \times 10^{-11} M$

57. **C** The number of moles of iron in the sample is given by the following expression:

$$\text{moles} = \frac{\text{grams}}{\text{atomic mass}} = \frac{(10.0)}{(55.9)}$$

Now use Avogadro's number (6.02×10^{23}) to find the number of atoms in the sample.

$$\text{atoms} = (\text{moles})(6.02 \times 10^{23}) = \frac{(10.0)}{(55.9)}\left(6.02 \times 10^{23} \right) = \frac{(10.0)\left(6.02 \times 10^{23} \right)}{(55.9)}$$

58. **B** The half-life of a radioactive material is the time that it takes for half of the sample to decay. After 1 half-life, 50 percent of this sample remains; after 2 half-lives, 25 percent remains. If two half-lives are 40 minutes, then 1 half-life is 20 minutes long.

59. **C** Potassium (K) is in group 1A of the periodic table, between sodium (Na) and rubidium (Rb). Remember from your knowledge of periodic trends that the value of potassium's first ionization energy will fall between that of sodium and rubidium.

60. **D** In the expression for the equilibrium constant, the products are in the numerator, the reactants are in the denominator, and the coefficients become exponents. So the correct expression is

$$K = \frac{[NO]^2 [Cl_2]}{[NOCl]^2} .$$

61. **E** According to Le Châtelier's principle, equilibrium shifts to relieve any stresses placed on it. If NOCl is added, the equilibrium will shift to the right, and the concentration of Cl_2 will be increased, so I is wrong. If NO is added, the equilibrium will shift to the left and decrease the concentration of Cl_2, so II is correct. If the volume is decreased, the equilibrium will shift to the left, which has fewer moles of gas, and the concentration of Cl_2 will be decreased, so III is correct.

62. **A** You can see from the balanced equation that for every mole of NOCl consumed, 1 mole of NO is produced, so (A) is correct.

63. **D** Organic chemistry is the study of carbon compounds. Methane (CH_4) is the only compound listed that contains carbon.

64. **C** The equivalence point in a titration is the point at which enough base has been added to neutralize all the acid that was initially present in the solution. This point is in the middle of the steep part of a titration curve. In this case, when a strong acid is titrated by a strong base, the pH at the equivalence point will be 7, and the solution will be neutral.

65. **B** The atomic *mass* of fluorine is 19; the atomic *number*, which is the number of protons in the nucleus, is 9. All of the other statements about fluorine are true.

66. **E** Atoms react with other atoms to fill their valence electron shells, so the single most important factor in determining the reactivity of an atom is the makeup of its valence electron shell.

67. **A** The addition of sodium chloride (NaCl) will introduce more Cl^- ions to the solution. Because of the common ion effect, these Cl^- ions will affect the equilibrium of the copper(I) chloride (CuCl) with its dissociated ions. The addition of extra Cl^- ions will cause the reformation and precipitation of CuCl.

68. **D** The rule with chemical pH indicators is simple: They change color at a pH that's about equal to their pK_a. Therefore, if bromothymol blue has a pK_a around 7, it will change color around pH 7.

69. **B** If a nonionic substance has a high boiling point, that means that a large amount of energy must be put into the substance to overcome its intermolecular attractions and convert it to the gas phase. So a high boiling point is an indication of very strong intermolecular attractive forces.

70. **D** CF_4 and NH_3 are covalent compounds and would have the lowest melting point of the choices. For ionic substances, the melting point is based on Coulombic energy. The ions in CaO have greater charges than those in $MgCl_2$, and the ions in CaO are also smaller than the ions in BaS. These two factors give CaO the greatest Coulobmic energy and the highest melting point.

HOW TO SCORE PRACTICE TEST 2

When you take the real exam, the proctors will collect your test booklet and bubble sheet and send your answer sheet to a processing center, where a computer looks at the pattern of filled-in ovals on your answer sheet and gives you a score. We couldn't include even a small computer with this book, so we are providing this more primitive way of scoring your exam.

Determining Your Score

STEP 1 Using the answer key, determine how many questions you got right and how many you got wrong on the test. Remember: questions that you do not answer don't count as either right or wrong answers.

STEP 2 List the number of right answers here.

(A) _____

STEP 3 List the number of wrong answers here. Now divide that number by 4. (Use a calculator if you're feeling particularly lazy.)

(B) _____ ÷ 4 = (C) _____

STEP 4 Subtract the number of wrong answers divided by 4 from the number of correct answers. Round this score to the nearest whole number. This is your raw score.

(A) _____ − (C) _____ = _____

STEP 5 To determine your real score, take the number from Step 4 above, and look it up in the left column of the Score Conversion Table on the next page; the corresponding score on the right is your score on the exam.

PRACTICE TEST 2
SCORE CONVERSION TABLE

Raw Score	Scaled Score
85	800
84	800
83	800
82	800
81	800
80	800
79	800
78	790
77	780
76	780
75	780
74	780
73	780
72	770
71	770
70	750
69	750
68	740
67	740
66	740
65	730
64	730
63	710
62	710
61	710
60	700
59	700
58	690
57	690
56	680
55	680
54	680
53	670
52	670
51	660
50	650
49	650
48	630
47	630
46	630

Raw Score	Scaled Score
45	620
44	620
43	610
42	610
41	600
40	590
39	590
38	580
37	580
36	570
35	560
34	560
33	550
32	550
31	540
30	530
29	530
28	520
27	520
26	520
25	510
24	510
23	500
22	500
21	490
20	480
19	480
18	470
17	470
16	460
15	450
14	450
13	440
12	440
11	430
10	420
9	420
8	410
7	410
6	400

Raw Score	Scaled Score
5	390
4	390
3	380
2	380
1	370
0	370
−1	370
−2	360
−3	360
−4	350
−5	340
−6	340
−7	330
−8	330
−9	320
−10	310
−11	310
−12	300
−13	300
−14	290
−15	280
−16	280
−17	270
−18	270
−19	260
−20	250
−21	250

Chapter 17
Practice Test 3

PRACTICE SAT SUBJECT TEST IN CHEMISTRY–TEST 3

You are about to take the third practice SAT Subject Test in Chemistry. The bubble sheet can be found near the back of the book; feel free to tear it out for use. (Just don't lose it!)

After answering questions 1–23, which constitute Part A, you'll be directed to answer questions 101–116, which constitute Part B. Then, begin again at question 24. Questions 24–70 constitute Part C.

When you're ready to score yourself, refer to the answer key and scoring instructions on pages 348 and 362. Full explanations regarding the correct answers to all questions start on page 349.

MATERIAL IN THE FOLLOWING TABLE MAY BE USEFUL IN ANSWERING THE QUESTIONS IN THIS EXAMINATION.

PERIODIC TABLE OF THE ELEMENTS

DO NOT DETACH FROM BOOK.

1																		2
H 1.0079																		**He** 4.0026
3 **Li** 6.941	4 **Be** 9.012											5 **B** 10.811	6 **C** 12.011	7 **N** 14.007	8 **O** 16.00	9 **F** 9.00	10 **Ne** 20.179
11 **Na** 22.99	12 **Mg** 24.30											13 **Al** 26.98	14 **Si** 28.09	15 **P** 30.974	16 **S** 32.06	17 **Cl** 35.453	18 **Ar** 39.948
19 **K** 39.10	20 **Ca** 40.48	21 **Sc** 44.96	22 **Ti** 47.90	23 **V** 50.94	24 **Cr** 52.00	25 **Mn** 54.938	26 **Fe** 55.85	27 **Co** 58.93	28 **Ni** 58.69	29 **Cu** 63.55	30 **Zn** 65.39	31 **Ga** 69.72	32 **Ge** 72.59	33 **As** 74.92	34 **Se** 78.96	35 **Br** 79.90	36 **Kr** 83.80
37 **Rb** 85.47	38 **Sr** 87.62	39 **Y** 88.91	40 **Zr** 91.22	41 **Nb** 92.91	42 **Mo** 95.94	43 **Tc** (98)	44 **Ru** 101.1	45 **Rh** 102.91	46 **Pd** 106.42	47 **Ag** 107.87	48 **Cd** 112.41	49 **In** 114.82	50 **Sn** 118.71	51 **Sb** 121.75	52 **Te** 127.60	53 **I** 126.91	54 **Xe** 131.29
55 **Cs** 132.91	56 **Ba** 137.33	57 *****La** 138.91	72 **Hf** 178.49	73 **Ta** 180.95	74 **W** 183.85	75 **Re** 186.21	76 **Os** 190.2	77 **Ir** 192.2	78 **Pt** 195.08	79 **Au** 196.97	80 **Hg** 200.59	81 **Tl** 204.38	82 **Pb** 207.2	83 **Bi** 208.98	84 **Po** (209)	85 **At** (210)	86 **Rn** (222)
87 **Fr** (223)	88 **Ra** 226.02	89 †**Ac** 227.03	104 **Rf** (261)	105 **Db** (262)	106 **Sg** (266)	107 **Bh** (264)	108 **Hs** (277)	109 **Mt** (268)	110 **Ds** (271)	111 **Rg** (272)	112 **§** (277)						

§ Not yet named

*Lanthanide Series

58 **Ce** 140.12	59 **Pr** 140.91	60 **Nd** 144.24	61 **Pm** (145)	62 **Sm** 150.4	63 **Eu** 151.97	64 **Gd** 157.25	65 **Tb** 158.93	66 **Dy** 162.50	67 **Ho** 164.93	68 **Er** 167.26	69 **Tm** 168.93	70 **Yb** 173.04	71 **Lu** 174.97

†Actinide Series

90 **Th** 232.04	91 **Pa** 231.04	92 **U** 238.03	93 **Np** 237.05	94 **Pu** (244)	95 **Am** (243)	96 **Cm** (247)	97 **Bk** (247)	98 **Cf** (251)	99 **Es** (252)	100 **Fm** (257)	101 **Md** (258)	102 **No** (259)	103 **Lr** (262)

GO ON TO THE NEXT PAGE ➡

SAT SUBJECT TEST IN CHEMISTRY–TEST 3

Note: For all questions involving solutions and/or chemical equations, assume that the system is in pure water unless otherwise stated.

Part A

Directions: Each set of lettered choices below refers to the numbered statements or questions immediately following it. Select the one lettered choice that best fits each statement or answers each question, and then fill in the corresponding oval on the answer sheet. A choice may be used once, more than once, or not at all in each set.

Questions 1–4 refer to the following.

    (A) Carbon
    (B) Nitrogen
    (C) Oxygen
    (D) Neon
    (E) Argon

1. Is the third most abundant gas in Earth's atmosphere

2. At standard conditions, has an allotrophic form that is a good electrical conductor

3. The key element delivered in soil fertilizer

4. Allotrope of this element is the primary absorber of UV solar radiation in Earth's atmosphere

Questions 5–8 refer to the following.

    (A) Standard voltaic potential
    (B) Entropy
    (C) Enthalpy
    (D) Reaction rate
    (E) Gibbs free energy

5. Increased with the addition of a catalyst

6. A property that must decrease when a gas condenses into a liquid

7. Is always positive for a spontaneous chemical reaction

8. Is zero for a crystalline solid that is elementally pure at 0 K

GO ON TO THE NEXT PAGE

Questions 9–12 refer to the following.

   (A) Alkali metals
   (B) Alkaline earth metals
   (C) Noble gases
   (D) Halogens
   (E) Transition metals

9. The most unreactive family of elements

10. Form negative ions in an ionic bond

11. Consist of atoms that have valence electrons in a *d* subshell

12. Members possess the lowest first ionization energy in their respective period

Questions 13–16 refer to the following.

   (A) O_2
   (B) KI
   (C) CCl_4
   (D) $AgNO_3$
   (E) $CaCO_3$

13. A product of a neutralization of a strong acid with a strong base

14. A volatile covalent liquid at 25°C and 1 atm

15. Releases a gas with the addition of dilute acid

16. Is a strong oxidizing agent

GO ON TO THE NEXT PAGE

Questions 17–19 refer to the following.

  (A) Gamma decay
  (B) Nuclear fusion
  (C) Alpha decay
  (D) Positron emission
  (E) Nuclear fission

17. Is the principle reaction responsible for the energy output of the Sun

18. Is a nuclear process that results in no change in the mass number and atomic number of a nuclide

19. The nuclear process that transmutes uranium-238 into thorium-234

Questions 20–23 refer to the following.

  (A) 0.1 M $MgCl_2$
  (B) 0.1 M $HClO_4$
  (C) 0.1 M NH_4OH
  (D) 0.1 M KOH
  (E) 0.1 M $LiNO_3$

20. Has a pH of 13

21. The solution with the lowest freezing point temperature

22. The solution with the highest boiling point temperature

23. Indicates a red flame when ionized with a Bunsen burner

GO ON TO THE NEXT PAGE

SAT SUBJECT TEST IN CHEMISTRY–TEST 3—*Continued*

PLEASE GO TO THE SPECIAL SECTION LABELED CHEMISTRY AT THE LOWER RIGHT-HAND CORNER OF THE ANSWER SHEET YOU ARE WORKING ON AND ANSWER QUESTIONS 101-116 ACCORDING TO THE FOLLOWING DIRECTIONS.

Part B

Directions: Each question below consists of two statements, I in the left-hand column and II in the right-hand column. For each question, determine whether statement I is true or false and whether statement II is true or false, and fill in the corresponding T or F ovals on your answer sheet. Fill in oval CE only if statement II is a correct explanation of statement I.

EXAMPLES:

I		II
EX 1. H_2SO_4 is a strong acid	BECAUSE	H_2SO_4 contains sulfur.
EX 2. An atom of oxygen is electrically neutral	BECAUSE	an oxygen atom contains an equal number of protons and electrons.

SAMPLE ANSWERS

	I	II	CE
EX 1	● F	● F	○
EX 2	● F	● F	●

	I		II
101.	Transition metal compounds are often colored	BECAUSE	they frequently possess partially filled *d* orbitals.
102.	Chemical reactions slow down with lower temperature	BECAUSE	the energy barrier for the formation of products decreases with decreasing temperature.
103.	Exothermic reactions absorb heat	BECAUSE	breaking covalent bonds always requires energy.
104.	The solubility of gases in liquids does not depend upon pressure	BECAUSE	the vapor pressure of a substance is independent of external pressure.
105.	MgO has a high melting point	BECAUSE	highly charged ions result in strong ionic forces and high lattice energies.

GO ON TO THE NEXT PAGE

I		**II**
106. The ground state electron configuration orbitals of elemental Cu is [Ar] $4s^1 3d^{10}$	BECAUSE	completely half-filled and filled d bestow special electronic stabilization.
107. Isotopes of a particular element have nearly identical chemical behavior	BECAUSE	they have identical electron configurations.
108. The addition of acid to a solution buffered to pH 7 slightly lowers the pH	BECAUSE	the addition of acids to any neutral solution always lowers the pH.
109. Saltwater boils at a higher temperature than pure water	BECAUSE	the presence of salt increases the vapor pressure of water.
110. BF_3 has a tetrahedral geometry	BECAUSE	the central B atom does not have a complete stable octet.
111. Hydrogen peroxide, H_2O_2, is a good oxidizing agent	BECAUSE	the hydrogen in H_2O_2 has a +1 oxidation number.
112. Hydrogen gas (H_2) is considered a perfectly ideal gas	BECAUSE	hydrogen atoms interact with each other via hydrogen bonds.
113. Gas particles have a wider range of velocity distributions as temperature increases	BECAUSE	the velocity for all of the particles in the gas will increase.
114. By mass, oxygen is the most abundant element in the human body	BECAUSE	it is principally found as O_2 in the bloodstream.
115. LiOH is considered a strong base	BECAUSE	it undergoes neutralization reactions with acids.

GO ON TO THE NEXT PAGE ⟹

RETURN TO THE SECTION OF YOUR ANSWER SHEET YOU STARTED FOR **CHEMISTRY** AND
ANSWER QUESTIONS 24–70.

Part C

Directions: Each of the questions or incomplete statements below is followed by five suggested answers or completions. Select the one that is best in each case and then fill in the corresponding oval on the answer sheet.

24. A balloon has an internal pressure of 1 atm and a volume of 5.0L. If the temperature is 25° C where I am holding the balloon, what will be the volume of the balloon if I release it, and it floats to a height where the temperature is –123° C and the pressure is 0.5 atm?

    (A) 1.25L
    (B) 2.5L
    (C) 5.0L
    (D) 7.5L
    (E) 10.0L

25. Which of the following shows the correct math needed to determine the mass of 3.0L of hydrogen gas at STP?

    (A) $3 \times \dfrac{1}{22.4} \times \dfrac{2}{1} = 0.27$ g

    (B) $\dfrac{1}{3} \times 22.4 \times \dfrac{1}{2} = 3.73$ g

    (C) $3 \times \dfrac{1}{22.4} \times \dfrac{4}{2} = 0.27$ g

    (D) $\dfrac{3}{22.4} \times \dfrac{1}{2} = 0.07$ g

    (E) $3 \times \dfrac{1}{22.4} \times \dfrac{4}{1} = 0.54$ g

26. A student analyzed a 0.1 M sample of an unknown hydrocarbon in the lab and determined a yield of 3.6 g of carbon and 0.6 g of hydrogen. What is the empirical formula of the molecule?

    (A) CH_3
    (B) C_2H_4
    (C) C_2H_6
    (D) C_3H_3
    (E) C_3H_6

27. Assuming constant temperature, ammonia gas occupies a volume of 500 ml at a pressure of 720 mm Hg. What volume will the gas occupy at a pressure of 900 mm Hg?

    (A) 4 ml
    (B) 40 ml
    (C) 400 ml
    (D) 4 L
    (E) 40 L

GO ON TO THE NEXT PAGE

28. Four of the following elements are pairs of isotopes and one is two different elements. Which answer is NOT a pair of isotopes?

    (A) Element Q has 27 protons and 32 neutrons. Element R has 27 protons and 33 neutrons.
    (B) Element S has 56 protons and 81 neutrons. Element T has 56 protons and 82 neutrons.
    (C) Element U has 17 protons and 18 neutrons. Element V has 18 protons and 17 neutrons.
    (D) Element W has 92 protons and 143 neutrons. Element X has an atomic number of 92 and an atomic mass of 145.
    (E) Element Y has an atomic number of 20 and an atomic mass of 40. Element Z has an atomic number of 20 and an atomic mass of 41.

29. A student is given a sample of gallium oxide (Ga_2O_3). She finds that her sample contains 9 moles of oxygen. Knowing that the molar mass of gallium is 70 g/mole and the molar mass of oxygen is 16 g/mole, what is the total mass of her sample?

    (A) 86 g
    (B) 188 g
    (C) 276 g
    (D) 564 g
    (E) 752 g

30. Which of the following options is a viable set of quantum numbers for an electron in a $3d$ orbital?

    (A) $(3, 2, -1, \frac{1}{2})$

    (B) $(3, 1, 0, -\frac{1}{2})$

    (C) $(3, 2, 3, \frac{1}{2})$

    (D) $(2, 2, 1, \frac{1}{2})$

    (E) $(4, 1, 0, -\frac{1}{2})$

31. Identify the correct ground state electron configuration for Cr.

    (A) $[Ar]\ 3s^2 3d^4$
    (B) $[Ar]\ 3s^2 3d^5$
    (C) $[Ar]\ 4s^2 3d^5$
    (D) $[Ar]\ 4s^2 3d^4$
    (E) $[Ar]\ 4s^1 3d^5$

32. What is the hydroxide concentration for a solution with a pH of 10 at 25°C ?

    (A) $10^{-14}\ M$
    (B) $10^{-10}\ M$
    (C) $10^{-7}\ M$
    (D) $10^{-4}\ M$
    (E) $10^{-1}\ M$

33. The correct name of the compound $CrCO_3$ is:

    (A) chromium carbonate
    (B) chromium(I) carbonate
    (C) chromium(II) carbonate
    (D) chromium(III) carbonate
    (E) chromium(IV) carbonate

34. Five hundred milliliters of solution of 0.1 M NaBr has how many milligrams of bromine?

    (A) 200 mg
    (B) 400 mg
    (C) 2,000 mg
    (D) 4,000 mg
    (E) 20,000 mg

35. According to the ideal gas law, what is the approximate volume that will be occupied by 0.5 mole of an ideal gas at 30°C and 3 atm pressure (gas constant R = 0.0821 L·atm/mol·K)?

    (A) Less than 1 L
    (B) 5 L
    (C) 10 L
    (D) 15 L
    (E) More than 20 L

GO ON TO THE NEXT PAGE ⟶

36. The correct formula for the compound diphosphorus tetroxide would be:

    (A) PO_4
    (B) P_5O_2
    (C) P_2O_5
    (D) P_4O_7
    (E) P_2O_4

37. Given that $\Delta G = \Delta H - T\Delta S$, how is the spontaneity of an endothermic reaction expected to change with decreasing T ?

    (A) Becomes less spontaneous
    (B) Becomes more spontaneous
    (C) Does not change
    (D) Decreases at first but then increases
    (E) Insufficient information to make a conclusion

38. Identify the element with the greatest first ionization energy.

    (A) Ce
    (B) C
    (C) Cr
    (D) Ca
    (E) Cs

39. Which of the following correctly lists the strength of the three primary types of intermolecular forces in compounds of similar size from strongest to weakest?

    (A) London dispersion > H-bonding > Permanent dipoles
    (B) London dispersion > Permanent dipoles > H-bonding
    (C) Permanent dipoles > H-bonding > London dispersion
    (D) H-bonding > Permanent dipoles > London dispersion
    (E) H-bonding > London dispersion > Permanent dipoles

40. When a sample of liquid H_2S boils, which of the following is the strongest type of force that is being neutralized?

    (A) Hydrogen bonding
    (B) Permanent dipoles
    (C) London dispersion forces
    (D) Covalent bonds
    (E) Ionic bonds

$$2Ca_3(PO_4)_2 + 6SiO_2 + 10C \rightarrow P_4 + \ldots CaSiO_3 + 10CO$$

41. Which coefficient balances the reaction given above?

    (A) 2
    (B) 4
    (C) 5
    (D) 6
    (E) 8

42. What is the percent by mass of NaCl in a solution created when 10.0 g of NaCl is dissolved in 40.0 mL of water?

    (A) 10%
    (B) 20%
    (C) 25%
    (D) 33%
    (E) 40%

43. A 100-milliliter solution containing $AgNO_3$ was treated with excess NaCl to completely precipitate the silver as AgCl. If 5.7 g AgCl was obtained, what was the concentration of Ag^+ in the original solution?

    (A) 0.03 M
    (B) 0.05 M
    (C) 0.12 M
    (D) 0.30 M
    (E) 0.40 M

GO ON TO THE NEXT PAGE

44. Identify which of the following statements is FALSE.

    (A) The vapor pressure of a liquid decreases with increasing atmospheric pressure.
    (B) The value of an equilibrium constant is dependent on temperature.
    (C) The rate of a spontaneous reaction cannot be determined solely by its Gibbs free energy.
    (D) During a phase transition, the temperature of a substance must be constant.
    (E) The addition of a catalyst to a reaction at equilibrium has no net effect on the system.

45. In which of the following gas laws does the temperature NOT have to be measured in Kelvins?

    (A) Charles' Law
    (B) Boyle's Law
    (C) Gay-Lussac's Law
    (D) Combined Gas Law
    (E) Ideal Gas Law

46. Which of the following compounds would be expected to have the greatest lattice binding energy?

    (A) $LiNO_3$
    (B) LiF
    (C) KI
    (D) NH_4Br
    (E) $CsNO_3$

47. The daughter nucleus formed when ^{18}F undergoes positron emission is

    (A) ^{14}N
    (B) ^{16}O
    (C) ^{18}O
    (D) ^{19}F
    (E) ^{20}Ne

48. Which of the following elements would be the strongest reducing agent?

    (A) Fluorine
    (B) Nickel
    (C) Xenon
    (D) Phosphorus
    (E) Sodium

49. Which of the following reactions produces a yellow precipitate?

    (A) $NaOH(aq) + HCl(aq) \rightarrow NaCl(s) + H_2O$
    (B) $NaOH(aq) + BaCl(aq) \rightarrow BaOH(s) + NaCl(aq)$
    (C) $Pb(NO_3)_2(aq) + 2KI(aq) \rightarrow 2KNO_3(aq) + PbI_2(s)$
    (D) $CuO(s) + Mg(s) \rightarrow Cu(s) + MgO(s)$
    (E) $4Fe + 3O_2 \rightarrow 2Fe_2O_3$

$$Zn(s) \mid ZnCl_2(aq) \mid\mid Cl^-(aq) \mid Cl_2(g) \mid C(s)$$

50. When mixed with water, which of the following acids will react and cause the formation of bubbles?

    (A) H_2CO_3
    (B) H_2SO_4
    (C) HF
    (D) $HC_2H_3O_2$
    (E) HCl

51. Given the reaction $A \rightarrow B + C$, where ΔH_{rxn} is negative, what effect would increasing the temperature (at constant pressure) have on the system at equilibrium?

    (A) No change
    (B) Cannot be determined
    (C) Shift to the right
    (D) Shift to the left for $K < 1$ and to the right for $K > 1$
    (E) Shift to the left

GO ON TO THE NEXT PAGE

52. An unknown acid solution was presumed to be either HCl or H_2SO_4. Which one of the following salt solutions would produce a precipitate when added to H_2SO_4 but not when added to HCl ?

    (A) $LiNO_3$
    (B) NH_4NO_3
    (C) $CsNO_3$
    (D) $Ba(NO_3)_2$
    (E) $AgNO_3$

$$Ca_3(PO_4)_2(s) \rightleftharpoons 3Ca^{2+}(aq) + 2PO_4^{3-}(aq)$$

53. What is the equilibrium expression for the dissolution of $Ca_3(PO_4)_2$ where the above is true?

    (A) $K_{sp} = [Ca^{2+}]^3[PO_4^{3-}]^2$
    (B) $K_{sp} = [Ca^{2+}]^2[PO_4^{3-}]^3$
    (C) $K_{sp} = [Ca^{2+}][PO_4^{3-}]/[Ca_3(PO_4)_2]$
    (D) $K_{sp} = [Ca^{2+}]^3[PO_4^{3-}]^2/[Ca_3(PO_4)_2]$
    (E) $K_{sp} = [Ca^{2+}]^2[PO_4^{3-}]^3/[Ca_3(PO_4)_2]$

54. Which of the following represents a conjugate acid/base pair?

    (A) Na^+/Cl^-
    (B) HCl/H^+
    (C) H_2CO_3/CO_3^{2-}
    (D) NH_3/NH_4^+
    (E) K^+/OH^-

55. An unknown solution having a pH of 3.5 was titrated with 0.1 M NaOH. Analysis of the resulting titration curve showed a single equivalence point at pH 7. Therefore, which of the following could be the unknown solute in the initial solution?

    (A) HF
    (B) HCl
    (C) LiOH
    (D) NH_3
    (E) H_2SO_4

56. Acid/base titration experiments could be used to determine all of the following directly EXCEPT

    (A) the acid concentration of an acidic solution
    (B) the alkalinity of a basic solution
    (C) the pK_a of an unknown weak acid
    (D) whether an unknown acid is monoprotic or polyprotic
    (E) the molecular weight of an unknown acid or base

57. What is the correct term for the phase change from gas directly to solid?

    (A) Deposition
    (B) Sublimation
    (C) Liquefaction
    (D) Fusion
    (E) Vaporization

58. What is the correct name for a straight-chained organic compound with the molecular formula C_3H_8 ?

    (A) Methane
    (B) Ethane
    (C) Methylethane
    (D) Propane
    (E) Isopropane

59. If the pH of a solution is changed from 1 to 3 with the addition of an antacid, what percentage of $[H^+]$ was neutralized?

    (A) 2%
    (B) 10%
    (C) 20%
    (D) 90%
    (E) 99%

GO ON TO THE NEXT PAGE

60. Which of the following statements is the most accurate with regard to the significance of Avogadro's number, 6.02×10^{23} ?

(A) It is the conversion factor between grams and atomic mass units.
(B) It is a universal physical constant just as the speed of light.
(C) It is the number of particles that is required to fill a 1-liter container.
(D) It is the inverse diameter of an H atom.
(E) It is the number of electrons in the universe.

Questions 61–64 refer to the following data at standard conditions.

	Appearance	Reactions with dilute HCl	Reaction with dilute HNO_3
Unknown metal #1	Dull gray solid with white oxide coating	Dissolved with bubbles of clear gas	Dissolved with bubbles of clear gas
Unknown metal #2	Solid; lustrous, smooth silver-gray surface	No reaction	Dissolved with bubbles of orange gas

61. Unknown metal #1 could be

(A) mercury
(B) copper
(C) zinc
(D) iron
(E) silver

62. Unknown metal #2 could be

(A) carbon
(B) copper
(C) zinc
(D) sodium
(E) silver

63. The addition of dilute HCl to unknown metal #1 produced a transparent gas. What is the likely identity of this gas?

(A) Cl_2
(B) H_2
(C) O_2
(D) CO_2
(E) NO_2

64. The addition of dilute HNO_3 to unknown metal #2 produced an orange gas. What is the likely identity of this gas?

(A) Cl_2
(B) H_2
(C) O_2
(D) CO_2
(E) NO_2

GO ON TO THE NEXT PAGE

65. Which of the following solutions is the product of the neutralization reaction between 10 ml 0.2 *M* KOH and 10 ml 0.2 *M* HI ?

    (A) 0.1 *M* KI_3
    (B) 0.1 *M* KI
    (C) 0.2 *M* KI
    (D) 0.4 *M* KI
    (E) 0.4 *M* HOH

66. Which of the following is true regarding an Ne atom with a mass number of 20 and an O^{2-} ion with a mass number of 16 ?

    (A) They contain the same number of protons.
    (B) They contain the same number of neutrons.
    (C) They contain the same number of protons plus neutrons.
    (D) They are isoelectronic.
    (E) They are isomers.

67. Which of the following statements is NOT correct regarding chemical catalysts?

    (A) They are not consumed during the chemical reaction.
    (B) They cannot make nonspontaneous reactions occur.
    (C) They do not have to be the same phase as the reactant molecules.
    (D) They shift equilibrated reactions to the product's side.
    (E) Enzymes are biological catalysts.

68. Most elements are solids at 25°C and 1 atm pressure, the exception being the 11 elements that are gases and 2 that are liquids. What 2 elements are liquids?

    (A) Hg and Br
    (B) Hg and I
    (C) Ag and Kr
    (D) Au and Kr
    (E) Pt and Co

69. A student conducted an experiment and obtained three values during three repetitive trials: 1.65, 1.68, 1.71. Later, the student discovered that the true value was 2.37. In contrast to the real value, the experimental results should be characterized as

    (A) not accurate and not precise
    (B) accurate but not precise
    (C) not accurate but precise
    (D) accurate and precise
    (E) accurate, precise, but unreliable

70. Sulfurous acid, H_2SO_3 , is a weak diprotic acid. It will dissociate once into $HSO_3^- + H^+$, and then the HSO_3^- will dissociate again into SO_3^{2-} and H^+. Which of the following products would be present in the lowest concentration in a gaseous solution of sulfurous acid and water vapor?

    (A) H_2SO_3
    (B) HSO_3^-
    (C) SO_3^{2-}
    (D) H^+
    (E) H_2O

STOP

**If you finish before time is called, you may check your work on this section only.
Do not turn to any other section in the test.**

Chapter 18
Practice Test 3:
Answers and
Explanations

PRACTICE TEST 3 ANSWER KEY

Question Number	Correct Answer	Right	Wrong	Question Number	Correct Answer	Right	Wrong
Part A				**Part C**			
1.	E	___	___	24.	C	___	___
2.	A	___	___	25.	A	___	___
3.	B	___	___	26.	E	___	___
4.	C	___	___	27.	C	___	___
5.	D	___	___	28.	C	___	___
6.	B	___	___	29.	D	___	___
7.	A	___	___	30.	A	___	___
8.	B	___	___	31.	E	___	___
9.	C	___	___	32.	D	___	___
10.	D	___	___	33.	C	___	___
11.	E	___	___	34.	D	___	___
12.	A	___	___	35.	B	___	___
13.	B	___	___	36.	E	___	___
14.	C	___	___	37.	E	___	___
15.	E	___	___	38.	B	___	___
16.	A	___	___	39.	D	___	___
17.	B	___	___	40.	B	___	___
18.	A	___	___	41.	D	___	___
19.	C	___	___	42.	B	___	___
20.	D	___	___	43.	E	___	___
21.	A	___	___	44.	A	___	___
22.	A	___	___	45.	B	___	___
23.	E	___	___	46.	B	___	___
				47.	C	___	___
Part B				48.	E	___	___
101.	T, T, CE			49.	C	___	___
102.	T, F			50.	A	___	___
103.	F, T			51.	E	___	___
104.	F, T			52.	D	___	___
105.	T, T, CE			53.	A	___	___
106.	T, T, CE			54.	D	___	___
107.	T, T, CE			55.	B	___	___
108.	T, T, CE			56.	E	___	___
109.	T, F			57.	A	___	___
110.	F, T			58.	D	___	___
111.	T, T			59.	E	___	___
112.	F, F			60.	A	___	___
113.	T, F			61.	C	___	___
114.	T, F			62.	E	___	___
115.	T, T			63.	B	___	___
				64.	E	___	___
				65.	B	___	___
				66.	D	___	___
				67.	D	___	___
				68.	A	___	___
				69.	C	___	___
				70.	C	___	___

PRACTICE TEST 3 EXPLANATIONS

Part A

1. **E** The composition of Earth's atmosphere is approximately 78% N_2, 20% O_2, 1% Ar, 0.5% H_2O, 0.4% CO_2, and 0.1% other trace gases.

2. **A** Allotropes are different forms or molecular arrangements of the same element. Carbon has three common allotrophic forms at standard conditions (25°C and 1 atm): amorphous carbon (charcoal), graphite, and diamond. Graphite is unique among nonmetals in that it conducts electricity.

3. **B** Two elements that are essential to plant growth but are depleted in most soils are nitrogen and phosphorous. Phosphorous is not given as a choice, but nitrogen is. Plants cannot utilize atmospheric nitrogen gas because the strong triple bond in N_2 makes it virtually inert to biological processing.

4. **C** Again, allotropes are different forms or molecular arrangements of the pure element. Oxygen has two allotropic forms at standard conditions: molecular oxygen, O_2, and ozone, O_3. Ozone (and to a lesser extent, molecular oxygen) is the primary absorber of UV light in Earth's atmosphere.

5. **D** A catalyst decreases the activation energy, or energy barrier, that must be overcome for reactants to become products. In this way, catalysts increase the rate of chemical reactions.

6. **B** Entropy, S, is the measure of the amount of disorder in a molecular system. When a gas condenses into a liquid, the molecules become more organized, so the entropy of the system decreases.

7. **A** It may be tempting to choose (E), but remember that by definition, the change in Gibbs free energy, ΔG, must be negative for a reaction to be spontaneous. Standard voltaic potential, $E°$, is related to $\Delta G°$ by the equation

    $$\Delta G° = -nFE°$$

    where n is the number of transferred electrons and F is Faraday's constant. Since n and F are always positive numbers, you can see that for a spontaneous reaction—where $\Delta G°$ is negative—$E°$ will always be positive.

8. **B** By definition, entropy for a pure element in crystalline form at absolute zero (0 K) is zero.

9. **C** The atoms of noble gas elements have filled valence shells and, therefore, are extremely unreactive—more so than any other family.

10. **D** To form a negative ion, an atom needs to *acquire* electrons. This sounds like a nonmetal, not a metal. Eliminate (A), (B), and (E). Noble gases are essentially inert, so that leaves the halogens. Halogens need 1 valence electron to complete their valence shell and so will readily gain an electron and form an anion.

11. **E** When the test writers start talking about the *"d"* subshell, think "transition metals."

12. **A** Ionization energy is needed to remove an electron from an atom. Which kind of elements tend to give up electrons? Metals, of course. Of the metals, alkali metals, having only 1 valence electron per atom, will lose an electron most easily because this allows an alkali metal atom to assume a stable noble gas electron configuration.

13. **B** Given that the strong acids are HCl, HBr, HI, HNO_3, H_2SO_4, and $HClO_4$ and the strong bases are LiOH, NaOH, KOH, RbOH, and CsOH, the only compound that could result from a neutralization between a strong acid and strong base is KI.

14. **C** Compounds composed of only nonmetal elements tend to form covalent bonds, while compounds composed of metals and nonmetals tend to form ionic bonds. Therefore, N_2 and CCl_4 are expected to be covalent compounds. However, N_2 is a gas at standard conditions; only CCl_4 is a liquid.

15. **E** Carbonates, CO_3^{2-}, and bicarbonates, HCO_3^{-}, form CO_2 gas when mixed with acid. That's why baking soda ($NaHCO_3$) fizzes when added to vinegar (acetic acid).

16. **A** Oxygen gas is able to effectively take electrons from most metals, oxidizing them. This process is also colloquially known as rusting.

17. **B** The primary source of solar energy is energy released by the nuclear fusion of hydrogen at high pressure and temperature to form helium. $4^1H \rightarrow {}^4He + 2$ electrons + lots of energy.

18. **A** The only nuclear process that does not change the number of protons and neutrons of a nucleus is gamma decay. Gamma decay involves stabilization of a nucleus by loss of energy in the form of a gamma ray photon.

19. **C** Given the nuclear reaction

$$^{238}_{92}U \rightarrow {}^{234}_{90}Th + ?$$

When conserving mass and charge, the missing particle must be ^4_2He. Therefore, the nuclear process responsible for this transmutation is alpha decay.

20. **D** A pH of 13 indicates a basic solution; therefore, there must be a base in solution in the first place. NH_4OH and KOH are bases. However, a pH of 13 means that the pOH is 1, i.e., $[OH^-] = 0.1\ M$. For the $[OH^-]$ to be the same as the base, that base must completely dissociate and be strong. KOH is the only strong base given.

21.　**A**　This is a question about the colligative property freezing point depression. Remember that for all colligative properties, the greater the number of dissolved particles, the greater the effect. Therefore, this question is really asking which solution has the greatest number of dissolved particles. Since all of them have the same molar concentration, this is really just a contest of which compound breaks up into the most individual particles.

$$MgCl_2 \rightarrow Mg^{2+} + Cl^- + Cl^- \qquad \text{(3 particles)}$$

$$HClO_4 \rightarrow H^+ + ClO_4^- \qquad \text{(2 particles)}$$

$$NH_4OH \rightarrow NH_4^+ + OH^- \qquad \text{(2 particles)}$$

$$KOH \rightarrow K^+ + OH^- \qquad \text{(2 particles)}$$

$$LiNO_3 \rightarrow Li^+ + NO_3^- \qquad \text{(2 particles)}$$

Therefore, the winner is $MgCl_2$.

22.　**A**　This is a question about the colligative property boiling point elevation. As in question 21, recall that for all colligative properties, the greater the number of dissolved particles, the greater the effect. Therefore, this question is really asking which solution has the greatest number of dissolved particles. Since all of them have the same molar concentration, this too is a contest of which compound breaks up into the most individual particles.

$$MgCl_2 \rightarrow Mg^{2+} + Cl^- + Cl^- \qquad \text{(3 particles)}$$

$$HClO_4 \rightarrow H^+ + ClO_4^- \qquad \text{(2 particles)}$$

$$NH_4OH \rightarrow NH_4^+ + OH^- \qquad \text{(2 particles)}$$

$$KOH \rightarrow K^+ + OH^- \qquad \text{(2 particles)}$$

$$LiNO_3 \rightarrow Li^+ + NO_3^- \qquad \text{(2 particles)}$$

Again, the winner is $MgCl_2$.

23.　**E**　Certain metal ions produce characteristic colors when ionized in a flame—that's how fireworks are made to have different colors. Here are the most common ions, and the color they produce.

Red:　　　Lithium, strontium

Orange:　Calcium

Yellow:　Sodium

Green:　　Barium, copper

Violet:　　Potassium

Therefore, lithium ions, Li , will produce a red flame—(E).

Part B

101.   **T, T, CE**

Divide and conquer. Both statements are true. Nearly all colored compounds fall into two categories: 1) those that are colored because they are organic molecules that have conjugation, and 2) those that are colored because they have transition metal atoms with partially filled *d* subshells. That's why sodium oxide is colorless, but iron(II) oxide is orange.

102. **T, F**   Divide and conquer. The first statement is true. It is a fundamental law of chemical kinetics that all chemical processes slow down at lower temperatures—that's why refrigerating food retards the growth of microbes. At lower temperatures, reactant molecules have less kinetic energy to use to overcome the energy barrier for the formation of products, called the activation energy. The second statement is false. The only way to lower activation energy is to add a catalyst.

103. **F, T**   Divide and conquer. Exothermic reactions *release* heat energy (notice *exo-* looks like *exit*), endothermic reactions *absorb* energy (notice *endo-* looks like *enter*), so the first statement is false. The second statement is true and is an important law in chemistry.

104. **F, T**   Divide and conquer. The first statement is false. The solubility of a gas in a liquid is very sensitive to pressure, such that the solubility of gases in liquids increases with increasing pressure. That's why when we release the pressure trapped in a bottle of soda by opening it, a sudden surge of carbon dioxide bubbles races to get out of the container. The second statement is true but has no relevance to the solubility of gases.

105.   **T, T, CE**

Divide and conquer. All ionic compounds have relatively high melting points (all are solids at room temperature) because ionic forces between ions are very strong. In the case of MgO, the +2 and –2 charges on Mg and O, respectively, result in very strong intermolecular forces. Not surprisingly, MgO has a melting point—it's about 2,000°C.

106.   **T, T, CE**

Divide and conquer. According to the Aufbau principle, subshells need to be completely filled before moving up to the next higher one. However, completely half-filled and filled *d* subshells bestow extra stabilization to an atom. Therefore, Cr and Cu actually violate the Aufbau principle and promote a 4*s* electron to become [Ar] $4s^13d^5$ and [Ar] $4s^13d^{10}$, respectively. Remember this important exception.

107.   **T, T, CE**

Divide and conquer. Isotopes are atoms of the same element that have differing numbers of neutrons. They have nearly identical chemical behavior because the number of protons and electrons in an atom (two quantities that are identical between isotopes) govern an atom's chemical properties.

108. **T, T, CE**

Divide and conquer. No matter how complicated acid/base chemistry can appear, never forget that *adding acid to any solution, buffered or not, always lowers the pH; adding base to any solution always raises the pH.* A buffer does *not* prevent the pH from changing in these cases; it simply lessens by how much the pH changes.

109. **T, F** Divide and conquer. The first statement is true. Remember the colligative properties: Adding any solute to a liquid always raises the boiling point temperature of the resulting solution—that's called boiling point elevation. This occurs because adding a solute to a liquid always lowers the vapor pressure of the solution—vapor pressure depression. Recall two more things: 1) The vapor pressure of a liquid always gets higher with higher temperature, and 2) a liquid boils when its vapor pressure is equal to the atmospheric pressure. So if the vapor pressure of a solution is lowered by the addition of a solute, you have to heat the solution to a higher temperature before the vapor pressure equals the atmospheric pressure and the solution will boil again.

110. **F, T** Divide and conquer. The Lewis dot structure for BF_3 is

Now, count the groups of electrons around the central atom (B), keeping in mind that every pair of nonbonding electrons, every single bond, every double bond, and every triple bond counts as one group. So here, boron is surrounded by three groups of electrons. Any atom that is surrounded by three groups of electrons has an sp^2 hybridization and a *trigonal planar* geometry. Of course, the second statement is true because this B doesn't have a stable octet—it has only 6 electrons.

111. **T, T** Divide and conquer. Like all peroxides, hydrogen peroxide is a good oxidizing agent. It is also true that the hydrogen atoms in H_2O_2 have a +1 oxidation number. However, the oxidizing tendency of this molecule is not due to the H, but rather to the fact that each O has a –1 oxidation number, instead of the usual –2.

112. **F, F** Divide and conquer. Both statements are false. There are no ideal gases—end of story. Furthermore, H's in H_2 are bonded together via a covalent bond. Hydrogen bonding refers to a specific dipole interaction between two or more different molecules where an H covalently bonded to an F, O, or N is electrostatically attracted to an F, O, or N on another molecule.

113. **T, F** As the temperature increases, the overall energy level of the gas increases. However, due to the randomized distribution of velocities, it's impossible say that ALL of the particles will have more energy (and thus greater velocities). Yes, the average velocity of the gas particles will be greater, but there will still be some particles at the same, or even lower, velocities.

114. **T, F** Divide and conquer. Over $\frac{3}{4}$ of the mass of the average human is oxygen. However, most oxygen atoms in the bloodstream, over 99.99 percent of them, are in the form of H_2O, not as O_2. The first statement is true, but the second is false.

115. **T, T** Divide and conquer. Strong acids and strong bases are those that undergo 100 percent dissociation in water.

The strong acids are HCl, HBr, HI, HNO_3, H_2SO_4, and $HClO_4$.

The strong bases are LiOH, NaOH, KOH, RbOH, and CsOH.

Mixing any acid with any base will produce a neutralization reaction, regardless of whether the acid and base are strong or weak.

Part C

24. **C** $\frac{P_1V_1}{T_1} = \frac{P_2V_2}{T_2}$ so $\frac{1 \text{ atm} \times 5L}{300K} = \frac{0.5 \text{ atm} \times V_2}{150K}$

All ideal gas calculations must be done with the temperature in K, so we have to change 25°C to approximately 300K, and –123°C to 150K. Since the pressure has halved and the temperature has halved also, the volume will not change, so V_2= 5.0L.

25. **A** For this question, set up the equation as if you were going to do the actual math: you must also remember that hydrogen exists as H_2, not H.

$$3L \times \frac{1 \text{ mole of gas}}{22.4 \text{ L}} \times \frac{2g}{1 \text{ mole of } H_2}$$

26. **E** A 0.1M sample with 3.6g of carbon would yield 36g of carbon for a 1.0M sample. Since carbon is 12 g/mole, that would give us 3 moles of carbon. A yield of 0.6 g of hydrogen in a 0.1M sample would yield 6g for a 1.0M sample. Since Hydrogen is 1 g/mole, that would give us 6 moles of hydrogen.

27. **C** $\frac{P_1V_1}{T_1} = \frac{P_2V_2}{T_2}$, but at constant temperature, $P_1V_1 = P_2V_2$

720 mm Hg × 500 ml = 900 mm Hg × V_2

360,000 = 900 × V_2 so the new volume will be $\frac{36,000}{900}$ = 400 ml

28. **C** Isotopes are elements with same number of protons (or atomic number) and different numbers of neutrons (or atomic mass). Therefore, (C) is the correct answer.

29. **D** Since the formula of the molecule indicates 3 moles of oxygen, take the 9 moles you are told you have, and divide by the 3 moles in the formula. The result is 3. That means that we have triple the formula weight. Find the formula weight by taking $70 \times 2 + 16 \times 3 = 140 + 48 = 188$ g for the formula, then multiply that by 3 since we have triple the formula. $188 \times 3 = 564$ g.

30. **A** The first quantum number refers to the energy level, so it would be 3. A d-orbital is represented by a 2, giving us the second number. For the third number, the five possible numerical representations for a d-orbital orientation are –2, –1, 0, 1, or 2. The final quantum number, representing the spin, could be either $\frac{1}{2}$ or $-\frac{1}{2}$.

31. **E** First, according to the periodic table, Cr has 24 electrons. You can eliminate (B) and (C) because those configurations have 25 electrons. Choice (A) is wrong because the $3s$ subshell is already accounted for in the [Ar] core—i.e., [Ar] stands for $1s^2 2s^2 2p^6 3s^2 3p^6$. Now, according to the Aufbau principle, completely fill subshells before moving up to the next higher one. So the best answer would appear to be (D). However, remember that completely half-filled and filled d subshells bestow extra stabilization to an atom. Therefore, Cr and Cu actually violate the Aufbau principle and promote a $4s$ electron to become [Ar] $4s^1 3d^5$ and [Ar] $4s^1 3d^{10}$, respectively. Choice (E) is the correct ground state configuration for Cr.

32. **D** At 25°C, pH + pOH = 14 for any solution. Therefore, if the pH is 10 for this solution, the pOH is $14 - 10 = 4$. Taking the negative antilog of 4 gives 10^{-4}, (D).

33. **C** Chromium is a transition metal, so the charge on the cation in this compound must be specified. Carbonate has a charge of negative two, and to balance it, the chromium must have a charge of positive two.

34. **D** First, find the number of moles of Br^-.

    molarity = moles/volume or moles = molarity × volume

    $$= 0.1 \, M \times 0.5 \, L$$

    $$= 0.05 \text{ moles}$$

    Then figure out how much 0.05 moles of Br^- weighs.

    grams = molecular weight × moles

    $$= 80 \text{ g/mole} \times 0.05 \text{ moles}$$

    $$= 4 \text{ grams or } 4{,}000 \text{ mg (D)}$$

35. **B** This is another math problem, but this one involves the ideal gas law. A couple of things first: 1) since you don't have a calculator, round off the value of R to 0.1 L•atm/mol•K, and 2) remember that T must be in K, not °C, for $PV = nRT$ to work correctly. So

$PV = nRT$ or $V = nRT/P$

$\qquad$ = (0.5 moles × 0.1 L•atm/mol•K × 300 K)/3 atm

$\qquad$ = (15 L•atm)/3 atm

$\qquad$ = 5 (B)

36. **E** For covalent compounds, a *di-* prefix signifies two, and the *tetra-* prefix signifies four.

37. **E** Recall that when ΔG is negative, a reaction is spontaneous, and when ΔG is positive, a reaction is nonspontaneous. The question indicates that the reaction in question is endothermic—i.e., ΔH is positive. Looking at the equation provided, the effect that decreasing T has will depend on the sign of ΔS. But the question doesn't tell you the sign of ΔS, nor can you figure it out on your own. Therefore, there is no way to make any conclusions—(E).

38. **B** First, ionization energy is a periodic trend that increases up and to the right on the periodic table. After looking at the position of these elements on the periodic table, carbon is clearly the best answer—(B).

39. **D** Hydrogen bonding is the strongest type of intermolecular force. Other types of permanent dipoles would be next strongest, and the temporary dipoles created through London dispersion forces would be the weakest type of intermolecular force.

40. **B** H_2S is a covalent substance, and when covalent substances undergo phase changes the intermolecular forces between various molecules must be neutralized. The strongest type of IMF present in a sample of H_2S is permanent dipoles. Note that H_2S does not have hydrogen bonding because the hydrogen is not bonded to N, O, or F.

41. **D** According to the reaction, 6 Ca atoms are present in the reactants. Therefore, 6 $CaSiO_3$ must be present as products, (D).

42. **B** Percent by mass is calculated by dividing the mass of the solute by the total mass of the solution. 40.0 mL of water would have a mass of 40.0 g (density of water = 1.0 g/mL), so the total mass of the solution would be 10.0 g + 40.0 g = 50.0 g. Then, (10.0 g/50.0 g) × 100% = 20%.

43. **E** Given that the molecular weight of AgCl is 143.4 g/mol, the number of moles of AgCl precipitated is

Moles AgCl = 5.70 g/143.4 g/mol

= 0.040 moles

Since the molar ratio of Ag+ in AgCl is 1, the number of moles of Ag^+ in the original solution was also 0.040. Therefore, the concentration of the original solution was

Molarity Ag^+ = moles Ag^+/volume (L)

= 0.040 moles/0.100 L

= 0.40 M (E)

44. **A** Choices (B), (C), (D), and (E) are all true statements. Choice (A) is a false statement—the vapor pressure of a substance depends only upon 1) the substance's temperature, and 2) its mole fraction when it's in solution (see the colligative property of vapor pressure depression).

45. **B** This is a bit of a trick question; when using any gas law that involves temperature the Kelvin scale must be used. However, Boyle's Law ($P_1V_1 = P_2V_2$) is only used when temperature is held constant, and thus, the temperature never enters into the calculations.

46. **B** Since these are all ionic compounds, electrostatic forces can be assumed to be entirely responsible for the cohesive forces on the lattice. According to Coulomb's Law

$F = Kq_1q_2/r^2$ where Energy = Kq_1q_2/r

Since the charges for all of the ion pairs given in the choices (q_1 and q_2) are ±1, it is the internuclear distance, r, of each ion pair that is the determinant factor. According to the equations above, the smaller the r, the greater the energy. So using the periodic trend in atomic/ion size, LiF (B) is the ion pair with the smallest internuclear distance.

47. **C** Positron emission is a type of beta decay. During beta decay, nuclear mass remains constant. Therefore, (C) is the only possible answer.

$^{18}_{9}F \rightarrow \, ^{?}_{?}? + \, ^{0}_{+1}e$

Conserving mass (superscript) and charge (subscript) gives (C).

48. **E** A reducing agent describes a species that will lose electrons easily in a redox reaction. This in turn causes another species to gain electrons and thus be reduced. Out of the choices, sodium loses its one valence electron to form Na^+ ions very readily. This also means that sodium would be very high on the activity series.

49. **C** Recall the solubility rules. Choices (A) and (B) are incorrect because neither NaCl nor BaOH are insoluble and therefore would not precipitate out of the aqueous solution. Because lead salts are insoluble except for their nitrates and perchlorates, lead iodide would precipitate out of solution as (C) depicts. Choices (D) and (E) are examples of oxidation-reduction reactions.

50. **A** H_2CO_3 is carbonic acid, and when carbonic acid is mixed with water it dissociates. One of the products of that dissociation is carbon dioxide gas, CO_2, which will then bubble up out of the solution.

51. **E** According to Le Châtelier's principle, the direction in which an equilibrium is disturbed can be predicted if ΔH_{rxn} is known (eliminate (B)). A straightforward way of solving this is to write "HEAT" into the reaction either as a reactant for endothermic reactions or as a product for exothermic reactions. Here, the reaction is exothermic, so

$$A \rightleftharpoons B + C + \text{"HEAT"}$$

Then, since temperature is a measure of "HEAT," increasing T, or "HEAT," would be expected to shift the system to the left. Choice (E) is the answer.

52. **D** Recall some fundamental solubility rules.

- All group 1 metals and NH_4^+ salts are *soluble*.

- All NO_3^- and ClO_4^- salts are *soluble*.

- All silver, lead, and mercury salts are *insoluble*.

Therefore, the addition of Li^+, NH_4^+, or Cs^+ would not produce a precipitate with either acid (eliminate (A), (B), and (C)). Silver, Ag^+, would form precipitates with both acids (eliminate (E)). Ba^{2+} is somewhat unique, even among other group 2 elements, because $BaCl_2$ is soluble, while $BaSO_4$ is not, (D).

53. **A** Writing equilibrium expressions is a three-step process.

1. First, ignore any molecule that is in the solid (*s*) or liquid (*l*) phases.

2. Second, write $K = [products]/[reactants]$

3. Third, all coefficients in front of molecules become exponents in the equilibrium expression.

Therefore, the correct choice is (A).

54. **D** A conjugate acid/base pair is a set of 2 molecules/ions that have identical molecular formulas, except that one of them has one more H^+ than the other. Only (D) represents a true pair of conjugates.

55. **B** The starting solution has a pH of 3.5. Therefore, the starting solution must be acidic. You can eliminate (C) and (D) because they are bases. The subsequent titration experiment revealed a single equivalence point, so the acid in question must be monoprotic—eliminate (E). Since the equivalence point comes at pH 7, the unknown acid must be *strong*. HCl is the only monoprotic strong acid given, (B).

56. **E**   Statements (A) through (D) can all be determined with data obtained from a titration experiment.

57. **A**   The phase changes associated with the terms are

deposition (gas → solid)

sublimation (solid → gas)

liquefaction (gas→ liquid)

fusion (solid → liquid)

vaporization (liquid → gas)

58. **D**   The molecular formulas associated with the IUPAC names for organic molecules are

methane:	CH_4
ethane:	CH_3CH_3
methylethane:	does not exist in the IUPAC system
propane:	$CH_3CH_2CH_3$
isopropane:	does not exist in the IUPAC system

59. **E**   First, figure out the concentration of $[H^+]$ at pH 1 and pH 3.

pH = 1; $[H^+]$ = 0.1 M pH = 3; $[H^+]$ = 0.001 M

Then realize that 0.001 M is 1 percent of (or 100 times smaller than) 0.1 M. Therefore, 99 percent of the H^+ is neutralized when going from pH 1 to pH 3.

60. **A**   Avogadro's number is nothing more than the conversion faction among two measures of mass, atomic mass units, and grams. Just as you can say that there are 2.54 centimeters in an inch, so too can you say there are 6.02×10^{23} amu in a gram.

61. **C**   POE is the best tool to use here. First, we can eliminate mercury, (A), because mercury metal is a liquid at standard conditions, yet the table indicates that unknown metal #1 is a solid. Second, we can eliminate copper, (B), because copper metal is brownish, yet the table says unknown metal #1 is dull gray. Now, consider the presence of the white oxide coat. The oxide of iron, better known as rust, is orange brown, not white, so eliminate (D). Last, the oxide of silver is gray-black, better known as tarnish, so eliminate (E). Therefore, zinc is the best choice—(C).

62. **E** Again, POE is the best tool to use here. First, you can eliminate carbon, (A), because carbon is not a metal. Second, you can again eliminate copper, (B), because copper metal is brownish, yet the table says unknown metal #2 is silver-gray. Third, you can eliminate zinc, (C), because it is a fairly reactive metal that always has a whitish oxide coat in air. Fourth, you can definitely eliminate sodium because sodium metal explodes with yellow flame on contact with even plain water, let alone acidic solutions—the table doesn't report any explosions! Finally, the best choice is silver, a relatively inert metal along with copper, gold, and platinum (it's no accident that these metals are used for jewelry and coinage)—(E).

63. **B** There are several ways to approach this one. Again, POE is very useful here. Chlorine, (A), and nitrogen dioxide, (E), gases are colored—greenish and orange, respectively. Therefore, they cannot be the gas in question. Furthermore, it's difficult to choose carbon dioxide, (D), because there are no carbon atoms anywhere in this experiment. Finally, as a rule of thumb, a colorless gas produced from reactions between metals and acids is hydrogen—(B).

64. **E** This requires a bit of general chemistry knowledge. The colors of the gases are

Cl_2—green

H_2—colorless

O_2—colorless

CO_2—colorless

NO_2—orange/brown

Choice (E) is the best answer.

65. **B** First, the neutralization reaction that occurs here is

$$KOH + HI \rightarrow KI + H_2O$$

The trick is to realize that the number of K's and I's are not changing during the reaction; but since the solutions are being added, the volume is doubling. If the volume doubles, then the initial solution concentrations (0.2 M) are halved (0.1 M).

66. **D** An O^{2-} ion has gained 2 electrons to fill its outer shell. This gives an O^{2-} ion the same electron configuration as Ne. That is, the 2 are isoelectronic.

67. **D** The addition of a catalyst to a system at equilibrium has NO effect. That's because all a catalyst does is increase the rate at which a nonequilibrated system reaches equilibrium.

68. **A** It's important to know the phase of the elements at standard conditions (25°C at 1 atm).

Gases: hydrogen, helium, nitrogen, oxygen, fluorine, neon, chlorine, argon, krypton, xenon, and radon

Liquids: mercury and bromine (A)

Solids: the rest of the elements

69. **C** By definition, accuracy is the measure of how close experimental data are to true data, while precision is the measure of how similar experimental data are to one another. Clearly, the student's data is very precise; the values of 1.65, 1.68, 1.71 vary by no more than 4 percent. However, the average value of the experimental data is nearly 50 percent off the true value, meaning these results are not very accurate—(C).

70. **C** As a weak acid, very little H_2SO_3 actually dissociates, meaning the H_2SO_3 molecule itself will be present in the highest concentration. Each ensuing dissociation is weaker than the previous one, and thus the ion that is only created after the final dissociation will be present in the lowest concentration.

HOW TO SCORE PRACTICE TEST 3

When you take the real exam, the proctors will collect your test booklet and bubble sheet and send your answer sheet to a processing center, where a computer looks at the pattern of filled-in ovals on your answer sheet and gives you a score. We couldn't include even a small computer with this book, so we are providing this more primitive way of scoring your exam.

Determining Your Score

STEP 1 Using the answer key, determine how many questions you got right and how many you got wrong on the test. Remember: questions that you do not answer don't count as either right or wrong answers.

STEP 2 List the number of right answers here.

(A) _____

STEP 3 List the number of wrong answers here. Now divide that number by 4. (Use a calculator if you're feeling particularly lazy.)

(B) _____ ÷ 4 = (C) _____

STEP 4 Subtract the number of wrong answers divided by 4 from the number of correct answers. Round this score to the nearest whole number. This is your raw score.

(A) _____ − (C) _____ = _____

STEP 5 To determine your real score, take the number from Step 4 above, and look it up in the left column of the Score Conversion Table on the next page; the corresponding score on the right is your score on the exam.

PRACTICE TEST 3
SCORE CONVERSION TABLE

Raw Score	Scaled Score	Raw Score	Scaled Score	Raw Score	Scaled Score
85	800	45	620	5	390
84	800	44	620	4	390
83	800	43	610	3	380
82	800	42	610	2	380
81	800	41	600	1	370
80	800	40	590	0	370
79	800	39	590	−1	370
78	790	38	580	−2	360
77	780	37	580	−3	360
76	780	36	570	−4	350
75	780	35	560	−5	340
74	780	34	560	−6	340
73	780	33	550	−7	330
72	770	32	550	−8	330
71	770	31	540	−9	320
70	750	30	530	−10	310
69	750	29	530	−11	310
68	740	28	520	−12	300
67	740	27	520	−13	300
66	740	26	520	−14	290
65	730	25	510	−15	280
64	730	24	510	−16	280
63	710	23	500	−17	270
62	710	22	500	−18	270
61	710	21	490	−19	260
60	700	20	480	−20	250
59	700	19	480	−21	250
58	690	18	470		
57	690	17	470		
56	680	16	460		
55	680	15	450		
54	680	14	450		
53	670	13	440		
52	670	12	440		
51	660	11	430		
50	650	10	420		
49	650	9	420		
48	630	8	410		
47	630	7	410		
46	630	6	400		

FORMULA REFERENCE GUIDE

- $\text{Density} = \dfrac{\text{mass}}{\text{volume}}$

Heat

- $q = mc\Delta T$

  q = Heat ΔT = Temperature change

  m = mass

  c = specific heat

Spontaneity

- $\Delta G = \Delta H - T\Delta S$

  $\Delta G < 0$ means that a reaction is spontaneous at this temperature

  $\Delta G > 0$ $\begin{cases} +\Delta H, \text{ Low temp} \\ -\Delta S, \text{ High temp} \\ -\Delta H, +\Delta S, \text{ Any temp} \end{cases}$

  $\Delta G < 0$ $\begin{cases} -\Delta H, +\Delta S, \text{ Any temp} \\ +\Delta S, \text{ High temp} \end{cases}$

  - $\Delta H > 0$ Endothermic
  - $\Delta H < 0$ Exothermic

- $\Delta T = kmi$

  Freezing Point Depression
  & Boiling Point Depression

  i: whole number equaling the number of particles a substance dissolves into

  k: solvent constant

  m: molality (NOT molarity)

  $\text{molarity} = \dfrac{\text{moles of solute}}{\text{liters of solution}}$

  $\text{molality} = \dfrac{\text{moles of solute}}{\text{kilograms of solvent}}$

  $\text{mole fraction} = \dfrac{\text{moles of solute}}{\text{total moles of solution}}$

Ideal Gas Law

- $PV = nRT$

  P = pressure in atm (or mmHg or torr)

  V = volume in liters

  n = number of moles of gas particles in the container

  R = the ideal gas constant

  T = temperature in Kelvin

  To calculate the ideal gas constant, use the following formula:

  $$R = .08 \; \frac{L \cdot atm}{mol \cdot k}$$

Conversions

- Pressure:

  1 ATM = 760 torr = 760 mmHg

- Energy (Heat):

  1 Calorie = 1000 calories = 4000 joules

- Temperature:

  0°C = 273 Kelvin

  25°C = 298 K

Facts to Know

- To find the mass of a mole of a substance, multiply the formula weight by the number of moles.

- 1 mol of gas at STP occupies 22.4 L of volume.

Solubility

- All alkali and ammonium (NH_4^+) compounds are soluble. The alkali metals are included in group IA (Li^+, NA^+, K^+, Rb^+, Cs^+).

- All acetates (CH_3COO^-), chlorates (ClO_3^-), nitrates (NO_3^-), and perchlorates (ClO_4^-) are soluble.

- Pb^{n+}, Hg^{n+}, and Ag^{n+} salts are insoluble, unless they are paired with one of the anions from the previous rule.

Oxidation Rules

1. When oxygen is in a compound, its oxidation state is usually –2 (it has been reduced). One important exception is oxygen in a peroxide such as hydrogen peroxide (H_2O_2). In a peroxide, oxygen has an oxidation state of –1.

2. When an alkali metal (Li, Na, etc.) is involved in a compound, its oxidation state is always +1 (it's been oxidized).

3. When an alkaline earth metal (Be, Mg, etc.) is involved in a compound, its oxidation state is +2.

4. When a halogen (F, Cl, etc.) is involved in a compound, its oxidation state is often –1. The oxidation state of fluorine in a compound is always –1.

5. When hydrogen is combined with a nonmetal, its oxidation state is +1. When hydrogen is combined with a metal, its oxidation state is –1.

6. In any compound, the sum of all oxidation states is zero.

Constants

- Avogadro's number: 6×10^{23} molecules/mole

Prefixes

Prefixes for Organics

Meth- 1

Eth- 2

Prop- 3

But- 4

Pent- 5

Hex- 6

Hep- 7

Oct- 8

Non- 9

Dec- 10

Prefix	Symbol	Notation
nano-	n	10^{-9}
micro-	μ	10^{-6}
milli-	m	10^{-3}
centi-	c	10^{-2}
kilo-	k	10^{-3}
mega-	M	10^{6}

Electrochemistry

OIL

<u>O</u>xidation <u>I</u>s <u>L</u>osing Electrons

AN OX

<u>O</u>xidation <u>O</u>ccurs at <u>A</u>node

RIG

<u>R</u>eduction <u>I</u>s <u>G</u>aining Electrons

RED CAT

<u>R</u>eduction <u>O</u>ccurs at <u>C</u>athode

- Galvanic Cell: $E°_{cell} > 0$ means reaction is spontaneous and energy is released (battery).

- Electrolytic Cell: $E°_{cell} < 0$ means the reaction is NOT spontaneous and requires a voltage source (electro plating).

Equilibrium

- $K_{eq} = \dfrac{[\text{Products}]}{[\text{Reactants}]}$

  Reactants $\rightleftharpoons$ Products for $aA + bB \rightleftharpoons cC + dD$

  $K_{eq} = \dfrac{[C]^c[D]^d}{[A]^a[B]^b}$

  $K_{eq} > 1$: Products favored

  $K_{eq} < 1$: Reactants favored

Periodic Trends

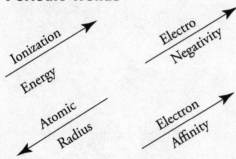

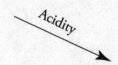

Acid-Base

$$pH = pK_a + \log \frac{[A]}{[HA]}$$

$$pH = -\log_{10}[H^+]$$

pH > 7: Basic

pH = 7: Neutral

pH < 7: Acidic

Strong Acids:

HCl, HI, H_2SO_4, HBr, $HClO_4$, HNO_3

Strong Bases:

All Group I Hydroxides

Completely darken bubbles with a No. 2 pencil. If you make a mistake, be sure to erase mark completely. Erase all stray marks.

1.

YOUR NAME: _____
(Print)
Last — First — M.I.

SIGNATURE: _____ DATE: __/__/__

HOME ADDRESS: _____
(Print)
Number and Street

_____
City — State — Zip Code

PHONE NO.: _____

IMPORTANT: Please fill in these boxes exactly as shown on the back cover of your test book.

2. TEST FORM

_____

6. DATE OF BIRTH

Month		Day		Year	
◯ JAN					
◯ FEB	⓪	⓪	⓪	⓪	
◯ MAR	①	①	①	①	
◯ APR	②	②	②	②	
◯ MAY	③	③	③	③	
◯ JUN		④	④	④	
◯ JUL		⑤	⑤	⑤	
◯ AUG		⑥	⑥	⑥	
◯ SEP		⑦	⑦	⑦	
◯ OCT		⑧	⑧	⑧	
◯ NOV		⑨	⑨	⑨	
◯ DEC					

3. TEST CODE

⓪	Ⓐ	Ⓙ	⓪	⓪
①	Ⓑ	Ⓚ	①	①
②	Ⓒ	Ⓛ	②	②
③	Ⓓ	Ⓜ	③	③
④	Ⓔ	Ⓝ	④	④
⑤	Ⓕ	Ⓞ	⑤	⑤
⑥	Ⓖ	Ⓟ	⑥	⑥
⑦	Ⓗ	Ⓠ	⑦	⑦
⑧	Ⓘ	Ⓡ	⑧	⑧
⑨			⑨	⑨

4. REGISTRATION NUMBER

⓪	⓪	⓪	⓪	⓪	⓪	⓪
①	①	①	①	①	①	①
②	②	②	②	②	②	②
③	③	③	③	③	③	③
④	④	④	④	④	④	④
⑤	⑤	⑤	⑤	⑤	⑤	⑤
⑥	⑥	⑥	⑥	⑥	⑥	⑥
⑦	⑦	⑦	⑦	⑦	⑦	⑦
⑧	⑧	⑧	⑧	⑧	⑧	⑧
⑨	⑨	⑨	⑨	⑨	⑨	⑨

7. GENDER
◯ MALE
◯ FEMALE

The Princeton Review®

5. YOUR NAME

First 4 letters of last name				FIRST INIT	MID INIT
Ⓐ	Ⓐ	Ⓐ	Ⓐ	Ⓐ	Ⓐ
Ⓑ	Ⓑ	Ⓑ	Ⓑ	Ⓑ	Ⓑ
Ⓒ	Ⓒ	Ⓒ	Ⓒ	Ⓒ	Ⓒ
Ⓓ	Ⓓ	Ⓓ	Ⓓ	Ⓓ	Ⓓ
Ⓔ	Ⓔ	Ⓔ	Ⓔ	Ⓔ	Ⓔ
Ⓕ	Ⓕ	Ⓕ	Ⓕ	Ⓕ	Ⓕ
Ⓖ	Ⓖ	Ⓖ	Ⓖ	Ⓖ	Ⓖ
Ⓗ	Ⓗ	Ⓗ	Ⓗ	Ⓗ	Ⓗ
Ⓘ	Ⓘ	Ⓘ	Ⓘ	Ⓘ	Ⓘ
Ⓙ	Ⓙ	Ⓙ	Ⓙ	Ⓙ	Ⓙ
Ⓚ	Ⓚ	Ⓚ	Ⓚ	Ⓚ	Ⓚ
Ⓛ	Ⓛ	Ⓛ	Ⓛ	Ⓛ	Ⓛ
Ⓜ	Ⓜ	Ⓜ	Ⓜ	Ⓜ	Ⓜ
Ⓝ	Ⓝ	Ⓝ	Ⓝ	Ⓝ	Ⓝ
Ⓞ	Ⓞ	Ⓞ	Ⓞ	Ⓞ	Ⓞ
Ⓟ	Ⓟ	Ⓟ	Ⓟ	Ⓟ	Ⓟ
Ⓠ	Ⓠ	Ⓠ	Ⓠ	Ⓠ	Ⓠ
Ⓡ	Ⓡ	Ⓡ	Ⓡ	Ⓡ	Ⓡ
Ⓢ	Ⓢ	Ⓢ	Ⓢ	Ⓢ	Ⓢ
Ⓣ	Ⓣ	Ⓣ	Ⓣ	Ⓣ	Ⓣ
Ⓤ	Ⓤ	Ⓤ	Ⓤ	Ⓤ	Ⓤ
Ⓥ	Ⓥ	Ⓥ	Ⓥ	Ⓥ	Ⓥ
Ⓦ	Ⓦ	Ⓦ	Ⓦ	Ⓦ	Ⓦ
Ⓧ	Ⓧ	Ⓧ	Ⓧ	Ⓧ	Ⓧ
Ⓨ	Ⓨ	Ⓨ	Ⓨ	Ⓨ	Ⓨ
Ⓩ	Ⓩ	Ⓩ	Ⓩ	Ⓩ	Ⓩ

1. Ⓐ Ⓑ Ⓒ Ⓓ Ⓔ
2. Ⓐ Ⓑ Ⓒ Ⓓ Ⓔ
3. Ⓐ Ⓑ Ⓒ Ⓓ Ⓔ
4. Ⓐ Ⓑ Ⓒ Ⓓ Ⓔ
5. Ⓐ Ⓑ Ⓒ Ⓓ Ⓔ
6. Ⓐ Ⓑ Ⓒ Ⓓ Ⓔ
7. Ⓐ Ⓑ Ⓒ Ⓓ Ⓔ
8. Ⓐ Ⓑ Ⓒ Ⓓ Ⓔ
9. Ⓐ Ⓑ Ⓒ Ⓓ Ⓔ
10. Ⓐ Ⓑ Ⓒ Ⓓ Ⓔ
11. Ⓐ Ⓑ Ⓒ Ⓓ Ⓔ
12. Ⓐ Ⓑ Ⓒ Ⓓ Ⓔ
13. Ⓐ Ⓑ Ⓒ Ⓓ Ⓔ
14. Ⓐ Ⓑ Ⓒ Ⓓ Ⓔ
15. Ⓐ Ⓑ Ⓒ Ⓓ Ⓔ
16. Ⓐ Ⓑ Ⓒ Ⓓ Ⓔ
17. Ⓐ Ⓑ Ⓒ Ⓓ Ⓔ
18. Ⓐ Ⓑ Ⓒ Ⓓ Ⓔ
19. Ⓐ Ⓑ Ⓒ Ⓓ Ⓔ
20. Ⓐ Ⓑ Ⓒ Ⓓ Ⓔ
21. Ⓐ Ⓑ Ⓒ Ⓓ Ⓔ
22. Ⓐ Ⓑ Ⓒ Ⓓ Ⓔ
23. Ⓐ Ⓑ Ⓒ Ⓓ Ⓔ

24. Ⓐ Ⓑ Ⓒ Ⓓ Ⓔ
25. Ⓐ Ⓑ Ⓒ Ⓓ Ⓔ
26. Ⓐ Ⓑ Ⓒ Ⓓ Ⓔ
27. Ⓐ Ⓑ Ⓒ Ⓓ Ⓔ
28. Ⓐ Ⓑ Ⓒ Ⓓ Ⓔ
29. Ⓐ Ⓑ Ⓒ Ⓓ Ⓔ
30. Ⓐ Ⓑ Ⓒ Ⓓ Ⓔ
31. Ⓐ Ⓑ Ⓒ Ⓓ Ⓔ
32. Ⓐ Ⓑ Ⓒ Ⓓ Ⓔ
33. Ⓐ Ⓑ Ⓒ Ⓓ Ⓔ
34. Ⓐ Ⓑ Ⓒ Ⓓ Ⓔ
35. Ⓐ Ⓑ Ⓒ Ⓓ Ⓔ
36. Ⓐ Ⓑ Ⓒ Ⓓ Ⓔ
37. Ⓐ Ⓑ Ⓒ Ⓓ Ⓔ
38. Ⓐ Ⓑ Ⓒ Ⓓ Ⓔ
39. Ⓐ Ⓑ Ⓒ Ⓓ Ⓔ
40. Ⓐ Ⓑ Ⓒ Ⓓ Ⓔ
41. Ⓐ Ⓑ Ⓒ Ⓓ Ⓔ
42. Ⓐ Ⓑ Ⓒ Ⓓ Ⓔ
43. Ⓐ Ⓑ Ⓒ Ⓓ Ⓔ
44. Ⓐ Ⓑ Ⓒ Ⓓ Ⓔ
45. Ⓐ Ⓑ Ⓒ Ⓓ Ⓔ
46. Ⓐ Ⓑ Ⓒ Ⓓ Ⓔ

47. Ⓐ Ⓑ Ⓒ Ⓓ Ⓔ
48. Ⓐ Ⓑ Ⓒ Ⓓ Ⓔ
49. Ⓐ Ⓑ Ⓒ Ⓓ Ⓔ
50. Ⓐ Ⓑ Ⓒ Ⓓ Ⓔ
51. Ⓐ Ⓑ Ⓒ Ⓓ Ⓔ
52. Ⓐ Ⓑ Ⓒ Ⓓ Ⓔ
53. Ⓐ Ⓑ Ⓒ Ⓓ Ⓔ
54. Ⓐ Ⓑ Ⓒ Ⓓ Ⓔ
55. Ⓐ Ⓑ Ⓒ Ⓓ Ⓔ
56. Ⓐ Ⓑ Ⓒ Ⓓ Ⓔ
57. Ⓐ Ⓑ Ⓒ Ⓓ Ⓔ
58. Ⓐ Ⓑ Ⓒ Ⓓ Ⓔ
59. Ⓐ Ⓑ Ⓒ Ⓓ Ⓔ
60. Ⓐ Ⓑ Ⓒ Ⓓ Ⓔ
61. Ⓐ Ⓑ Ⓒ Ⓓ Ⓔ
62. Ⓐ Ⓑ Ⓒ Ⓓ Ⓔ
63. Ⓐ Ⓑ Ⓒ Ⓓ Ⓔ
64. Ⓐ Ⓑ Ⓒ Ⓓ Ⓔ
65. Ⓐ Ⓑ Ⓒ Ⓓ Ⓔ
66. Ⓐ Ⓑ Ⓒ Ⓓ Ⓔ
67. Ⓐ Ⓑ Ⓒ Ⓓ Ⓔ
68. Ⓐ Ⓑ Ⓒ Ⓓ Ⓔ
69. Ⓐ Ⓑ Ⓒ Ⓓ Ⓔ
70. Ⓐ Ⓑ Ⓒ Ⓓ Ⓔ

PART B

	I		II		CE
101.	Ⓣ	Ⓕ	Ⓣ	Ⓕ	◯
102.	Ⓣ	Ⓕ	Ⓣ	Ⓕ	◯
103.	Ⓣ	Ⓕ	Ⓣ	Ⓕ	◯
104.	Ⓣ	Ⓕ	Ⓣ	Ⓕ	◯
105.	Ⓣ	Ⓕ	Ⓣ	Ⓕ	◯
106.	Ⓣ	Ⓕ	Ⓣ	Ⓕ	◯
107.	Ⓣ	Ⓕ	Ⓣ	Ⓕ	◯
108.	Ⓣ	Ⓕ	Ⓣ	Ⓕ	◯
109.	Ⓣ	Ⓕ	Ⓣ	Ⓕ	◯
110.	Ⓣ	Ⓕ	Ⓣ	Ⓕ	◯
111.	Ⓣ	Ⓕ	Ⓣ	Ⓕ	◯
112.	Ⓣ	Ⓕ	Ⓣ	Ⓕ	◯
113.	Ⓣ	Ⓕ	Ⓣ	Ⓕ	◯
114.	Ⓣ	Ⓕ	Ⓣ	Ⓕ	◯
115.	Ⓣ	Ⓕ	Ⓣ	Ⓕ	◯

Completely darken bubbles with a No. 2 pencil. If you make a mistake, be sure to erase mark completely. Erase all stray marks.

1.

YOUR NAME: _____
(Print)   Last   First   M.I.

SIGNATURE: _____   DATE: ___ / ___ / ___

HOME ADDRESS: _____
(Print)   Number and Street

_____
City   State   Zip Code

PHONE NO.: _____

IMPORTANT: Please fill in these boxes exactly as shown on the back cover of your test book.

2. TEST FORM

_____

6. DATE OF BIRTH

Month		Day		Year	
⭘ JAN					
⭘ FEB	⓪	⓪	⓪	⓪	
⭘ MAR	①	①	①	①	
⭘ APR	②	②	②	②	
⭘ MAY	③	③	③	③	
⭘ JUN		④	④	④	
⭘ JUL		⑤	⑤	⑤	
⭘ AUG		⑥	⑥	⑥	
⭘ SEP		⑦	⑦	⑦	
⭘ OCT		⑧	⑧	⑧	
⭘ NOV		⑨	⑨	⑨	
⭘ DEC					

3. TEST CODE   4. REGISTRATION NUMBER

⓪	Ⓐ	Ⓙ	⓪	⓪	⓪	⓪	⓪	⓪	⓪	⓪	⓪
①	Ⓑ	Ⓚ	①	①	①	①	①	①	①	①	①
②	Ⓒ	Ⓛ	②	②	②	②	②	②	②	②	②
③	Ⓓ	Ⓜ	③	③	③	③	③	③	③	③	③
④	Ⓔ	Ⓝ	④	④	④	④	④	④	④	④	④
⑤	Ⓕ	Ⓞ	⑤	⑤	⑤	⑤	⑤	⑤	⑤	⑤	⑤
⑥	Ⓖ	Ⓟ	⑥	⑥	⑥	⑥	⑥	⑥	⑥	⑥	⑥
⑦	Ⓗ	Ⓠ	⑦	⑦	⑦	⑦	⑦	⑦	⑦	⑦	⑦
⑧	Ⓘ	Ⓡ	⑧	⑧	⑧	⑧	⑧	⑧	⑧	⑧	⑧
⑨			⑨	⑨	⑨	⑨	⑨	⑨	⑨	⑨	⑨

7. GENDER

⭘ MALE
⭘ FEMALE

The **Princeton** Review®

5. YOUR NAME

First 4 letters of last name				FIRST INIT	MID INIT
Ⓐ	Ⓐ	Ⓐ	Ⓐ	Ⓐ	Ⓐ
Ⓑ	Ⓑ	Ⓑ	Ⓑ	Ⓑ	Ⓑ
Ⓒ	Ⓒ	Ⓒ	Ⓒ	Ⓒ	Ⓒ
Ⓓ	Ⓓ	Ⓓ	Ⓓ	Ⓓ	Ⓓ
Ⓔ	Ⓔ	Ⓔ	Ⓔ	Ⓔ	Ⓔ
Ⓕ	Ⓕ	Ⓕ	Ⓕ	Ⓕ	Ⓕ
Ⓖ	Ⓖ	Ⓖ	Ⓖ	Ⓖ	Ⓖ
Ⓗ	Ⓗ	Ⓗ	Ⓗ	Ⓗ	Ⓗ
Ⓘ	Ⓘ	Ⓘ	Ⓘ	Ⓘ	Ⓘ
Ⓙ	Ⓙ	Ⓙ	Ⓙ	Ⓙ	Ⓙ
Ⓚ	Ⓚ	Ⓚ	Ⓚ	Ⓚ	Ⓚ
Ⓛ	Ⓛ	Ⓛ	Ⓛ	Ⓛ	Ⓛ
Ⓜ	Ⓜ	Ⓜ	Ⓜ	Ⓜ	Ⓜ
Ⓝ	Ⓝ	Ⓝ	Ⓝ	Ⓝ	Ⓝ
Ⓞ	Ⓞ	Ⓞ	Ⓞ	Ⓞ	Ⓞ
Ⓟ	Ⓟ	Ⓟ	Ⓟ	Ⓟ	Ⓟ
Ⓠ	Ⓠ	Ⓠ	Ⓠ	Ⓠ	Ⓠ
Ⓡ	Ⓡ	Ⓡ	Ⓡ	Ⓡ	Ⓡ
Ⓢ	Ⓢ	Ⓢ	Ⓢ	Ⓢ	Ⓢ
Ⓣ	Ⓣ	Ⓣ	Ⓣ	Ⓣ	Ⓣ
Ⓤ	Ⓤ	Ⓤ	Ⓤ	Ⓤ	Ⓤ
Ⓥ	Ⓥ	Ⓥ	Ⓥ	Ⓥ	Ⓥ
Ⓦ	Ⓦ	Ⓦ	Ⓦ	Ⓦ	Ⓦ
Ⓧ	Ⓧ	Ⓧ	Ⓧ	Ⓧ	Ⓧ
Ⓨ	Ⓨ	Ⓨ	Ⓨ	Ⓨ	Ⓨ
Ⓩ	Ⓩ	Ⓩ	Ⓩ	Ⓩ	Ⓩ

1. Ⓐ Ⓑ Ⓒ Ⓓ Ⓔ
2. Ⓐ Ⓑ Ⓒ Ⓓ Ⓔ
3. Ⓐ Ⓑ Ⓒ Ⓓ Ⓔ
4. Ⓐ Ⓑ Ⓒ Ⓓ Ⓔ
5. Ⓐ Ⓑ Ⓒ Ⓓ Ⓔ
6. Ⓐ Ⓑ Ⓒ Ⓓ Ⓔ
7. Ⓐ Ⓑ Ⓒ Ⓓ Ⓔ
8. Ⓐ Ⓑ Ⓒ Ⓓ Ⓔ
9. Ⓐ Ⓑ Ⓒ Ⓓ Ⓔ
10. Ⓐ Ⓑ Ⓒ Ⓓ Ⓔ
11. Ⓐ Ⓑ Ⓒ Ⓓ Ⓔ
12. Ⓐ Ⓑ Ⓒ Ⓓ Ⓔ
13. Ⓐ Ⓑ Ⓒ Ⓓ Ⓔ
14. Ⓐ Ⓑ Ⓒ Ⓓ Ⓔ
15. Ⓐ Ⓑ Ⓒ Ⓓ Ⓔ
16. Ⓐ Ⓑ Ⓒ Ⓓ Ⓔ
17. Ⓐ Ⓑ Ⓒ Ⓓ Ⓔ
18. Ⓐ Ⓑ Ⓒ Ⓓ Ⓔ
19. Ⓐ Ⓑ Ⓒ Ⓓ Ⓔ
20. Ⓐ Ⓑ Ⓒ Ⓓ Ⓔ
21. Ⓐ Ⓑ Ⓒ Ⓓ Ⓔ
22. Ⓐ Ⓑ Ⓒ Ⓓ Ⓔ
23. Ⓐ Ⓑ Ⓒ Ⓓ Ⓔ

24. Ⓐ Ⓑ Ⓒ Ⓓ Ⓔ
25. Ⓐ Ⓑ Ⓒ Ⓓ Ⓔ
26. Ⓐ Ⓑ Ⓒ Ⓓ Ⓔ
27. Ⓐ Ⓑ Ⓒ Ⓓ Ⓔ
28. Ⓐ Ⓑ Ⓒ Ⓓ Ⓔ
29. Ⓐ Ⓑ Ⓒ Ⓓ Ⓔ
30. Ⓐ Ⓑ Ⓒ Ⓓ Ⓔ
31. Ⓐ Ⓑ Ⓒ Ⓓ Ⓔ
32. Ⓐ Ⓑ Ⓒ Ⓓ Ⓔ
33. Ⓐ Ⓑ Ⓒ Ⓓ Ⓔ
34. Ⓐ Ⓑ Ⓒ Ⓓ Ⓔ
35. Ⓐ Ⓑ Ⓒ Ⓓ Ⓔ
36. Ⓐ Ⓑ Ⓒ Ⓓ Ⓔ
37. Ⓐ Ⓑ Ⓒ Ⓓ Ⓔ
38. Ⓐ Ⓑ Ⓒ Ⓓ Ⓔ
39. Ⓐ Ⓑ Ⓒ Ⓓ Ⓔ
40. Ⓐ Ⓑ Ⓒ Ⓓ Ⓔ
41. Ⓐ Ⓑ Ⓒ Ⓓ Ⓔ
42. Ⓐ Ⓑ Ⓒ Ⓓ Ⓔ
43. Ⓐ Ⓑ Ⓒ Ⓓ Ⓔ
44. Ⓐ Ⓑ Ⓒ Ⓓ Ⓔ
45. Ⓐ Ⓑ Ⓒ Ⓓ Ⓔ
46. Ⓐ Ⓑ Ⓒ Ⓓ Ⓔ

47. Ⓐ Ⓑ Ⓒ Ⓓ Ⓔ
48. Ⓐ Ⓑ Ⓒ Ⓓ Ⓔ
49. Ⓐ Ⓑ Ⓒ Ⓓ Ⓔ
50. Ⓐ Ⓑ Ⓒ Ⓓ Ⓔ
51. Ⓐ Ⓑ Ⓒ Ⓓ Ⓔ
52. Ⓐ Ⓑ Ⓒ Ⓓ Ⓔ
53. Ⓐ Ⓑ Ⓒ Ⓓ Ⓔ
54. Ⓐ Ⓑ Ⓒ Ⓓ Ⓔ
55. Ⓐ Ⓑ Ⓒ Ⓓ Ⓔ
56. Ⓐ Ⓑ Ⓒ Ⓓ Ⓔ
57. Ⓐ Ⓑ Ⓒ Ⓓ Ⓔ
58. Ⓐ Ⓑ Ⓒ Ⓓ Ⓔ
59. Ⓐ Ⓑ Ⓒ Ⓓ Ⓔ
60. Ⓐ Ⓑ Ⓒ Ⓓ Ⓔ
61. Ⓐ Ⓑ Ⓒ Ⓓ Ⓔ
62. Ⓐ Ⓑ Ⓒ Ⓓ Ⓔ
63. Ⓐ Ⓑ Ⓒ Ⓓ Ⓔ
64. Ⓐ Ⓑ Ⓒ Ⓓ Ⓔ
65. Ⓐ Ⓑ Ⓒ Ⓓ Ⓔ
66. Ⓐ Ⓑ Ⓒ Ⓓ Ⓔ
67. Ⓐ Ⓑ Ⓒ Ⓓ Ⓔ
68. Ⓐ Ⓑ Ⓒ Ⓓ Ⓔ
69. Ⓐ Ⓑ Ⓒ Ⓓ Ⓔ
70. Ⓐ Ⓑ Ⓒ Ⓓ Ⓔ

PART B

	I		II		CE
101.	Ⓣ	Ⓕ	Ⓣ	Ⓕ	⭘
102.	Ⓣ	Ⓕ	Ⓣ	Ⓕ	⭘
103.	Ⓣ	Ⓕ	Ⓣ	Ⓕ	⭘
104.	Ⓣ	Ⓕ	Ⓣ	Ⓕ	⭘
105.	Ⓣ	Ⓕ	Ⓣ	Ⓕ	⭘
106.	Ⓣ	Ⓕ	Ⓣ	Ⓕ	⭘
107.	Ⓣ	Ⓕ	Ⓣ	Ⓕ	⭘
108.	Ⓣ	Ⓕ	Ⓣ	Ⓕ	⭘
109.	Ⓣ	Ⓕ	Ⓣ	Ⓕ	⭘
110.	Ⓣ	Ⓕ	Ⓣ	Ⓕ	⭘
111.	Ⓣ	Ⓕ	Ⓣ	Ⓕ	⭘
112.	Ⓣ	Ⓕ	Ⓣ	Ⓕ	⭘
113.	Ⓣ	Ⓕ	Ⓣ	Ⓕ	⭘
114.	Ⓣ	Ⓕ	Ⓣ	Ⓕ	⭘
115.	Ⓣ	Ⓕ	Ⓣ	Ⓕ	⭘

Completely darken bubbles with a No. 2 pencil. If you make a mistake, be sure to erase mark completely. Erase all stray marks.

1.

YOUR NAME:
(Print) _____
Last   First   M.I.

SIGNATURE: _____   DATE: / /

HOME ADDRESS:
(Print) _____
Number and Street

_____
City   State   Zip Code

PHONE NO.: _____

5. YOUR NAME

First 4 letters of last name				FIRST INIT	MID INIT
Ⓐ	Ⓐ	Ⓐ	Ⓐ	Ⓐ	Ⓐ
Ⓑ	Ⓑ	Ⓑ	Ⓑ	Ⓑ	Ⓑ
Ⓒ	Ⓒ	Ⓒ	Ⓒ	Ⓒ	Ⓒ
Ⓓ	Ⓓ	Ⓓ	Ⓓ	Ⓓ	Ⓓ
Ⓔ	Ⓔ	Ⓔ	Ⓔ	Ⓔ	Ⓔ
Ⓕ	Ⓕ	Ⓕ	Ⓕ	Ⓕ	Ⓕ
Ⓖ	Ⓖ	Ⓖ	Ⓖ	Ⓖ	Ⓖ
Ⓗ	Ⓗ	Ⓗ	Ⓗ	Ⓗ	Ⓗ
Ⓘ	Ⓘ	Ⓘ	Ⓘ	Ⓘ	Ⓘ
Ⓙ	Ⓙ	Ⓙ	Ⓙ	Ⓙ	Ⓙ
Ⓚ	Ⓚ	Ⓚ	Ⓚ	Ⓚ	Ⓚ
Ⓛ	Ⓛ	Ⓛ	Ⓛ	Ⓛ	Ⓛ
Ⓜ	Ⓜ	Ⓜ	Ⓜ	Ⓜ	Ⓜ
Ⓝ	Ⓝ	Ⓝ	Ⓝ	Ⓝ	Ⓝ
Ⓞ	Ⓞ	Ⓞ	Ⓞ	Ⓞ	Ⓞ
Ⓟ	Ⓟ	Ⓟ	Ⓟ	Ⓟ	Ⓟ
Ⓠ	Ⓠ	Ⓠ	Ⓠ	Ⓠ	Ⓠ
Ⓡ	Ⓡ	Ⓡ	Ⓡ	Ⓡ	Ⓡ
Ⓢ	Ⓢ	Ⓢ	Ⓢ	Ⓢ	Ⓢ
Ⓣ	Ⓣ	Ⓣ	Ⓣ	Ⓣ	Ⓣ
Ⓤ	Ⓤ	Ⓤ	Ⓤ	Ⓤ	Ⓤ
Ⓥ	Ⓥ	Ⓥ	Ⓥ	Ⓥ	Ⓥ
Ⓦ	Ⓦ	Ⓦ	Ⓦ	Ⓦ	Ⓦ
Ⓧ	Ⓧ	Ⓧ	Ⓧ	Ⓧ	Ⓧ
Ⓨ	Ⓨ	Ⓨ	Ⓨ	Ⓨ	Ⓨ
Ⓩ	Ⓩ	Ⓩ	Ⓩ	Ⓩ	Ⓩ

IMPORTANT: Please fill in these boxes exactly as shown on the back cover of your test book.

2. TEST FORM

_____

3. TEST CODE

⓪	Ⓐ	Ⓙ	⓪	⓪
①	Ⓑ	Ⓚ	①	①
②	Ⓒ	Ⓛ	②	②
③	Ⓓ	Ⓜ	③	③
④	Ⓔ	Ⓝ	④	④
⑤	Ⓕ	Ⓞ	⑤	⑤
⑥	Ⓖ	Ⓟ	⑥	⑥
⑦	Ⓗ	Ⓠ	⑦	⑦
⑧	Ⓘ	Ⓡ	⑧	⑧
⑨			⑨	⑨

4. REGISTRATION NUMBER

⓪	⓪	⓪	⓪	⓪	⓪	⓪
①	①	①	①	①	①	①
②	②	②	②	②	②	②
③	③	③	③	③	③	③
④	④	④	④	④	④	④
⑤	⑤	⑤	⑤	⑤	⑤	⑤
⑥	⑥	⑥	⑥	⑥	⑥	⑥
⑦	⑦	⑦	⑦	⑦	⑦	⑦
⑧	⑧	⑧	⑧	⑧	⑧	⑧
⑨	⑨	⑨	⑨	⑨	⑨	⑨

6. DATE OF BIRTH

Month		Day		Year	
◯ JAN					
◯ FEB	⓪	⓪	⓪	⓪	
◯ MAR	①	①	①	①	
◯ APR	②	②	②	②	
◯ MAY	③	③	③	③	
◯ JUN		④	④	④	
◯ JUL		⑤	⑤	⑤	
◯ AUG		⑥	⑥	⑥	
◯ SEP		⑦	⑦	⑦	
◯ OCT		⑧	⑧	⑧	
◯ NOV		⑨	⑨	⑨	
◯ DEC					

7. GENDER

◯ MALE
◯ FEMALE

1. Ⓐ Ⓑ Ⓒ Ⓓ Ⓔ
2. Ⓐ Ⓑ Ⓒ Ⓓ Ⓔ
3. Ⓐ Ⓑ Ⓒ Ⓓ Ⓔ
4. Ⓐ Ⓑ Ⓒ Ⓓ Ⓔ
5. Ⓐ Ⓑ Ⓒ Ⓓ Ⓔ
6. Ⓐ Ⓑ Ⓒ Ⓓ Ⓔ
7. Ⓐ Ⓑ Ⓒ Ⓓ Ⓔ
8. Ⓐ Ⓑ Ⓒ Ⓓ Ⓔ
9. Ⓐ Ⓑ Ⓒ Ⓓ Ⓔ
10. Ⓐ Ⓑ Ⓒ Ⓓ Ⓔ
11. Ⓐ Ⓑ Ⓒ Ⓓ Ⓔ
12. Ⓐ Ⓑ Ⓒ Ⓓ Ⓔ
13. Ⓐ Ⓑ Ⓒ Ⓓ Ⓔ
14. Ⓐ Ⓑ Ⓒ Ⓓ Ⓔ
15. Ⓐ Ⓑ Ⓒ Ⓓ Ⓔ
16. Ⓐ Ⓑ Ⓒ Ⓓ Ⓔ
17. Ⓐ Ⓑ Ⓒ Ⓓ Ⓔ
18. Ⓐ Ⓑ Ⓒ Ⓓ Ⓔ
19. Ⓐ Ⓑ Ⓒ Ⓓ Ⓔ
20. Ⓐ Ⓑ Ⓒ Ⓓ Ⓔ
21. Ⓐ Ⓑ Ⓒ Ⓓ Ⓔ
22. Ⓐ Ⓑ Ⓒ Ⓓ Ⓔ
23. Ⓐ Ⓑ Ⓒ Ⓓ Ⓔ

24. Ⓐ Ⓑ Ⓒ Ⓓ Ⓔ
25. Ⓐ Ⓑ Ⓒ Ⓓ Ⓔ
26. Ⓐ Ⓑ Ⓒ Ⓓ Ⓔ
27. Ⓐ Ⓑ Ⓒ Ⓓ Ⓔ
28. Ⓐ Ⓑ Ⓒ Ⓓ Ⓔ
29. Ⓐ Ⓑ Ⓒ Ⓓ Ⓔ
30. Ⓐ Ⓑ Ⓒ Ⓓ Ⓔ
31. Ⓐ Ⓑ Ⓒ Ⓓ Ⓔ
32. Ⓐ Ⓑ Ⓒ Ⓓ Ⓔ
33. Ⓐ Ⓑ Ⓒ Ⓓ Ⓔ
34. Ⓐ Ⓑ Ⓒ Ⓓ Ⓔ
35. Ⓐ Ⓑ Ⓒ Ⓓ Ⓔ
36. Ⓐ Ⓑ Ⓒ Ⓓ Ⓔ
37. Ⓐ Ⓑ Ⓒ Ⓓ Ⓔ
38. Ⓐ Ⓑ Ⓒ Ⓓ Ⓔ
39. Ⓐ Ⓑ Ⓒ Ⓓ Ⓔ
40. Ⓐ Ⓑ Ⓒ Ⓓ Ⓔ
41. Ⓐ Ⓑ Ⓒ Ⓓ Ⓔ
42. Ⓐ Ⓑ Ⓒ Ⓓ Ⓔ
43. Ⓐ Ⓑ Ⓒ Ⓓ Ⓔ
44. Ⓐ Ⓑ Ⓒ Ⓓ Ⓔ
45. Ⓐ Ⓑ Ⓒ Ⓓ Ⓔ
46. Ⓐ Ⓑ Ⓒ Ⓓ Ⓔ

47. Ⓐ Ⓑ Ⓒ Ⓓ Ⓔ
48. Ⓐ Ⓑ Ⓒ Ⓓ Ⓔ
49. Ⓐ Ⓑ Ⓒ Ⓓ Ⓔ
50. Ⓐ Ⓑ Ⓒ Ⓓ Ⓔ
51. Ⓐ Ⓑ Ⓒ Ⓓ Ⓔ
52. Ⓐ Ⓑ Ⓒ Ⓓ Ⓔ
53. Ⓐ Ⓑ Ⓒ Ⓓ Ⓔ
54. Ⓐ Ⓑ Ⓒ Ⓓ Ⓔ
55. Ⓐ Ⓑ Ⓒ Ⓓ Ⓔ
56. Ⓐ Ⓑ Ⓒ Ⓓ Ⓔ
57. Ⓐ Ⓑ Ⓒ Ⓓ Ⓔ
58. Ⓐ Ⓑ Ⓒ Ⓓ Ⓔ
59. Ⓐ Ⓑ Ⓒ Ⓓ Ⓔ
60. Ⓐ Ⓑ Ⓒ Ⓓ Ⓔ
61. Ⓐ Ⓑ Ⓒ Ⓓ Ⓔ
62. Ⓐ Ⓑ Ⓒ Ⓓ Ⓔ
63. Ⓐ Ⓑ Ⓒ Ⓓ Ⓔ
64. Ⓐ Ⓑ Ⓒ Ⓓ Ⓔ
65. Ⓐ Ⓑ Ⓒ Ⓓ Ⓔ
66. Ⓐ Ⓑ Ⓒ Ⓓ Ⓔ
67. Ⓐ Ⓑ Ⓒ Ⓓ Ⓔ
68. Ⓐ Ⓑ Ⓒ Ⓓ Ⓔ
69. Ⓐ Ⓑ Ⓒ Ⓓ Ⓔ
70. Ⓐ Ⓑ Ⓒ Ⓓ Ⓔ

PART B

	I		II		CE
101.	Ⓣ	Ⓕ	Ⓣ	Ⓕ	◯
102.	Ⓣ	Ⓕ	Ⓣ	Ⓕ	◯
103.	Ⓣ	Ⓕ	Ⓣ	Ⓕ	◯
104.	Ⓣ	Ⓕ	Ⓣ	Ⓕ	◯
105.	Ⓣ	Ⓕ	Ⓣ	Ⓕ	◯
106.	Ⓣ	Ⓕ	Ⓣ	Ⓕ	◯
107.	Ⓣ	Ⓕ	Ⓣ	Ⓕ	◯
108.	Ⓣ	Ⓕ	Ⓣ	Ⓕ	◯
109.	Ⓣ	Ⓕ	Ⓣ	Ⓕ	◯
110.	Ⓣ	Ⓕ	Ⓣ	Ⓕ	◯
111.	Ⓣ	Ⓕ	Ⓣ	Ⓕ	◯
112.	Ⓣ	Ⓕ	Ⓣ	Ⓕ	◯
113.	Ⓣ	Ⓕ	Ⓣ	Ⓕ	◯
114.	Ⓣ	Ⓕ	Ⓣ	Ⓕ	◯
115.	Ⓣ	Ⓕ	Ⓣ	Ⓕ	◯

STUDY GUIDE FOR THE SAT SUBJECT TEST IN CHEMISTRY

Bad news first: there's no one right way to study for a test. If you're looking for a surefire shortcut, there simply isn't one. The good news, however, is that if you're reading this, you're already on the right track—you're putting in the three key resources for successful study habits: time, energy, and focus. The following study guide features a few suggested ways to tackle the SAT Subject Test in Chemistry, depending on whether the test is just around the corner (1 Week Cram) or if you've got more time to practice (7 Week Stretch).

Remember that these plans are simply suggestions; everybody learns in their own way and at their own pace. When choosing where to begin, use what you know about your own study habits. If cramming for a test hasn't been effective for you in the past, perhaps it's time to try spreading out your practice over a longer period of time. On the other hand, if you find yourself forgetting key material just before the test, you might want to try an intense refresher in the week leading up to the exam.

If you're not sure how best to prepare, we recommend using Practice Test 1 (pages 39–58) as a diagnostic, which means giving yourself enough time to mirror what will be allotted to you on test day, and then working in a quiet and uninterrupted environment. When you're done, check answers against the key on page 60. If you're happy with your results, you might just spend a week focusing on the specific section for which you had wrong answers. On the other hand, if you're struggling across the board, you may be best served by building up those content gaps over the course of a few months. Here are our recommendations.

1 Week Cram

The following schedule is an extremely abbreviated way of gaining maximum exposure to the course. It involves reinforcement over a limited amount of time, so you'll be touching on each bit of content four times—once when you skim the chapter to get a general sense of the ideas within, again when you read the summary to remind yourself of what you're expected to have learned, a third time when you test your knowledge against the drill questions, and finally when you mark key terms that you remain unfamiliar or uncomfortable with. If you have extra time on any given day, we recommend reading the portions of each content chapter that you feel least comfortable with.

Day 0, Sunday [2 hours]

Take Practice Test 1. Keep the results of the test in mind as you go through the next week, and slow down your skimming when you hit a section where you struggled.

Day 1, Monday [1 hour]

- Review Chapter 1, "Introduction"
- Familiarize yourself with the exam format and our test-taking strategies in Chapter 2, "Test Strategies"
- Skim Chapter 3, "Some Basic Stuff"

Day 2, Tuesday [1.5 hours]

- Review Summary (page 37) for Chapter 3

- Complete Drill 1 (page 34) in Chapter 3

- Skim Chapter 4, "Atoms: The Building Blocks of Matter" and Chapter 5, "Chemical Reactions and Stoichiometry"

Day 3, Wednesday [2 hours]

- Review Summary (page 90) for Chapter 4

- Complete Drill 1 (page 87) in Chapter 4

- Review Summary (page 111) for Chapter 5. Circle any items you don't know.

- Complete Drills 1 and 2 (pages 95, 108) in Chapter 5

- Skim Chapter 6, "Electron Configuations and Radioactivity"; Chapter 7, "The Periodic Table and Bonding"; and Chapter 8, "Phases: Gases, Liquids, and Solids"

Day 4, Thursday [2.5 hours]

- Review Summary (page 130) for Chapter 6. Circle any items you don't know.

- Complete Drills 1 and 2 (pages 122, 127) in Chapter 6

- Review Summary (page 157) for Chapter 7. Circle any items you don't know.

- Complete Drills 1 and 2 (pages 139, 155) in Chapter 7

- Review Summary (page 182) for Chapter 8. Circle any items you don't know.

- Complete Drills 1 and 2 (pages 167, 180) in Chapter 8

- Skim Chapter 9, "Solutions"; Chapter 10, "Kinetics and Equilibrium"; and Chapter 11, "Acids and Bases"

Day 5, Friday [3 hours]

- Review Summary (page 192) for Chapter 9. Circle any items you don't know.

- Complete Drill 1 (page 190) in Chapter 9

- Review Summary (page 209) for Chapter 10. Circle any items you don't know.

- Complete Drill 1 (page 206) in Chapter 10

- Review Summary (page 226) for Chapter 11. Circle any items you don't know.

- Complete Drill 1 (page 223) in Chapter 11

- Skim Chapter 12, "Oxidation and Reduction"; Chapter 13, "Organic Chemistry and Environmental Chemistry"; and Chapter 14, "Laboratory"

Day 6, Saturday [3.5 hours]

- Review Summary (page 239) for Chapter 12. Circle any items you don't know.

- Complete Drill 1 (pages 236) in Chapter 12

- Review Summary (page 253) for Chapter 13. Circle any items you don't know.

- Complete Drill 1 (page 251) in Chapter 13

- Review Summary (page 268) for Chapter 14. Circle any items you don't know.

- Complete Drills 1 (page 266) in Chapter 14

- Take Practice Test 2 (pages 295–312)

- Review Answers and Explanations for Practice Test 2 (pages 313–325)

Day 7, Sunday [2 hours]

- Take Practice Test 3 (pages 329–345)

- Review Anwers and Explanations for Practice Test 3 (347–361)

This is it, your final chance to review. Look at all the circled Key Terms and look at the questions you got wrong on Practice Test 2. If there's any overlap between the two, that's a clear sign that you need more practice in that section, so spend any remaining time reviewing that content. That said, you've been working hard, so don't burn yourself out by pushing for more than two hours. Rest is an important part of studying, too: it's when the mind processes everything.

7 Week Stretch

This schedule doesn't break things into a day-to-day calendar, but helps to establish what you should aim to accomplish within a given week. For some, that may be a matter of evenly distributing the reading material across the week. For others, it may be to spend one day studying, one day reviewing, and one day testing.

We have arranged the material by EARLY, MID, and LATE week.

Week 1

- EARLY: Read Chapters 1–3

- MID: Review the Summary for Chapter 3

- LATE: Complete Drill 1 in Chapter 3. Complete Practice Test 1, score your test, read through all Answers and Explanations.

Week 2

- EARLY: Read Chapters 4–6

- MID: Review the Summary for Chapters 4, 5, and 6

- LATE: Complete Drill 1 in Chapter 4; Drills 1–2 in Chapter 5; and Drills 1–2 in Chapter 6

Week 3

- EARLY: Read Chapters 7–9

- MID: Review the Summary for Chapters 7, 8, and 9

- LATE: Complete Drills 1–2 in Chapter 7; Drills 1–2 in Chapter 8; and Drill 1 in Chapter 9

Week 4

- EARLY: Read Chapters 10–12

- MID: Review the Summary for Chapters 10, 11, and 12

- LATE: Complete Drill 1 in Chapter 10; Drill 1 in Chapter 11; and Drill 1 in Chapter 12

Week 5

- EARLY: Read Chapters 13, 14

- MID: Review the Summary for Chapters 13, 14

- LATE: Complete Drill 1 in Chapter 13; Drill 1 in Chapter 14

Week 6

- EARLY: Complete Practice Test 2, score your test, read through all Answers and Explanations

- MID: Carefully review Drills and Drill Answers and Explanations for Chapters 3–9

- LATE: Carefully review Drills and Drill Answers and Explanations for Chapters 10–14

Week 7

- EARLY: Complete Practice Test 3

- MID: Score your completed Practice Test 3 and read through all Answers and Explanations

- LATE: Read all Chapter Summaries for Chapters 3–14

FINAL NOTES

Don't feel as if you have to limit yourself to one of these templates. This is your test and your book; the most effective practice is likely to be that which you feel most comfortable with and able to commit to. That said, here are a few final pointers for adapting the book:

- Spread out the practice tests so that you can track progress and learn from mistakes.

- Don't gloss over reviewing answers, even to problems that you got right, especially if you guessed.

- If possible, don't cram. Your goal isn't to remember material for a single day—unless you're taking the test tomorrow—so the more that you can check back in on how much you remember from a section over the course of your review, the more you'll be able to retain for test day.

Feel free to use other resources! We've given you the best content review and practice tests at our disposal, but if you're still struggling over a difficult concept, and your teacher can't help, another perspective can only help. (Just make sure you fact-check the source!) The College Board's website features an overview of each Subject Test as well as practice questions: **https://collegereadiness.collegeboard.org/sat-subject-tests/subjects/science/chemistry**

NOTES